LIT

*Active Leadership in Education
Enterprise and Engagement*

'ISH CAN

The management of projects

Peter W. G. Morris

Thomas Telford, London

Published by Thomas Telford Services Ltd, Thomas Telford House, 1 Heron Quay, London
E14 4JD

First published 1994

Distributors for Thomas Telford books are
USA: American Society of Civil Engineers, Publications Sales Department, 345 East 47th
Street, New York, NY 10017-2398
Japan: Maruzen Co Ltd, Book Department, 3–10 Nihonbashi 2-chome, Chuo-ku, Tokyo 103
Australia: DA Books and Journals, 648 Whitehorse Road, Mitcham 3132, Victoria

A catalogue record for this book is available from the British Library

Classification
Availability: Unrestricted
Content: Original analysis
Status: Refereed
User: Project managers

ISBN: 0 7277 1693 X

Typeset in Great Britain by MHL Typesetting Ltd, Coventry
Printed in Great Britain by Redwood Books, Trowbridge, Wiltshire

Contents

Preface

For a long time, almost my whole professional life, I have been fascinated by project management. I have read most of its literature and have been blessed with a wide experience of its practice. I am convinced that it is a field of great importance, yet I am acutely aware that it has still to be established effectively as a major discipline. It lacks the academic and professional support that many other, arguably less important, disciplines receive. It is widely misperceived as a collection of planning and control techniques rather than as a rich and complex management process. Indeed, many of the project management specialists themselves perhaps do not fully recognize the real scope of the discipline.

This book has been written with the aim of describing the full scope of what is involved in really managing projects. It does so largely through a historical account of the development of the modern practices of managing projects, concluding with a summary of the discipline and its possible future development. This rather unusual, chronologically based format was chosen deliberately. There is still confusion over the use of many of project management's tools and ideas, and part of the trouble lies in the lack of information on the contexts in which they were developed. Describing these contexts in a chronological industry-specific format may, I hope, lead to a fuller appreciation of the purposes behind project management's key ideas and techniques. As a further benefit, it may also furnish students of the discipline with a useful sourcebook for further research and understanding.

The great majority of publications on project management deal with techniques and procedures rather than management practice. Too much of the writing is dry and mechanistic. Little conveys the challenge and exhilaration of working on real projects. There is a shortage of case studies; there are even fewer studies comparing the project management practice between industries or between countries. Without this cross-industry, cross-cultural analysis, much of project management continues to be seen primarily within industry-specific contexts. One of the greatest challenges still facing the discipline is thus to develop genuine generic practices and terminology. Configuration Management is a good example: although it is regarded in aerospace, electronics and information technology as a fundamental project management practice, most project managers in construction would find difficulty even in describing it. The cross-industry comparisons in this book may, I hope, facilitate the development of a generic body of project management knowledge.

Let me expand on the question of the proper scope of project management, which is a major preoccupation of this book. In the early 1980s my education in project management was subject to major shock. I realized that *the discipline as normally described is often incapable of fulfilling its objectives*. I was analysing the public record of projects' out-turn costs and schedules against their budgeted, or baseline, estimates. I had data on 1449 projects — all that I could then find in the public record; of these, incredibly, only 12 had out-turn costs below or on budget! (Later I repeated the exercise with over 3000 projects, with similar results.) Not only did this seem to be a substantial indictment of the projects' management but, more significantly, the reasons given for these overruns were factors that hardly ever appeared in the textbooks on project management — factors such as poor estimating; increased order quantities; poor technology management; design faults; contracting and legal difficulties; governmental, labour or social issues; and geophysical problems! The data clearly showed that in order for project management to fulfil its stated objective of accomplishing projects 'on time, in budget, to technical specification', a whole class of generally strategic factors such as these needed to be addressed in addition to the intra-project, organizational issues and tools and techniques normally covered in the writing.

The discipline, I felt, was mis-focused. Surely it should really be the '*management of projects*' rather than 'project management': i.e. the management of the process of establishing the project's objectives and its definition; of assessing it so that it is set up with the maximum chance of being successful technically, commercially, socially, etc. for all the parties ('stakeholders') it affects; and of accomplishing it efficiently and effectively.

At its most basic, project management is a deceptively simple discipline. It is the process of *integrating* everything that needs to be done (typically utilizing a number of special project management tools and techniques) as the project evolves through its *life cycle* (from concept definition through implementation to handover) in order to ensure that its objectives are achieved. The broader discipline of the management of projects is evidently more ambitious, involving the setting of appropriate objectives and subtle definitions of success, and requiring management of some sophistication in dealing with a broad range of specialized and strategic matters, ranging from finance, environment and technology to procurement and people management.

These, then, were the motivations behind this book. In writing it I have sought to provide its readers with

- a record of the seminal events and documents in the development of the modern practice of the management of projects

- a detailed picture of how project management is and has been practised in different industries, countries and cultures (although I recognize that a great many, regrettably, are not covered)
- a sense of the drama and excitement of the real world of projects
- an international perspective to the discipline — we cannot now afford not to think internationally (or even globally)
- a model (chapter 8) of best practice as I currently perceive it
- a vision of how the discipline will evolve over the next decade or so (chapter 9).

This is a thick brew, and in many ways I regret its density. I can only say that the story is a large one: I hope my readers will find it stimulating and will let me know where I have gone wrong or omitted something important!

What I clearly have not written is a textbook. This is not a 'how to' manual. Hundreds of these have been written already, and are referenced in these pages, although of course more are required — partly, perhaps, to reflect the scope of the broader discipline of the *management of projects* which this book introduces, partly also to reflect the exciting developments noted in chapter 9, particularly Total Quality, new data management techniques, Simultaneous Engineering and so on. Meanwhile, what I have provided, I hope, is a map of the discipline — a guide that others may find useful; an indication of where, and how, the profession must develop.

In saying this, I do not wish to appear arrogant. I know too well that the experience and preoccupations of many in the field will be different from what is covered in this book. Some will be working only on detailed implementation issues. Many, perhaps, will claim that this book is too dominated by large, often international, 'single-shot' projects and that their concern is more, say, with multi-project or intra-organizational management. Of the many readers who will inevitably feel that their experience does not match the project models developed in these pages, I can only ask for patience and trust. It is true that I have tended to use the large single-shot project as a basis for much of the book. I have done so quite deliberately, since I believe that it best describes the full potential range of issues that managers of projects may have to face. Do not dismiss others' experience too quickly: in a few years' time you, too, quite unexpectedly, possibly even without at first realizing it, will have to face new issues of the kinds described here.

There is much experience and work behind this book, most of it belonging to people other than myself. There are great people and personalities in these pages. Many of them are my personal friends. I honour them all. They have vision, integrity and a tremendous capacity for work.

I should acknowledge in particular the debts that I owe in my own professional development — to Joseph Graubard, then of Booz, Allen & Hamilton; Dr Albert J. Kelley, my boss as President of Arthur D. Little Program Systems Management Company; and Sir Frank Lampl, Chairman of the Bovis Construction Group. I should also mention David Rolt of Sir Robert McAlpine & Sons, who gave me much rope in my early years; Uwe Kitzinger, the first President of Templeton College, Oxford; Frank Davidson of MIT, the leading light in the macro-engineering discipline; Derek Fraser and Allen Sykes of the Major Projects Association; and George Steel of Indeco, who is a touchstone of project management good sense.

Three ladies have typed innumerable drafts of this book — Anne Scott, Pat Brien and Hazel Williams. They are special people and I would like to recognize their patience, kindness and effort.

I could not close without a note of my family: my mother and father, who introduced me very directly and bluntly to the world of construction in Liverpool in the 1950s and 1960s; my parents-in-law who, through ICI, knew more about project management in the 1970s than I at first realized; and my wife Carolyn, and three children, Simon, David and Charlotte, all of whom I love dearly and who put up with much because of my great interest in this special, and important, subject of the management of projects.

Peter Morris,
Sutton Courtenay,
Oxfordshire,
January 1994

Publisher's note
In this book certain terms such as 'Systems Management' and 'Earned Value' are capitalized to reflect their meanings in the context of this book, which are more precise than would otherwise be clear. The spelling in the American style of usage in the terms 'Program Management' and 'Program Manager' reflects the provenance of such terms and, again, imbues them with the precise, contextual implications of their use.

1. Introduction

Managing projects is one of the oldest and most respected accomplishments of mankind. We stand in awe of the achievements of
the builders of the pyramids, the architects of ancient cities, the
masons and craftsmen of great cathedrals and mosques; of the might
and labour behind the Great Wall of China and other wonders of
the world. Today's projects, too, command our attention. We were
riveted at the sight of Americans landing on the Moon. We are
impressed as a new road or bridge is opened, as a major building
rises, as a new computer system comes on line or as a spectacular
entertainment unfolds.

All of these endeavours are projects, like many thousands of
similar task-oriented activities, yet the skills employed in managing
projects, whether major ones such as these or more commonplace
ones such as constructing a house, are not well-known other than
to the specialists concerned. The contribution that our knowledge
of managing projects can make to management at large is greatly
underrated, and generally poorly known. For years, project
management was derided as a low-tech, low-value, questionable
activity. Only recently has it been recognized as a central
management discipline. Major industrial companies now use
project management as their principal management style.
'Management by projects' has become a powerful way to integrate
organizational functions and motivate groups to achieve higher
levels of performance and productivity.

In fact, even the practices of the specialists working on the
various areas of project management differ significantly.
Defence/aerospace managers, for example, may miss commercial
and contractual insights developed in construction; civil engineers
may miss aspects of technology and design management developed
in aerospace and information technology; both may learn valuable
lessons on quality, flexibility and speed from the automotive and
pharmaceutical industries.

What then do we know about managing projects? What corpus
of knowledge is available? What do we mean by the management
of projects, and where can we find it practised? Where is it going?
What are the issues in its successful application and development?

We can identify many different situations where project
management is practised on one form or another. The most obvious
are the heavily project-based industries: building and civil
engineering, power, petrochemicals, pharmaceuticals, oil and gas,
the extractive industries, shipbuilding, information systems and
telecommunications, and defence/aerospace. A second group might

include sectors that are frequent users of projects although not necessarily organized primarily on a project basis: manufacturing, emergency and social services, entertainment, education, consulting, financial services and many others.

The development of the art and science of the management of projects in these industries is the subject of this book. How did the discipline grow? What is it? What lessons have been learned (often painfully)? How can the collective wisdom of so many thousands who have toiled, suffered and failed or succeeded be distilled into practical advice for those who now wish to create and implement successful projects?

Project management or the management of projects?

Modern project management emerged between the 1930s and the 1950s. The evolution of project management has been closely related

(a) to the development of systems engineering in the US defence/aerospace industry and to engineering management in the process engineering industries
(b) to developments in modern management theory, particularly in organization design and team building
(c) to the evolution of the computer, on which project management's planning and control systems are now generally run.

Despite its long development, the concepts and techniques of project management now available to the general practitioner, however advanced and specific they may be, are often inadequate to the overall task of managing projects successfully. For, as previous research by my colleague Dr George Hough and me has demonstrated, the successful accomplishment of a project may well require attention to a range of factors not treated by the traditional project management literature.[1,2] Design and technology management, the management of political forces (governmental and non-governmental, and 'political with a small p' — business, labour and community), cost−benefit management and the raising and management of the project's finance, the management of the timing or phasing of the project (something quite different, incidentally, from the theory and practice of project scheduling), and even contract strategy and administration: all these are frequently ignored in the professional and academic writings and teachings of today's project management. As a result, there is not yet an adequate conceptual basis to the discipline. On the best projects these matters are of course recognized and tackled, but in others, where people may lack experience or resources, they may be overlooked and omitted.

The major themes of this book, therefore, are that the current formal view of, and indeed practices of, project management are often inadequate to the task of managing projects successfully; and that we would do better to enlarge the subject to the broader one of the '*management of projects*', including specifically the topics mentioned above, than to keep to the more narrowly defined areas of '*project management*' as it has typically been conceived and taught. This account of the subject thus addresses not only the traditional core 'project management' topics such as scheduling, cost control, Work Breakdown Structures and team building, but also these 'newer' topics of strategy, technology, finance, politics, the environment and so on.

For reasons given below, a review of the development of the modern practices and theories of the management of projects should start with an analysis of events that occurred around 1940−1955. However, there were important precursors to modern project management in the late 19th and early 20th centuries, and indeed throughout recorded history. These are dealt with briefly in chapter 2.

References

1. Morris, P. W. G. and Hough, G. H. *The anatomy of major projects.* Wiley, Chichester, 1988.
2. Morris, P. W. G. Initiating major projects — the unperceived role of project management. *Proc. Int. Association of Project Managers 9th World Congress on Project Management*, September 1988.

2. Developments prior to the 1940s

In reviewing previous generations of projects, there is a danger of launching too freely into an account of engineering, military and other project achievements. The challenges posed in building large ancient structures, whether socio-religious monuments such as Stonehenge and the Pyramids or utilitarian structures such as the aqueducts, roads and fortifications of the Romans, have been studied and described by generations of archaeologists.

Projects have always enjoyed a symbolic, often even religious, connotation. Some consider the Creation as the first great project — the timing was certainly impressive — but the first of man's great projects is often held to be the Tower of Babel. Not only was this a huge and mighty enterprise: its schedule control was clearly awful. Communications were dreadful. It has been the task of the project manager ever since to find a common project language — to integrate the work of others (note 1).

The ancient projects involved enormous numbers of people, with an extremely high ratio of 'labourers' to 'managers'. The ancient mega-structures such as Stonehenge and the pyramids were notable for their involvement of the whole community, an important consequence of which was the cementing of secular and sacred authority (note 2). The civil and military undertakings of the Greeks, Persians, Romans, Chinese and others, on the other hand, often used slaves who were the property of the government or contractors. Contracts for the construction work were generally awarded, as today, for either the whole of the work or just part. The Long Walls in Athens, for example, were managed as a whole by the architect Callicrates, with the work let to ten contractors; the Colosseum was build by four contractors. Contracts contained detailed specifications of the work to be carried out, the material to be used, the guarantees to be given and the method of payment. Typically, these projects were constructed with great consciousness of the importance of time.

The medieval cathedrals represented the dominance of heavenly beauty — of sacred values — over the meanness of day-to-day life. Unlike previous mega-projects, the length of time taken to build these great structures was generally immense, in some cases covering several generations. Engineering and artistic aspirations typically overrode secular considerations of urgency. Scale and timing did not, generally, depend on the short-term ability to fund the project or on the press of personal vanity to produce a monument quickly.

Fig. 1. Rievaulx Abbey   Between the 15th and 17th centuries, large projects were relying increasingly on emerging concepts of engineering science. Typically, they were again emphasizing the importance of timely completion. The projects of Restoration architects such as Wren (Fig. 1), Hawksmore and others show the architect working not just as designer but as estimator, purchaser, organizer, inspector and paymaster. As the commercial sophistication of society developed rapidly, contractual transactions became a significant part of the realization of most projects.

As the 16th gave way to the 17th and 18th centuries, the engineering sophistication of projects increased steadily. By the mid-18th century, Louis XIV's *'génies civils'* — the first civil engineers — such as Vauban and the graduates of the Ecole des Ponts et Chaussées (founded in 1747), and English engineers such as Brindley, Smeaton and Rennie were concentrating on the preparation of engineering designs and estimates for work that would be realized by others. Those who built the projects were now organizationally and contractually separate from those who designed them, far more than in Restoration building (note 3). This, then, was the birth of the professional, or consulting, engineer and architect (note 4).

It is important at this point to recognize that of all the industries in which modern project management is typically practised today, by far the oldest are building and civil engineering. Indeed, the industries in which modern project management was formed — as we shall see, process engineering but particularly aerospace — were hardly born by the time building and civil engineering acquired their current dominant form: that of the professional designer 'representing' the owner's interests in preparing a design and awarding and administering the contract between the builder and the owner. Only recently, as the general lessons of project management have developed in these more modern industries and slowly trickled back into building and civil engineering, have the practices of managing construction projects begun to change, as described later.

The mid-19th to mid-20th centuries saw a prodigious development of the earth's infrastructure and a flourishing of new inventions and products. A 'second generation' of building, civil engineering and related technologies (structural steel frames, the elevator, electrical systems, sewer and water systems, indoor plumbing, central heating, the highway and the subway) together with the emergence of numerous new mass-production industries (steel, petroleum, petrochemicals and pharmaceuticals, electric power, telephony, aircraft, medicine and other sectors) created an era of outstanding projects. There were thousands of construction achievements: skyscrapers, dams, canals, railways (and hence bridges and tunnels) and other transportation achievements; vast cabling and telephone installation projects; potable and waste water systems; progressive electrification with all that this implied in fuel extraction and supply, together with the development of other utilities; and the development of totally new products, not least aircraft and petrochemicals.[1-10]

Government involvement at this time was generally light; taxes were low. This was the era of the private financier and the entrepreneur. The railways, power, mining and telephone companies, and automobile and aircraft manufacturers, were all generally privately owned. Capital was not scarce, regulations were not complex, people wanted work. The early theories of management — Weber's on bureaucracy, for example,[11-13] and Taylor, Gilbreth and Gantt's on scientific management[14-18] (all, incidentally, still used in modern project management) — emphasized simple rules of administration and organization. Only in wartime did this pattern alter.

The history of the First World War is the history, in a sense, of a technologically unsophisticated, imperialistic, military caste. Only slowly did the General Staffs realize that the methods used to subdue their colonies were inappropriate for the Western Front (note 5). As the great powers began to countenance defeat and bankruptcy, new impetus was given to the development of more

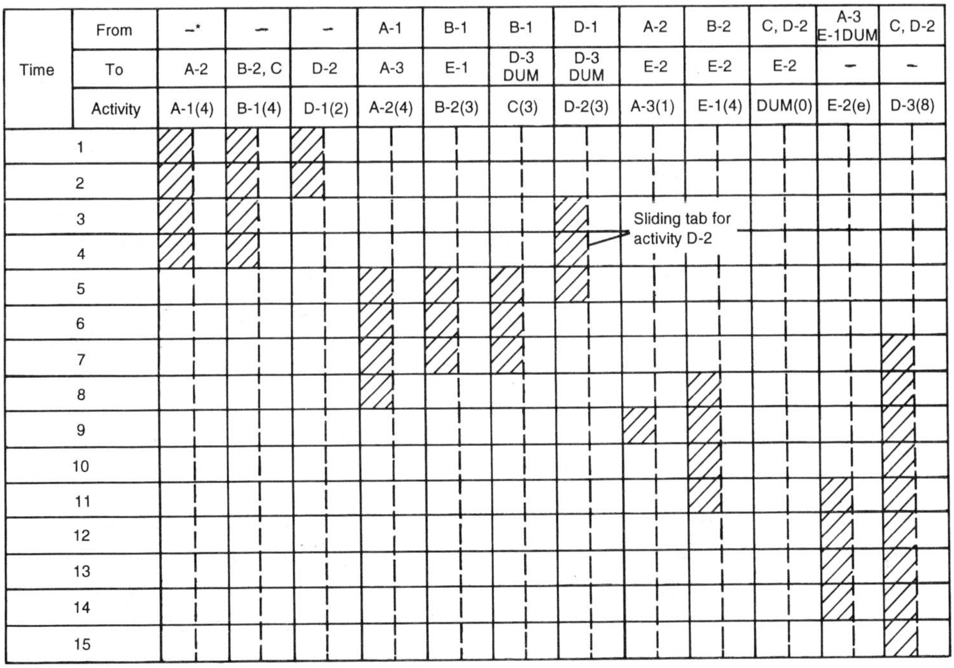

Time	From	—*	—	—	A-1	B-1	B-1	D-1	A-2	B-2	C, D-2	A-3 E-1DUM	C, D-2
	To	A-2	B-2, C	D-2	A-3	E-1	D-3 DUM	D-3 DUM	E-2	E-2	E-2	—	—
	Activity	A-1(4)	B-1(4)	D-1(2)	A-2(4)	B-2(3)	C(3)	D-2(3)	A-3(1)	E-1(4)	DUM(0)	E-2(e)	D-3(8)
1													
2													
3								Sliding tab for activity D-2					
4													
5													
6													
7													
8													
9													
10													
11													
12													
13													
14													
15													

*The first column or strip represents activity A-1, where (4) indicates the estimated time to perform this activity. The dash in the 'From' row indicates that activity A-1 has no predecessor activities, and the A-2 in the 'To' row indicates that it is a successor to A-1.

Fig. 2. Adamiecki's Harmonygraph (from Moder, Phillips and Davis[19])

scientific ways of organizing and undertaking complex operations: the convoy system, for example, developed in 1917.

The scientific school gave birth to two *project planning techniques*. The Gantt bar chart, developed by Henry Gantt in the USA for production scheduling at the Frankford Arsenal in 1917, is widely used today in an essentially unaltered form. Adamiecki's Harmonygraph (Fig. 2), however, is little known. Adamiecki developed the Theory of Work Harmonization around 1896 in Poland. This was the forerunner of work-flow network planning, which was to become so popular 60 years later with CPM and PERT. The final version of the Harmonygraph was published in 1931 (note 6).[20] Another precursor of networks is path analysis, developed by Wright in 1918 as a way of decomposing relationships and of expressing their causal intensity statistically.[21–24]

An early forerunner of project management was the development in the mid-to-late 1920s by Procter and Gamble of *product management* (under the term 'brand management'). Product management is the practice of making a manager responsible for the overall marketing, planning and control of a brand or product. Like project management, product management stresses *the integration of those functions influencing the successful outcome of a venture*. It does not have the same implementation or development emphasis as project management; however, the antecedent is a strong one. Gaddis, for example, in his seminal article on the project manager in the *Harvard Business Review* of 1959[25] begins: 'Generally speaking, the project manager's business is to create a *product*' (emphasis in original) — see p. 36.

During the 1930s, the US Air Corps' Materiel Division moved progressively towards a *project office* function to monitor the development and progress of aircraft. At the same time, Exxon and other (comparatively young) process engineering companies began to develop a *Project Engineer* function: an engineer who could follow a project as it progressed through its various functional departments. The prevailing pattern of organization at this time, however, was almost without exception along pyramidal or *functional* lines. Following Weber, management writers such as Henri Fayol were emphasizing the administrative skills required in the management of hierarchically organized enterprises. In 1937, however, Urwick, one of Fayol's 'school', edited a book in which Gulick wrote a paper proposing that a co-ordinator might be appointed to pull together the administration of a task involving several functional areas (note 7). This was the first appearance of the horizontal, or task, form of organization in the academic writings on management.[26]

By 1939, then, at the outbreak of the Second World War, modern project management was just emerging as an embryonic discipline, although probably evident only to a very few, mostly in the military and process engineering industries.

References

1. Armythe, W. G. H. *A social history of engineering*. Faber & Faber, London, 1961.
2. Beatty, C. *De Lesseps*. Harper, New York, 1956.
3. Burton, P. *The impossible railway: the building of the Canadian Pacific — a triumphant saga of exploration, politics, high finance and adventure*. Knopf, New York, 1972.
4. Hadfield, C. *The canal age*. Praeger, New York, 1969.
5. Howard, R. W. *The great iron trail: the story of the first trans continental railroad*. Bonanza, New York, 1952.
6. Mazlish, B. (ed.). *The railroad and the space program; an exploration in historical analogy*. MIT Press, Cambridge, MA, 1965.
7. McCullogh, D. *The path between the seas: the creation of the Panama Canal 1870–1915*. Simon & Schuster, New York, 1977.
8. Schodek, D. L. *Landmarks in American civil engineering*. MIT Press, Cambridge, MA, 1988.
9. Wendt, H. *The romance of water*. Hill & Wang, New York, 1973.
10. Hughes, T. P. *Networks of power: electrification in Western society, 1880–1930*. Johns Hopkins University Press, Baltimore, 1983.
11. Weber, M. *The theory of social and economic organizations*. Oxford University Press, New York, 1947.
12. Lupton, T. *Management and the social sciences*. Penguin, Harmondsworth, 1971.
13. Tillerd, A., Kempner, T. and Wills, G. (eds). *Management thinkers*. Penguin, Harmondsworth, 1970.

14. Taylor, F. W. *Principles of scientific management*. Harper, New York, 1911.
15. Gilbreth, F. B. *Field system*. Myron C. Clarke, New York, 1908.
16. Gantt, H. *Organizing for work*. Harcourt, Brace & Hove, New York, 1919.
17. Rathe, A. W. (ed.). *Gantt on management*. American Management Association, New York, 1961.
18. Urwick, L. and Brech, E. F. L. *Making of scientific management: Vol. 1, 13 pioneers*. Sir Isaac Pitman, London, 1966.
19. Moder, J. J., Phillips, C. R. and Davis, E. W. *Project management with CPM, PERT and precedence diagramming*. Van Nostrand Reinhold, New York, 3rd edn, 1983.
20. Adamiecki, K. Harmonygraph. *Przeglad Organizacji*, Warsaw, 1931. *O nauce organizacji, panstwowe wydawnictwo ekonomiczw*, Warsaw, 1970.
21. Blalock, H. M. Causal inferences, closed populations, and measures of association. *American Political Science Review*, 1967.
22. Duncan, O. D. Path analysis: sociological examples. *The American Journal of Sociology*, 1966.
23. Wright, S. *Corn and hog correlations*. US Department of Agriculture, Bulletin 1300, Government Printing Office, Washington DC, 1925.
24. Wright, S. Statistical methods in biology. *Journal of the American Statistical Association*, 1931.
25. Gaddis, P. O. The project manager. *Harvard Business Review*, 1959, May—June, 89—97.
26. Gulick, L. Notes on the theory of organization. In *Papers on the science of administration*, Urwick, L. (ed.), Institute of Public Administration, Columbia University Press, New York, 1937, pp. 1—46.

3. The Second World War

Military operations have a distinctly project-like nature (although this may be more obvious in their preparation than in their execution). They generally have clear objectives, need careful planning, rely heavily on the quality of leadership, follow an operational life cycle, and require detailed planning and clear communications and control — characteristics that closely parallel those of project management.

The Second World War, given the prominence that science came to play in its management and the enormous number of complex technologically-driven operations it involved, demonstrates surprisingly little of the tools, language and formal project concepts that have come to comprise modern project management. This is not to say that many military operations were not managed with clarity and attention to 'project' requirements, but, critically, we see in the Second World War few of the formal techniques or practices that project managers today recognize as clearly 'project management' ones.

Three Second World War candidates are commonly put forward as bearing the seed of modern project management: the early work of Operations Research, 'Overlord' (the D-Day landings and the Battle for Normandy) and the Manhattan Project (the USA's development of the atomic bomb). I regard only the Manhattan Project as a valid contributor to the subsequent practice of project management, for the reasons set out below; even the Manhattan Project's contribution to the lexicon of modern project management is not major.

Operational Research

Operational Research (OR) is the collection and analysis of data on everyday operations using scientific principles of research and investigation. Throughout the Second World War, a relatively small number of scientists applied these principles to improving the efficiency of military operations. Their efforts were initially concentrated on improving bombing accuracy and in assisting fighter control — both through radar, but in the case of bombing accuracy also through work on bomb sights, the Pathfinder practice, aircraft formations, and measurement of the effects of bombing damage. OR also worked with coastal command on submarine interception, air flight optimization and depth charges; with the army in applying work study and analysing artillery and armament matters; with civil defence on anti-aircraft defences; and with the navy on ship protection and enemy interception.[1]

None of these have any direct relation to the concepts, tools or practices of project management, with the possible exception of work study, which was in any case invented before the Second World War by Frederick Taylor, Henry Gilbreth and others of the 'scientific' school of management.

'Overlord':
D-Day and the
Battle of
Normandy

Operation Overlord presents a more difficult judgement in terms of project management. D-Day was a hugely successful endeavour involving an enormous amount of planning. It had a clear objective and was 'managed' by a 'Supreme Commander'. Yet, while I do not wish to detract from its formidable accomplishments:

(a) D-Day was not actually an event with a single clear objective, nor was Overlord — the Battle for Normandy was one of a series of battles being waged in 1944, and was soon transformed into the invasion of the Low Countries and the Allies' approach to the Rhine

(b) while the invasion was enormously complex logistically and strategically in almost every way, its execution was made harder in many instances by the personal animosities and political compromises that were such a feature of the Allies' senior command

(c) many of what were later to become key practices of the modern management of projects and programmes, such as technology management, matrix or project organization and principles of contracting, are not found explicitly in Overlord.

The quantities of men and material landed on D-Day were vast and impressive (note 1). Overlord, though, was much more than an achievement in logistics. It was a battle plan involving land, sea and air strategies; detailed resource planning; considerations of French political arrangements; and, crucially, deception plans, secrecy and intelligence gathering (Fig. 3).

Plans for Overlord had begun with the Casablanca conference in January 1943, at which it was accepted that a large-scale cross-Channel invasion would be unlikely before the spring of 1944. Nevertheless, in April 1943, Lt General Morgan was appointed Chief of Staff to the Supreme Allied Commander (COSSAC), to be responsible with an independent US—British staff for the 'control, planning and training of cross-Channel operations'.[2] The first version of Overlord had been produced by July 1943; invasion was planned for 1 May 1944. Preconditions of the plan were that the German Air Force must have been substantially reduced, facilities must have been devised to sustain operations without the use of a great port for at least three weeks, and land opposition must be kept at bay for at least three months. However, no Supreme Commander was appointed until December 1943, and

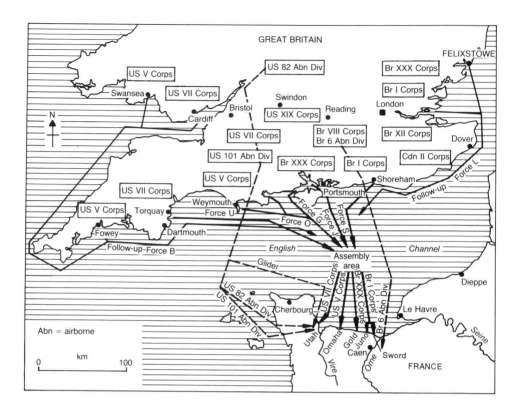

Fig. 3. Normandy and the D-Day Landings

Morgan and his staff were compelled to prepare the plan under the direction of the Chiefs of Staff, who proved unwilling to allocate sufficient resources to the invasion. It was only when General Montgomery arrived in London in December 1943 as Commander-in-Chief, 21st Army Group, that adequate resources were assigned. On reviewing COSSAC's plan, Montgomery immediately insisted that the proposed front be broadened extensively; when told that this was not possible since resources were not available to cover a broader front, he insisted that they be made available, simultaneously relieving Morgan and his staff in their entirety. Eisenhower, the newly appointed Supreme Allied Commander, approved Montgomery's plan on 23 January 1944, shortly after his arrival in London.

There then began 17 weeks of intense planning. Greatly increased numbers of landing craft were now required to be brought over from the USA; in fact this became the 'critical path' item, 3–5 June 1944 becoming the earliest date, consonant with tides and moon, by which sufficient numbers of landing craft could be made available to ship the larger quantities of men and material now to be landed. Inventories were drawn up, loading programmes developed, convoys routed and naval escorts arranged; beach landings and (more importantly) exits were planned and estimates made of possible German counter-movements (the biggest risk was thought to be not the D-Day landings but around 14–20 days later, by which time the Germans might be able to deploy five to six divisions more than the Allies).

Air support was vital: the Allied commanders were fearful of the toll the German Air Force might exact (in fact this was to prove negligible). To secure air cover and to damage the German transportation system, Eisenhower insisted that the Allied air forces come under his command. Such was the independence of the US and British air commanders, however, that it was only with the greatest difficulty and not until April 1944 that Eisenhower was given authority over them.

The Allied commanders were under no illusion as to the fighting capability of the Germany army. Recognizing their vulnerability in numbers during the first few weeks after D-Day, the Allied planners went to exceptional lengths to ensure that the Germans had not the slightest suspicion of either the date or the place of the invasion; further, every effort was made to lead the Germans to believe that the Pas de Calais was to be the real invasion area and that Normandy was only a feint. In both respects they were brilliantly successful, particularly in the 'Fortitude' deception plan, which played a crucial role in keeping the German 15th Army Group locked in Calais in the early days following the landings.[3]

The commanders themselves were not a happy lot. Most of Eisenhower's immediate subordinates were British — Tedder, Montgomery, Ramsay, Leigh-Mallory. Few of them have been regarded as first-rate by their commander, their peers or historians. American–British resentments were frequent and fierce. Eisenhower was not respected by Montgomery, who scorned his commander's complete lack of battle-front experience. Eisenhower's greatest quality, however, was 'his extraordinary generosity of spirit to his difficult subordinates . . . It remains impossible to conceive of any other Allied soldier matching his achievement'.[4]

To portray Eisenhower only as a leader of a team would be to do him a considerable injustice. He faced, and made, many hard decisions — perhaps none harder than to proceed with the invasion on 6 June despite the adverse weather forecasts and against the advice of his subordinates. Yet his greatest strength was undoubtedly as a welder and leader of a strongly disparate team, a team riven by powerful forces, both psychological and political.

Whether this colossal story adds up to a case of modern project management in the making must in the end, I feel, be doubted. The web is too complex, the tools too traditional, the centre too weak. 'The great operation was preparing itself in a thousand different ways throughout the country. The strategic authorities meanwhile were concerned more directly with ensuring that its necessary conditions should be achieved'.[5] Such was not the case with the last of our Second World War cases: the Manhattan Project.

The Manhattan Project

The Manhattan Project — the development of the first atomic bomb — was one of the greatest industrial research and development (R&D) projects ever undertaken. It involved some 600 000 Americans and over $2bn expenditure, entailed huge risks and was of great complexity.

When the project began formally in 1942, the theoretical physics required to control a nuclear chain reaction was still not understood; only microscopic quantities of fissionable material were available and all the research work was being conducted in laboratories. By 1944, $2\frac{1}{2}$ years later, huge plants were nearing completion to produce tons of fissionable material, heavy water and, of course, the bomb (or more precisely, the bombs). All this was carried out in the utmost secrecy under the direct command of President Roosevelt, with the knowledge and authority of only a handful of his most senior Cabinet officers, and under the direct command of one man, General Leslie M. Groves.

Groves took charge of the project in September 1942 (note 2). 'The basic research and development are done', he was told, 'You just have to take the rough designs, put them into final shape, build some plants and organize an operating force and your job will be finished and the war will be over'.[6] The only mistake was the word 'just'.

The principle of the bomb was that sufficient amounts of the uranium isotope, uranium-235, or the plutonium isotope, plutonium-239, could be caused to 'go supercritical' — i.e. for neutrons to cause uranium to fission (break down) at a faster rate than they could escape from the assembly, thereby releasing huge quantities of energy (note 3). Einstein had warned President Roosevelt of the threat of Nazi Germany developing a fission bomb in 1939. Roosevelt appointed an Advisory Committee on uranium in early 1940, uranium 235 and plutonium being identified as fissionable elements in the same year. The committee reported to the President in the spring of 1941 that no nuclear explosion was likely before 1945, and that it would be 18 months before a nuclear chain reaction could be manufactured. Both the British and Americans stepped up their nuclear research, and in December 1941 the USA entered the war. In June 1942 the historic decision was taken to proceed simultaneously with the development of all promising production methods.

The aim of the Manhattan Project was, as the Secretary of War, Henry L. Stimson, put it, 'to bring the war to a successful end more quickly than otherwise would be the case and thus save American lives'.[6] (One might add Japanese, British, Commonwealth and many thousands of other lives.)

The essence of the Manhattan Project was *urgency* — or rather, urgency and *technical uncertainty* — together with security. There was concern throughout the war that Nazi Germany was well on the way to developing a nuclear bomb. It was recognized immediately, and to the considerable credit of the scientists advising the President, that the problems faced in developing an atom bomb were largely *organizational* and *engineering*, even though in 1942 many of the scientific principles were still not understood. Accordingly, the US Army Corps of Engineers was asked to organize the construction work. To provide a security framework, the project was nominally located at first in the Corps' Manhattan Engineering District of New York — hence its title.

At this time the scope of the project was still vastly under-appreciated. The level of expenditure that would eventually be required was completely unrecognized. The urgency that was to grip the project was still unperceived. Nevertheless, the Corps did recognize that the engineering work required was beyond its resources. It therefore hired Stone & Webster as Architect/Engineer for the project. It was decided to concentrate all the facilities for uranium separation at one site — Clinton, in Tennessee — where 25 000 acres were purchased (the facility later became known as Oak Ridge). Contracts for the various facilities were placed in late 1942. The two main uranium separation processes at Oak Ridge were the electromagnetic and the gaseous diffusion processes. The electromagnetic plant (Project Y-12) involved separating ions by passing them through a magnetic field and collecting them into different groups according to their weight. Doing this on a large scale involved a huge programme of physical and chemical research as well as facilities of very great size. The work was conducted under the leadership of Dr Ernest O. Lawrence, with the plant being operated by Eastman Kodak. Construction of the work (by General Electric, Westinghouse and Allis-Chalmers) began in February 1943 and was completed, at a cost of about $330m, in November that year (a not inconsiderable feat!). The technical problems were colossal: the specifications were rough, equipment did not arrive in an orderly sequence, and manufacturing quality problems were sometimes severe. Until 31 December 1946, this was the only plant producing fully enriched uranium (Fig. 4).

The gaseous diffusion process (Project K-25) was designed to separate ^{235}U from ^{238}U by passing uranium gas through a porous barrier: the lighter ^{235}U molecules would pass through more quickly than the heavier ^{238}U molecules. The work had been pioneered by Columbia University and the plant was constructed by M. W. Kellogg. Enriched uranium was first produced in early 1945. In all, 25 000 men worked on K-25, which cost $275m.

A major concern for the Oak Ridge facilities was the supply

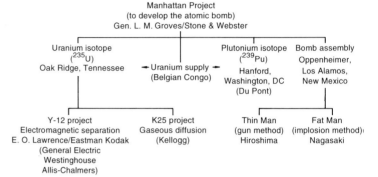

Fig. 4. Work Breakdown Structure of the Manhattan Project

of uranium ore. By good fortune, bravery and decency, a considerable stock of uranium ore was made available to the USA by Union Minière of the Belgian Congo.

Following its highly successful experience in managing the development of nylon on a crash basis,[7] E. I. Du Pont de Nemours was asked to design, construct and operate the plutonium production plant. Du Pont was extremely uneasy about the project, not only because there were at this time no engineering data to speak of — the major plant decisions being taken before theoretical confirmation of the practicability of recovering plutonium — but also because so far only minute quantities of plutonium had been produced. Large amounts were now required, although the scientists could say how much only within a factor of ten. The reactors that would produce the plutonium required considerable quantities of cooling water and had to be isolated, for safety reasons. Hanford in Washington State was chosen as the site for the production facility; 45 000 men and over 10 000 subcontractors were to work on its construction.

The bomb itself (or rather bombs, for two kinds were being developed) was to be designed at Los Alamos in New Mexico. Groves selected J. Robert Oppenheimer to be the director of Los Alamos (Project Y) — a choice demonstrating vision and courage, since Oppenheimer had evinced 'suspect' left-wing views in the past and many establishment figures were against his nomination. Oppenheimer collected about him, under conditions of the most intense security, a group of distinguished scientists and engineers. His ability to weld a team out of such extraordinary personalities operating in physical conditions of considerable discomfort showed leadership of a rare and truly outstanding calibre.[8,9] In the early stages the work was extremely theoretical. Estimates as to the optimum length of the explosion reaction were little more than guesses, and varied greatly. It was not known whether the fissionable material would be ^{235}U or plutonium, or both.

Two types of bomb were developed: the Thin Man and the Fat Man. Thin Man used the gun assembly method in which a subcritical mass of fissionable material was shot at another subcritical mass, the impact causing the material to become supercritical. This was the bomb eventually dropped on Hiroshima. In 1943, Neddermeyer, von Neumann, Teller and others at Los Alamos developed another design, the implosion bomb: subcritical material was imploded to such an extent that it went supercritical. This became the Fat Man bomb, which was later dropped on Nagasaki.

By 1944, the Manhattan Project was huge — spending $1bn a year — and in difficulties. Virtually every stage of the project was experiencing problems. Recovery in the electromagnetic process (Y-12) was only 50%, the diffusion plant (K-25) was not yet working, there were problems in finding satisfactory barriers, the first reactor at Hanford had shut itself down as soon as it was started up, at Los Alamos it had been concluded that plutonium would not work on the gun assembly method. These difficulties caused delay; this delay meant that the target gradually changed from Germany to Japan.

In April 1945, following Roosevelt's dealth, President Truman was briefed for the first time on the project. The design of the ^{235}U gun had now been frozen but, he was told, there would not be sufficient ^{235}U until about August. Enough plutonium-239 would be available for an implosion test in July. This was successfully accomplished at Almogordo on 16 July (note 4). Bombers had meanwhile been adapted and facilities built at Tinian, 1500 miles south of Japan. ^{235}U was shipped out to Tinian, arriving on 26 July on board the cruiser Indianapolis. (The Indianapolis was sunk by a Japanese submarine with the loss of over 900 lives four days later.) The Thin Man bomb was dropped on Hiroshima, untested, on 6 August. Two-thirds of the city was destroyed. The Fat Man bomb was then dispatched for Kokura on 11 August, but owing to poor visibility the B-29 crew followed their fall-back plan and dropped their bomb on Nagasaki instead. Slightly less than half the city was destroyed. The Japanese began surrender negotiations four days later.

Groves characterized the Manhattan Project as presenting great difficulties, bearing a small chance of success, and incurring great costs. He attributed the success of the project to five factors.[6]

> First we had a clearly defined, unmistakable, specific objective ... Second, each part of the project had a specific task. These tasks were carefully allocated and supervised so that the sum of their parts would result in the accomplishment of our overall mission ... Third, there was positive, clear-cut, unquestioned direction of the project at all levels. Authority was invariably delegated with responsibility, and this delegation was absolute and without reservation ... Fourth, the project made maximum use of already existing agencies, facilities and services ... Consequently, our people were able to devote themselves exclusively to the task at hand, and had no reason to engage in independent empire building. Fifth, and finally, we had the full backing of our government with the nearly infinite [availability of resources].

Groves also stressed 'the cohesive entity that was such a factor in the project's success'.[6] Edward Teller quotes Sir James Chadwick to make the additional point that Groves himself was essential to the project's success.[6]

The Manhattan Project may not have used network scheduling — in fact its scheduling problems were chronic — or Work Breakdown Structures or similar project management tools which were to be the buzzwords of 20 years later, but it certainly displayed the principles of organization, planning and direction that typify the modern management of projects. It also displayed many of the problems, such as cost overruns and concurrency (note 5), that have characterized defence projects ever since (note 6).

References

1. McCloskey, J. F. The beginning of Operations Research. *Operations Research*, 1987, **35**, Nos 1, 3, 6, 143–152, 453–470, 910–925.
2. Howard, M. *Grand strategy*. Vol. 4, HMSO, London, 1972.
3. Hinkey, F. H., Thomas, E. E., Simkins, C. A. G., and Ransom, C. F. G. *British intelligence in the Second World War*. Vol. 3, No. 2, HMSO, London, 1988, p. 182.
4. Hastings, M. *Overlord*. Pan, London, 1985, pp. 34–35.
5. Ehrman, J. *Grand strategy*. Vol. 5, HMSO, London, 1956, pp. 856–857, 216–219, 283.
6. Groves, L. M. *Now it can be told: the story of the Manhattan Project*. Harper, New York, 1962 (reprinted De Capo Press, New York, 1983).
7. Galison, P. and Hevly, B. *Big science: the growth of large-scale research*. Stanford University Press, 1992.
8. Goodchild, P. *J. Robert Oppenheimer: shatterer of worlds*. Houghton Mifflin, Boston, 1981.
9. Lawrence, W. L. *Man in atoms*. Simon & Schuster, New York, 1959.

4. The 1950s: the development of Systems Management

Groves' masterful display of successful project management naturally received very little publicity — the process of developing atomic weapons was of the utmost sensitivity and secrecy. By the early 1950s, then, there had been little or no development in the formalization of the arts and mechanics of managing projects. Yet by the end of the decade the situation was to be utterly different. PERT and CPM would both be developed — almost to the point of being household terms — while Systems Management and Engineering were the up-and-coming jargon terms of a new technologically sophisticated coterie.

The earliest obvious development of Program and Project Management began in the early 1950s in the US Air Force (USAF). It was caused initially by sudden pressures to develop and produce large numbers of increasingly sophisticated planes, and later by the programme to develop long range rockets on an extremely urgent basis. Both these major production efforts gave rise to a host of new systems and project techniques.

It is now time, therefore, to start getting more specific in this account of who did what, and why and how successfully they did it, in the development of the formal discipline of the management of projects.

USAF procurement in the early 1950s

As the USAF entered the 1950s it was still organizing its defence projects with engineering and production organized by separate project offices. With the onset of the Korean War in the summer of 1950, however, there was a sharp increase in production orders for the B47 bomber. This led to an increased need to improve co-ordination between engineering and production. As a result, 'joint project offices' were established in February 1951. The B52 programme followed suit shortly afterwards, and by January 1952 joint project offices had become common practice in the USAF.

In April 1951, this practice was extended. A new USAF command, Air Research and Development Command (ARDC), was established to create a research and development organization concentrating on the long-term development of weapons systems. The joint engineering and production project offices continued to work well, although they now came under two commands: ARDC and the Air Materiel Command (AMC). Formal Joint Project Offices were established in late 1953. In early 1954 the practice was further extended, as *Weapon System Project Offices* (WSPOs) were created.

The language used in defining WSPO responsibilities is very interesting. Suddenly, modern systems and project terminology emerges in full force, including terms that still seem current in the 1990s, 40 years later. For example, within the WSPO, the USAF said that

> [ARDC was responsible for] planning system development, overseeing technical integration of components, assuring compatibility of interdependent subsystems, insuring system reliability, conducting flight tests, and furnishing procurement data. Meanwhile, AMC was responsible for procurement of the system, programming deliveries, assuring maintainability, and insuring adequate supply support.[1]

This practice was not without difficulties. Defining exactly which person was responsible for which action was a particular problem, being especially prone to continual reinterpretation and debate when a difficulty arose or a major decision had to be taken.

By now, however, a more significant event was arising which was to prove of more long-term importance to the development of project management practice. This was the need, felt increasingly urgently, to develop long-range missiles rapidly to counter the perceived major Soviet threat of nuclear-armed intercontinental ballistic missiles.

The Atlas missile programme and the emergence of Systems Management in the USAF

During the early 1950s, popular and political concern over the rapid progress seemingly being made by the Soviet Union in developing long-range ballistic missiles began to increase markedly. By the end of the decade, it was forecast, the Soviet Union would possess a force of intercontinental ballistic missiles (ICBMs) armed with nuclear warheads. For the first time ever, the continental mainland of the USA would be vulnerable to direct and devastating aerial bombardment. And, as if this were not traumatic enough, the bombardment would be atomic. Armageddon was around the corner! The US government thus began to come under strong criticism for not having developed US counter-systems more quickly and efficiently (note 1).

With the arrival of the Eisenhower Administration in 1953, new impetus was given to the creation of US ICBMs. Eisenhower's Secretary of the Air Force, Harold E. Talbott, appointed Trevor Gardner as his special assistant for research and development. Before long, Gardner was expressing major concern at the estimate that at best it would be another ten years before the USA had an atomic-armed and appropriately guided ICBM. In June 1953, the Secretary of Defense asked Gardner to review the overall programmes of all three of the US military services. Gardner organized a prestigious committee, the Strategic Missiles Evaluation Committee, to conduct this study under the chairmanship of John von Neumann of Princeton University. Two members of the committee were Dr Ramo and Dr Woolridge, who had recently left the Hughes Aircraft Company to found their own company, Ramo Woolridge Corporation (later to become TRW). Gardner now began to think of Ramo Woolridge as providing some kind of development agency outside the USAF bureaucracy.

The von Neumann Committee reported on 10 February 1954. The committee's estimates were more optimistic than previous reports: it believed that the ICBM then being developed by the USA — Atlas (Fig. 5) — could be operational by 1962, but proposed nevertheless that a new development group should 'be given direct responsibility for the entire project' and that 'the type of directional team needed is of the calibre and strength that may require the creation of a special group by a drafting operation performed by the highest level government executives in university, industry, and government organizations'.[2] These organizational requirements, the committee considered, were more critical to the programme's success than any of the then outstanding technical problems. A Rand report at the same time came to a strikingly similar conclusion, observing in passing that the Atlas programme was being burdened by unnecessarily onerous performance requirements.

The USAF's response to these two reports was one of scepticism. In particular, it feared that Gardner might be setting himself up as the manager of another Manhattan Project. The USAF recognized the technical validity of the report's proposals, however, and argued that ARDC should establish 'a very competent military—civilian group which would be given a year in which to produce in full detail a redirected, expanded, and accelerated program'.[3] This proposal was accepted by Gardner and Talbott. On 1 June 1954, Brigadier Bernard A. Schriever was placed in charge of the ICBM effort as head of the USAF Western Development Division, Ramo Woolridge Corporation having received a contract to provide systems support to this effort on 3 May 1954.

The concept of a *systems support contractor* had grown directly from ARDC's experience in developing the first jet aircraft in the early 1950s, which indicated that 'the traditional practices of designing components to be fitted into aircraft as necessary should be replaced by a policy of specifying the total system and designing components to perform within it . . . . The complete weapon system — the aircraft or guided missile, its components, supporting equipments and USAF preparation for its implementation as a weapon — should be planned, scheduled, and controlled, from design through test, as an operating entity (ref. 1, p. 6). Basic to this approach were the assumptions that

- performance requirements could be specified
- careful detailed preplanning could eliminate subsequent configuration and engineering changes

Fig. 5. Atlas rocket with a Mercury capsule attempting lift-off (courtesy NASA)

Fig. 6. Polaris A3 (courtesy Jane's Information Group)

- speed and efficiency of development could be maximized by selecting the contractor proposal best calculated to meet this specification, carefully planning the research and development required, and assigning the task to a 'single prime contractor'.

These concepts, it will be seen, *are fundamental to all modern Project and Program Management*, to some degree at least. For example, the integration of everything necessary to ensure that defined technical, cost and schedule performance requirements are met, and the emphasis on a prime contractor taking overall responsibility for implementation, remain as basic project management concepts to this day (note 2).

Unfortunately, while these ideas contained the seed of much that has proved good in Project and Program Management, they also contained that which has proved less than good. The practice of systems management soon came to emphasize the process of managing others — of procedures, paperwork and bureaucracy — rather than of performing engineering and integration directly, and these 'front-line' tasks came to be the responsibility primarily of the contractor(s). Worse, with the system specifiers now organizationally separated from those who would actually engineer and build the system, it became more likely that inoptimum or unrealistically ambitious specifications would be set. *The setting of excessive standards has been a major system engineering/project management problem in advanced technology projects for most of the period covered in this book.*

The immediate consequences of the USAF's acceptance of the von Neumann Committee's recommendations, however, were highly beneficial and practical, for General Schriever quickly proved himself not just an able administrator but also a forceful and effective leader. A personable, intelligent and patient man, he was to employ all his remarkable skills of leadership in creating a radically new form of organization structure within the USAF in order to give the Atlas programme the resources and support it was soon seen to need.

During the second half of 1954, the USAF decided to reject the idea of a single prime contractor since, it was felt, no single firm possessed the range of skills or industrial capacity required. Instead, an unprecedented structure was devised whereby the USAF management would be advised by a special contractor. The Ramo Woolridge Corporation was charged with assembling the scientific and industrial skills and abilities not only to advise the USAF, but also to perform the overall systems engineering and integration for the Atlas programme. Development and fabrication were contracted at the major subsystem level: air frame and assembly, propulsion, guidance and nose cone. All major system engineering and integration decisions were reserved to the government office and executed through Ramo Woolridge as system engineering and technical direction contractor.

Urgency and technical uncertainty were of the essence in the programme. In June 1954 Schriever won the overwhelming (USAF) 'political' support he needed (just as Groves had for the Manhattan Project) when it was announced that 'The Atlas program will be reoriented and accelerated to the maximum extent that technological development will permit .... The Atlas will be given the highest program priority in the Air Force. Processing any aspect of this program will be given precedence over any others in the Air Force' (ref. 2, pp. 180—181).

In view of the great urgency of the programme, Schriever also introduced (in fact, he pioneered) the practice of testing major systems simultaneously rather than consecutively, a technique later used on Apollo (see p. 54) and the precursor of 'concurrency'. This method evidently poses an increased risk of failure, as the number of 'chances' one has to catch problems is reduced. To deal with this increased risk one must put more effort into supervision, integration and quality at the workplace. Schriever was thus forcing management down the organization, and emphasizing further the importance of systems and project management.

These technical and managerial innovations notwithstanding, by mid-1955 the programme was still experiencing difficulties, due largely to resentment felt by the USAF hierarchy and the lack of adequate funding provided by the USAF. Schriever and Gardner therefore sought further radical changes to the USAF management and review procedures. They recognized, however, that given the already serious opposition, such change would have to come from above. Their chance came in late 1954, when the Soviet Union displayed the 'Bear', its first long-range bomber, and at the 1955 May Day parade, when the 'Bison', another long-range bomber comparable in many respects to the US B52, was presented. This demonstration of an increased Soviet military 'threat' immediately created Congressional pressure to expedite the development of a US ICBM capability.

With Congress thus now highly supportive of programme acceleration, Gardner ordered a new working group, the Gillette Committee (which included General Schriever), to recommend ways in which the USAF's ICBM management could be streamlined. By October 1955, the Gillette Committee recommended the removal of several levels of managerial approval: financial appropriations would be made by a Ballistic Missile Committee, which would co-ordinate and speed up the review, approval and funding of requests prepared by the programme management office. These proposals helped to integrate ARDC and AMC and to reduce the overall time required to achieve funding. Effective though such measures were for the ICBM programme, however, they were inevitably unpopular with the mainstream of the USAF hierarchy, and by November 1959 had effectively been abandoned.

The general concepts of Systems Engineering and Program Management developed for the ICBMs were, despite the resentment felt for Gardner and his initiatives, soon promoted further within the USAF. The Robertson Committee report of September 1956 recommended that procedures and methods for the development of manned aircraft weapons systems be organized on 'product' rather than 'functional' lines, and that there be a general elevation of the project manager function/office within the USAF management organization.

Once again, the USAF hierarchy resisted such proposals, and functionally organized commands remained in ARDC and AMC for some time, in fact until Sputnik and the arrival of President

Kennedy and his Defense Secretary, Robert McNamara, forced the integration necessary within the Pentagon. Meanwhile, another ballistic missile programme had begun which was to prove of even greater importance to the development of Project and Program Management: the US Navy's Polaris programme.

The fleet ballistic missile: Polaris

Even more than Atlas, Polaris (Fig. 6) elevated the authority of 'the Program' within the organization as opposed to the traditional functional orientation. Polaris demonstrated, like Atlas, the prime importance of outstanding leadership on such challenging programmes. But unlike Atlas, Polaris developed a management control procedure, PERT; this, together with CPM, was the progenitor of the management systems which over the next 20 years were to become (almost too) synonymous with project management.

During the early-to-mid 1950s, as the importance of ballistic missiles became steadily more apparent, the USAF benefited while the US Navy suffered. The Navy developed proposals for its own ballistic missile programme (in the early autumn of 1955), after the USAF's and the Army's, at the insistence of Admiral Burke, who was conscious of the Navy's failure so far to find a role in the USA's deployment of this vitally important new technology and determined to push the Navy to the forefront of the new era of weaponry. Unfortunately, the Navy was also the first to feel the effect of the new budget stringencies: its proposal was rejected and it was told to collaborate with the Army. This it did, with some reluctance, proposing that the liquid-fuelled intermediate-range ballistic missile (IRBM) Jupiter be developed into a Fleet Ballistic Missile (FBM) for use on board ships or submarines.

Having established Jupiter as the FBM, Admiral Burke turned to the question of who would be responsible for developing the missile. Recognizing the latent rivalry between the Navy's Bureau of Aeronautics and Bureau of Ordnance, Burke and the Navy Secretariat created a new organization, the Special Projects Office (SPO), under the command of Admiral William F. Raborn on 17 November 1955. (Significantly for project management, the SPO was a programme office one hierarchical level higher than that created in the USAF. It was established, incidentally, just three days after the Gillette Committee published its recommendations.)

From the outset, the Navy made it clear to the Army that it preferred a solid- to a liquid-fuelled rocket, mainly for size reasons. Without the approval of either the Department of Defense (DoD) or the Navy Secretariat, senior Naval officers began researching solid-fuel possibilities early in 1956. The first design, Jupiter S, was an unacceptable monster. In the summer of 1956, however, the Navy organized a 'summer study' — a national gathering of scientists and their families — at Woods Hole, Massachusetts. This was to have a profound impact on the FBM programme in that it gave rise to the recognition that the FBM was based on two systems — the submarines and the missiles — whose technologies were at different states of evolution. Edward Teller, 'the father of the H-bomb', one of those resident at the 'school', pointed out that the pace of development of thermonuclear technology, in which warhead weight was being steadily reduced, was such that in a few years it should be possible for warheads to fit on rockets the size of large torpedoes. The FBM missile performance specifications were of 1958 vintage and took no account of this trend, although the submarine was not scheduled for service until 1965. 'Why use a 1958 warhead in a 1965 weapon system?' asked Teller.

This episode in the Polaris story makes two vitally important points about managing projects. First, Teller saw the complete system — rocket plus submarine — while everyone else was concentrating on a part of the total system. *Defining the 'total' project is critical to success*: generally it is obvious but sometimes it is not, particularly in major projects where 'external' factors can emerge to affect the project or related projects or systems — for example the Shuttle for the Space Station (p. 328, note 38). Second, *forecast rate of technological change* was being consciously examined. Too often in projects this is ignored — in any system, let alone the total project system, as here. Inaccurate assessment of the rate of technological change (especially underestimation) has been the cause of a huge number of project failures.

Burke and Raborn picked up Teller's point. Burke, convinced that the Navy's future rested on the successful development of the FBM, ordered the switch from Jupiter in September 1956.

Obtaining DoD approval was no easier now than it had been a year earlier. This time, however, the Navy was politically more astute. It indicated first that Polaris would offer a one-third cost saving over Jupiter. It then voted with the USAF in the Joint Chiefs of Staff to assign responsibility for all land based ICBMs with a range of 200 miles or more to the USAF. In December 1956 the Navy was authorized to initiate the Polaris FBM programme.

Admiral Raborn promoted the Special Projects Office as an elite force within the Navy. The programme and the SPO were soon making huge demands in both money and personnel. Not surprisingly, they were also stirring up opposition, both within the Navy and, particularly, from the USAF which saw the FBM as a threat to its own missile programmes. Some of this criticism was unhelpful, but in the end, as Sapolsky has documented,[4] much of it improved the performance of Polaris.

Admiral Raborn was outstanding as a *champion, leader* and *manager* of the Polaris programme. He championed the programme's organizational independence by developing a broad base of support for it and by engendering confidence in the managerial capability of the SPO. The SPO operated on a wartime basis, with officers always in uniform, flags flying over facilities, personnel working extended hours, and messages red-stamped and often hand-carried. Those working on it showed a deep commitment to the programme's success. Urgency was paramount. Raborn spoke often and enthusiastically to outside groups, not least to Congress, and drew into the programme potential critics as well as the country's leading scientists. Special efforts were made to ensure the support of Admiral Rickover (of the Bureau of Ships' Nuclear Power Directorate (note 3)) and the Navy's submariners. Raborn was also careful to avoid attacking his competitors. In the main, his strategy was to display moderation.

Like Atlas, Polaris employed contractors for the bulk of its R&D, management support and procurement. As a result, the programme schedule was not only accelerated but also its base was broadened further. By 1961, it was estimated that 250 prime contractors and 9000 subcontractors were working on the programme. Employing so many contractors, however, brought costs as well as benefits. Although the SPO staff were technically more involved in the engineering of the FBM than the USAF officers were on Atlas (since the USAF relied heavily on the Ramo Woolridge Corporation), detailed technical knowledge about the system generally rested with the contractors. Under this way of working, the systems management function was not formalized as clearly as in General Schriever's Division within the USAF. Main responsibility for systems engineering rested with the Chief Engineer in the SPO's Technical Directorate, whose task was to establish system boundaries and monitor interface relationships.

The SPO's propensity for detailed control was carried forward by Gordon Peterson, the head of its Plans and Programs Division. Peterson believed that government was generally more concerned with the control of inputs than outputs, and sought instead 'to create integrated management control systems that would focus decision making. .... on program costs only in relation to program performance' (ref. 4, p. 66). Out of this idea was to evolve PERT (Fig. 7).

The Program Evaluation Review Technique (PERT)

In early 1956, Admiral Raborn had ordered the SPO Plans and Programs Division to survey the systems employed by other companies and organizations accustomed to working on large-scale programmes. Visits were made to Chrysler, General Motors, Du Pont and other companies. Little of value to the SPO seems to have been found. A few months later Raborn persuaded Peterson to join the programme.

In January 1957 Raborn outlined his thoughts on the features that the control system should have: 'I must be able to reach down to any level of Special Projects Office activity and find a plan and performance report that logically and clearly can be related to the

Fig. 7 (below and facing page). PERT scheduling techniques: an early example adapted from Battersby[19]

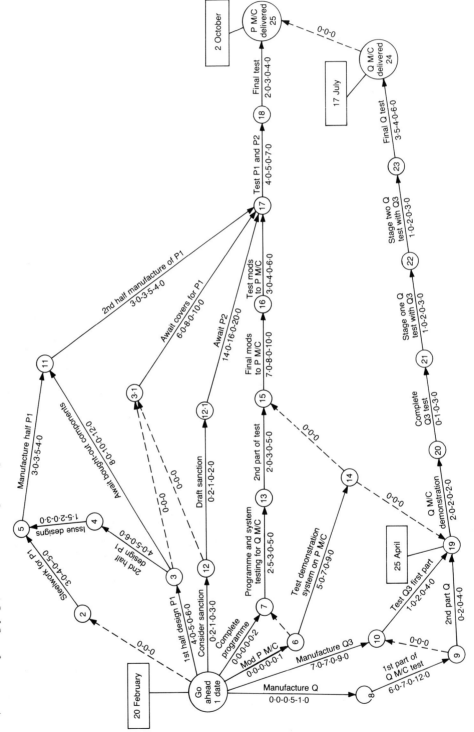

English Electric Computing Services—Programme Assessment

Report Date:	5 February 1962				PERT				Slack order
Customer:	Computer Development								
Project:	P & Q Machines								
Event	Critical neighbour	Landmark	Actual date	Expected date (1962)	Latest date (1962)	Schedule date (1962)	Slack	Std Dev.	Prob.
1		Go ahead date		19 February	12 February		−1·0		
8	1	Q delivered to engineers		23 February	16 February		−1·0	0·1	
9	8	Q machine half tested		17 April	10 April		−1·0	0·9	
10	9	Start testing Q 3		17 April	10 April		−1·0	0·9	
19	10	Q ready to demonstrate		2 May	25 April	25 April	−1·0	0·9	0·15
20	19	Demonstration finished		16 May	13 May		−0·4	0·9	
21	20	Q 3 fully tested		24 May	21 May		−0·4	1·1	
22	21	Stage one Q test done		7 June	4 June		−0·4	1·1	
23	22	Stage two Q test done		21 June	18 June		−0·4	1·2	
24	23	Deliver Q machine		20 July	17 July	17 July	−0·4	1·2	0·37
6	1	P machine modified		20 February	7 March		2·1	0·1	
14	6	P ready to demonstrate		10 April	25 April		2·1	0·7	
15	14	Q system fully tested		10 April	12 May		4·5	0·7	
16	15	P machine last mods. done		6 June	8 July		4·5	0·8	
17	16	P machine mods. tested		5 July	6 August		4·5	0·9	
18	17	Test P 1 and P 2		10 August	11 September		4·5	0·9	
25	18	Deliver P machine		31 August	2 October	2 October	4·5	1·1	1·0
3	1	P 1 half designed		26 March	29 April		4·8	0·2	
4	3	P 1 fully designed		30 April	3 June		4·8	0·2	
5	4	Start making P 1		14 May	17 June		4·8	0·4	
11	5	P 1 half designed		8 June	12 July		4·8	0·4	
7	6	Start programme testing		20 February	29 March		5·2	0·1	
13	7	Q system half tested		14 March	20 April		5·2	0·4	
12	1	Start drafting sanction		27 February	7 April		5·5	0·4	
121	12	Order P 2		6 March	14 April		5·5	0·5	
31	3	Order covers for P 1		26 March	11 June		11·0	0·2	
2	1	Order steelwork for P 1		19 February	20 May		12·8		

total job we have to do'.[5] Raborn already had several of the components of the later PERT system in place by this time: a Progress Analysis Branch whose job it was to audit actual rather than officially reported progress; a 'Management Center' acting as a 'war room' or *control room* (an idea taken from the Army's Jupiter programme); and a system of 'weekly staff meetings' in which progress was reported systematically. Measuring performance against plan was a central objective of SPO control.

At the weekly staff meetings, terms such as 'good shape' or 'minor weakness' were used to describe status. Clearly these were subjective and imprecise. A more objective measure was sought. Although *line-of-balance* (LOB) techniques provided a measure of productivity (note 4), they were not useful for predicting development progress in an R&D environment. To develop a method for doing this, Peterson established in December 1956 a small team of SPO staff and outside contractors — the management consultants Booz, Allen & Hamilton and the Lockheed Corporation.

The team quickly developed a number of criteria for the required project control system:

- a careful time estimate for each activity, no matter how far in the future
- since such time estimates involve uncertainty, the exposure of this uncertainty — 'ideally, for each activity we should have a probability distribution of the times that the activity might require'
- 'precise knowledge of the sequencing required or planned in the performance of activities'.[6]

Work began formally on 27 January 1957. The study team recognized that the status of the FBM programme was a function of the resources employed, the technical performance of those constructing the system, and the time that the various programme activities would take. Only the last, it was soon realized, was amenable to systematic evaluation. Diagrams were therefore constructed showing the relation between activities and events on the Polaris programme.

In addition to this technique of networking, core concepts of PERT included the collection of estimates from bench engineers of the time required to accomplish specific events, the use of a mathematical formula for determining the expected time of achieving the event (note 5), and the identification of the '*critical path*', i.e. *the sequence of events in the project that required the longest time for completion.*

Development of the basic PERT concepts took only about four weeks. By July 1957, the first PERT procedures had been published, and PERT was being run on computers that October. In mid-1958, Admiral Raborn and the SPO public relations machinery began publicizing PERT, hailing it as 'the first management tool of the nuclear and computer age' (Raborn never did things by half!). So effective was the publicity that when the first Polaris missile was launched in 1960, press coverage of PERT was almost as great as the coverage of the launch itself. By 1962, the US Government had issued 139 different documents and reports on the technique. By 1964, the bibliography on PERT comprised nearly 1000 books and articles. The technique has become almost a household word, synonymous in some people's minds with project management itself (and of course it is still used by many people to describe network scheduling in general). There is, however, considerable evidence that the method was deliberately oversold, with the aim of keeping Congressional and other external critics at arm's length (ref. 4, pp. 129–130). *Raborn used PERT as a tool to manage his external environment.*

In fact, by 1959 only a small portion of the Polaris programme was on PERT. SPO technical staff were suspicious of their estimates being fed back to them as a PERT result which might be wholly unacceptable yet whose computation they could not trust and which would be unverifiable. Contractors resented being asked to estimate pessimistic schedule dates, and, like the SPO staff, they were reluctant for 'their' data to be processed outside their control, to produce a result with which they might not be happy. Both SPO and contractor staff queried the basic assumptions underlying PERT. Admiral Raborn, however, endorsed and championed the system — his vote was in fact the deciding one at the SPO Board meeting that approved the implementation of PERT in October 1958.

As Raborn made continued and effective use of PERT, in presenting an image of efficiency and control of the programme, ·opposition within the SPO diminished. Variants of PERT were developed — *PERT/Cost* added a budgeting and cost monitoring module in 1961–1962 (see p. 44) and, later, the Reliability Management (later, Maturity) Index (RMI) was added to monitor technical reliability of activities — these proved far less successful than basic PERT, and the RMI never really worked. Early in the 1960s, when NASA adopted PERT — PERT systems having become a contract requirement on DoD, NASA and Atomic Energy Commission programmes in 1962 — it dropped the requirement for a threefold estimate of event and activity times (note 6).

By the early 1960s, the outbreak of project management planning and control systems seemed to be getting almost out of control. Philip Geddes, in his famous 1962 article 'The year of management systems', identified 52 'techniques that can help your management problems' spawned by 'DoD attitudes on long range planning and management efficiency'.[7] The decade was if anything, as described below, over-dominated by this emphasis on management systems.

Before moving on to the 1960s and this discussion, however,

we must discuss the other network scheduling system developed at about the same time as PERT. This is the Critical Path Method (CPM).

Construction project management and CPM

The account of post-war project management given above is set largely in the US military domain. There were, however, other antecedents to modern project management.

While the building and civil engineering industries continued to operate along the lines established at the end of the 19th century, with the architect or engineer administering the contract between the owner and the contractor — meaning that no one person or group was actively and comprehensively directing the project from the top — the oil, gas and petrochemical industries continued, in the main, to emphasize the integrated approach to project identification and development that they had pioneered before the Second World War. In general, though, the huge amount of rebuilding after the war was carried out largely using traditional organizational relationships and management practices. (As one old hand put it, on the 'slug it out' method of management.)

During the 1950s in the UK, much interest was shown in the construction industries in the techniques of Work Study, i.e. Time Measurement and Method Study. Operational Research (being scientific and therefore more respectable!) was also given considerable support by the intellectual side of British industry. At ICI's Billingham works, a technique was developed in 1955 using 'the controlled sequence duration' for plant maintenance scheduling;[8] in a similar attempt to plan plant shutdown more efficiently, the UK's Central Electricity Generating Board (CEGB) developed in 1957 a technique to identify the 'longest irreducible sequence of events' in the overhaul of generating plants — what was later termed the 'major sequence'.[9] Both were direct precursors of what was soon to be known as the 'critical path'. Neither the ICI method nor the CEGB's were widely publicized, however, and effectively they had little impact on general engineering management practice (note 7).

Meanwhile, in the USA, E. I. Du Pont de Nemours was investigating uses for its newly acquired Univac computer, one of whose possibilities was to determine the best trade-off between the time and the cost of plant overhaul, maintenance and construction. In particular, Du Pont wished to determine the optimum (that is, minimum total cost) duration for a large project where the activity durations could be calculated with some reliability. Formal investigations were begun in December 1956 — a year earlier than Peterson's on Polaris. By 1957 a pilot scheme had been developed and run using the arrow diagram method, but the studies were not finished and published until February 1959.[10,11]

CPM is strikingly similar to PERT — both use the network

technique, both use 'arrows' to represent activities — although neither group became aware of the other's work until early 1959. Du Pont's business — construction — was fundamentally different from the Navy's in that the technologies and processes were largely known. In contrast to the R&D world of Polaris, Du Pont could calculate how long each activity would take with some accuracy — so many feet of pipe at so many feet per hour, etc. Hence its method naturally emphasized *activity duration* whereas the Navy's naturally emphasized the *probability of an event happening* around a future date (Fig. 8).

Further, the environment of the ballistic missile programmes was intensely schedule driven, with very little consideration for cost control (which is why, of course, PERT/Cost came later than PERT itself). Du Pont, on the other hand, was operating in a commercial environment in which costs mattered greatly. Since Du Pont was searching for a way to optimize costs and schedules, it required basic data on both.[12] Du Pont thus developed its

Fig. 8. Evolution of CPM compared with PERT (source: Archibald and Villoria[18])

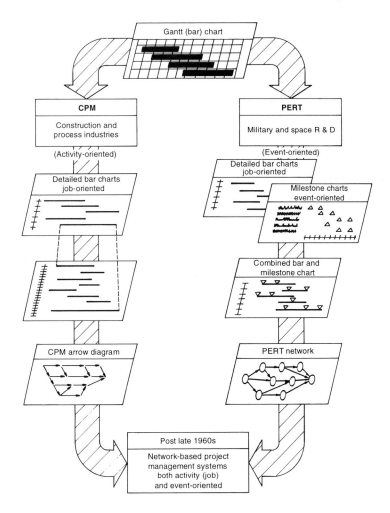

approach by calculating various schedule durations according to varying resource utilization: two different resource allocations were in fact allowed for each activity (note 8). The costs of the different resource loadings were then compared against savings in indirect costs such as overheads. CPM, in other words, dealt not only with *costs* but also with *resource allocation*; PERT, at least until around 1962, dealt only with schedule matters.

CPM was developed by a very small group of Du Pont engineers led by Morgan R. Walker, with the assistance of computer and mathematics experts from Remington Rand Univac led by James E. Kelley. Du Pont was cautious in promoting the technique, partly to avoid conflicts with its customers. Thus by the late 1950s PERT was clearly receiving considerably more attention than CPM. The founders of CPM left Du Pont in 1959, however, and formed their own consulting firm, Mauchly Associates. CPM then became much better known.[13,14] By the late 1960s it had become the basic method of most construction scheduling, and was generally more commonly used than PERT.

A third important scheduling technique — precedence — was to be developed soon, in the early 1960s. Before turning to the 1960s, however, we should return to the history of US defence procurement to note the impact of Sputnik on the promotion of a more streamlined and integrated systems development process in US defence.

The impact of Sputnik on US systems acquisition practices

The USAF, it will be recalled, had not been overly enthusiastic about the Robertson Committee's 1955 recommendation that manned aircraft acquisition should follow the practice of ballistic missile development and become structured primarily along product (or project) lines. By the summer of 1957, however, the question seemed to be not so much the way systems acquisition was organized, but the more critical one of whether the level of funding would be sufficient to meet the various programmes' needs. Increased prices and a peaking of funding for the ICBM development meant that either the national debt ceiling would have to be raised or, as the Eisenhower Administration would have preferred, programmes would have to be trimmed.

In the midst of this budget crisis, on 4 October 1957, the Soviet Union launched Sputnik. The US nation was shocked. 'No event since Pearl Harbor set off such repercussions in public life' (ref. 3, p. 142). The Soviet Union was perceived to be technologically ahead of the USA; if the Soviets could master guidance and re-entry problems, they would have the ability to deliver nuclear warheads from Soviet soil on to the continental mainland of the USA. The Gaither Committee, originally appointed to evaluate fallout shelter needs, reported coincidentally just a few weeks later. The committee had soon concluded that civil defence could not be separated from other defence requirements; its report thus became an overall judgement on the state of national defence. The USA, it concluded, would become a second-class power unless missile production was rapidly increased. As a consequence of Sputnik, the committee's report had a dramatic impact on the nation; indeed, with the ensuing 'missiles gap' debate it also significantly affected the conduct and outcome of the 1960 Presidential campaign.[15] Once the Armed Forces Select Committee (under Senator Lyndon Johnson) had heard accounts of management problems on the missile programmes, funding increases were soon authorized.

Of more long-term significance to project management and its implications was the fact that, as a result of the Sputnik launch, the DoD was reorganized and centralized in 1958. Detailed attention began to be given to the examination of management practices at a department-wide level, while the USAF began to refine its practices of acquiring major weapons. It was also of long-term project management significance, and also largely a consequence of Sputnik, that the National Aeronautics and Space Administration (NASA) was created in 1958 to conduct all research, development and operations in space that did not have a military character (note 9).[16] The DoD's interest in systems acquisition practices and NASA's management practices in the 1960s were to have a critical impact on the development of modern project management.

By 1959, it was clear that existing management practices were no longer satisfactory. New families of weapons systems were emerging in the electronic, ballistic missiles and space arenas, employing vastly more complex technology; the potential for cost increases was consequently seen to be dangerously high. Urgency continued to be very great — many systems were developed on the 'concurrency' basis, where production and development start before the design is complete. Heavy reliance was placed on contractors, many of whom were awarded contracts to develop systems on a cost-plus-fixed-fee basis.

A Weapons Systems Management Study Group (known as the Anderson Committee after its Chairman, General Anderson, Commander of Air Materiel Command) was formed in 1959 to review policies and procedures for weapons systems management. Its findings were to have a major impact on the USAF's practices of systems acquisition (and hence, via NASA and NATO, in the 1960s, on project management as a whole).

The group was exceedingly impressed with the benefits of the ICBM systems management practices and with the Gillette Committee proposals. There was remarkable consensus within the group on its recommendations. Product management across functional lines was seen as increasingly necessary for major programmes. The dual-command character of USAF system acquisition should, it was recommended, be replaced by 'packaged' programmes evolving through a three-phase *life cycle* — concept, creation, operation — with one command responsible for the programme throughout all three phases. There should be greater *front-end feasibility analysis* before a major development was embarked on. Again, all these are absolutely fundamental principles of modern project management.

The Commanders of ARDC and AMC favoured some form of unified command, with authority given to the Program Manager, per Gillette. The USAF Chief of Staff decided against the group's recommendations, however, although several of its ideas were nevertheless implemented in a set of regulations, the '375 series', first published in August 1960 (ref. 1, p. 18). These included the 'package' programme, the three-phased life cycle, and the establishment of a System Program Office (SPO) for compilation and execution of the package programme (note 10).

Gaddis and the first *Harvard Business Review* article on project management

The 1950s were to end on a fortuitous note, at least in terms of the development of project management. From this perspective, the decade had until mid-1959 been characterized by two streams of activity: the development first of a weapons systems acquisition practice, and second of network scheduling tools. In May 1959, Paul O. Gaddis published his article 'The project manager' in the most widely read management journal at that time, *The Harvard Business Review*.[17] While positioning his essay very much in the context of US high technology, Gaddis pointed to a number of organizational issues that merited attention, and were indeed to receive it in the 1960s and 1970s, such as the project manager's *style*, his need for *organizational support*, the need to take *sub-optimal decisions* for the sake of maintaining progress, the importance of *conflict* in projects, and the problems of *authority* and *responsibility*. Drawing a useful analogy with product development, Gaddis brought many mainstream managers face to face, perhaps for the first time, with the burgeoning new discipline of project management.

References

1. Putnam, W. D. *The evolution of air force system acquisition management*. Report R-868-PW, Rand Corporation, Santa Monica, CA, 1972, p.5.
2. Beard, E. *Developing the ICBM*. Colombia University Press, New York, 1976, p.161.
3. McDougall, W. A. *The heavens and the earth: a political history of the space age*. Basic Books, New York, 1985.
4. Sapolsky, H. *The Polaris system development: bureaucratic and programmatic success in government*. Harvard University Press, Cambridge, MA, 1972, p.14.
5. Raborn, W. F. *Special projects office management of the fleet ballistic missile program*, quoted in Massey, R. S. *Program evaluation review technique: its origins and development*. The American University, Washington, DC, Master's thesis, 1963, p.11.
6. Malcolm, D. G., Roseboom, J. H., Clarke, C. E. and Fazar, W. P.

Application of a technique for research and development program evaluation. *Operations Research,* **7**, 1959, Sept.−Oct., 648.

7. Geddes, P. The year of management systems. *Aerospace Management,* 1962, March, 89−91.

8. Andrew, S. P. S. *A job planning system for the rapid overhaul of large units of plant.* Report G & P/SPSA/JD, 1956, ICI Billingham Division.

9. Lockyer, K. G. *Introduction to critical path analysis.* Pitman, London, 3rd edn, 1969, chapter 1.

10. Kelley, J. E. An historical view of CPM. *Proc. SAM National CPM Conf., Princeton, NJ,* 1970.

11. Kelley, J. E. and Walker, M. R. The origins of CPM, *PM NETwork,* **3**, No. 2, 1989, Feb., 7−22.

12. Sayer, J. S. Du Pont Engineering Department in the 1950s. *PM NETwork,* **3**, No. 2, 1989, Feb., 23−25.

13. Kelley, J. Critical path planning and scheduling: mathematical basis. *Operations Research,* **9**, No. 3, 1961, May−June, 296−321.

14. Kelley, J. E. and Walker, M. R. Critical path planning and scheduling. *Proc. Eastern Computer Conf.,* Boston, 1−3 December, 1959, 160−170.

15. Halpern, M. H. The Gaither Committee and the policy process. *World Politics,* 1961, April, 360−384.

16. Anderson, F. W. *Orders of magnitude. A history of NACA and NASA, 1915−80.* SP-4403, NASA, Washington DC, 1981.

17. Gaddis, P. O. The project manager. *Harvard Business Review,* 1959, May−June, 89−97.

18. Archibald, R. and Villoria, R. L. *Network-based management systems (PERT/CPM).* Wiley, New York, 1967.

19. Battersby, A. *Network analysis for planning and scheduling.* Macmillan, London, 1964.

5. The 1960s: Apollo and the decade of management systems

If the 1950s had been a decade of increasing systems integration (often despite strong opposition) and, towards the end, of the development of new project management planning and control tools, the 1960s were to see a veritable explosion in the development and use of both. By the end of the decade a theoretical basis, in organizational terms, for the need for such management integration had been developed and despite, or possibly because of, a generally very bad record of project overruns, interest was being shown worldwide in the new management discipline of project management.

The arrival of Robert McNamara as US Secretary of Defense

On his election in 1960, President-elect John F. Kennedy appointed a series of task forces to advise him on problems he would have to face once he assumed office. One of these, under the President's Science Advisor, Jerome B. Wiesner, was charged with reviewing the status of the ballistic missile programme. Wiesner's group was very critical of the missiles' programme management, commenting adversely on the slow rate of production (but missing the crucial point that the Gillette procedures had been effectively revised away). This concern with Program Management was taken up by Robert S. McNamara, the incoming Secretary of Defense, who sought a detailed plan to improve USAF internal management and organization.

Implementation of the Anderson Committee proposals had not run smoothly during the second half of 1960, as USAF reorganizations were now announced. Early in 1961, McNamara ordered that the USAF have R&D responsibility for all military space programmes. Eleven days later, on 17 March 1961, he created three new commands to handle functions previously the responsibility of ARDC and AMC: the Office of Aerospace Research, Air Force Systems Command (headed by Schriever) and Air Force Logistics Command. The systems management recommendations of the Anderson Committee became the established procedures for these new commands.

McNamara initiated a period of centralization of defence planning and authority. Among the practices introduced during his tenure were the Five Year Defense Plan; the Planning, Programming, Budgeting System (PPBS); Systems Analysis; Life-Cycle Costing; greater emphasis on front-end Concept Formulation and Contract Definition; new planning and reporting systems requirements

(C/SCSC, SAIMS and SAR) (note 1); Should–Cost analysis; Integrated Logistics Support, Quality Assurance, Value Engineering, Technical Data Management; Configuration Management; and the Work Breakdown Structure.[1] All these practices and techniques, except perhaps for PPBS and Systems Analysis, have become core tools of modern project management (and are described later in this book).

Many of these tools and techniques were developed by military and civilian personnel working independently of McNamara, as described below, but their development was undoubtedly fostered by his enthusiasm for systems management and management science. McNamara also oversaw a reorganization of DoD contract administration which resulted in the establishment of the Defense Supply Agency, the Defense Contract Administration Service and the Defense Contract Audit Agency. Improvements were also made in proposal evaluation and source selection practices. Importantly, as described below, increased emphasis came to be placed on competition and incentive contracts.

Many of these tools and techniques were also implemented on NASA programmes, where they achieved considerable publicity through the Apollo programme. There was, in fact, extensive interchange of both people and practices between the USAF and NASA during the late 1950s and early 1960s. George Mueller (pronounced 'Miller'), for example, NASA's Associate Administrator for Manned Space Flight, had been a Vice-President of Space Technology Laboratories, Inc. (the name given to the Ramo Woolridge Corporation after a reorganization in the late 1950s), and Brigadier General Samuel C. Phillips of the USAF was brought in to act as Apollo Program Director. Phillips brought with him about 20 officers from the Minuteman programme on which he and Mueller had been working. Both Mueller and Phillips had developed sophisticated tools for managing the technical cost and schedule requirements of Minuteman, which were then developed further on Apollo, as described below.

McNamara's desire to achieve integration and systematization within DoD procurement was, as shown in chapter 4, not untimely. His efforts, and the tools and techniques he fostered, clearly made an immensely valuable contribution to the improvement of DoD project efficiency. Not everything he touched worked well, however, and one case — the F-111 — offers some interesting lessons on how projects can go wrong, particularly if the initial specifications are not right.

The F-111

The USAF had been working on a successor to the F-105 for some time. A statement of requirements (SOR-183) was issued on 14 June 1960. Curiously, however, although the SOR called for a fighter aircraft (hence the programme was given the generic acronym TFX), in fact only its bomb loading was defined —

nothing being specified, for example, on manœuvrability or weapons requirements. In parallel, meanwhile, the US Navy was looking for a Fleet Air Defense Fighter (FADF) to replace its Phantoms, the principal criterion for which was the longest possible time on combat air patrol.

McNamara's interest in streamlining the Pentagon's project planning and implementation practices led him to seek the greatest possible 'commonality' between the TFX and the FADF — which looked like being programmes of several thousand planes. The services objected vigorously: the USAF wanted a fighter—bomber, with air-to-air combat as only a secondary capability; the Navy wanted primarily an air-to-air combat plane, capable of acting as a missile platform and of operating long-endurance missions. Against the wishes of both the USAF and the US Navy, however, a joint programme was established and, in the face of 'almost all expert opinion', a contract was awarded for General Dynamics' F-111 'swing wing' design in November 1962 because it showed greater commonality between its USAF (F-111A) and Navy (F-111B) models than the Boeing proposals preferred by the military.

In the event, the Navy programme was not a success and was halted in 1968. A strategic bomber version of the F-111 was developed from 1964 (the FB-111A), going into production in 1968. (A remarkable transformation from the SOR-183 TFX air attack specification!) 'Flyaway costs' rose dramatically, largely because of development difficulties with the engines and avionics, the cost overruns on the bomber being particularly severe.

The F-111 (Fig. 9) underscores the importance of the most vulnerable part of the systems integration process: the project specification. McNamara clearly misread the USAF and Navy's requirements, and was intellectually convinced of the need for commonality and willingness to compromise performance. The Tornado, which in a sense succeeded the F-111 in Britain and became one of the first of the highly successful European collaborative defence aircraft (see p. 137), was better able to handle the conflicts in specifications between the European air

Fig. 9. F-111 with Paveway laser-guided bombs (courtesy Jane's Information Group)

forces because of the less entrenched views of those (techno-logically less developed) forces. Failure to achieve agreement on project specifications will always cause project problems. *The systems management ideal elaborated in the 1950s works effectively only if the specifications are appropriate.*

Precedence diagramming

While McNamara was creating major changes in US defence systems acquisition practices, another development was occurring which at first was hardly noticed but has since proved of great significance in that most fundamental aspect of project management: scheduling. This was the development, largely by John W. Fondahl at Stanford University, of *precedence diagramming*.

In their network methodology, both PERT and CPM represent activities by arrows. Fondahl and his colleagues had begun to examine (before Kelley and Walker's publication of CPM[2]) two issues with which the computer-based PERT and CPM methods had difficulty (since at that time all computer processing was done in batch on mainframe in a special computer facility). These were the updating of schedule data in the field and the improvement of time−cost trade-offs and resource levelling. The diagramming method used by the Stanford researchers was a 'circle and connecting line', derived from industrial engineering, in which a circle represents an activity or event.

The methodology was published in 1961 in a widely reviewed report.[3] One of its features was the use of 'precedence' matrices and 'lag' values. The idea of lags (which has subsequently proved a powerful one in scheduling) was in fact probably first developed by B. Roy of the Metra Group in France in 1958, in the Metra Potential Method (MPM) (note 2).[4] Lags were also used on another European activity-on-node system developed in Germany in 1960 by Walter and Rainer Schleip: Regeltechnischen Planning und Steuerung, (RPS, note 3).[5] However, Fondahl appears not to have known of either the MPM or the RPS method.

In 1962, IBM began the development of its Project Control System for use with the IBM 1440. J. David Craig, one of its principal authors, developed an extended node system of scheduling which he called precedence diagramming, in which complex overlaps, lags and leads between activities could be represented with great simplicity (Fig. 10). This system was published in early 1964, shortly before Joseph Moder and Cecil Phillips published the first edition of what has since become the standard text on network scheduling, *Project management with CPM and PERT.*[6]

Moder and Phillips coined the term '*Activity on Arrow*' to describe the PERT/CPM approach. Fondahl was just about to publish a second report on Stanford's research with the Navy, and had to select a terminology for his system. Although tempted to use '*Activity on Node*', he chose instead to adopt the IBM term, precedence. (To a purist today, Activity on Node is generally

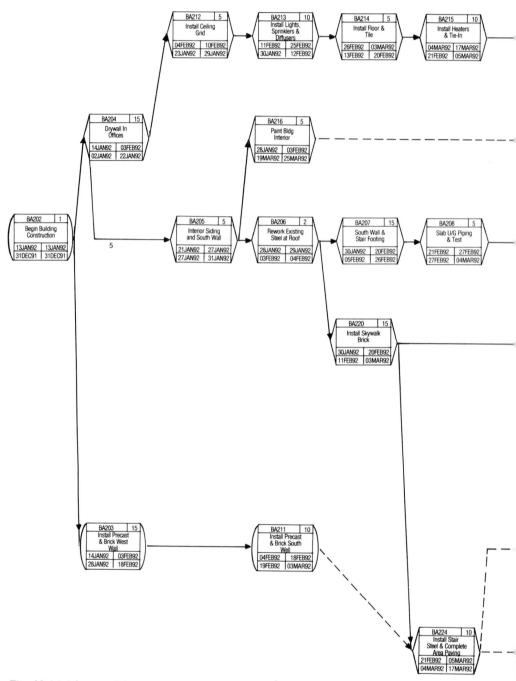

Fig. 10 (a) (above and facing page). Precedence scheduling: an example based on a construction project, showing how activities are based on nodes

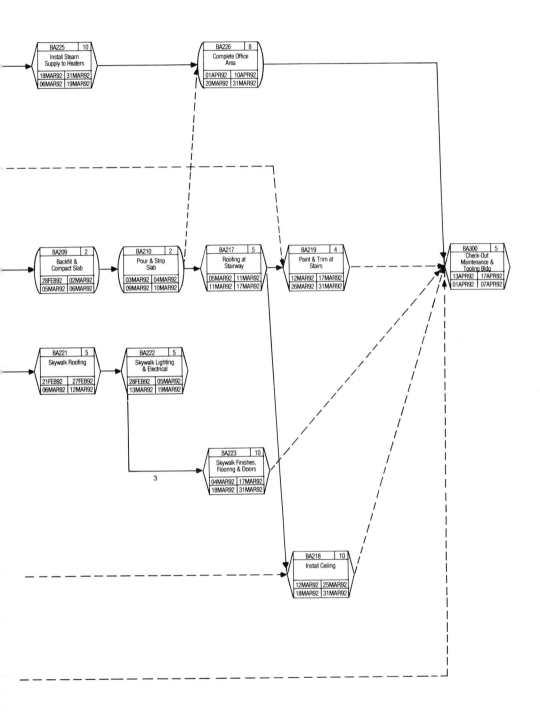

BA225	10
Install Steam Supply to Heaters	
18MAR92	31MAR92
06MAR92	19MAR92

BA226	8
Complete Office Area	
01APR92	10APR92
20MAR92	31MAR92

BA209	2
Backfill & Compact Slab	
28FEB92	02MAR92
05MAR92	06MAR92

BA210	2
Pour & Strip Slab	
03MAR92	04MAR92
09MAR92	10MAR92

BA217	5
Roofing at Stairway	
05MAR92	11MAR92
11MAR92	17MAR92

BA219	4
Paint & Trim at Stairs	
12MAR92	17MAR92
26MAR92	31MAR92

BA300	5
Check-Out Maintenance & Tooling Bldg	
13APR92	17APR92
01APR92	07APR92

BA221	5
Skywalk Roofing	
21FEB92	27FEB92
06MAR92	12MAR92

BA222	5
Skywalk Lighting & Electrical	
28FEB92	05MAR92
13MAR92	19MAR92

3

BA223	10
Skywalk Finishes, Flooring & Doors	
04MAR92	17MAR92
18MAR92	31MAR92

BA218	10
Install Ceiling	
12MAR92	25MAR92
18MAR92	31MAR92

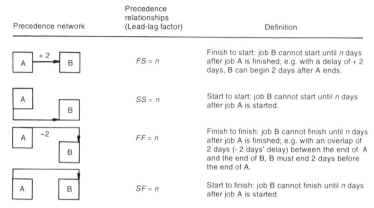

Precedence network	Precedence relationships (Lead-lag factor)	Definition
A +2 B	$FS = n$	Finish to start: job B cannot start until n days after job A is finished; e.g. with a delay of + 2 days, B can begin 2 days after A ends.
A B	$SS = n$	Start to start: job B cannot start until n days after job A is started.
A -2 B	$FF = n$	Finish to finish: job B cannot finish until n days after job A is finished; e.g. with an overlap of 2 days (- 2 days' delay) between the end of A and the end of B, B must end 2 days before the end of A.
A B	$SF = n$	Start to finish: job B cannot finish until n days after job A is started.

Fig. 10(b). Precedence scheduling: the conventions that allow leads and lags to be shown easily

used as the generic term for this type of scheduling, Precedence being the special case where there are lags.)

Precedence grew in popularity at a much slower rate than CPM or PERT had, for the obvious reasons that it was not such a novelty and received less promotion. Nevertheless, by 1965 *Engineering News Record* was claiming that contractors were shifting to precedence diagramming.[7] However, although it is indeed substantially easier to demonstrate complex activity interrelations with precedence, it was perhaps not until the second half of the 1970s that the method became generally more popular than Activity on Arrow.

PERT/Cost, Work Breakdown Structure, Earned Value, C/SCSC and the new USAF and NASA Systems Procurement Procedures

The Polaris Special Projects Office had been conscious since PERT's development in 1957 that a major shortcoming was its inability to handle cost as well as schedule control. The Navy had thus begun working with several contractors, notably Lockheed, General Electric, the Mitre Corporation and Stanford University, in the late 1950s to develop a version of PERT that included a cost-control dimension. The development team visited some 40 defence and aerospace contractors, where it found that, unlike on most commercial work, defence contractors did not maintain records for the planned or budgeted value of work performed, and that, while it would be extremely difficult to obtain cost data based on network *activities*, it would be easier based on a *Work Breakdown Structure*, as was done 'on most large commercial development and production programs'.

The outcome of this study was published jointly by the Department of Defense and NASA in June 1962 as the *DoD and NASA guide, PERT/Cost Systems Design*.[8] This study was notable not just for its emphasis of the cost control aspects of 'PERT-type systems' (NASA had now abandoned the threefold time estimate that was such a central feature of the original PERT system), but for its formal introduction into government programme management for the first time of the *Work Breakdown Structure* tool.

The Work Breakdown Structure (note 4)[9]

> begins at the highest level of the program with the identification of project end items (hardware, services, equipment or facilities). The major end items are then divided into their component parts (e.g. systems, subsystems, components) to successively lower levels, reducing the dollar value and complexity of the units at each level, until it reaches the level where the end item subdivisions finally become manageable units for planning and control processes. The end item subdivisions appearing at this last level of work breakdown structure are then divided into major work packages (e.g. engineering, manufacturing, testing).[10]

This concept, it will be seen, is a direct descendant of the Anderson Committee's approach to USAF systems acquisition.

The use of work breakdown structures represented only a part of the contribution of the DoD−NASA Guide. Its other major contribution was its conceptual emphasis on milestone and interface planning, and on cost estimating and control of man-hours and costs by groups of activities (which might or might not be contiguous on the PERT network). The top−down approach of the guide, emphasizing planning and control primarily at key *milestone events*, has subsequently proved of great importance (note 5), as indeed has the emphasis on project management as an *interface management* function (note 6). Unfortunately, this emphasis was largely missed: the guide was applied primarily not at the conceptual but at the detailed level, where it was widely misinterpreted both by industry and in government as requiring that work packages be accommodated *within* network activities. (It was not properly appreciated 'that the work breakdown structure, not the network, was the basis for cost planning and control'.[11]) As a result, before long several government agencies were requiring detailed budget and cost data to be presented for each network activity. Vast amounts of data were thus generated, in far too great a level of detail.

By 1964, with over ten variants of PERT/Cost in government as well as numerous contractor versions, many of which were claimed — and agreed — as justifying additional overhead payments, the situation appeared to be getting out of hand. The USAF thus decided to adopt a simpler procedure, which had been developed in 1963 by Brigadier General Phillips on the Minuteman program, known as the Minuteman Contractor *Performance Measurement* system. This employed an improved version of the PERT/Cost work package concept known as the *Earned Value* system. Earned Value was to become another central project management technique in the years ahead.

In developing PERT/Cost, DoD had noticed that a particularly common problem was the accurate relation of physical and financial

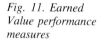

*Fig. 11. Earned
Value performance
measures*

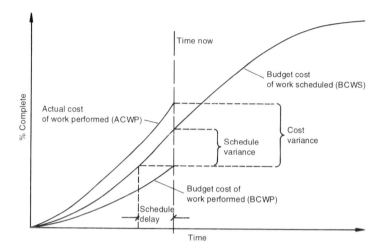

*Table 1. Key
performance measures*

Element	Item	Acronym
Work planned	Budgeted cost for work scheduled	BCWS
Work accomplished/ earned value	Budgeted cost for work performed	BCWP
Cost of work accomplished	Actual cost of work performed	ACWP
Work authorized	Budgeted cost at completion	BAC
Estimate of final cost	Estimated cost at completion	EAC
Cost variance	Cost variance (BCWP minus ACWP)	CV
Schedule variance	Schedule variance (BCWP minus BCWS)	SV
At-completion variance	At-completion variance (BAC minus EAC)	ACV

progress. A project could be ahead on its spend rate but behind in physical accomplishment, for example: unless these two measures were somehow correlated, the programme faced a nasty shock! The Earned Value method did this by measuring actual progress by the budgeted cost of work performed (BCWP) (Fig. 11, Table 1). With this 'target', (i) the budgeted cost of work scheduled (BCWS) — planned work, and (ii) the actual cost of work performed (ACWP) — actual cost, were then compared. These three measures provided information on the project's schedule variance (BCWP−BCWS) and cost variance (BCWP−ACWP). This simple process is the essence of Earned Value.

In 1964, the Office of the Secretary of the Air Force defined a standard whereby if a contractor's internal company cost-management systems fulfilled certain criteria, as embodied in PERT/Cost and Earned Value, the contractor would no longer have to use PERT/Cost itself. Under this approach the WBS concept was retained, but cost data no longer had to be reported in PERT/Cost format. This procedure was refined in 1964–1965 with the assistance of McKinsey & Co., management consultants, as the 'Specification Approach'.[11]

In 1966, in an attempt to improve contractor reporting and keep it where possible in line with the Earned Value approach, DoD initiated a two-part Contractor Performance Measurement programme. Part 1 required contractors to use internal planning and control systems to meet minimum government control criteria known as *Cost and Schedule Control System Criteria' (C/SCSC)*. (To correct the misapprehension that had arisen that PERT/Cost required cost estimates by individual activities, C/SCSC made it clear that network activities could be grouped together for purposes of cost estimating and cost control.) Part 2 required contractors to submit Cost Performance Reports regularly on the budgeted value of work performed. The C/SCSC reporting requirement was intended to make it clear contractually that contractors' cost reports had to be a direct summary of the budgets for work actually performed; that work authorization documents had to contain appropriate budgets and schedules and that costs had to be accumulated on the same basis as budgets; and that reporting had to be based strictly on the number of tasks completed to date. The lowest level reporting unit was to be the work package; this was to be of no more than a few weeks' duration — or two months at the maximum. The aim was to stop periodic retroactive adjustments to the plan — the so-called rubber baseline — and the keeping of different sets of cost reports to obfuscate reporting.

C/SCSC was not imposed mandatorily, however. Indeed, its implementation was slow — it was seen as yet more DoD bureaucracy — and by 1972 only 36 defence contractors had complied with the criteria.

Resistance to DoD's burgeoning procedures had in fact been mounting rapidly during the early 1960s. By 1965, DoD control and reporting requirements appeared so onerous that US defence aerospace contractors officially and strongly expressed concern about the proliferation of management systems and the growing number of reporting requirements now imposed on them (note 7). These requirements were felt, not unreasonably, to be inconsistent with the practice of fixed-price and incentive contracting. The Aerospace Industries Association formed a Systems Management Analysis Group which issued an 'appeal for disengagement' (ref. 1, p. 26) in a report of May 1966 which highlighted

- conflicts between existing DoD management systems
- the need to match appropriate systems with the type of contract
- the need to tailor the degree of management to the complexity of the programme.

The report urged that any system imposed should produce results that justified its cost of operation. As a result of this industry plea, DoD issued its Directive 7000.1, *Resource Management Systems for the Department of Defense*, on 22 August 1966. This marked a further move towards the control systems specification approach of C/SCSC.[12]

Two important families of procedures — the Air Force Regulation (AFR) 375 series and, later, the Air Force Systems Command Manuals (AFSCM) 375 series — were published and/or revised during 1963 and 1965. These became immensely powerful through their effect on US aerospace management practice in the 1960s and indeed ever since — their concepts and practices were taken up with vigour by NASA, which published its own version as its 500 series; through NATO and NASA they have come to form the basis of most Western project and systems development practices. The procedures were, however, bureaucratic and dictatorial, and by no means popular with industry.[13] The USAF procedures in particular were immensely long.

The AFR series, published in November 1963, comprised

- *Management of system programs* (AFR 375-1)
- *System program office* (SPO) (AFR 375-2)
- *System program director* (AFR 375-3)
- *System program documentation* (AFR 375-4)
- *Definition phase of system life cycle* (AFR 375-5).

The AFSCM series manuals, first published in 1960 and revised in 1968, dealt with

- *System program management* (AFSCM 375-4)
- *System program office* (AFSCM 375-3)
- *Configuration management* (AFSCM 375-1)
- *Systems engineering management* (AFSCM 375-5)
- *Management of contractor data and reports* (AFSCM 310-1).

(Curiously, numerical ordering was not a strength of the series.) Of these, *System program management* (375-4) was the 'parent', introducing the basic concepts and requirements for programme control, configuration management, procurement and production, engineering and testing, and deployment.

Underlying the whole process was the structure of the *system development life cycle* concept proposed by the Anderson Committee. The four basic stages of the life cycle were

- concept formulation — develop the system concept and establish its feasibility
- contract definition — define the system sufficiently and undertake the necessary engineering and development
- acquisition — physically acquire the system (detail design, development, procurement and testing)

Fig. 12. NASA rockets and capsules, from left to right: Mercury, Gemini, Apollo, Skylab, Apollo–Soyuz Test Project, Space Shuttle (top); Mercury/Atlas, Gemini/Titan II, Saturn V/Apollo, Saturn V/Skylab, Saturn 1B/Apollo, Space Shuttle/Orbiter (bottom) (courtesy NASA)

• operation — deliver and place the system in use.

There is of course nothing magical about the identification of such a sequence. It is common sense, and has in effect been used by those developing projects for thousands of years. The method adopted by DoD and NASA at this time proved important, however, for two reasons. First, it provided a framework under which modern practices of *engineering management*, particularly regarding the physical and technical configuration, could be consistently and rigorously managed. Second, more generally, it provided an integrated approach to project development and control — something that at this time was still receiving minimal attention in many of the construction industries, for example.

Both these aspects of Project and Program Management were now given increased visibility in what is probably the most highly regarded of all modern project management endeavours: the Apollo lunar programme.

Apollo: paradigm of modern project management

Apollo (Fig. 12) could be discussed simply in terms of how it employed project management techniques of the kind described above. However, a broader view, that looks at its history in order to understand better the range of techniques, concepts, approaches, concerns, philosophies and practices that those responsible for this remarkable project employed, has much to commend it. For Apollo was much more than the deployment of a set of special management tools and techniques. As with Polaris, Manhattan and the other major projects we have so far considered, those responsible for Apollo were operating in fact across a full range of management and organizational dimensions. Apollo, with its enormous public visibility and its virtuoso demonstration of the modern approach to project management, became for many — in business, academia, government and the lay public — the paradigm of modern project management. To most, however, the paradigm is only partially perceived.

The technological challenges of the programme were awesome; the management demands huge. The public image, fostered willingly — and necessarily, given the need to secure annual Congressional funding — was of an exceedingly professionally managed, clearly defined programme. Yet, without belittling it, one can say that the programme had many fuzzy edges. There is no doubt, however, that it was conceived and implemented by a group of innovative and extremely dedicated individuals who honed and applied the techniques of *Systems Management (Systems Engineering and Program Management)* to a fine art.

In October 1957 (the month Sputnik was launched), a NASA committee under H. Gryford Stever of the Massachusetts Institute of Technology was set up to look at US aerospace projects and practices. In February 1958, following Sputnik, the committee concluded that exploration of the solar system would require manned spaceflight. NASA's attention moved quickly to the possibility of manned landings on the moon, the German rocket pioneer Wernher von Braun taking a lead in outlining the options open to NASA.

There was at this time much debate as to whether the military or civilian agencies should lead the US space effort, and indeed whether man really needed to be in space at all. NASA acquired the Jet Propulsion Lab in October 1958, and von Braun and the Army missile team in January 1960, as Eisenhower ordered an acceleration of the super-booster programme. From now on, all US space programmes came under the aegis only of the USAF or NASA. As for 'spam in the can' — the astronauts' early term for man in space (note 8) — Eisenhower and Nixon came down strongly in favour of man's presence, not for scientific or engineering reasons but for political prestige, aimed particularly at the uncommitted Third World. The military implications were just an excuse. The Mercury programme was initiated in December 1958 'frankly [as] a stopgap aimed at getting a manned capsule into space as quickly and safely as possible'.[14]

In 1959, Congress released a study that indicated a high level of consensus on the desirability of a mission around the moon within a decade.[15] A launch vehicle programme was initiated at the same time, with von Braun beginning work on the Juno V rocket (now renamed Saturn). Significant funding approval was still unforthcoming by July 1960, however, when 1300 government, industry and academic aerospace officials were called to a two-day NASA—industry planning session to review NASA's plans for manned and unmanned spaceflight. A further meeting was held in August, after which contracts were awarded to study the feasibility of a circumlunar manned space programme. These studies showed that there should be no insurmountable technical problems and that the programme cost would be around $25bn−$38bn! However, it was soon realized that Congress was unlikely to supply this level of funding for a programme that did not entail an actual landing on the moon; the requirements for a lunar landing thus began to receive increased study.

The period of late 1960 and early 1961 was an unsettled one for NASA. The incoming Kennedy Administration showed no indication that it wished to promote the USA's role in space; meanwhile, the Weisner Committee review was causing considerable uncertainty for US aerospace organization and management. On 30 January 1961, very much with Vice-President Lyndon Johnson's support, Kennedy appointed James E. Webb as the new Administrator of NASA. Webb was another in the mould familiar in this account of the origins of modern project management: tough, charismatic, politically astute, 'a genius for extemporization'.[16] Webb appointed Robert E. Seamans as his operating vice-president and, working from recommendations made by Lawrence A. Kimpton, the Chancellor of the University of Chicago, for Webb's predecessor, T. Keith Glennan, soon began to reorganize NASA along project lines. Project offices were to be responsible for managing projects, and NASA was to rely more on contracting outside support.

On 12 April 1961, Yuri Gagarin circled the earth in Vostok 1. Congress reacted vigorously: there was immediate talk of 'beating the Russians'. Funding was stepped up. By May, as the feasibility studies began to come in, a NASA working group was formed to estimate the technical feasibility and cost of landing a man on the moon within the decade. It reported favourably to President Kennedy, who announced on 25 May 1961, just six weeks after Gagarin's flight

> I believe that this nation should commit itself to achieving the goal, before this decade is out, of landing a man on the moon and returning him safely to earth.

Congress approved more funds for NASA without delay and with virtually no dissent.

The lay-myth of the Apollo programme is that at this time the venture was clearly planned, and from here on 'project management' methods realized these plans within time and more or less within budget. Certainly at this point we see the birth, in extraordinarily clear profile, of a project task: technically, get a man on the moon and return him safely to earth; schedule, by the end of the decade. As to cost, it is generally accepted that the budget for the programme from here on was $20bn. (In fact, it is said, the hard-figure estimate for the programme submitted to Webb was $13bn; recognizing the strength of support for the programme in Congress at that time, Webb immediately decided to add $7bn of contingency.) The reality of the Apollo project specification, then, is that the technical, schedule and budgetary objectives were indeed starkly clear, but the means by which these ends were to be achieved were still subject to considerable uncertainty. 'What NASA did was to establish broad program objectives to serve as a foundation within which detailed planning could take place. It was recognized that this latter facet of planning had to be flexible, for it was a continuing exercise influenced by myriad political, technological, fiancial, and other inputs. NASA planning had to reflect Webb's repeated observation that "at NASA, the name of the game is uncertainty".'[17]

Technically, the first and biggest question was the sequence of flying to the moon and back. In the planning of May 1961 — conducted very much on a rush basis — it was assumed there would be a direct flight from the earth to the moon. This was soon seen as likely to require exceedingly large rockets, however, and so alternative 'rendezvous' options were considered — either earth-orbit rendezvous (EOR), which would need less propellant and could be done with a single yet-to-be-developed Saturn C-3, or lunar-orbit rendezvous (LOR), in which a landing craft would descend from the orbiting spacecraft, land and then take off again to orbit with the mother craft before returning to earth. This uncertainty over the mode of flying to the moon constrained NASA's ability to define specifications for the spacecraft hardware contract, and was to continue for over a year, during which it represented the biggest uncertainty of the whole project.

During 1961 and 1962 NASA had to grow at a very fast pace in order to step up to the Apollo schedule. There was a huge amount of work, for example, even while the early schedules were extremely rough, in preparing the major system contract specifications. For most of 1961 there simply were not enough people in NASA to staff an Apollo project office; the work was therefore done by ad hoc committees and task groups drafted from other organizations. Many of the recruits joining NASA came from the Air Force, Army and Navy. NASA's manpower numbered 6000 in 1961: with Apollo it grew tenfold. Its ability to assimilate so many new groups so effectively was remarkable. And crucially, from a project management viewpoint, not only did this transfer of staff permit work to be done on schedule, but it also ensured that the latest concepts and practices of systems and project management were transferred directly from these people into the agency.

A major organization study ordered by Webb in late 1960 examined how NASA could better integrate its many research centres without killing off the *flexibility* it required. The answer was to create a state within a state: the Office of Manned Space Flight. Also, individual initiative would be encouraged and the discipline of systems integration would be stressed. In September 1961, D. Bramerd Holmes was appointed HQ Director of the Office of Manned Space Flight; shortly afterwards Joseph F. Shea was appointed Holmes' deputy, to concentrate on systems engineering. (Shea came from Space Technology Laboratories, the successor to the Ramo Woolridge Corporation.) Manned space flight projects and spacecraft engineering and development were to be managed at a new major facility in Houston (later renamed the Johnson Space Center); rockets were to be developed at a new facility at Huntsville, Alabama; launching would take place from a huge new spaceport (later named the Kennedy Space Center) in Florida. The facilities and construction work required to create these centres were enormous; responsibility for providing them was entrusted to the US Army Corps of Engineers. A little later, in January 1962, separate project offices were set up for Mercury, Gemini and Apollo.[18]

By December 1961, NASA had decided not to develop a solid fuel rocket for manned lunar landing and had agreed on the Saturn C-5 as the rocket that should be developed. The mode of flight at this stage was very strongly favoured to be EOR. The Langley Research Center, however, was interested in the potential attractions of LOR. By February 1962 the newly formed Apollo Spacecraft Project Office at the Manned Spacecraft Center became convinced that LOR should be the preferred mode. It was recognized that the mode decision had now to be made if the overall programme schedule was to be met: LOR would offer the 'cleanest management interfaces', would probably be about $1·5bn cheaper, and could be accomplished six to eight months sooner than the other modes.[19] The decision was announced in June–July 1962, but immediately came under fierce and continued criticism from the President's Science Advisor Jerome Wiesner and his staff, which continued until Webb threatened to take the matter to the President in November 1962.

This fundamental decision having been made, attention now turned to development, testing and installing of the various components in the 'Apollo stack', and to selecting and training astronauts and other operations personnel. A crucial feature of the 'stack' was the enormous complexity of the many interdependencies. Several important management systems were in place by 1962 to help achieve proper co-ordination. Examples included the practice of *interface control* — 'somewhere along the line, some piece of Apollo's two million functional parts assembled in one place had to meet and match with a piece put together in another place . . . these interface documents were essential in laying out just where and how the parts would come together';[16] the hiring of General Electric as troubleshooting systems engineering specialists to help Holmes and his headquarters staff make technical decisions; and system review meetings sponsored by Shea at the Office of Manned Space Flight.

A significant moment in the programme came in June 1963 when Holmes resigned following disagreements with Seamans and Webb, who refused to provide the programme with additional funds. He was replaced by George E. Mueller, who was Vice-President for Research and Development at Space Technology Laboratories Inc. Mueller asked Brigadier General Samuel C. Phillips to join him as Apollo Program Director 'to help him apply to Apollo the kind of configuration and logistics management procedures [they had] established for Minuteman' (note 9) (ref. 16, p. 128). In mid-1963, Mueller became responsible for Huntsville, Houston and Canaveral — the three centres working on manned missions — and reorganized his office on a *matrix* basis, dividing the 'functions' along the lines of programme control, systems engineering, test, flight operations, and reliability and quality (note 10). Mueller retained direct control over Apollo (Fig. 13).

On taking over, Mueller conducted a project risk analysis. To his shock he discovered that the chances of achieving a lunar landing by 1970 were no more than one in ten. As a result, he ordered that the Saturn I manned flight programme be eliminated from the Apollo programme, and that flight testing procedures be radically streamlined: there would no longer be piece-by-piece, stage-by-stage prequalification flights; each part would now be delivered thoroughly tested ready for the ultimate mission (the approach pioneered by Schriever on Atlas).

Testing and reliability concepts were pushed even harder in mid-1964, with NASA's decision that, to save weight, astronauts would not be expected to carry tools and spare parts into space. Instead, spacecraft reliability would be secured through a series of redundant systems. If something went wrong, the crew would switch to a back-up system. This put much greater emphasis on manufacturing reliability, and manufacturers were asked to upgrade their 'failure reporting practises, manufacturing schedules, engineering change controls, test plans, traceability methods, means of standardizing interface control documents, and ground support equipment provisioning' (ref. 16, p. 135). Concurrently, NASA implemented a *subsystem manager* practice whereby engineers became mini-project managers responsible for seeing their components developed from design to test, on time, in budget, to specification.

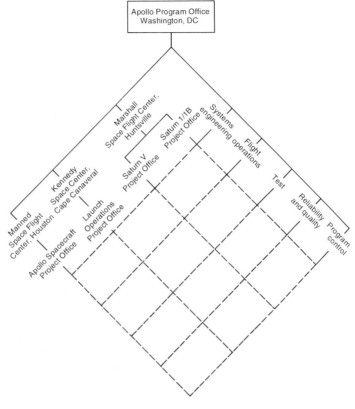

The diagram shows:

Apollo Program Office, Washington, DC

Manned Space Flight Center, Houston

Apollo Spacecraft Project Office

Kennedy Space Center, Cape Canaveral

Launch Operations Project Office

Marshall Space Flight Center, Huntsville

Saturn V Project Office

Saturn 1/1B Project Office

Systems engineering

Flight operations

Test

Reliability and quality

Program control

Fig. 13. (Left) Apollo 11 lunar module Eagle 60 miles above the moon (courtesy NASA); (right) Apollo matrix organization

Weight growth in both the lander and command modules was becoming a very serious problem during 1964 and 1965. Weight savings were sought assiduously in every part of the stack. Among the components subjected to fierce scrutiny during this 'scrub-down' were the TV cameras, which were retained because of their publicity value and consequent funding importance.

Several specification, contracting and design practices that emerged about this time on the programme have remained as fundamental project management practices, two of the most important being *Phased Project Planning* and *Configuration Control*. (The two are naturally closely related.) Phased Project Planning, which was based on a similar DoD practice initiated in July 1965, became NASA policy in November 1965 as a means of defining the project and making appropriate contract commitments progressively as the programme developed. Four programme phases were defined: *Phase A — Preliminary Analysis, Phase B — Definition, Phase C — Design, Phase D — Operation*.

The practice of configuration management had first been formalized as a set of technical and administrative procedures to identify and document the functional and physical characteristics of a system and particularly to control — i.e. to review and document — proposed changes to that system. This became

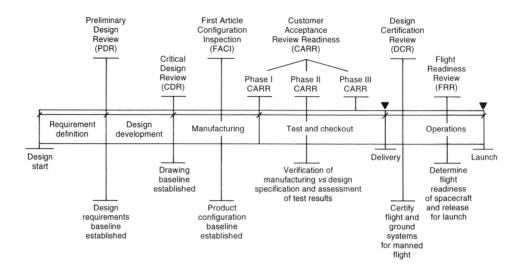

*Fig. 14. NASA's
Program Development
Plan*

particularly important with the growth in weight and the increasing
schedule slippage that occurred during 1964–1965. In mid-August
1965, Mueller and Phillips established a programme checkpoint
review procedure (ref. 17, p. 283) (Fig. 14) outlined as follows

(*a*) Preliminary Design Review (PDR) — to review the basic
design during the detailed design phase

(*b*) Critical Design Review (CDR) — to check specifications
and engineering drawings before their release for
manufacture

(*c*) Flight Article Configuration Inspection (FACI) — to
compare hardware with specifications and drawings and
to validate acceptance testing (FACI could be repeated to
make sure that any deficiencies had been corrected; it
would also be repeated on every vehicle that departed
significantly from the basic design)

(*d*) Certification of Flight Worthiness (COFW) — to certify
completion and flight-qualification of each vehicle stage
or spacecraft module

(*e*) Design Certification Review (DCR) — to verify the
airworthiness and safety of each spacecraft and launch
vehicle design (DCRs would include all government and
contractor agencies with major parts of the programmes
and would formally review the development and
qualification of all stages, modules, and subsystems)

(*f*) Flight Readiness Review (FRR) — a two-part review
before each flight, held by the mission director in
Washington, to confirm the readiness of hardware and
facilities (the mission period would then begin with the
commitment of support forces around the world).

Mueller, invaluably assisted by Phillips, was relentless in

pushing the programme schedule. On 15 January 1965 Phillips issued his Apollo *Program Development Plan*.[20] This described in comprehensive detail how the Apollo programme directives would be reached, how changes would be managed, and how the programme was organized. There were *sections specifying procedures for scheduling, procurement, data management, configuration management, logistics, facilities, funds and manpower, and systems engineering*. The practices embodied in this plan, which became widely discussed in the aerospace industry, were to prove extremely powerful in promoting the basic techniques of modern project management.

This plethora of procedures and techniques should not be seen as an infallible system for managing projects. NASA and its contractors continued to experience management problems. Grumman, for example, the lunar module contractor, had major problems with cost growth and schedule slippage in 1965. As a result, NASA sent a review team to Grumman in June 1966. A few months later Grumman began to implement the practice of *work package estimating* — a revolution for the aerospace manufacturer, which had always estimated and monitored costs by commodities and other cost elements! Implementation of the new system did not go well, however, and there were still problems by the end of the year.

As Apollo progressed through 1966 towards the first manned flight, scheduled for February 1967, hundreds of problems arose that NASA considered serious enough for special task forces and committees to be set up. The *task force approach* was an outstanding characteristic of NASA's approach to the programme. Several major problems required radical management measures to keep the programme on schedule. Of these, two of the most dramatic were the fatal fire on 27 January 1967 on the first manned rocket, in which the astronaut crew lost their lives, and the decision to make Apollo 8 a lunar-orbit mission, which was made before Apollo 7 had qualified the spacecraft. Only by accelerating the schedule in this way, it was felt, might a lunar landing still be feasible by the end of the decade. The repercussions of the fire were considerable, particularly in design. In the implementation of the design modifications, great emphasis was placed on strengthening contractor management, particularly of the support contractors. Boeing was given a central technical integration and evaluation contract; General Electric was asked to strengthen its systems analysis and ground support activity.

Ultimately, as everyone knows, Apollo was a major success. Armstrong and Aldrin touched down on the Sea of Tranquillity on 20 July 1969. In all there were to be six Apollo visits to the moon (fewer than originally planned — the programme was curtailed at the insistence of the new Nixon administration). Experiments were set up on the moon, and some 800 lbs of moon rock was brought back to earth. Whether or not all this was worth $25·5bn — the total cost of Apollo — remains one of the open questions of modern high-technology programme management.

Contracting practices and development strategies

As NASA began to wrestle with Grumman to bring the lunar module's schedule and cost progress back to plan in mid-1965, it tried simultaneously to convert Grumman's contract from a cost-plus to an incentive basis, partly because Congress had begun to impose a budgetary squeeze on the agency. But NASA's desire to change its contracting base reflected a more fundamental shift that was occurring throughout the US defence/aerospace industry, and indeed in other project sectors elsewhere in the world — for example the UK power and petrochemicals industries, as described below.

In 1962, a report published by two Harvard academics, M. J. Sherer and F. W. Peck, examined in great detail the state of contemporary US weapon acquisition practices. *The weapons acquisition process: an economic analysis* showed that US defence procurement still had many inefficiencies, that US systems development at times appeared uncompetitive with the Soviet Union's, and that excessive regard was often given to quality at the expense of costs and schedules, of which there were consequently frequent overruns.[21] The report recommended that 'gold plating' be eliminated, that cost control be given greater weight, that there be greater front-end competition, and that the number of cost-reimbursable type contracts be reduced. McNamara accepted these recommendations and, largely as a result of this study, DoD began to reduce the amount of its *cost-plus contracting* (generally *cost plus fixed fee — (CPFF)*) and moved instead toward incentive-type contracts such as *firm fixed price (FFP)*, *fixed price incentive (FPI)* and *cost plus incentive fee (CPIF)*. NASA agreed to follow suit.

The move was a controversial one. Critics pointed out that incentive contracts require clear programme definition in order to work effectively. Often this is not immediately available, and in any event agreement on the contract terms entails lengthy, and expensive, negotiations. Nor, it was claimed, was it necessarily the case that industry sought to maximize its profit on all cost-reimbursable contracts — given that government was the *only* client in defence and space, many firms managed their contracts with an eye on being awarded future work as much as maximizing profit on existing jobs (see p. 131 and p. 322, note 45). There were also objections that the government public servants had less bargaining ability than industry's senior executives, and that this would lead to weak targets being agreed.[22]

DoD and NASA disagreed with these contentions, claiming that incentives would place more responsibility on those actually performing the work. While it was true that incentive contracts required greater attention to front-end definition, this, DoD and NASA felt, was no bad thing.

In any event, a massive shift in contracting policy occurred in DoD and NASA in the mid-1960s, the results of which were to come under substantial scrutiny later in the decade and in the 1970s (see pp. 60−61 and pp. 128−130), with the conclusion that the results had not been as obvious as expected. (Grumman changed to an incentive form in December 1965; it then completed its work within contract budget and schedule.)

Cost and schedule overrun data

The concern over programmes overrunning their budget and schedule targets intensified within DoD throughout the 1960s. Several studies were initiated on the problem following that of Peck and Scherer (who had reported 0−600% cost increases and 0−130% schedule increases on the twelve US weapon systems they had studied). Many of these studies, and certainly the best known, were conducted by the Rand Corporation.

- A. W. Marshall and W. H. Meckling studied the cost and schedule performance of 22 US weapons systems, reporting in 1959 200−300% cost growth and 30−50% schedule slippage, due largely to technological uncertainty and advances.[23]
- R. Summers reported in 1965 on 22 different US weapon systems showing 15−150% cost overrun, due largely to technological uncertainty and programme length.[24]
- R. L. Perry et al. studied US weapon systems, reporting in 1969 0−460% cost growth, due largely to government- and contractor-induced scope changes.[25]

Work carried out by Rand on overruns in the 1970s (see chapter 6, note 38) confirmed these orders of magnitude as still typical in later years, and for similar reasons. Rand's work on cost growth of weapons systems largely ceased thereafter and its studies on cost growth and schedule slippage were transferred to the construction sector — particularly power and process plants which, as we shall see, became an area of major project concern during the 1970s (note 11).

Summer's work was reprinted in a major study by Thomas Marschak and Thomas K. Glennan, also of Rand, published in 1967.[26] Marschak and Glennan reviewed the development strategies of most major USAF radars, engines, fighter aircraft and jet bombers produced between the Second World War and the mid-1960s, together with the Sidewinder missile. Their conclusions focused on the importance of the early stages of a project's development. While pointing out that *technical uncertainty* was a principal cause of overrun, Marschak and Glennan showed that in its early phases a major weapons system project faces two strategic options. A large commitment can be made early on: this allows long lead time items to be initiated quickly, but requires that there be fairly detailed knowledge of what is needed if cost and schedule overruns are to be avoided. Alternatively, a small commitment can be made at the outset, in which case long lead items cannot be initiated very early but a large jump in programme definition can be quickly achieved; as a result, estimates should be more accurate before the commitment to proceed is made.

Marschak and Glennan did not propose that one method was better than the other, they merely pointed out that the two methods are different. 'It has been the tendency of most large organizations to adopt procedures appropriate to the image they hold of the "ideal" development. Experience has shown that there is no ideal, and that procedures should be flexible enough to allow strategies appropriate to each development' (ref. 26, p. 48).

The Total Package Procurement concept

Concurrently with these studies, the DoD heard from a number of sources in both government and industry that contractors were purposely 'buying-in' to contracts by underestimating the cost of development programmes. Once the contractor was secured as a sole source supplier, profits could be made on subsequent follow-on contracts. To mitigate this trend, Assistant Secretary of Defense Robert H. Charles conceived the 'Total Package Procurement' (TPP) concept, which was implemented in 1966. Under TPP, contractors were asked at the outset to bid on the total programme package, including not just the development of the system but also its production and the supply of spare parts. Total programme packages were to be awarded on a competitive bid basis, generally on a fixed price contract. Profit was decided initially through competition, but determined ultimately by the quality of product and by management efficiency. Suppliers would thus, it was argued, be motivated to design for economical production and buying-in would be eliminated. Risk was in effect being shifted substantially from government to industry.

Several Total Package Procurement contracts were let during the latter half of the 1960s including the DD-963 Navy destroyer, the Army Cheyenne helicopter (AH-56A), the short-range attack missile (SRAM) and the Air Force Galaxy transport (C-5A). Nearly all these programmes ran into serious technical and cost overrun problems, due partly to the 'heating up' of the economy and the onset of inflation in the late 1960s, and partly to technical difficulties and uncertainties combined with pressures of programme urgency and lack of management flexibility. 'Contractors had to make substantial production commitments to meet delivery schedules before completion of design and verification by testing. Costly design and rework followed. Continued trade-off analysis was stifled because of the rigidity of the contracts' (ref. 1, p. 26). So severe were the problems on the C-5A and the Cheyenne helicopter that the contracts were eventually converted to cost-reimbursement, and the contractor, Lockheed in both instances, was forced to sustain substantial losses.

The Total Package Procurement concept was abolished in 1972, the DoD deciding that the task of systems acquisition was too complex and too sensitive to turn over in such a manner to industry. In particular, it was seen as unrealistic to expect estimates for future service demands, military threats and technological requirements to be sufficiently accurately assessed at the concept stage of a programme to allow accurate bid preparation and pricing by industry at such a comprehensive level.

(The problems of the C-5A, Cheyenne and SRAM in particular were to prompt renewed attention to the special project management difficulties of *concurrency*, i.e. the initiation of the development and production of a programme before the design is stable.[27,28] These projects illustrated dramatically the problems of Project and Program Management in such conditions: the situation is logically obvious — clearly it will be much harder to bring a project in on time, in budget and to technical specification if the specification keeps changing while one is building the product — but is often unavoidable. Concurrency, as we shall see, was to be a major cause of problems on many major projects in the 1960s and 1970s.)

The end of the dominance of the aerospace industry and the mega-project paradigm

So far, this account of the evolution of modern project management has necessarily been dominated by the US defence/aerospace sector, since virtually all the basic techniques and concepts were pioneered there. From around the mid-1960s, however, this was no longer to be the case. There was soon to be a dramatic rise in the number of projects in the construction industry that used modern project management techniques. There were large increases in the volume and types of construction activity, largely as a result of the steep increase in the price of oil between 1967 and 1972 — huge increases in Third World projects, more refinery capacity, the development of North Sea oil, bigger power generation plants. All these stretched management's ability to manage projects; in some cases, arguably, beyond its competence. Many of these projects posed major technical and organizational challenges. As the challenges were tackled, new insights into the management of projects were developed and became absorbed into the lexicon of modern project management.

A further push to the development of project management was the awakening of intellectual interest in the subject at this time in business schools, general academia and industry. As awareness of the discipline grew in academia and industry, its central concepts began to receive more rigorous examination and discussion, and it was disseminated more widely into the management community at large.

Both these developments — the expansion of project management into construction, with the new insights this entailed, and the introduction of the discipline into academia and general industry — meant that slowly the special focus of defence/aerospace project management began to broaden.

Fig. 15. Project Matrix Organization (based on Reis de Carvalho and Morris's[147] description of the Açominas matrix) showing the various responsibilities in a matrix of the project and functional groups, and their relation: in large organizations (e.g. Açominas, see p. 104), there can be second- and even third-order matrices — matrices within matrices

One of the early signs of this broadening was the adoption in the early-to-mid 1960s in several large project-based institutions — from large architect/engineer organizations such as Bechtel to several acquisition arms of DoD — of the *matrix* form of organization in which functional staff are assigned to projects, technically therefore serving two masters within the one-organization (see Fig. 15). The US Army Materiel Command was organized on a project/matrix basis in 1962; indeed, as we have seen, NASA experimented with various matrix/project arrangements in 1960–1963. *A massively important implication of this switch was that thousands more people were now working in project organizations.* Projects and project management was no longer reserved for the mega-effort; project managers did not have to be champions in the heroic mould of Groves, Schreiver, Raborn *et al.* Projects became more everyday experiences, with

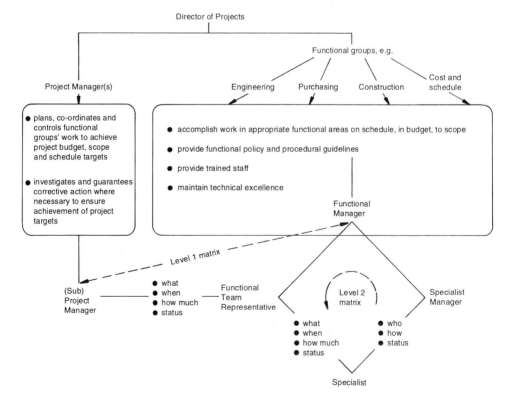

problems of implementation becoming even more commonplace. For most of the 1960s, and a large portion of the 1970s, these were typically to be problems of *perception and authority, systems and bureaucracy.*

This important expansion in the development of project management is very much the subject of the next chapter of this book — the 1970s. First, however, it might be useful to look at the status of project management in the UK — a country which, through Operations Research, had after all been a pioneer in the development of the scientific approach to management, yet which had a substantially different culture of engineering management from that of the USA.

A useful review of project management practice in the UK in the second half of the 1960s is given in ref. 29.

Bloodhound

Metcalfe and Rowley (in ref. 29) discussed the project management of the Bloodhound ground-to-air missile — one of Britain's major aerospace successes in the 1960s and 1970s (Fig. 16). Bloodhound offers an excellent window onto the issues being faced on major hi-tech projects in the UK at this time.

Bloodhound was begun in 1950. Not surprisingly, there was next to no project management in the early years of the project. Network scheduling was not used; cost estimating and control were rudimentary. Contracts were let on a cost-plus basis for phase 1 of the project, whose development cost was estimated to be £1·5m (the actual figure was £32m!). A project office was created only during the development phase, first by the contractor and much later by the owner (note 12).

Bloodhound was commercially a very successful project for its makers, being sold to several foreign countries. (The prime

Fig. 16. Bloodhound (courtesy Jane's Information Group)

contractor was the British Aircraft Corporation.) For one of the principal contractors, Ferranti, however, the project was embarrassingly over-successful. Disturbed by the way the costs of missiles were exceeding estimates by quite large margins, the Ministry of Defence (MoD) decided in 1955 that Ferranti's contract (and others') for Bloodhound would be fixed price (note 13). The contract price was agreed as £12·824m, of which the profit component had been estimated as £0·81m. Production was conducted efficiently (delivery was (only) six weeks late on a four-year programme) and Ferranti's direct and indirect costs were low. As a result, its actual profit was higher: £5·773m. This was discovered and there was political uproar. The matter was debated in the House of Commons, a committee of inquiry was set up, and ultimately Ferranti agreed to refund 85% of its profit on the contract (note 14).

The committee of inquiry (the Lang Committee) reported in July 1964 on the Ferranti contract (and on the general system of pricing in February 1965).[30,31] Several lessons were drawn that were relevant to the desire, on both sides of the Atlantic, to develop appropriate contracting policies. The most important was that *fixed price contracts may not be suitable for projects that are first-time products* or where the manufacturer is a dominant supplier (since political sensitivities will become overriding if the costs are too far above or below estimate, as of course happened with Ferranti). In such cases, the Lang Committee recommended, *target contracts* may be more appropriate, since the contractor then has an incentive to limit his costs and political realities are respected. (These findings in retrospect seem eminently sensible, certainly more so than the philosophy of Total Package Procurement which was just about to be launched in the USA.)

Bloodhound added a *commercial dimension* to the management of projects which had largely been overlooked by the earlier US defence and space projects. But, much more significantly, Bloodhound, through the Ferranti affair, affected the UK defence establishment for decades to come. For many in MoD, it was *not now considered proper for contractors to make large profits, no matter how large the risks they had borne!* Years later, MoD officials were still asking to audit the profits made on fixed-price work. Even more damagingly, civil servants and military officers sought to 'engineer' products through specifications in order to prevent the supplier from 'milking' MoD. Bloodhound, like the F-111, illustrates the limitations of the systems engineering approach, in this case caused by distrust and consequent lack of openness on the part of the specifier.

The next British major aerospace *cause célèbre*, the TSR-2, was to reveal technology/weapons systems development problems and commercial/industrial strategy issues in awful abundance.

TSR-2

The TSR-2 (Tactical Strike Reconnaissance 2) was designed as a light bomber to replace Britain's first jet bomber, the Canberra, during the period 1955–1959 (Fig. 17). General Operational Requirement (GOR) 339, outlining the general strategic and technical requirements for the aircraft, was issued in mid-1954.

The organization of Britain's aircraft industry was, it was recognized, too ill-focused and poorly structured to meet adequately

Fig. 17. TSR-2: (a) general arrangement; (b) the aircraft (photograph courtesy S. R. Temblett)

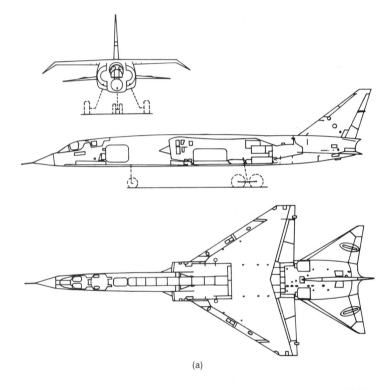

(a)

(b)

the increasingly complex, sophisticated needs of modern aircraft production at the time of issue of GOR 339; the way the industry organized itself to meet the requirement would, it was seen, have a lasting and profound effect on its future structure. In January 1959 the Ministry of Supply announced that the aircraft would be named TSR-2 and that the chief contract would go to Vickers, probably with work shared with English Electric. The engine would be developed by Bristol Siddeley.

The weapons procurement policies in Britain at this time were to influence significantly the way in which this major project was managed. A 1957 House of Commons Select Committee[32] had made several criticisms of and recommendations for the UK defence procurement practices of the time

- operational requirements were controlled by the Defence Research Policy Committee (DRPC) without reference to or adequate liaison with other relevant government departments such as the Treasury and the Ministry of Supply (note 15)
- in general, there was poor control of changes
- Royal Air Force (RAF) procurement personnel were posted-on too frequently and without due regard to the continuity demands of the project
- an aircraft must be viewed as a total weapons system
- in future, development aircraft should be prepared in batches of a dozen or so rather than in one or two prototypes
- the technical 'steps' by which aircraft are developed should be small and frequent.

In 1961 the Ministry of Defence adopted a 'step-by-step' concept of weapon system procurement proposed by Sir Claud Gibb and Solly Zuckerman — the *Gibb−Zuckerman* procedures.[33] Since much detailed work is necessary before project go-ahead can be given, the Gibb−Zuckerman approach was a way of keeping a promising project going, subject to review, without making premature commitment or incurring excessive costs. Unfortunately, the procedure allowed scientific establishments to *refer the project 'back' to earlier stages for reworking without anyone having authority to defend the project's interest against such decisions*; as a result, the procedures came to be associated with exceptional delays in gaining project approval. The TSR-2 was held by many in industry to have been one of the victims in this regard.

TSR-2, which represented substantial technical advances in virtually all its major systems, was something of a guinea pig for testing the new weapons procurement practices developed as a consequence of the 1957 Select Committee recommendations. This was especially true of the engine, which became virtually a new design, and the avionics, which at this time were reflecting a complete new generation of electronic miniaturization. In this respect, the TSR-2 differed fundamentally and crucially from its US 'rival', the F-111. The US practice at this time was the *building block* approach, in which defence technology was advanced over a broad front so that individual weapons systems used technology that was largely already developed. The primary requirement on the US system thus became *systems integration*. The British considered this policy too expensive, and instead adopted a *spearhead* approach whereby a new weapons system was used to spearhead new technology. *Technology development was thus added to the problem of systems integration.*

Because of the substantial technical advances that TSR-2 involved, estimation of the project's costs proved very difficult. The engine, for example, was initially thought of as simply an upgrading of the existing Olympus 200 series, and an estimate was prepared of £7·3m. By March 1964 this had risen to £32·5m, largely as a result of an under-appreciation of the magnitude of the technical challenge. Partly, though, it was caused by the complexity of the interaction between the development of the airframe, the electronics and the engine.

The problem of integration was particularly badly handled with regard to managerial and contractual responsibilities. The Ministry of Aviation maintained that the aircraft industry alone was capable of managing design, development and production. Theoretically, the British Aircraft Corporation (Vickers) was the prime contractor, but in practice it was responsible for only about 30% of the project expenditure. Contracts for the rest — primarily the engines and the electronics — came under the direct responsibility of the Ministry of Aviation/Technology. Also, various items of equipment were provided directly by the RAF. In practice, then, the British Aircraft Corporation never had the contractual authority to control the whole project effectively, no matter how vigorously the Ministry of Aviation urged it to do so.

To make matters worse, *the 'owner' did not have any one party clearly in charge of the total project.*

> The Ministry of Supply regarded themselves as servants of the Air Ministry, while the aircraft firms merely did what the Ministry of Supply told them, but fed back ideas about refinements and additions to projects to the Air Ministry. As a result . . . there [was] no effective way to relate those detailed changes in specification seen as appropriate by the [Air] Ministry to their monetary cost, or to the slippage in the programme that might result. Those co-ordinating or liaison committees that did exist had little effect on Air Ministry actions in such areas, as the Air Ministry had no direct accounting responsibility for weapons development programmes and traditionally demanded the best equipment available.[34]

That is, *technical, schedule and cost performance did not all come together at one place. There was no integrating project management.*

This lack of project management was clearly manifest in the difficulty in finalizing the TSR-2's design. The Air Ministry kept demanding specification changes without being able to relate them to their effect on cost growth or schedule slippage. The comparison with Apollo and Minuteman could not be more acute (note 16).

In January 1963 the Ministry of Aviation realized that this situation was untenable. Large amounts of money were being spent on the project while there was effectively next to no project control (note 17). In May 1964, at the Ministry's request, new cost control and value engineering systems were introduced together with PERT, while a senior director of BAC was appointed project manager.

In October 1964 the Labour party was elected to form a new government. On 5 April 1965 TSR-2 was cancelled, mainly on the grounds that it would be more cost-effective to purchase the F-111 from America. Other expensive aircraft projects such as the HS-681 and P-1154 were also cancelled at this time (as Concorde would have been were it not for the refusal of the French, with whom the British shared a treaty for design, development and production which could be terminated only by mutual consent).

Plowden, Polaris and Downey

Several important lessons were drawn from the TSR-2 debacle which decisively influenced future UK weapons systems procurement practices. First, it became accepted, following the influential recommendations of the 1965 Plowden Report,[35] that Britain should no longer attempt to maintain a full range of aerospace capabilities, but should instead collaborate with other countries on projects that promised a reasonable relationship between market sales and development costs. Thus, by the end of the 1960s, Anglo-French *collaboration* was a significant facet of UK aerospace work, with projects such as Concorde, the Jaguar bomber and the Martel missile. (The lessons of these collaborative projects are discussed on pp. 137–139 and p. 323, note 55.) Where Britain's needs required disproportionate development efforts (e.g. in missiles), it should, Plowden further recommended, purchase such systems from the USA. Second, the spearhead approach to technology development was rejected in favour of the building block approach.[36] Third, responsibility for managing projects was to be placed unequivocally in the hands of industry.

While the RAF struggled with the question of how to develop advanced aerospace projects, a much more integrated approach to project management was being demonstrated by the Royal Navy in its development of a Polaris fleet. Britain acquired the Polaris missile in 1963. With Polaris, not only were the technical challenges less than for the TSR-2, but also the project management techniques developed by Raborn's Special Projects Office were available. A *Polaris Executive* was created for the British Polaris programme early in 1963 (note 18).[37] This differed from the

SPO in that it was not given such high rank or overriding priority within the Navy. Nevertheless, the Polaris Executive retained the core concept of a small administrative and managerial cadre, directly responsible for the organization, planning and progress of the project, co-ordinating the activities of the functional departments relevant to the programme. The Chief Polaris Executive had right of access to the Admiralty Board. Staff numbered not more than 500, of whom about 40 comprised the central executive group. There was also a management service unit responsible for co-ordinating the planning and monitoring of the project progress. As well as developing the overall programme plan, this group gave guidance on the use of network schedules to both Polaris Executive field officers and manufacturers. *Polaris was one of the first projects on which British contractors were required contractually to use advanced project management systems*; its championing within the Ministries of Defence and Technology undoubtedly did much to promote these systems' use in the mid-1960s in the UK.

The practice of British defence project management was reviewed comprehensively in 1966 by the Steering Group on Development Cost Estimating chaired by W. G. Downey of the Ministry of Aviation.[38] The practices covered in Downey, as the report was thereafter known, have largely remained unchallenged, though not always observed, ever since. The Downey report provides an interesting picture of the state of project management in the industry at the end of the 1960s — *not enough time spent in front-end definition and preparation; wide variations in standards of cost and schedule control; inadequate control over design changes* — as well as comparing UK with US and French approaches to weapons system development. The report also provided a project management manual, in which techniques such as *work breakdown structures, task responsibility matrices, estimating methodologies*, and *cost and schedule monitoring* and *reporting systems* are described in detail.

Downey's comments on comparisons of the British, American and French systems are interesting. Downey was not convinced of the validity of the American practice of not beginning engineering development until the technical requirement and programmes were defined. This, as we have seen, was an argument that would persist for many years, obvious 'good management practice' contrasting with the needs of urgency (hence leading to the 'concurrency' situation). France's ministerial structures were seen as more compact and as having more authority and independence than the UK's; design changes were rigidly controlled and the government had the statutory right to obtain data on actual costs on all contracts. The French were believed to be 'behind' the Americans and British, however, in not requiring detailed project definition as early as possible.

Finally, Downey examined incentive contracting, advocating its greater use in the UK but noting, again, that a benefit of the American building block approach was that unexpected technical risks should not be too frequent; this would be less the case in the UK. The British, Downey noted, concentrated more on target cost forms of incentive contracts as compared with the Americans' emphasis on performance and delivery incentives; American industry, being larger, could offer more competition than the British and could better absorb losses where these occurred. (Downey's report, of course, was written before Total Package Procurement collapsed, precisely because of industry's problems with unstable technical requirements, and before the Pentagon's consequent decision to bail out Lockheed on the C-5 and Cheyenne helicopter contracts!)

The UK process industries

Project management in the UK construction sector at this time was essentially practised only in the process industries. The challenges were not so much in the area of technological development (as with defence/aerospace) as in design management and site management. The other speakers at the 1969 symposium[29] where Rowley and Metcalfe spoke on Bloodhound were three from the Central Electricity Generating Board (CEGB).

Howard Gott, the last of the CEGB's speakers (note 19), emphasized the importance of *firm technical definition*, the problem of discovering the real difficulties only after detailed engineering and/or production had begun (in this the construction industry differs from aerospace in that prototyping is generally not possible), the need to *schedule the design work and to link it into production requirements*, and the importance of firm *change control* (ref. 35, pp. 30–41). The 1968 Wilson Committee which examined the problems of the CEGB in completing power stations on schedule emphasized the same points.[39] In the 36 power plants constructed during the 20 years following the end of the Second World War, 43% of the units had schedule overruns of a year or more: the principal causes of the overruns were *adverse site conditions, manufacturing difficulties, design faults* and *labour problems*.

The British site was (and to an extent, still is) characterized by multiple managements and multiple unions — each requiring its own programming and co-ordination. Site productivity for a similar task performed by a similar crew could vary substantially, depending on the way the work was programmed, restrictive practices, contract disputes or communication difficulties.

The problems of cost and schedule overruns on large process plant sites was in fact so widespread and serious[40] in the late 1960s that a special working party was established in July 1968 by the UK's National Economic Development Office (NEDO) 'to inquire into the problems of organization of large industrial

construction sites with particular reference to labour relations ... '.
There were reckoned to be over 50 such sites in Britain at the time
— power stations; oil, gas and chemical plants; steelworks and
non-ferrous metal plants — virtually all of which were prone to
delay and cost growth caused by late design changes, late delivery
of materials and plant, low labour productivity, labour disputes,
skills shortages and so on. The working party's findings, which
were taken extremely seriously by the industry and represented
a milestone in its development, concentrated on improvements to
contract strategy, industrial relations and the *better management
of design.*[41]

The contracting basis on which the UK process industries had
operated during the Second World War and for 10–15 years
afterwards was largely a cost-reimbursable one, as capacity was
rebuilt on an emergency basis; the performance of many projects
during this period had been far from satisfactory. In the 1960s,
however, this contracting practice changed. Suppliers were now
asked to take fixed price responsibility, unfortunately even in
situations where they could neither control their contractual
environment effectively nor bear the cost of failure should they
be forced to default — a situation, indeed, not dissimilar to that
of the Total Package Program concept described above. In the
UK nuclear power industry in the late 1960s, for example, the
supply consortia were asked to take fixed-price responsibility for
the construction of major operating plants using an as yet
undeveloped technology — the Advanced Gas Cooled Reactor
design — these high-performance risks being in no sense matched
by a corresponding financial strength within the consortia. The
result, in the early 1970s, was to be little short of disastrous.[42]
Partially in recognition of the difficulties this blanket and often
inequitable (and foolish) contracting philosophy represented,
NEDO in 1970 recommended a greater use of reimbursable and
negotiated contracts (in practice this proved to be too simplistic,
not to say naïve), fewer contracts on a project and *the use of a
specialist integrating engineer–constructor contractor.*

The *industrial relations* record was little short of dreadful.
NEDO's solution was a comprehensive national agreement on
industrial relations for the industry. Although this recommendation
was regarded as fundamental, it was not in fact taken up for over
a decade (note 20).

The CEGB's projects in the late 1960s were headed not by a
project manager but by a project engineer. The task was to ensure
that the engineering (design, manufacture, erection, test,
commission) of what had been defined was carried out efficiently
(note 21). As a result, thinking on matters such as the
appropriateness of the project definition, contract types,
organization behaviour and structure, and quality — even industrial
relations — tended to be underpowered. The NEDO working party

proposed instead that *owners should exercise more comprehensive project management authority*, extending their activities over the whole project life cycle, and that there should be more thorough *programming*, particularly at the design stage. Since late *design changes* were held to be the single biggest cause of delays in projects, it was recommended that 'clients reappraise the value of allowing the design and construction phases of a project to overlap' and that the need for changes be monitored more closely.

In fact, Britain's construction industries in general at this time were dominated by the design professions — engineering, architecture, etc. — and indeed, as we shall see, the engineers were further dominated by scientists who were often concerned more with experimentation and knowledge than with efficient 'project' completion. 'Management' was not yet accepted as a valid central intellectual organizing force. To this day, management of British construction projects — building, civil, mechanical, chemical — is largely dominated by the standard forms of contract and the patterns of work promulgated by the professional institutions (Institutions of Civil, Mechanical and Chemical Engineers, Royal Institute of British Architects — or more accurately in building, the Joint Contracts Tribunal).

The UK building and civil engineering industries

The difficulties of design management, of a fragmented industrial structure and of site management were just as important in the building and civil engineering industries as in the process ones, and the project management problems were compounded by the fact that these industries had neither a discipline of integrating design and production nor a structure that lent itself to active management at the 'project' level (note 22). As we have seen, the process by which the various parties in the building and civil engineering industries were organized had been formalized in the UK largely in the late 19th century (note 23).

In civil engineering, design and production were not separated in as draconian a fashion as in building, but the Consulting Engineer in practice adopted a very similar stance to the Architect *vis-à-vis* the Contractor. Both were to act as the administrator of the contract between the Owner (Client) and the Contractor; both would adjudicate this contract on the Owner's behalf; the Contractor would typically enter the project only after the designs had been completed and an estimate had been prepared by a Quantity Surveyor. The Contractor would submit a programme and a price for doing the job in accordance with the drawings and specifications; if these were changed during the project, he was entitled under the standard forms of contract to seek extra payment. And he did, generally with energy and forethought.

Under such arrangements there was *no-one in overall active management of the project* — no-one balancing cost and schedule requirements against the designers' wishes. Construction expertise typically was being brought in too late; teamwork was generally poor. As the noted student of the British building industry, Marion Bowley, wrote in 1966, 'It is quite time that an end was put to the sacrifice of possible improvements of efficiency in design and production to the idol of competitive tenders on finished designs.'[43]

Two official committees, the Emerson Committee and the Banwell Committee, came to similar conclusions in 1962 and 1964 for civil engineering as well as building.[44,45] These rumblings of discontent were given added voice by a study commissioned between 1963 and 1965 on communications in the building industry, which was carried out by the Tavistock Institute of London and attracted some notoriety.[46,47] The study reached three conclusions. First, there had to be more efficient forms of organization and contractual arrangements than those prevailing at the time. Second, the decision-making process in the industry could be improved if studied along 'systems design' lines. Third, the efficiency of the building process should be reviewed further 'from the point of view of the client/user/community'. Regrettably, the building industry took fright and ceased funding Tavistock's work in 1967. Its insights were, however, to be developed in both practice and theory during the following decade.

The Tavistock Institute was not an inappropriate group to study project management since, by the mid-to-late 1960s, a growing and important theoretical dimension was being developed in universities and research institutes to support the emerging 'project view' of the need at times in organizations for special efforts to achieve cross-functional integration (note 24). The origins of this work lie chiefly with the development of General Systems Theory and the effect of this on organization theory. The work provides in effect *theoretical grounds for the organizational base of project management*.

The systems and organization theory basis of project management

During the 1920s and 1930s, biologists had noticed that living organisms share many common principles of organization — the way energy and information are exchanged between systems and their environment in order for the systems to grow and to maintain equilibrium through the feedback principle, the tendency towards differentiation, and other processes, many of which they described in esoteric language. Gestalt psychologists added to this 'open systems' schema, and by the 1950s General Systems Theory was being embraced by economists, anthropologists, geographers, sociologists and others (note 25).

Another important intellectual stream influencing this emerging 'holistic' approach in the 1950s was the (largely computer-based) quantitative one, of which the USAF/Rand-type systems engineering was one of the best examples.

The major tenet of the systems approach is a concern with overall effectiveness.[48-50] The starting point is the definition of the system — what its aims are and what, and who, will be involved in realizing these. (This approach, of course, is mirrored exactly in project management, as writers such as Kast and Rosenzweig in 1963 and particularly Cleland and King in 1968 have shown.[49, 50-52])

'Open' systems, such as living organisms, interact with their environment; 'closed' systems, such as most simple machinery, do not. Open systems, as Fred Emery of the Tavistock Institute pointed out in his 1959 pioneering work on what he termed 'socio-technic systems' (note 26), emphasize survival (rather than structure), adaptability and internal differentiation, interaction and interdependency.[50,53-59] Important in the socio-technic school, then, were interrelationships between environment, organizational form and participants' views.[50,60]

Using the systems approach, Tavistock writers extended the vocabulary of management in ways that resemble much of project management terminology. In 1965, for example, Emery and Trist pointed to the importance of *boundary management* functions — those parts of the organization responsible for monitoring, controlling and adapting (if need be) the organization's structure.[61-63] Miller and Rice showed in 1967 that an organization's boundaries are best positioned where there are clear discontinuities in time, technology or territory (note 27).[48-50,64]

During the second half of the 1960s, other writers began to give increased attention to the influence on management of technology and in particular to the challenges of *differentiation* and *integration*. The impact of technology was studied from several angles.[65-67] Joan Woodward of Imperial College found that there would be greater overlap between design and scheduling (programming) not only where there was greater environmental uncertainty and rate of change, as some researchers had predicted, but also where there was technological uncertainty.[68-70] In project management terms, *greater technical and environmental uncertainty would lead to a greater need for project management.*

Later in the decade, Paul Lawrence and Jay Lorsch, of Harvard, published a study in which they analysed how and under what conditions an organization needed to put more effort into integrating its various parts.[71,72] James Thompson of Indiana University showed that as the *interdependence* between organizational parts increased, so would the amount of integration required.[73] In project management terms, these two studies showed that there would be *a need for more project management the more that groups had to work together towards shared goals, the more they overlapped, and the greater the differences between them.*

In 1968, Jay Galbraith of MIT tested these ideas at Boeing, showing that there was a continuum of integrating devices.[74] Integration was now seen to be increasingly necessary (*a*) the more that the parts of an organization needed to work together, (*b*) the greater the environmental, technical and organizational rate of change and complexity, and (*c*) the greater the degree of differentiation between the parts of the organization. Program Management, according to Galbraith, Burns and others of the Lawrence and Lorsch school, was an important way of achieving such integration.[75,76]

Put simply, *the need for integration would increase as the project became larger, more urgent, or more complex. A range of integrating structures was available: liaison, expeditor, special teams, project co-ordinator, project manager, full project team, matrix — greater integrative power being provided as one moved along this continuum* (Fig. 18).

Writings on project management

While organization theory thus developed a relatively satisfactory explanation of *project management as a form of integration* (Fig. 18), other writers were articulating, contextualizing and popularizing this new form of management. The 1960s saw the first flood of writing, both technical and popular, on this exciting 'space-age' form of management.

The earliest writings on project management had tended to explain the approach within the context of a specific industry — process engineering, new product development, R&D, defence, information systems, etc.[77-83] During the 1960s, many writings on the organizational aspects of project management were produced, with a particularly heavy output around 1965–1967. Articles on *project organization* matters by Lanier,[84] Johnson and

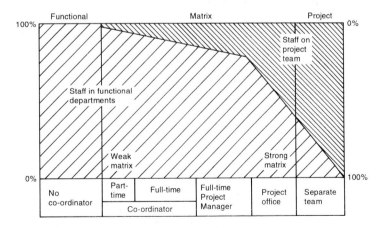

Fig. 18. Project Integration models (after Youker[148]): this shows how, as more staff are assigned to work on a project on a dedicated basis, one moves to a strong matrix/project organization; with fewer staff working on a dedicated basis on a project, one has a weak matrix or an entirely functional organization; moving from a weak to a strong matrix, one also moves from a co-ordinator position to a project management role

Jones[85] and Gaddis[86] had appeared in the late 1950s; the subject of the *project manager's authority* was first aired in 1960 by Janger[87,88] (and has been of perennial interest ever since). In 1965, Marquis and Straight[89] at MIT published research on the relevance of organizational factors to project performance, while Mee[90] and Schull[91] published some of the first writings on the *matrix* form of organization. 1967 saw a flurry of further writing on organizational aspects of project management, with Cleland[92] and Goodman[93] on the problem of defining and exercising *project management authority*, Rubin and Seilig[94] on the *selection of project managers* and Middleton[95] and Lawrence and Lorsch[96] obtaining considerable exposure through their articles in the *Harvard Business Review*, Middleton's in March 1967 on how to set up a project organization and Lawrence and Lorsch's in November 1967 on 'the new management job: the integrator'.

Writings on cost and scheduling, meanwhile continued to appear regularly. Dozens of articles describing *CPM, PERT, precedence* and the other scheduling techniques appeared each year during the 1960s, while comprehensive textbooks on scheduling were published by Battersby[97] and Moder and Phillips in 1964,[6] by Antill and Woodhead[98] and O'Brien[99] in 1965, by Archibald and Villoria[100] in 1967 and by Lockyer[101] in 1969. 1969 also saw Wiest and Levy[102] publish a comprehensive review of the use of CPM and PERT.

The second half of the 1960s saw a shift away from this preoccupation with scheduling and organizational aspects towards more comprehensive texts on project management. The first of these was published in 1963 by Baumgartner;[103] Hajek[104] published *Project engineering* in 1965 (articles on project management were now beginning to appear regularly); in 1967 Silverman[105] published *The technical program manager's guide to survival*; 1968 saw Cleland and King's[106] *Systems analysis and project management*, which has since become a classic of the genre, Lock's[107] *Project management* and Steiner and Ryan's[22] *Industrial project management*.

Meanwhile, management writers were beginning to take note of and feed off project and systems management, so that management thinking in general began to be influenced by its concepts, tools and techniques. Kast and Rosenzweig[51] published *Organization and management: a systems approach* in 1963, a section of which dealt with Program Management and matrix organization; in July 1969, with the first landing of man on the moon, *Fortune*[108] wrote of project management as 'the unexpected pay-off from Apollo'; in the same year James Webb,[109] the NASA Administrator for much of Apollo, wrote an account of his NASA experiences entitled *Space age management*; in 1970 Alvin Toffler's[110] best-selling book *Future shock* described project management as an example of the increased tendency for organizations to restructure themselves frequently, terming this process 'the new adhocracy': 'it is important to recognize that the rise of ad hoc organization is a direct effect of the speed-up of change in society as a whole' (ref. 110, p. 135).

The writings of Webb and others presented NASA's systems management skills as a new weapon for social development. Society had to move forward increasingly, Webb wrote — presaging the views of the macro-project societies a decade or two later — through its 'ability to organize the complex and do the unusual [by using] adaptive, problem-solving, temporary systems of diverse specialists, linked together by co-ordinating executives in organic flux'.[109] The Manhattan Project, Tennessee Valley Authority, Panama Canal — these, Webb asserted, were tomorrow's type of organization. No doubt Webb genuinely believed this. In retrospect, however, one cannot help being conscious of the limitations of such an argument, *limitations that were soon to become apparent as major projects stumbled in the 1970s*; limitations that two distinguished academics, Leonard R. Sayles and Margaret K. Chandler, were to observe in their detailed study of NASA's management practices in 1971.[111]

Sayles and Chandler's *Managing large systems* is a serious book reflecting a view that the future 'will be characterized by large engineering systems matched by, and reflected in, large organizational systems' (ref. 112, p. 1). Sayles and Chandler correctly perceived that in Apollo, NASA deployed many more management skills than those simply of programme management. As well as perceptively analysing the functions of systems integration, project control and the project manager (the 'organization metronome', see chapter 10), they touched all the bases that we shall see in this study as being *important in the successful management of projects: the environment; collaboration between industry, government and academia; the relative roles of scientists and technologists; the subtleties of effective management of technology; the need for a phased approach to project planning.* Yet in reading this worthy book one soon tires, partly because of the jargon and the repetition, but mainly because its optimism was already dated when it was published in 1971.

In a prophetic concluding chapter, Sayles and Chandler indicated the decisive difference between the 1960s and the 1970s.

But compared to some of the socio-technical programs [now] on the horizon, NASA had a simple life. NASA was a closed loop — it set its own schedule, designed its own hardware, and used the gear it designed ... The populace did not feel threatened by the program; on the whole the popular mood was supportive ... As one moves into the socio-technical area, this luxury disappears. [Housing and environmental protection, for example] will have to deal with political complexities NASA never dreamed of — interfaces that are more readily identified than managed ... We are not saying that there are two types of large-scale systems; rational types such as AEC and space programs that brook no political nonsense [note 28] and political types such as urban development which quickly become a morass of competitive and conflicting interests. All large development organizations constitute political—business systems ... [but] management and organizational skills will be many times more critical in these inherently unwieldy public—private systems than in more traditional organizations.

For by the late 1960s, even as Armstrong and Aldrin set foot on the Sea of Tranquillity, doubt and disillusion were beginning to arise in the world of projects. Some of the earlier and still vaunted project management practices were being criticized with increasing effect. More importantly, perhaps, several major projects were experiencing traumatic difficulties — programmes ranging from the US defence Total Package Procurement projects such as the C-5A to European aerospace projects such as Concorde and the Rolls-Royce RB-211 engine (see pp. 90—92 and 136), from the US Supersonic Transport to the Trans Alaskan Pipeline, from San Francisco's Bay Area Rapid Transit to the British third London airport (see pp. 92—100) — indeed, one might even add the US space programme itself (see pp. 139—142). Some of these projects (e.g. Concorde) experienced problems precisely because project management was being hardly applied at all: although this was not an indictment of project management, the image of large projects became tarnished as a result. Large, highly focused, multi-organizational projects and programmes were seen by many, not least their potential sponsors in government and industry, as anything but 'organizations for the future'. Rather, *pace* Sayles and Chandler, they were becoming enterprises at best to be avoided wherever possible, and at worst, to be treated with the greatest caution and scepticism. As regards the development of project management as a discipline, curiously, *many of the difficulties that these projects were experiencing were due to issues that project management had not yet addressed formally — notably, technical uncertainty and contract strategy, and the emergence of a new class of external factors, in particular community opposition and the project's environmental impact.*

The resolution of these shortcomings occupied the development of the *discipline of managing projects* for some time. Before moving' on to the 1970s, however, this description of project management practice in the 1960s should be concluded with a brief mention of further developments in project management planning and control techniques. It is important to do this not just for the sake of completeness, but because interest in the subject at this level was to be central to the professional project management societies created in the 1960s and 1970s, which took up the banner of developing project management as a professional discipline. Their concentration on such techniques, unfortunately, directed the development of the discipline away from more fundamental issues.

Planning and control techniques in the late 1960s

When we last discussed project planning and control systems, it was to note the difficulties that both US contractors and government agencies had experienced in implementing *PERT*, and the consequent development and slow adoption first by the USAF and later by other government agencies of the *Cost/Schedule Control Systems Criteria* approach and *Earned Value*. Despite these difficulties, network scheduling, cost control and other project management tools had been implemented with gusto by project management enthusiasts throughout North America and Europe, and elsewhere.

During the 1960s and 1970s, hundreds of articles were published on network scheduling alone (many, as Wiest has shown,[112] in the Soviet Union). Not everyone was convinced of the overriding value of the method, however. Several authors had supplied critiques of the statistical basis of PERT,[113–115] while in the late 1960s a number of influential articles were published questioning the real contribution of such techniques and systems to the success of projects.[116–119]

Nevertheless, interest in such project management tools and techniques continued to be extremely strong. Indeed, two further developments were initiated in this area before the decade was out, namely *GERT* and *Resource Scheduling*.

In 1966 Alan Pritsker, following pioneering work by Freeman,[120] Eisner[121] and Elmaghraby[122] on alternative ways of portraying alternative paths in a project graphically by use of new node types, published the first of his papers on GERT — the Graphical Evaluation and Review Technique.[123–127] In PERT, one *must* follow the flow of arrows and nodes; in this sense, PERT, CPM and precedence are all deterministic in that once an activity is complete, one must proceed to the next node in accordance with the logic of the network diagram. In reality, however, one often has a choice: if the product passes its quality check, for example, one can proceed to stage *X*; if it does not, one may have to go to stage *Y*. Representation of this option requires a probabilistic network, which is what GERT allows. GERT also allows for looping back in the net and for different probability distributions at the node (not just a beta distribution, as in PERT).

Pritsker developed GERT as part of Rand's work for NASA on developing automatic check-out procedures for Apollo. Arisawa and Elmahgraby[128] added a cost processing module in 1972; in 1975 Hebert[129] developed a version that could model resource constraints. By the late 1970s the program, incorporating these and other features, was known as Q-GERT.[130] The computation required to model activities using GERT, however, has proved very great. For this and other reasons, it was not used widely.

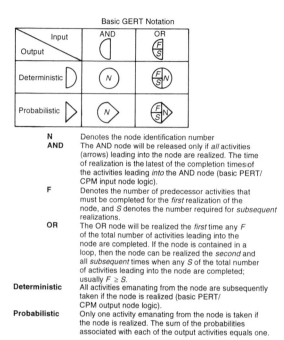

Output	Input	AND	OR
Deterministic		N	
Probabilistic		N	

Basic GERT Notation

N   Denotes the node identification number
AND   The AND node will be released only if *all* activities
            (arrows) leading into the node are realized. The time
            of realization is the latest of the completion times of
            the activities leading *into* the AND node (basic PERT/
            CPM input node logic).
F   Denotes the number of predecessor activities that
            must be completed for the *first* realization of the
            node, and S denotes the number required for *subsequent*
            realizations.
OR   The OR node will be realized the *first* time any F
            of the total number of activities leading into the
            node are completed. If the node is contained in a
            loop, then the node can be realized the *second* and
            all *subsequent* times when any S of the total number
            of activities leading into the node are completed;
            usually $F \geq S$.
Deterministic   All activities emanating from the node are subsequently
            taken if the node is realized (basic PERT/
            CPM output node logic).
Probabilistic   Only one activity emanating from the node is taken if
            the node is realized. The sum of the probabilities
            associated with each of the output activities equals one.

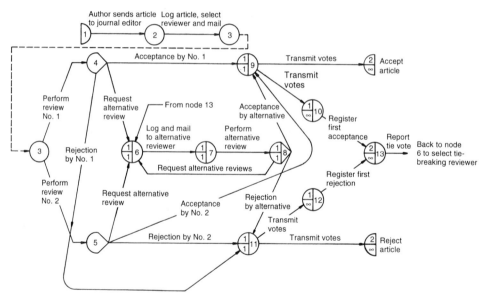

Fig. 19. A GERT diagram (from Moder, Phillips and Davis[131])

It was mostly used in the simulation of large projects (such as the scheme for the Alaskan gas pipeline) or in simulation by researchers (Fig. 19).[131] The 1990s, as shown in chapter 9, are currently seeing a rise in interest in the principles of GERT planning.

Another method offering a probabilistic network logic similar to GERT is *VERT*, the Venture Evaluation and Review Technique. Developed in 1972 by G. L. Moeller, VERT models technical performance more comprehensively than GERT. Like GERT,

VERT assesses the risks involved in undertaking a new venture by simulating the variety of relations a project may experience using deterministic and probabilistic nodes and arcs, a variety (up to 13) of statistical probability distributions being possible.[132-134] VERT has so far been used even less than GERT.

Resource scheduling had been an aspect of CPM from its inception in 1957−1958, and there had been steady interest in the topic throughout the 1960s. The ability of CPM to deal with variations in resources was exceedingly limited, however; it essentially comprised assessment of the impact on the network durations of the variation of individual activity according to the different level of resources being applied. This was adequate for *resource smoothing* — by shifting of slack tasks beyond periods of peak resource requirements[135,136] — but it did not help with the more common problem of deciding what would happen if sufficient resources were not available when required, the so-called *resource allocation* problem. Heuristics ('the rule of thumb' approach to problem solving) had been developed for tackling resource allocation around 1963−1966,[137-140] but by 1967 researchers were finding more analytical ways of expressing how to minimize project duration given a limited set of resources,[141] and these initiatives were given a considerable boost between 1968 and 1976 by the work of Davis and his colleagues.[142-146]

By the end of the 1960s, then, resource allocation was emerging as an important aspect of project scheduling. However, it was still a largely theoretical field, and was to remain so until the emergence of cheap, powerful, smaller computers in the late 1970s and early 1980s. Until then, the complexity required to model the various resourcing options was so great that it required unrealistically large amounts of expensive mainframe computing time and, more to the point, discouraged the project manager from experimenting with the computer programs in a useful way. The concept was tantalizing, however, since it was clearly relevant not just to single projects but to multi-project scheduling. Many Program Managers worked in multi-project environments but, because of this constraint, made little use of the project scheduling tools of the late 1960s (and most of the 1970s) to help schedule and plan their work effectively.

PMI and Internet: the new project management professional societies

In late 1968, a group of project managers in the USA came together to form a professional organization 'dedicated to advancing the state-of-the-art in project management '. The Project Management Institute (PMI) was formed in 1969 with the objectives of fostering professionalism in project management, improving communications 'about terminology and techniques', encouraging research, providing 'an interface between users and suppliers of hardware and software systems' and supporting project management education and career development. A journal, *Project Management*

Quarterly, was founded by the institute, its first publication being in April 1970.

PMI's European counterpart has had a different evolution. A meeting was held in Vienna in 1967 to take stock of the network planning techniques then believed necessary, or at least beneficial, for the management of modern projects. This meeting was entitled INTERNET 67. The subject stimulated such interest that it was decided five years later (after a second INTERNET congress in Amsterdam in 1969) to form a more permanent project management society: the International Management Systems Association (IMSA) was formed after the third INTERNET congress in Stockholm in 1972, still, however, with the emphasis on network planning and the management science aspects of project management tools, which it was to keep for most of the 1970s. IMSA was also different from PMI in having much more independent national organizations. Whereas PMI has local chapters whose function is to organize events at the local level, IMSA has national societies which exist in their own right with their own constitutions, officers and memberships. Project management publications have been created by IMSA at national and international levels. IMSA changed its name in 1979 to the International Project Management Association.

The 1970s and project externalities

While interest in the tools and techniques of project management and in the practical problems of organizing and running teams continued at a high level as the 1960s gave way to the 1970s, a major new dimension began to emerge which has continued to compromise the accomplishment of projects on time, in budget and to technical specification, namely community and environmentalist opposition. Some major projects were already experiencing difficulties with community opposition in the late 1960s, but the problem was to become acute during the 1970s.

References

1. Acker, D. D. The maturing of the DoD acquisition process. *Defense Systems Management Review*, 1980, **3**, No. 3, pp. 17–25.
2. Kelley, J. E. and Walker, M. R. Critical path planning and scheduling. *Proc. Eastern Joint Computer Conf.*, Boston, 1959, pp. 160–173.
3. Fondahl, J. W. *A non-computer approach to the critical path method for the construction industry*. Technical Report No. 9, Department of Civil Engineering, Stanford University, CA, 1961.
4. Roy, B. Graphs et ordonnancements. *Revue Française Operationelle*, 1962, **6**, No. 323.
5. Schleip, W. and Schleip, R. *Planning and control in management: the German RPS system*. Peter Peregrinus, Dusseldorf, 1972.
6. Moder, J. J. and Phillips, C. R. *Project management with CPM and PERT*. Litton, 1964; 2nd and 3rd edns Van Nostrand Reinhold, New York, 1968 and 1970.
7. *Engineering News Record*, 6 May 1965.
8. *DoD and NASA Guide PERT/Cost Systems Design*. Office of the Secretary of Defense and the National Aeronautics and Space Administration, US Government Printing Office, Washington, DC, June 1962.

9. Archibald, R. D. *Managing high technology programs and projects*. Wiley, New York, 1976.

10. *Project Management Journal*, 1987, **18**, No. 3, Sept.

11. Fox, J. R. *Arming America: how the US buys weapons*. Harvard University, Boston, 1974, p. 405.

12. Department of Defense Directive 7000.1. *Resource management systems for the Department of Defense*. Department of Defense, Washington, DC, 1966.

13. Morrison, E. J. Defense systems management: the 375 series. *California Management Review*, 1967, **9**, No. 4, Summer.

14. McDougall, W. A. *The heavens and the earth: a political history of the space age*. Basic Books, New York, 1985.

15. House Select Committee on Astronautics and Space Exploration. *The next ten years in space, 1959–69: staff report*. 86th Congress, First Session, House Document 115, 1959.

16. Brooks, C. G., Grimwood, J. M. and Svenson, L. S. *Chariots for Apollo: a history of manned lunar spacecraft*. National Aeronautics and Space Administration, Washington, DC, 1979, p. 24.

17. Seamans, R. and Ordway, F. I. The Apollo tradition: an object lesson for the management of large-scale technological endeavours. *Interdisciplinary Science Review*, 1977, p. 280.

18. Hacker, B. C. and Grimwood, J. M. *On the shoulders of titans: a history of Project Gemini*. National Aeronautics and Space Administration, Washington, DC, 1977, pp. 36–38.

19. Rosholt, R.L. *An administrative history of NASA, 1958–1963*. National Aeronautics and Space Administration, Washington, DC, 1966.

20. Office of Manned Space Flight, Apollo Program Office. *Apollo program development plan*. MPC Space C500, MA000–1, 15 January 1965.

21. Peck, M. J. and Scherer, F. M. *The weapons acquisition process: an economic analysis*. Harvard University Press, Cambridge, MA, 1962.

22. Steiner, G. A. and Ryan, W. E. *Industrial project management*. Macmillan, New York, 1968, pp. 88 ff.

23. Marshall, A. W. and Meckling, W. H. *Predictability of the costs, time and success of development*. Rand Corporation, P-1821, Santa Monica CA, December 1959.

24. Summers, R. *Cost estimates as predictors of actual weapon costs: a study of major hardware articles*. Rand Corporation, RM-3061-PR, Santa Monica, CA, March 1965.

25. Perry, R. L., DiSalvo, D., Hall, G. R., Harman, A. L., Levenson, G. S., Smith, G. K. and Stucker, J. P. *System acquisition experience*. Rand Corporation, RM-6072-PR, Santa Monica, CA, November 1969.

26. Marschak, T., Glennan, T. K. and Summers, R. *Strategy for R&D: studies in the microeconomics of development*, Springer-Verlag, New York, 1967.

27. Cochran, E. G., Patz, A. L. and Rowe, A. J. Concurrency and disruption in new product innovation. *California Management Review*, 1978, Fall.

28. Harvey, T. E. Concurrency today in acquisition management. *Defense Systems Management Review*, 1980, **3**, No. 1, Winter, 14–18.

29. Comparative Project Management Symposium. *Institution of Mechanical Engineers Proceedings 1968–69*, 183, Part 3K.

30. *First report of the Inquiry into the Pricing of Ministry of Aviation Contracts*. HMSO, London, Cmnd 2428, July 1964.

31. *Second report of the Inquiry into the Pricing of Ministry of Aviation Contracts*. HMSO, London, Cmnd 2581, February 1965.

32. *The supply of military aircraft*. Second Report of the Select Committee on Estimates. House of Commons Paper No. 34 of Session 1956–57, HMSO, London, 1957.

33. Ministry of Defence. *Management control of research and development*. HMSO, London, 1961.
34. Williams, G., Gregory, F. and Simpson, J. *Crisis in procurement: a case study of the TSR-2*. Royal United Services Institution, London, 1969.
35. *Report of the Committee of Inquiry into the Aircraft Industry*. Cmnd 2853, HMSO, London, 1965.
36. Select Committee on Science and Technology. *Defence research*. House of Commons Paper 213, Session 1968–69, HMSO, PLIV.
37. Nailor, P. *Nassau connection: organization and management of the British Polaris project*. Ministry of Defence, HMSO, London, 1988.
38. Ministry of Technology, *Report of the Steering Group on Development Cost Estimating*. HMSO, London, 1969.
39. Wilson, A. *Committee of Inquiry into Delays in Commissioning CEGB Power Stations*. HMSO, London, 1969.
40. National Economic Development Office. *Engineering construction performance*. HMSO, London, 1970, Appendix 5.
41. National Economic Development Office. *Large industrial sites*. HMSO, London, 1970.
42. Morris, P. W. G. and Hough, G. H. *The anatomy of major projects*. Wiley, Chichester, 1988, chapter 6.
43. Bowley, M. *The British building industry*. Cambridge University Press, London, 1966, p. 462.
44. *Survey of the problems before the construction industries* (The Emerson Report). HMSO, London, 1962.
45. *The placing and management of contracts for building and civil engineering work*. HMSO, London, 1964.
46. The Tavistock Institute. *Interdependence and uncertainty*. Tavistock, London, 1966, pp. 58–59.
47. Higgins, G. and Jessop, N. *Communications in the building industry*. Tavistock, London, 1965.
48. Morris, P. W. G. Managing project interfaces — key points for project success. In *Project management handbook*. Cleland, D. I. and King, W. R. (eds), Van Nostrand Reinhold, New York, 1988, chapter 2.
49. Checkland, P. *Systems thinking, systems practice*. Wiley, Chichester, 1981.
50. Emery, F. E. (ed.). *Systems thinking*. Penguin, Harmondsworth, 1969.
51. Kast, F. E. and Rosenzweig, J. E. *Organization and management: a systems approach*. McGraw-Hill, New York, 1963.
52. Cleland, D. I. and King, W. R. *Systems analysis and project management*. McGraw-Hill, New York, 1968.
53. Emery, F. E. *Characteristics of socio-technical systems*. Document No. 527 (mimeo), Tavistock Institute of Human Relations, London, 1959.
54. Ashby, W. R. *An Introduction to Cybernetics*. Chapman and Hall, London, 1958.
55. Boulding, K. E. *The organizational revolution*. Harper & Row, New York, 1953.
56. Von Bertalanffy, L. *General systems theory: foundations, development, applications*. George Braziller, New York, 1968.
57. Haire, M. (ed.). *Modern organization theory*. Wiley, New York, 1959.
58. Rice, A. K. *The enterprise and its environment*. Tavistock, London, 1963.
59. Vickers, G. *Freedom in a rocking boat*. Penguin, Harmondsworth, 1970.
60. Burns, T. and Stalker, G. M. *The management of innovation*. Tavistock, London, 1961.
61. Emery, F. E. and Trist, E. L. The causal texture of organizational environments. *Human Relations*, 1965, **18**, No. 1, 21–32.

62. Katz, D. and Kahn, R. L. *The social psychology of organizations*. Wiley, New York, 1966.

63. Hutton, G. *Thinking about organization*. Bath University Press, 1968.

64. Miller, E. J. and Rice, A. K. *Systems of organization — the control of task and sentient boundaries*. Tavistock, London, 1967.

65. Anderson, T. R. and Warkov, S. Organizational size and functional complexity, a study of administration in hospitals. *American Sociological Review*, 1961, **26**, No. 1, 23–28.

66. Hage, J. and Aiken, M. Routine technology, social structure and organizational goals. *Administrative Science Quarterly*, 1969, **14**, No. 3, 366–376.

67. Harvey, E. Technology in the structure of organizations. *American Sociological Review*, 1968, **33**, No. 2, 247–259.

68. Woodward, J. *Management of technology*. HMSO, London, 1958.

69. Woodward, J. *Industrial organization: theory and practice*. Oxford University Press, London, 1965.

70. Woodward, J. *Industrial organization: behaviour and control*. Oxford University Press, London, 1970.

71. Lawrence, P. R. and Lorsch, J. W. *Organization and environment: managing differentiation and integration*. Harvard University Press, Boston, 1967.

72. Lawrence, P. R. and Lorsch, J. W. Differentiation and integration in complex organizations. *Administrative Science Quarterly*, 1967, **12**, No. 1, 1–47.

73. Thompson, J. D. *Organizations in action*. McGraw-Hill, New York, 1967.

74. Galbraith, J. R. *Achieving integration through information systems*. Working Paper No. 361–68, Alfred, P. Sloan School of Management, Massachusetts Institute of Technology, 1968.

75. Burns, J. Effective management of programs. In *Studies in organization design*, Lorsch, J. R. and Lawrence, P. R. (eds), Irwin-Dorsey, Homewood, Il., 1970, chapter 5.

76. Galbraith, J. R. Environmental and technological determinants of organizational design. In *Studies in organization design*, Lorsch, J. R. and Lawrence, P. R. (eds), Irwin-Dorsey, Homewood, Il., 1970, chapter 7.

77. Baker, R. J. S. *The management of capital projects*. Bell, London, 1962.

78. Bowie, R. M. The project overlay in research organization. *IRE Transactions on Engineering Management*, 1957, Sept.

79. Fuchs, G. J. and Thompson, G. C. Management of a new product development. *Conference Board Business Record*, 1967, Oct.

80. Hackney, J. W. *Control and management of capital projects*. Wiley, New York, 1965.

81. Lecht, C. P. *The management of computer programming projects*. The American Management Association, New York, 1967.

82. McKenzie, G. The time and resource aspects of project management in the construction of chemical plants. *The Chemical Engineer*, 1967, June, 118–137.

83. Ramstrom, D. and Rhenham, E. A method of describing the development of an engineering project. *IEEE Transactions on Engineering Management*, 1965, **EM-13**, No. 3, Sept.

84. Lanier, F. Organizing for large engineering projects. *Machine Design*, 27 Dec. 1956, 54.

85. Johnson, S. D. and Jones, C. Organizing for a development? *Harvard Business Review*, 1957, May–June.

86. Gaddis, P. O. The project manager. *Harvard Business Review*, 1959, May–June, 89–97.

87. Janger, A. R. Organizing the corporate research function. *Management Records*, 1960, Dec.
88. Janger, A. R. Charting authority relationships. *Conference Board Record*, 1964, Dec.
89. Marquis, D. G. and Straight, D. M. *Organizational factors in project performance*. Working Paper No. 133–65, Sloan School of Management, Massachusetts Institute of Technology, August 1965.
90. Mee, J. F. Matrix organization. *Business Horizons*, 1964, Summer, p. 70.
91. Schull, F. A. *Matrix structure on project authority for optimizing organizational capacity*. Business Science Monograph No. 1, Business Research Bureau, Southern Illinois University, 1965.
92. Cleland, D. I. Understanding project authority. *Business Horizons*. 1967, Spring.
93. Goodman, R. A. Ambiguous authority definition of project management. *Academy of Management Journal*, 1967, Dec.
94. Rubin, I. M. and Seilig, W. Experience as a factor in the selection and performance of project managers. *IEEE Transactions on Engineering Management*, 1967, Sept., 131–135.
95. Middleton, C. J. How to set up a project organization, *Harvard Business Review*, 1967, Mar.–Apr., **45**, 73–82.
96. Lawrence, P. R. and Lorsch, J. W. The new management job: the integrator. *Harvard Business Review*, 1967, Nov.–Dec.
97. Battersby, A. *Network analysis for planning and scheduling*. Macmillan, London, 1964.
98. Antill, J. M. and Woodhead, R. W. *Critical path methods in construction practice*. Wiley, New York, 1965.
99. O'Brien, J. J. *CPM and construction management*. McGraw-Hill, New York, 1965.
100. Archibald, R. and Villoria, R. L. *Network-based management systems (PERT/CPM)*. Wiley, New York, 1967.
101. Lockyer, K. G. *Introduction to CPA*. Pitman, London, 1969.
102. Wiest, J. D. and Levy, F. K. *A management guide to PERT/CPM*. Prentice Hall, Englewood Cliffs, NJ, 1969.
103. Baumgartner, J. S. *Project management*. Richard D. Irwin, Homewood, Il., 1963.
104. Hajek, V. G. *Project engineering*. McGraw-Hill, New York, 1965.
105. Silverman, M. *The technical program manager's guide to survival*. Wiley, New York, 1967.
106. Cleland, D. I. and King, W. R. *Systems analysis and project management*. McGraw-Hill, New York, 1968.
107. Lock, D. L. *Project management*. Gower, London, 1968.
108. *Fortune*, 1969, June.
109. Webb, J. E. *Space age management: the large-scale approach*. New York, 1969.
110. Toffler, A. *Future shock*. Random House, New York, 1970 (page reference is to Bantam edition, 1974).
111. Sayles, L. R. and Chandler, M. K. *Managing large systems: organizations for the future*. Harper & Row, New York, 1971.
112. Wiest, J. D. Project network models: past, present and future. *Project Management Quarterly*, 1977, **8**, No. 4, 27–36.
113. Lukaszewicz, J. On the estimation of errors introduced by standard assumptions concerning the distribution of activity duration in PERT calculations. *Operations Research*, 1965, **13**, No. 2, Mar.–Apr., 326–327.
114. MacCrimmon, K. R. and Ryavec, C. R. An analytical study of PERT assumptions. *Operations Research*, 1964, **12**, Jan.–Feb., 16–37.

115. Welsh, D. J. A. Errors introduced by a PERT assumption. *Operations Research*, 1965, **13**, No. 1, Jan.–Feb., 141–142.

116. Avots, I. Why does project management fail? *California Management Review*, 1969, Fall.

117. Geddes, P. How good is PERT? *Aerospace Management*, 1961, **4**, Sept., 41–43.

118. Marquis, D. C. A project team plus PERT = success. Or does it? *Innovation*, 1969.

119. Vazsonyi, I. L'histoire de grandeur et la decadence de la methode PERT. *Management Science*, 1970, **16**, No. 8, Apr., B449–B450.

120. Freeman, R. J. A generalized PERT. *Operations Research*, 1960, **8**, No. 2, 281.

121. Eisner, H. A generalized network approach to the planning and scheduling of a research project. *Operations Research*, 1962, **10**, No. 1, 115–125.

122. Elmaghraby, S. E. An algebra for the analysis of generalized activity networks. *Management Science*, 1964, **10**, No. 3, 494–514.

123. Pritsker, A. A. B. *GERT: graphical evaluation and review technique*. Rand Corporation, RN-4973-NASA, Santa Monica, April 1966.

124. Pritsker, A. A. B. and Happ, W. W. GERT: Graphical Evaluation and Review Technique, Part 1 — fundamentals. *Journal of Industrial Engineering*, 1966, **17**, No. 5, 267–274.

125. Pritsker, A. A. B. and Whitehouse, G. E. GERT: Graphical Evaluation and Review Technique, Part 2 — probabilistic and industrial engineering applications. *Journal of Industrial Engineering*, 1966, **17**, No. 6, June, 293–301.

126. Pritsker, A. A. B. GERT networks. *The Production Engineer*, 1968, Oct.

127. Pritsker, A. A. B., Walters, L. J. and Wolfe, E. M. Multi-project scheduling with limited resources: a zero–one programming approach. *Management Science*, 1969, **16**, No. 1, 293–301.

128. Arisawa, S. and Elmaghraby, S. E. Optimal time–cost trade-offs in GERT networks. *Management Science*, 1972, **18**, No. 11, July, 589–599.

129. Hebert, J. E. *Critical path analysis and a simulation program for resource-constrained activity scheduling in GERT project networks*. Purdue University, PhD dissertation, 1975.

130. Pritsker, A. A. B. *Modelling and analysis using Q-GERT networks*. Wiley, New York, 1977.

131. Moder, J. J., Phillips, C. R. and Davis, E. W. *Project management with CPM, PERT and precedence diagramming*. Van Nostrand Reinhold, New York, 3rd edn, 1983, p. 333.

132. Kidd, J. B. A comparison between the VERT program and other methods of project duration estimation. *OMEGA*, 1987, **15**, No. 2, 129–134.

133. Moeller, G. L. and Digman, L. A. Operations planning with VERT. *Operations Research*, 1981, **29**, No. 4, July–Aug., 271–280.

134. Lee, S. M., Moeller, G. L. and Digman, L. A. *Network analysis for management decisions*. Kluwer-Nighoff, Boston, 1982.

135. Berman, E. B. Resource allocation in a PERT network under continuous activity time–cost functions. *Management Science*, 1964, July.

136. Clark, E. The optimum allocation of resources among the activities of a network. *Journal of Industrial Engineering*, 1961, Jan.–Feb.

137. Dewitte, L. Manpower levelling of PERT networks. *Data Processing for Science/Engineering*. 1964, Mar.–Apr.

138. Kelly, J. E. The critical path method: resources, planning and scheduling. In Muth, J. F. and Thompson, G. L. *Industrial scheduling*.

Prentice Hall, Englewood Cliffs, New Jersey, 1963, chapter 21.

139. Levy, F. K., Thompson, G. L. and Wiest, J. D. Multi-ship, multi-shop workload smoothing program. *Naval Research Logistics Quarterly*, 1962, **9**, Mar., 37–44.

140. McGee, A. A. and Markarian, M. D. *Optimum allocation of research engineering manpower within a multi-project organization structure.* IBM file number 61-907-171, Federal Systems Division, 1961.

141. Wiest, J. D. A heuristic model for scheduling large projects with limited resources. *Management Science*, 1967, **13**, No. 6, Feb., B359–B377.

142. Davis, E. W. and Heidorn, G. E. An algorithm for optimal project scheduling under multiple resource constraints. *Management Science*, 1971, **17**, No. 12, B803–B816.

143. Davis, E. W. Project scheduling under resource constraints — historical review and categorization of procedures. *AIIE Transactions*, 1973, Dec.

144. Davis, E. W. Project network summary measures and constrained resource scheduling. *AIIE Transactions*, 1975, June.

145. Davis, E. W. and Patterson, J. H. A comparison of optimal and heuristic solutions in resource-constraint project scheduling. *Management Science*, 1975, Apr.

146. Davis, E. W. and Patterson, J. H. Resource-based project scheduling: which rules perform best. *Project Management Quarterly*, 1975, **6**, No. 4, 25–31.

147. Reis de Carvalho, E. and Morris, P. W. G. Project matrix organizations — or how to do the matrix swing. *Proc. 1978 Project Management Institute Symp., Los Angeles*, Project Management Institute, Drexel Hill, PA, 1978.

148. Youker, R. Organizational alternatives for project management. *Project Management Quarterly*, 1977, **8**, No. 1.

6. The 1970s: the expansion of project management

The 1970s were to witness a formidable expansion of projects and project management activity, but the pattern of activity was to be totally different from that of the previous two or three decades. This was not a decade of a few mega-projects, employing extraordinary mission-oriented structures and heroic management, as in the 1960s. Although there certainly were such undertakings, project management became a more common management practice. Project-related organizations — most obviously the big process construction companies — increasingly used project managers and project management as an everyday line-management function, often employed in a matrix context. And while defence/aerospace matters continued to pose serious management challenges, they were not nearly as dominant within project management as they had been during the previous decades.

The projects of the 1970s — particularly the civil ones — were marked most by the consequences of the actions of the Organization of Petroleum Exporting Countries (OPEC), which in 1973 doubled the price of oil. This and later associated actions were to have an enormous impact on the world. In project terms, there were at least four specific consequences. First, with such a large change in the price of oil, the economics of power generation changed almost overnight; as a result, a new generation of power plants began to be constructed. Second, oil, gas and petrochemical activity increased markedly — hundreds of new facilities were constructed for both upstream (exploration and production) and downstream (refining). Third, with OPEC countries suddenly rich, and their revenues being on-lent by way of the commercial banking system, generally to Third World countries for new projects, the quantity of developing world projects increased enormously. Fourth, domestic economies had to adjust to this new economic situation; this particularly affected the pattern and pace of construction-related work.

A feature of the upsurge in construction project activity was that (as Sayles and Chandler had foreseen), in contrast to the defence world, this project management activity was *not shielded from public criticism* by national security considerations. This was to prove very important. The 1960s had seen a rising tide of public opposition against many kinds of major project; this trend was to continue and become extremely significant in the 1970s.

Concorde illustrates many of these points vividly. Although it was an aerospace project of the 1960s, its success was compromised not just by its technology management, which undoubtedly was challenge enough, but by the newly arising, unanticipated actions of the outside groups of the 1970s: OPEC and the environmentalist lobby.

Concorde

Concorde (Fig. 20) was the first of an important new breed of aerospace projects: those built through international collaboration. It was a huge technology-push 'spearhead' project, whose basic requirement was simply to carry passengers safely and supersonically (note 1). Its development represented a continual struggle to reconcile two entirely different requirements: sustained supersonic flight and subsonic approach. Its management practices were largely those of TSR-2; its cost escalation and schedule delays were huge. This occasioned much public criticism and governmental chagrin. The British governmental psyche was so traumatized that its response to suggestions for high-risk major projects for many decades subsequently was invariably one of nervous disinclination. However, Concorde was an economic disaster[1] not so much because of its huge developmental difficulties and costs as because of the unexpectedly high cost of fuel and the inability to obtain authorization to fly it supersonically over land.

Fig. 20. Concorde assembly line, Filton: 10th, 12th and 14th aircraft (courtesy British Aerospace plc)

Concorde was first proposed by UK government ministers in 1956. The feasibility of a supersonic transport was confirmed in

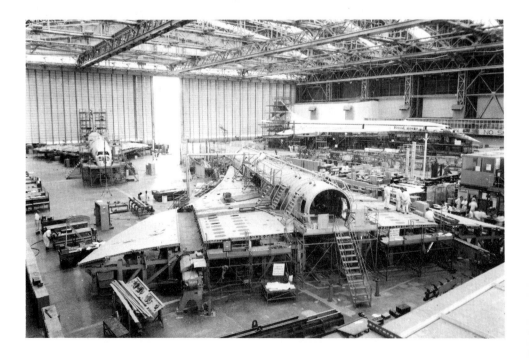

principle in 1959. In 1960–1962 the British and French governments discussed, at the initiative of the British, the prospect of the project being accomplished jointly. In 1962 a treaty was signed between the two governments for the joint design, development and production of a supersonic airliner. There was no break clause to the treaty, no performance requirements and no financial limits. Management structures and programmes (schedules) were proposed in the treaty, but generally in imprecise terms. The management structure, for example, comprised a series of hierarchical committees: the project was set up with little regard to the most basic rules of project management, such as a clearly identified owner organization; there was no owner and no one person 'in charge'. The first prototype flight was scheduled for the second half of 1966, with the Certificate of Airworthiness to be awarded at the end of 1969; in fact these were accomplished in October 1969 and December 1975 respectively. The project's financial estimate in November 1962 was £135·2m; by 1979 the cost of the programme had grown more than eightfold to around £1129m.

PERT scheduling and work package planning and estimating were introduced in 1964–1965 (note 2), but were formally abandoned in 1972 as unreliable and unworkable.

Between 1964 and 1970, Concorde's commercial prospects became increasingly doubtful. The pattern of air traffic began to change with the advent of wide-bodied aircraft; economy and price became the critical parameters rather than speed. The new Labour government of 1964 attempted to cancel the plane, along with TSR-2, the P-1154 and HS-681, but was rebuffed by the French, who threatened to sue the British government in the International Court of Justice if the Treaty was abrogated. The decision to go into production was taken in 1968 (note 3). Environmentalist opposition grew dramatically, particularly in the USA, where it effectively killed the US Supersonic Transport (US SST), as described below. With the rise in the price of fuel oil following the Yom Kippur war in 1973, the economics of operating Concorde became even more unfavourable, especially as its economic speed was designed to be Mach 2 rather than subsonic. In 1973, most of the options taken by airlines to buy Concorde were revoked. Obtaining permission to enter the USA proved extremely difficult, and it was not until May 1976, 20 years after the project's inception, that the first flight landed in Washington DC. Concorde did not land in New York until November 1977.

In the end, Concorde proved to be a commercial disaster for its developers (the two governments), although not for its builders or operators: a technological triumph yet a plane designed on the massive misconception that speed was the principal criterion for airliner success; an aircraft project that was set up with no regard to the most basic rules of project management, such as a clearly identified owner organization, and one which experienced severe problems of design and technology management; a project whose chances of success were severely compromised by the two external factors of changes in fuel prices and environmentalist opposition.

The US SST programme

Concorde's rival, the American supersonic transport (US SST, Fig. 21), showed even more starkly than Concorde the importance of *external factors*, in particular the environmentalist movement. Mel Horwitch, in his important book on the project, contends that *the US SST marked a turning point in the management of projects.*[2] Formal project management had so far been developed in a defence–aerospace sector largely shielded from public opposition. Manhattan, the ballistic missile programmes, Apollo, the various DoD programmes of the late 1960s — all had external threat and urgency as overriding criteria. The US SST did not. Conceived and managed by aerospace spacialists, the project grew 'into an all-out societal war' (ref. 2, p. 2) which in the end the environmentalists won. The US SST was the harbinger of many similar confrontations in the 1970s: the Trans Alaskan Pipeline, nuclear power, airports, transport projects — all were beginning to witness massive disruption due to environmentalist opposition.

However, the project did begin partly in response to an external threat: it was very much a race with the Europeans to develop the first intercontinental SST passenger airliner. Amazingly (and fortunately unlike its successor 25 years later), there were practically no commercial viability studies. While the British and French aimed for a Mach 2 airliner, the Americans pinned their hopes on a Mach 3 plane. 'To the winner', said Najeeb Halaby, the Federal Aviation Authority (FAA) Administrator, in 1963, 'the guy who produces the first commercially profitable, safe and efficient aircraft, goes a \$3–4bn market' (ref. 2, p. 41). President Kennedy announced the launch of the US SST programme on 5 June 1963. Many senior members of Kennedy's administration, however, not least Robert McNamara, were severely sceptical of the project, questioning the financial viability of the programme and worrying about the impact of sonic booms. Of particular concern was the airlines' unwillingness to commit any of their own funds to the project. The National Academy of Sciences reported on the sonic boom issue in January 1965, but in generally optimistic terms: there should not be any adverse physical or physiological consequences from the sonic booms; the FAA should develop effective public relations; but — prophetically — the fate of the

Fig. 21. Prototype Boeing SST (1970)

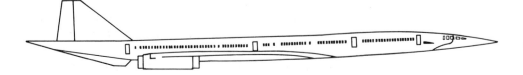

SST might depend on its ability to mobilize political support against protesters to the boom.

In July and August 1965 a new team took over at the FAA: USAF General William McKee as Administrator and USAF Brigadier General Jewell Maxwell as Director of the SST programme. Both were perceived as less gung-ho and more professional than Halaby, and the attitudes of McNamara and other programme sceptics eased considerably. It was now agreed that prototypes could and should proceed independently from questions of the plane's economic justification. Serious opposition to the sonic boom continued (from, for example, the Swede Bo Lundberg and the US Secretary of the Interior, Stewart Udall), but the FAA had by now been absorbed into the Department of Transportation and was able to use its greater economic muscle to smother this.

On 31 December 1966, Boeing and General Electric were awarded contracts for prototype development. In October 1968, however, the Boeing tilt-wing design had to be changed to fixed-wing. Re-evaluating the new design took until early 1969. This was the first of two or three major delays that collectively were to prove fatal to the programme, for environmentalist opposition now began to mount, and these *delays provided time for the opposition to gather the political force needed to halt the project*. Anti-SST articles had begun to appear in the press to a serious extent around 1966. In March 1967 William Shurcliff founded the 'Citizens' League Against the Sonic Boom' — a back-room, one-man operation that was to lead directly to the programme's demise just four years later.

22 April 1970 was proclaimed the first 'Earth Day'. All over the USA, groups met to demonstrate their concern for the environment. For the US SST, Earth Day proved a psychological watershed: people and politicians angrily focused on the programme and the damage it threatened to their lives and environment. William Macgruder was appointed the new director of the SST programme on the same day, and immediately faced a hostile set of hearings in Congress under Senator William Proxmire on the economic viability of the programme. The hearings provided further fuel to the environmentalists. The May–June Congress appropriations hearings voted the funds requested for the programme, but by now a near-avalanche of groups were opposing it: Shurcliffe in the van, with the Friends of the Earth, the Sierra Club, the Citizens' League, Environmental Action; and, in September, the Federation of American Scientists, several distinguished economists, John Lindsay the Mayor of New York, Common Cause, and Citizens Against Noise; in February 1971 Charles Lindbergh joined in opposition — Lindbergh was not only a famous aviator, but also a member of the board of Pan American, one of the SST's staunchest supporters. Macgruder, however, countered energetically, and by early 1971 was receiving support

from several leading politicians, including the President, as well as from industry, the unions and various specialist groups. By now, the SST had provoked the most visible and strident national argument.

Then, to the shock of many, on 18 March 1971 the House of Representatives voted 215 to 204 against continued SST funding. On 24 March the Senate also voted (51 to 46) against funding the SST. Attempts were made to find a way of continuing the programme; Gerald Ford seeking to introduce a supplemental appropriation for the project in May 1971, which the House in fact approved by 201 to 197. But William Allen, President of Boeing, quashed any hope of resurrecting the SST: to do so, he said, would cost at least half a billion dollars of extra funds. The project to build an American Concorde was over, killed by technical problems, political doubt, community opposition and a Program Management more attuned, initially, to promoting technology and speed than to the threats posed by citizen opposition. McNamara had brought in two top USAF officers to bring order, systems and Air Force management to the programme, as Phillips had done on Apollo, but these two had failed completely to read the environmental threat and its political consequences. Their *project management was inward-looking engineering-time management. They missed crucial external factors* in a way that Schriever or Raborn would probably never have done.

Transportation projects, community opposition and cost−benefit analysis

Concorde and the US SST demonstrate two serious difficulties of large-scale projects of this time. First, that of *assessing the value of the project*: whether it is worth investing in this particular project in this configuration at this time. Second, that of *community opposition* to the project, due either to its direct and adverse interference with people's lives or to concern for its impact on the environment. 1970s' projects to build major ground transportation systems such as roads, rail and airports experienced both these difficulties in abundance. They illustrate well the challenges of managing projects that have a major impact on the community. San Francisco's metro system, BART (Bay Area Rapid Transit, Fig. 22), for example, was the first of a whole generation of US metros that were overambitious, poorly assessed and managed, and ultimately both late and hugely over budget.

BART was conceived in the late 1940s/early 1950s as a 'technological and economic necessity'. ('We do not doubt that the Bay Area citizens can afford rapid transit: we question seriously whether they can afford not to have it'[3] — *the dangerous double negative of major projects*, seen later, e.g., in the Space Station, see p. 327, note 34.) BART's planning was developed on a methodology that was wider and employed a longer-range vision of urban growth than had previously been used. Finance was to come largely from specially raised property tax bonds and tolls.

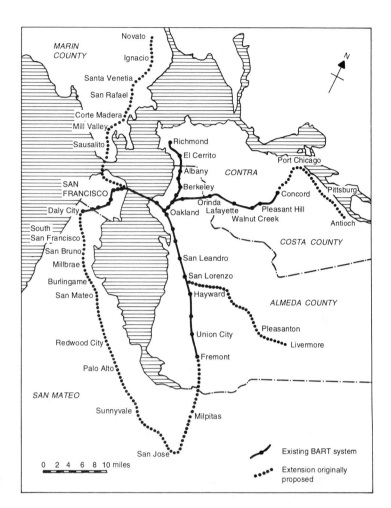

Fig. 22. Bay Area Rapid Transit system, California

In 1961–1962, however, two Bay Area counties withdrew from BART, leaving a truncated system estimated to cost $923·2m. Design work was begun in 1962. Not atypically of projects in this era, the project used very advanced and to some degree *unproven technology* — cars were to be controlled by computer and were made of advanced lightweight materials. BART's management was largely inexperienced: most of the work was carried out by consultants, and there was no overall systems engineering integrating the level of technology and its engineering into the total project and its management. Before long, problems were being experienced in many of these new technologies. The system was to have been complete on 1 January 1971: in fact, it was 1972–1974 before operation began. The final cost was $1·6bn (a cost increase of 73%), the extra funding having been sought unsuccessfully from additional bonds and tolls, and in the end raised from new sales taxes. Operationally BART was not a success: ridership was lower and operating costs were higher than expected.

BART was typical of all US rapid transit systems of the time. It failed, to the extent that it did, because of its failure to change traffic (rider) behaviour, the difficulties and delays in getting financing and getting all the counties to participate, the inability to systems-design the project as a whole, and the overenthusiastic use of advanced technology.

The situation in the UK was little better. Although most of Britain's motorways were constructed in the 1960s and 1970s, in the more sensitive 'environmental' areas community opposition slowly began to limit the initiation of proposed projects. The difficulty of getting large infrastructure projects accepted by the community — particularly a densely packed, articulate community as in the southern and south-eastern part of England — was epitomized by the debate over the siting of London's proposed third airport.

London's two principal airports, Heathrow and Gatwick, date from 1946 and 1954 respectively. (Neither site would pass today's criteria for location of a London airport.) In 1963 a government committee proposed Stansted in Essex, north of London, as the site for an additional airport which, it was predicted, would probably be needed around 1970. The recommendation was met by a storm of protest. A public inquiry was instituted, whose results were inconclusive and, in consequence, were not published for over a year, at which time the Government reiterated its intention to push ahead with Stansted. A new storm of protest erupted: *The case for reappraisal*, in which many of the assumptions underlying the Government's decision were challenged (note 4), was published in June 1967 by a Stansted working party composed of local residents and Members of Parliament.

There was now a change of government. The new minister, Anthony Crosland, was both genuinely concerned with the quality of the environment and attracted to the notion of a rigorous analysis of the costs and benefits of various sites. Accordingly, in February 1968 the Government announced a new inquiry, the Roskill Commission. This was to conduct the most comprehensive study of its kind ever seen in the UK, demonstrating the limits to which cost—benefit analysis can, and should, be put.

Robert McNamara had brought *cost-effectiveness analysis* into the Department of Defense from the Ford Motor Company in 1960—1961 under the term *Systems Analysis*. The method was used to analyse the effect of alternative decision options on profits. In the defence industry the approach was necessarily broadened, since there are inevitably a great many unknowns in defence that can influence the effectiveness of a decision, many of which are extremely difficult to quantify, particularly in monetary terms.

When McNamara became President of the World Bank in 1968 he brought with him many of the beliefs and tools of the DoD, including the use of *cost—benefit analysis*. The cost—benefit approach had already been used on social- and developmental-type projects;[4] its shortcomings had been recognized at the outset.[5] By the late 1960s to early 1970s, however, the systems approach to project identification and analysis had taken such a firm hold both intellectually and in practice, not least in the World Bank,[7–16] that the cost−benefit tool seemed natural when one was faced with a complex major decision like the choice of a site for an airport.

The Roskill Commission began by drawing up a list of 78 possible sites. Within seven months the choice was narrowed to four. Stansted, interestingly, was not one of these — it did not compare, the Commission felt, in terms of air traffic control, noise, impact or surface access. One of the four sites selected was, somewhat inconsistently, Maplin (also known as Foulness), an area on the Thames estuary ranking much better in terms of noise, air traffic control and defence, but much worse on surface access — it had in fact been positioned four places below Stansted! Maplin was included only because of its 'special' (i.e. non-cost−benefit) attractions. The commission's analysis of the costs and benefits of these four sites was without doubt the largest and most complex of its kind ever attempted anywhere. Direct and indirect costs were calculated for each site (note 5) and these, together with the overall cost−benefit analysis, were published for public discussion in early 1970. In the end, Cublington, a prettily little village in the affluent commuter belt north of London, emerged best; Maplin emerged worst.

Dramatically, however, just a few days before the Commission published its final report in January 1971, one of the Commissioners, Professor Colin Buchanan, announced that he could not accept the choice of Cublington. Buchanan produced an eleven-page note of dissent expressing, in emotional terms, deep distrust of the whole cost−benefit approach and his fear of the environmental disaster that the choice of Cublington or any of the sites other than Maplin would represent. On the publication of the report the public at large responded vigorously, the majority clearly agreeing with Buchanan. The Cublington residents immediately formed a resistance association. Press criticism raged, and in April 1971 the Government announced that London's third airport would be built not at Cublington but at Maplin.

In fact it was not. By early 1974, spurred partly by the suggestion that oil price rises would probably depress traffic volume and by continued worry over the ecological damage a new airport would cause, both governmental and national opinion had moved against starting construction of a new London airport. The new Labour government of February 1974, inheriting a rapidly deteriorating balance-of-payments situation, cancelled the Maplin project in July 1974 (note 6).

Estimation of the benefits of these large infrastructure projects, and their assessment against the costs involved, was thus proving enormously difficult. Cost—benefit analysis was seen to embody severe limitations due to 'its inability to distinguish among objectives other than that of pure economic efficiency and hence in the inflexibility of its approach when confronted with long-term environmental and social consequences'.[17] Planning Programming and Budgeting (another McNamara technique, of course) was introduced in the 1960s to tackle these difficulties by focusing more on objectives and inter-agency co-ordination,[18] but without much success. It was not until *Environmental Impact Analysis* became common in the 1980s (see pp. 165—166) that anything like a workable mechanism came into being for the handling of the numerous conflicting demands that inevitably surround a major project.

The Trans Alaskan Pipeline, NEPA and environmentalism

As a final seminal project of this period, illustrative of the practices of managing projects in the early 1970s, let us consider the Trans Alaskan Pipeline System (TAPS).[19,20]

TAPS is the archetypal 'major project' which was to become so characteristic of the 1970s. Like so many, its existence was intimately related to the 1973 OPEC oil crisis. Like the supersonic transport planes, the third London airport and other major projects of this time, it suffered difficulties both in cost—benefit estimating and in planning and realization. It was a massive endeavour, providing, among other things, important insights not only into the many environmental challenges such projects may face, but also into the organizational dimensions of their execution.

In January 1968, Arco announced that huge deposits of oil, possibly rivalling the Middle East fields in size, had been found in the Alaskan Prudhoe Bay area in the Arctic Circle (Fig. 23). The impact that a field this size would have on Alaska was difficult to conceive, for the State was (and is) mostly little more than wilderness. Oil deposits in such quantity immediately raised two fundamental environmental questions: how would oil change the life of this last great North American wilderness, and how was the oil to be transported out of Prudhoe Bay? The oil companies under-appreciated both these questions; they did not foresee the enormous environmental controversy that would soon surround the pipeline and have such an impact on its management.

To the oil companies, there was little doubt of the attractiveness of the project (note 7). The North Slope field was estimated to hold at least $9 \cdot 6$ billion barrels; eventual production was estimated at around 2 million barrels per day. Clearly, an efficient high-volume transportation system was essential. To the Federal Government, the strategic importance of the field was large: in 1969 it would have represented an increase in domestic oil production of about 15%. To the State of Alaska — which had been created only in 1959 and which, despite its obvious vast deposits of natural wealth, had yet to generate a strong economic

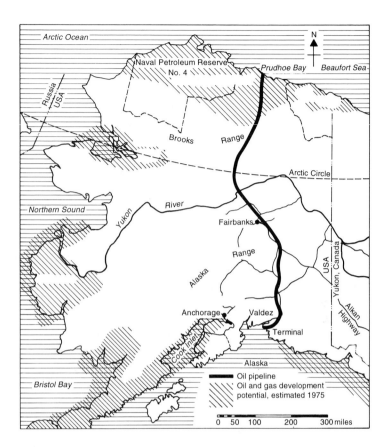

Fig. 23. Alaska and
the Trans Alaskan
Pipeline System

base — the oil represented an economic opportunity of major
importance. But to others — some native Alaskans, citizens who
preferred an unchanged way of life, environmentalists, and state
and federal agency officials charged with protecting the
environment — TAPS represented a huge threat. Many felt that
TAPS had been configured too quickly and that important economic
questions, such as the distribution of Alaskan oil to the USA's
Midwest and the question of what to do with the North Slope gas
(which, it was estimated could represent up to 10% of US reserves),
had not received adequate consideration.

The two methods commonly employed to transport oil are by
pipeline and tanker. Unfortunately, the presence of pack ice for
about ten months per year precluded the use of tankers. A pipeline
across Alaska to a warm-water port seemed to be the obvious
alternative. No detailed maps existed and it was realized from the
outset that the physical challenges were large: the route would cross
three mountain ranges and innumerable rivers; much of the ground
was affected by permafrost (note 8), which would present particular
problems if the oil was to be shipped in a 'hot' form; and the area
was one of very high seismic activity (Valdez, the site ultimately
selected as the warm-water port, had experienced a massive

earthquake — 8·5 on the Richter scale — in 1964). Also, the tankers carrying oil from Valdez would have to pass through several very narrow channels (note 9). Finally, although the planners hardly realized just how disruptive this was to prove, the pipeline would cross a land teeming with wildlife, much of it rare or endangered. In short, the environmental hazards the pipeline option would encounter were considerable. Nevertheless, the oil companies felt that, since a good pipeline was and always had been one that took care not to spill its contents, care of the environment would not be more different on TAPS than on other pipelines.

Somewhat naïvely, rule-of-thumb estimates based on 'lower 48' data (note 10) were made in order to derive a 'ballpark' estimate of over $900m. No contingency sum was included. In October 1968 Arco, Humble and BP formed the Trans Alaskan Pipeline System (TAPS) as an unincorporated joint venture. This was superseded in August 1970 when a formal project development, management and operating company, Alyeska, was created. Ed Patton, who was to display decisive leadership and drive, became its Chairman. The basic design was announced on 10 February 1969: a 500 000 barrels per day line to be completed by 1972, with additional capacity planned for 1975 and 1980. It was a schedule that was soon to be frustrated. TAPS would not become operational until 1977, by which time its costs would have risen ninefold to approximately $8bn.

On 6 June 1969, TAPS submitted a formal right-of-way application. The pipeline was to be hot-oil, constructed of 48 inch diameter pipe that would be buried for over 90% of its length. There would be eleven pumping stations and a large terminal at Valdez. A 390 mile construction road would be built along the right of way where access could not be gained from existing roads.

Instead of the speedy approval requested, however, the Interior Department replied with 79 questions on all aspects of the impact of TAPS on its habitat, including not only permafrost and seismic matters but animal migration routes and the care and resettlement of native Alaskans disturbed by the system.

On 7 January 1970 the National Environmental Policy Act (*NEPA*) was approved. This landmark legislation — which, as we shall see, *was to have a profound effect throughout the world on the way projects would be assessed in the future* by planning and regulatory authorities — provided, in general terms, a framework wherein the *environmental impact of a major project* could be debated. Specifically, Section 102 Part C required identification of adverse environmental impacts, consideration of alternatives, and public dissemination of relevant documents.

In March and April, native and environmentalist groups filed suits challenging TAPS' plans, claiming in particular that the Environmental Impact Statements required under NEPA had not been submitted. This was not upheld by the courts, however. The claimants then submitted that the width of the right of way being sought was greater than that allowed under the 1920 Mineral Leasing Act. This was upheld, and an injunction was placed on TAPS forbidding its construction. The project came to an abrupt halt.

There now began 30 months of legal battle, during which TAPS was pushed into a largely reactive posture and which was to end only as a consequence of the OPEC oil-price rise of 1973. By early 1971 influential politicians such as the new Secretary of Interior and the Governor of Alaska appeared to be taking an anti-TAPS stance: in July 1971 Alyeska submitted a three-volume project description to the Department of Interior together with 23 volumes of appendices; in the spring of 1972 the Department of Interior filed an Environmental Impact Statement with the Council on Environmental Quality (note 11) (at about the same time, Alyeska announced that TAPS's estimate had risen to $3bn); in August 1972 the injunction was dissolved but several environmentalist groups appealed against this decision; in February 1973 the Court of Appeals upheld their appeal, agreeing that the right of way violated the 1920 Minerals Leasing Act. In the spring of 1973 the Nixon Administration petitioned the Supreme Court to overrule the Appeals Court, but the petition was refused; at the same time, however, the US Senate approved a bill awarding TAPS the right of way sought, and in July, on a tie vote broken only by the casting vote of Vice-President Spiro Agnew, the Senate passed this bill, thereby authorizing construction. In October 1973 the Arab members of OPEC declared a total embargo on oil shipments to the USA; in November, amid public near-panic over petrol shortages and incredulity that their country was not able to ship its own oil to its population, Congress passed the Trans Alaskan Pipeline Authorization Act; rights-of-way permits were issued in January 1974. The cost of the pipeline — now heavily affected by the rate of inflation, which was running at record levels, as well as by design changes created largely in response to emerging geological data and fresh environmental considerations — was now estimated at over $4bn.

Construction work on TAPS began officially on 29 April 1974. Oil was introduced into the completed system on 20 June 1977, on schedule. During these three years, construction came to a complete standstill each winter due to the extremely harsh Alaskan conditions. Construction proceeded under a regime of unparalleled regulatory supervision: in accordance with the right-of-way provision, approval had to be given for Alyeska to proceed; this was done through a notice-to-proceed procedure administered by a Federal Authorized Officer, the State Pipeline Co-ordinator and the Joint Fish and Wildlife Advisory Team. These and other agencies had the power to halt the project if construction activities violated any of the legal provisions surrounding construction (note

12). At times TAPS's progress was help up substantially and considerable extra costs were incurred as a result of zealous implementation or conflicting regulatory instructions. The final cost of the project was just under $8bn.

TAPS and theories of the project matrix organization

The value of TAPS as a project management case lies not only in its environmentalist and regulatory aspects but also in the way in which the project was organized. It broke new ground, in particular in its use of specialist construction management firms and the adoption of a complex multi-layered hybrid matrix structure.

TAPS undoubtedly suffered initially from too long a chain of command. The eight firms that had shares in Alyeska (note 13) formed an Owners' Construction Committee which involved itself in a wide variety of issues through several ad hoc committees. Reporting to this committee was Alyeska. Alyeska recognized that it had insufficient construction expertise and recommended that Bechtel be retained to provide planning assistance, but the Owners' Construction Committee preferred Arctic Constructors, which, after some delay, was retained in August 1972. Alyeska continued to prefer Bechtel, however, and in June 1973 it was authorized, after some hesitation, to retain Bechtel for the construction management of the haul road and pipeline in October 1973. Under Bechtel were five Execution Contractors (ECs), who were directly responsible for performing the construction work. Fluor was hired in December 1972 for the pump stations and terminal.

There were soon problems in defining the roles of Alyeska, Bechtel and the ECs. Alyeska felt that there was 'gold plating' and that Bechtel was putting far too many people on to the project. Bechtel felt that more manpower was needed in order to do the job properly. Bechtel wanted to centralize operations further, while Alyeska favoured decentralization. As the snow began to fall for the 1974–1975 winter shutdown, Alyeska's pipeline project manager, Frank Moolin, backed by the Owners' Audit Committee, concluded that Bechtel's role should be drastically reduced: 'At about the 15% point of physical completion, in a bold and unprecedented move, Alyeska decided to decentralize the decision-making to the five basic geographical sections making up the project' (Fig. 24). Each section came to be managed as a separate project; decision-making was pushed down to EC level; the number of management levels between senior management and the 400 or so subcontractors was reduced from nine to three; and Bechtel was formally relieved of its Construction Management Contractor role, becoming Project Services Contractor for a limited number of tasks only, while being encouraged to work in a 'salt and pepper' fashion, interspersing its staff with Alyeska staff on an as-needed basis.

Alyeska — and Moolin in particular — was adamant that this

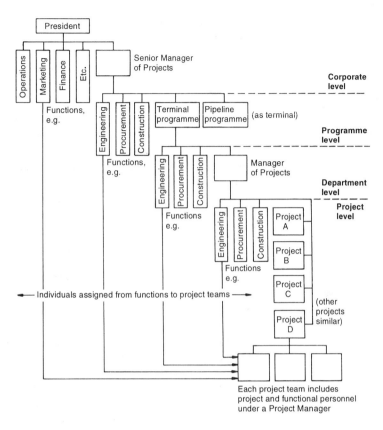

Fig. 24. The TAPS matrix (from Moolin and McCoy[104])

change to a flatter, decentralized form of organization was critical to the successful completion of TAPS. For although there were to be many problems during the next two-and-a-half construction seasons, the project was finished on time and was held by its owners and builders to have been a success.

(Not everyone agreed with this assessment of the project, however. As noted above, the final costs rose from $4·5bn in 1974 to nearly $8bn in 1977 (note 14). In a move that was to be replicated many times in the USA over the next 10−15 years, regulatory bodies were soon arguing in the courts that TAPS's cost overruns were due in part to grossly imprudent mismanagement (note 15). As a 'common carrier', TAPS's charges were subject to federal regulation, and there were fiscal benefits to the state and federal governments if it could be shown that the capital cost of the project was unreasonably high. In an out-of-court settlement, it was eventually agreed that the 'valid cost' of TAPS should be reduced by around $800m.)

Moolin's observations on the TAPS' reorganization were first presented at the Project Management Institute's 1979 symposium. A year earlier, at the 1978 PMI symposium, my colleague Emerson Reis de Carvalho and I had made strikingly similar observations derived from experience in implementing a project organization on a $5bn steel mill in Brazil — Açominas. In our paper we pointed out that the Açominas project was so large that *decentralization was essential as the project moved into the post-contract award/implementation phase* (note 16) — just as centralized decision-making had been necessary in the early concept/design phase. The result was a '*swing*' from a functional (centralized) organization to a (decentralized) matrix form.[21] And, crucially, as borne out by the experience of both TAPS and Açominas (and Apollo and several other large projects), *such large organizational change would be successful only if there were strong top-management leadership coupled with attention to 'soft' organizational issues* such as teamwork, communication and a clear understanding of how project management authority was articulated and exercised[22,23] (see Fig. 52, p. 250).

Project management — the new paradigm

The history of TAPS, and of the various transportation projects, illustrates that the management of projects in the late 1960s/early 1970s was operating in broader and more subtle contexts than were then normally recognized. As matrix-type organizations began to be implemented in thousands of institutions, project management came to be seen as a management tool to be employed when faced with a special task of some importance. *The common view of project management was of a collection of organizational, schedule and cost-control tools — a largely middle-management, intra-organizational skill.*

Yet this perception was falsely limited. TAPS and Açominas show that even the organizational issues of the matrix need to be seen in the context of the project's life cycle and managerial environment. (Indeed, these points are closely mirrored on Apollo.)

The projects of the early-to-mid 1970s were in fact pointing to a much fuller view of project management, i.e. that

(a)   *the impact of projects on their environment is an essential dimension of their chances of success*

(b)   *this 'environmental' impact is measured along several dimensions — economic, political, community, ecological*

(c)   *therefore, those responsible for the initiation or accomplishment of such projects should strive to influence the project's chances of success along these 'external' environmental dimensions, as well as ensuring that the internal project management functions are being carried out effectively.*

In effect, this amounts to a radical extension of the project management paradigm as developed just a decade previously on the DoD and NASA programmes. It was not that Webb, Raborn and others had not 'managed' their political environments; it was that the large projects of the late 1960s and early 1970s typically affected a wider swathe of the population, and were in turn being increasingly affected by changing external factors, such as economic uncertainty (the gathering pace of inflation) and the growing public concern over 'environmental' matters. Essentially, these conditions have obtained on most projects ever since.

The importance of managing the project within the context of its broad environment was, unfortunately, not yet recognized by the newly emergent project management community.

Writings on project management in the 1970s

'Project management' now had a professional voice through the (US) Project Management Institute and the (European) International Management Systems Association (more generally known as Internet). The attention of these societies was, however, very much on the tools and techniques that had emerged in the 1960s: they were less interested in the lessons of the BART, Concorde and other large projects. That this was so should really be no surprise. It was difficult to get information on these very large, complex projects — there was little focused research or teaching on the subject — and anyway such huge projects seemed very different from most project managers' experience. *Instead, therefore, of recognizing the important point that* all *projects require attention to a range of issues, varying from technical definition to economics and finance, and from organization and contracting to community attitudes, the activities both of project management writers in general and of these societies typically concentrated on more narrowly bounded matters, such as scheduling and cost control, teamworking, conflict management and debates over how a project manager could characterize his authority.*

Writings on project management during the decade included: in 1970, a textbook on scheduling by Kelly[24] as well as Bennigson's[25] *Project management* and Taylor and Watlings'[26] *Successful project management*; in 1971, Sayles and Chandler's[27] work, the Logistics Management Institute's[28] *Introduction to military program management* and Peart's[29] *Design of project management systems and records*; in 1972, Sapolsky's[30] study of Polaris and Wadsworth's[31] *EDP project management controls*; in 1973, Chapman's[32] *Project management in NASA*, Hoare's[33] *Project management using network analysis*, Metzger's[34] *Managing a programming project*, Pilcher's[35] *Appraisal and control of project costs*, Wearne's[36] *Principles of engineering organization* and Whitehouse's[37] *Systems analysis and design using network techniques*; in 1974, Ludwig's[38] *Applied project management for the process industries*; in 1976, Archibald's[39] *Managing high-technology programs and projects* (a classic!), Davis's[40] *Project management: techniques, applications and managerial issues*, Martin's[41] *Project management: how to make it work* (another great!), Peddie's[42] *The management of high technology projects* and Silverman's[43] *Project management: a short course for professionals*; in 1977, Snowden's[44]

Management of engineering projects; in 1978, Maciariello's *Program management control systems*; and in 1979 — like 1976, a bumper year — Adams, Brandt and Martin's[46] *Managing by project management*, Baumgartner's[47] *Systems management*, Davies, Demb and Espejo's[48] *Organization for program management*, Hill and White's[49] *Matrix organization and project management*, and Kerzner's[50] *Project management: a systems approach to planning, scheduling and controlling* (the most densely packed primer on the subject yet).

Other books of importance to the discipline included Cleland and King's[51] *Management: a systems approach* (1972); Johnson, Kast and Rosenzweig's[52] *The theory and management of systems*, Kingdon's[53] *Matrix organization: managing information technologies* and Pressman and Wildavsky's[54] *Implementation* (1973); Caro's[55] *The power broker* and Fox's[56] *Arming America* (1974); Squire and Van der Tak's[57] *Economic analysis of projects* and Wood's[58] *Project cancelled* (1975); Davis and Lawrence's[59] *Matrix* and Delp et al.'s[60] *Systems tools for project planning* (1977); Fisk's[61] *Construction project administration* (1978); and Stinchcombe's[62] work on North Sea oil project administration (1979).

In addition, several thousand articles, papers and reports on project management were published during the decade. Of these, 45 are listed in Table 2, some categorized by subject area.

Table 2. Key project management papers of the 1970s

Year	Organization	Tools and techniques	General
1970	Cicero and Wilemon[63] Gemmill and Wilemon[64]		
1971 (see refs 69–73)	Wilemon[65] Wilemon and Gemmill[66] Bennigson[67]	Bennigson[67]	Bennigson[67] Perry et al.[68] Olsen[71]
1972	Bennigson[75]	Arisawa and Elmaghraby[74]	
1973 (see ref. 79)	Butler[76]	Crandall[77] Davis[78]	
1974 (see refs 81–86)	Gemmill[80]		Murphy, Baker and Fisher[87]
1975 (see ref. 91)	Morton[88] Thamhain and Wilemon[89]		Barndt[90]
1976			Rondinelli[92,93]
1977 (see refs 99–101)	Baker and Wilemon[94] Wilemon and Thamhain[95] Youker[96]	Wiest[97]	Cook[98]
1978 (see ref. 103)			Cochran et al.[102]
1979 (see ref. 107)	Moolin and McCoy[104] Morris[105]		Merrow et al.[106]

Perry *et al.*[68] showed how cost overrun and schedule slippage were strongly correlated with technological uncertainty; the 1974 study by Murphy, Baker and Fisher[87] is extremely important, being the first substantial study to address the question of what factors are associated with project success (a subject that assumed increased importance in the mid 1980s, see pp. 180−182); Wilemon, Thamhain and Gemmill[64−66,80,89,95] provided original and insightful work on project managers' power and authority, and conflict management and team work in a project context; Youker[96] and Baker and Wilemon[94] provided what became classic synopses of organizational behaviour and structural options; Wiest's[97] is an important paper on resource allocation; and Merrow, Chapel and Worthing's[106] 1979 report presented Rand's first account of its studies into energy and process plant project development, using the frameworks developed over the previous 20 or more years in the study of defence programme developments.

The intra-project middle management issues so typically addressed by these project management writings were certainly important, but even in the 1960s they had been only part of the overall project management picture. Project management in the 1960s had been dominated by the technical challenges of designing, assembling and testing complex defence−aerospace systems to demanding technical specifications on time (and to a lesser extent, to budget). In the 1970s, extra challenges were being added — as we have seen, opposition from external groups and, as we shall see below with nuclear power and the oil and gas industries, difficulties of financing. Before turning to these industries, however, let us chart briefly how project management grew in popularity during the 1970s in another industry: building and civil engineering.

Construction management

As we have seen, the UK and US building and civil engineering industries' structures basically did not encourage a strong, owner-driven project management approach to development. By and large, building and civil engineering work was carried out by contractors that bid against drawings, specifications and other documents such as schedules of rates (US) or Bills of Quantities (UK) prepared by the design team and their cost engineers (US) or quantity surveyors (UK). The contractor's construction know-how came into the project only after the design was fixed. Production management know-how was thus excluded from design, so that designs were often inoptimum from a buildability point of view.

Further, this arrangement generally seemed to pitch the contractor somewhat as an outsider to the existing project team; certainly there was rarely the time or the inclination to involve the constructor as an integral member of the team. Since building and civil engineering designers typically had little tradition of design freeze, configuration or change management, or other design management techniques, design changes occurred regularly (design fees were generally a percentage of final project costs). Submission of claims for extra payment was thus an integral part of a contractor's management; the resulting disputes over authorization of claims further divided the contractor from his design 'project' colleagues. In short, there was next to no project integration, either structurally or behaviourally (note 17). The Thames Barrier, begun in 1971 and completed in 1982 some $3\frac{1}{2}$–4 years late and £329·3m over budget, is a classic example of this approach and the consequent inefficiencies (note 18).[108]

In the mid-to-late 1960s, however, the practice of employing professional construction management began to be used on large complex US projects, particularly where there was a premium on time. The practice had its origins partly in the systems design approaches adopted by US and UK prefabricated schools systems developed in the 1960s, such as California's SCSD, New York's SUCF and England's CLASP (note 19).[109–115] This building systems approach brought construction and operations factors much more systematically into the design phase; specifications were used to greater effect than before by increasing their scope to include these production and operations areas and by involving contractors and users in design development (note 20). By the mid-1960s the approach had spread to real estate development. New York's twin 100-storey, $550m World Trade Center, for example, employed the Tishman Company as construction manager: the project was split into 170 work packages which were let on a phased basis — the so-called fast-track approach. Tishman's tasks were the classic commonsense project management ones: preparation of budgets and detailed schedules, co-ordination of design work and use of value engineering to get better design value for money, assistance with procurement, progress supervision and change control. Several large US university campuses, hospitals and offices were built in a similar way during the late 1960s, as was the 56-storey Canadian Imperial Bank of Commerce in Toronto, although with separate construction management contracts for the general, mechanical and electrical work.[116,117]

In 1970, the US General Services Administration (GSA) published a report endorsing the construction management approach;[118] it also established within the GSA a project manager role to oversee and report on the project. (The powers of this project manager were in reality extremely weak: he was in effect little more than a project administrator.) As had been the case a decade earlier with the DoD, the adoption of a project management approach by a major spending US Federal agency proved a powerful stimulus to the widespread promotion of the practice.

In England, the practice was subtly, but importantly, different from that in America. Whereas in America the construction manager was essentially a consultant — a member of the professional design team — in the UK the constructor's input developed, at this time at least, as a contractor — a management contractor. As management contractor he still came in early and acted as a member of the professional team, but crucially, later in the project, all trades, or subcontracts, passed through him. The first UK project managed on this basis was probably the Horizon tobacco factory for John Player at Nottingham, with the design team of Ove Arup and the constructor Bovis acting as management contractor; this was followed shortly after by the Hartcliffe cigarette factory in Bristol for Wills, with the US firm Skidmore, Owings & Merril as architect and John Laing as management contractor.[119]

During the 1970s, the use of, and writings on, construction management increased hugely (note 21); by the middle of the decade attention was turning more to the use of purer project management. Articles began to appear in 1972–1973 on management contracting; the results of my study comparing project and construction management with the more traditional forms of building delivery system were published in 1973.[119–121] British public-sector institutions were inordinately slow to grasp the thrust of the changes being promoted, however. The 1975 Wood report published by NEDO talked of the value of an early contractor input in the project, but followed the GSA approach of seeing a project manager only as someone whose 'prime task would be that of co-ordinating client requirements such that clear instructions from a single source can be provided to the other parties involved',[122] in contrast, for example, to NASA's more dynamic, executive view of the project manager.

Towards the end of the 1970s, attention to these matters eased: partly because of the exposure they had already received, but largely, perhaps, because of the considerable demand most contractors were beginning to experience from overseas, as a result of the oil price rises, coupled with a decline in their volume of domestic work.

North Sea oil

Oil, gas and the petrochemical derivatives had, of course, been extremely important and active industries since their creation some 40–50 years previously, but the general rise in demand was given a sharp stimulus by the rise in the price of crude oil from around $3 to $12 per barrel between 1971 and 1973.

The first commercial North Sea oil find was made by Phillips Petroleum at Ekofisk in 1969. In 1970 BP discovered the huge Forties field. In 1971 a Shell–Esso joint venture, Shell Expro, announced a similar field — Brent. During the next two decades, over £60bn ($100–$120bn) was spent on oil and gas exploration and production facilities in the North Sea oil province (Figs 25 and 26).

The environmental–technical challenges of exploration and the building of production and shipment systems in the North Sea were

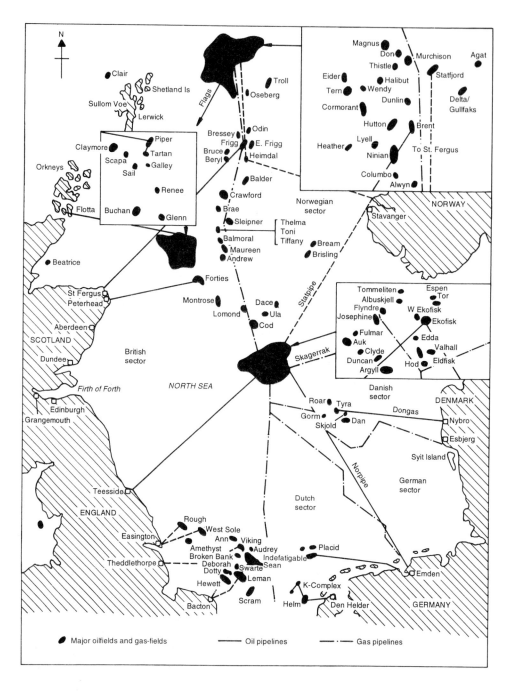

*Fig. 25. The North
Sea oil province*

enormous, particularly in the early days, when data on operating
conditions were scarce. Sea depths in the Northern section, where
the Brent and Forties fields were located, were two to three times
greater than had been encountered in previous offshore 'exploration
and production' work. The weather conditions of the area are often
very bad — 30 m waves are not uncommon — and the environ-

Fig. 26. Thistle A platform, North Sea (courtesy Offshore Engineer)

mental conditions that the structures would have to withstand were not at all clear. To these technical uncertainties were soon added problems of industrial overheating such as inflation, equipment supply and labour difficulties. Also, many of the companies lacked personnel with either the offshore or the project management experience appropriate for such large-scale operations.

These factors created problems of massive cost overruns on the early North Sea oil projects. Brent, for example (organized and developed by Shell Expro on largely functional as opposed to project or matrix lines) experienced substantial problems of redesign and delays in offshore hook-up and commissioning. By the mid-1970s, North Sea costs were escalating at around 100% per year.[123,124] Significantly, however, this was not of vital importance to most of the operators: the profitability of the developments was increasing despite such cost increases, since the price of crude oil was rising so strongly. And importantly, in view of the high net present value (NPV, note 22) of the oil at this time, although the fields were generally being completed way over budget, they were being completed on time.

The need for more professional project management expertise was now more widely recognized and, if not available in-house, 'pm' expertise was bought in, often on a project services contractor (PSC) basis.[125] The PSC form of project management structure was similar to TAPS's salt-and-pepper organization: contractors supply project management support to the owner by supplementing his project management functions as necessary (note 23).

The second-generation North Sea oil projects were undertaken in 1976–1984. During this period fiscal incentives were not so generous, fields were financially more marginal, and the expectation of similar rates of increase in the price of oil seemed less certain. As a result, this second generation of North Sea projects involved a much more considered effort to improve project management performance.[126,127] The technical requirements of the building of viable structures in the North Sea were now better known. As Davies observed, compared with the earlier fields, second-generation British fields were characterized by[128]

- a change in emphasis from minimum schedule times to greater cost·control
- longer schedules and better job definition
- a tendency towards fixed-price contracts, complicated by greater improvement of operators and some emphasis on operator–contractor teams
- a trend towards owner/operators acting as management over prime contractors
- the greater use of more sophisticated computerized project information systems
- a move away from the PSC approach.

The results were on the whole much better, although as my study of the Fulmar A platform — and other studies — showed, there were still plenty of difficulties and lessons to be learned: design management, contracting, project management authority and organization, training, etc.[129] (It was as well that project management performance did improve so much, since in 1983 the price of oil began to fall steeply. Third-generation fields have consequently had to put enormous emphasis on cost-effective engineering and project management.)

Limited-recourse financing

North Sea oil projects brought to greater prominence a form of financing that had so far been little used, but was to gain increased attention in the 1980s. Sometimes called 'project financing', the basis of the method is that the financing is secured on the project alone rather than the companies or institutions associated with it: in the case of default the lenders thus have no recourse, or only limited recourse, to the assets of the initiating companies. Originating in the oil and gas industry of the Southern USA, the method had had some success in the 1970s in the extractive industries in general. (RTZ's large Bougainville copper mine project had been financed on a limited-recourse basis in 1969, three bilateral agencies lending without sovereign guarantees (note 24).)

Project-specific guarantees can be provided in several ways. Where long-term purchase contracts are possible, security may be provided by take-and-pay (or take-or-pay) (note 25) contracts, in which a purchaser contracts to buy the product or service at a stated price and (or) to pay a sum.[130] Throughput contracts is another form of guarantee — an assured payment for a certain throughput is guaranteed. But, of course, securing of the income stream is just part of the project financing equation. Ensuring that the project is completed to technical specification, in budget and on schedule is also important. In other words, this form of financing puts great emphasis on the effective management of the project as an economic entity.

As limited-recourse financing became more widely used from the 1970s onwards, its contribution to the development of the discipline of the management of projects became increasingly valuable, primarily through its emphasis on comprehensive, thorough risk analysis. To reduce the overrun risk, the project financiers generally require a completion guarantee from the builders. Both builders (and their insurers) and financiers thus put the project through a much more severe *'project management' risk analysis* than might otherwise be the case. Technology, for example, will always be examined very carefully in project finance: bankers are loathe to hazard funds where the technological risk is high. Another important factor is political risk. This may cover regulatory controls, fiscal measures and even basic ownership. In the oil industry, for example, the process of granting licences has been of the utmost importance (note 26).

Unfortunately, since the lending security in project finance lies wholly in the legal documentation, arranging project financing is complex and time-consuming, and hence expensive. This has meant that it has been used predominantly for large projects. Initially the method was used primarily to keep debt off company balance sheets, although later in the 1970s it came to be used more as a way of shifting risk to lenders. And later still, in the 1980s, it was to become the basis of the build−own−operate method of project development and financing, one of the most important of conceptual developments in the management of infrastructure projects in the 1980s (see pp. 170−177).

Not all development in the North Sea by any means was carried out on a limited-recourse basis but, almost certainly, every development was looked at extremely carefully in terms of the likely production levels, other commercial risks, engineering challenges, and possible budget or schedule overruns to assess the prudence of going ahead with development. Although the industry was lucky that the price of oil rose substantially (tenfold) during the 10−15 years of maximum North Sea investment (before falling by over 50% in the mid-1980s), the discipline that the owners and their bankers and contractors brought to bear stood the industry in good stead throughout this period of extraordinary development. Such, unfortunately, was not the case in another area of major project activity accelerated by the OPEC price rise: Third World development projects.

Third World projects

The price of oil increased 900% betwen 1971 and 1979: from $3 per barrel in 1971 to $6 by 1973, then it doubled to $12 in 1973, increased to $15 by 1979, and again doubled in that year to $30 per barrel. As a result, oil-exporting countries saw their surpluses increase by over $400bn between 1973 and 1981.

Initially, there was concern that the world's financial systems would not be able to cope with this enormous disruption to capital flows. Deflation and protectionism seemed likely, and very dangerous. By 1976, however, thought of official intervention had been largely abandoned as the commercial banks, using the newly invented Eurodollar and syndicated loan instruments, appeared able to cope and on-lent the flood of petrodollars, most of it going to a small group of relatively high-income, fast growing newly industrialized countries ('nics'), notably Mexico, Brazil, Argentina, Venezuela, South Korea, the Philippines and Indonesia.

Commercial banks assumed that their loans were sovereign or sovereign-guaranteed, i.e. backed by sovereign nations, the theory being that since countries do not go bankrupt, the loans could not default. Additional reassurance was provided as developing countries' terms of trade improved in the mid-1970s and their growth prospects and foreign exchange reserves appeared to strengthen. Export credit guarantees further reduced the risk to exporters and their financiers. With an excess of funds over projects, commercial lending became highly competitive. In the heady conditions of the mid-1970s, sovereign lending to less developed countries became so frantic that 'loan pushing' became a feature of much commercial lending.

There was perhaps a preference for such lending to be for major projects. Typically being politically controlled, large projects attracted the sovereign guarantees that commercial bankers required. Further, they absorbed large amounts of capital quickly.

With the risks apparently being absorbed by borrowing governments and with high competition amongst lenders, the traditional disciplines of project appraisal were often applied only weakly (note 27). In addition, interest-rate risk was generally transferred to the borrowers, since the commercial bank lending was medium-term whereas the project pay-back periods were long-term. In these circumstances it was perhaps not surprising that the economic robustness of projects was often not given adequate attention.

Aid lending, both multilaterial and bilateral, increased markedly during this period. In general, however, aid projects were appraised and monitored much more carefully than projects financed through the commercial banking system. (Aid projects are discussed on pp. 116–118 and 166–170.)

It is very difficult to obtain data on the overall pattern of commercially financed Third World project activity. Kathleen Murphy, however, has analysed data on some 1600 projects described in the technical press between January 1970 and June 1979 and tracked by McKinsey & Co.[131] The data show a rapid increase in new project orders from 1973 to 1978, with a marked increase in average project size. Projects tended to be divided fairly consistently between infrastructure, hydrocarbon, metal, defence (note 28) and 'other' industry categories.

In general, these Third World projects were extremely difficult to manage efficiently, and the record of their accomplishment was often poor. Typically, they were located in places where the physical and social infrastructure was not adequate to support either the logistical or the managerial effort required, management practices were not as rigorously applied as one would normally expect for large complex projects (most projects had Third World parastatals as owners), and cost inflation was rampant. As a result, cost overruns and schedule delays were endemic. Most of Murphy's projects overran by 100% or more and by at least a couple of years.

Just as important, and even more difficult to manage, was the context within which the project was located: if it was a petrochemical project, say, what would be the prices of feedstock and output product in a few years' time, given the huge changes in world petrochemical business activity? If the project was of a telecommunications, road, port or other infrastructure type, what would the volume of traffic settle down to be, and to what extent could the nation's budget and trade balances bear the cost of these public-sector undertakings?

The delays on these projects were often extremely serious; many had a major impact on the developing nation's economic health. Delays in the completion of Sonatrach's liquid natural gas (LNG) project in 1976–1978, for example, meant delays in the receipt of desperately needed foreign exchange by Algeria, since natural gas was Algeria's major export commodity and the facilities at Arzew represented the first physical opportunity for this gas to be exported in significant quantities. Unfortunately, first the contractor that was building the facility, Chemico, went bankrupt, and then the purchase agreement with the US El Paso corporation, which had undertaken to purchase the gas (and invested several billion dollars in building LNG tankers and storage and distribution facilities on the US Eastern seaboard), collapsed. Because of these delays, Algeria had to increase its foreign exchange borrowing substantially in 1976–1978.

Some of the development projects in less developed countries were simplicity itself: clients were rich, project needs were obvious, everyone got on with the job. In the Arabian peninsula, for example, this was the case in hundreds of major projects. Other projects impacted more severely on issues of national economy.

The Iranian 2M56 programme, for example, was set up to install two million telephone lines across Iran; unfortunately Iran's oil revenues slumped during late 1975—1976 as consumers around the world tightened their belts while inflation soared; as a result just 12 exchanges were ultimately built. The mammoth Saudi Arabian programme to build industrial cities at Jubail and Yanbu, said to have cost up to $90bn, raised serious 'Saudiization' issues of population and culture — how could such industrial centres be staffed without damage to the strict Muslim culture of Saudi Arabia?

For the developed world companies, the boom in Third World major projects offered an assortment of opportunities and challenges. Hundreds of contractors, designers and suppliers obtained huge quantities of relatively straightforward, and sometimes — though by no means always — highly profitable, work. At another level, however, the opportunities were more complex. Many of the joint ventures pioneered at this time, for example, were the prelude to similarly sophisticated project-based trading arrangements which were to become a characteristic of the 1980s.

An important aspect of such ventures was the willingness of the supplier to participate directly in the sponsorship of the project (in this way paralleling the trend in project financing for the financiers to become more directly involved in the success of the project). Capital, market access and technology transfer were typically key variables for developers. Production sharing, concessionary financing, suppliers' credits, co-production deals, etc. became important vehicles for the securing of projects that made commercial sense.

Many of these development projects illustrated the importance of *seeing project management as part of the overall project deal*, particularly if, as was often the case, the project management company was being asked to take completion risk, currency risk or other significant risks. The Japanese, for example, demonstrated great flexibility in the way they structured their equity and contractual relationships. As large, complex deals were worked out, several contracting companies found themselves taking huge risks for relatively modest rewards, while others were taking large long-term rewards while bearing only minor short-term risks. The lesson here was to look at the duration of the contractual commitments as well as their absolute size; to look at the risks in relation to the company's broader, long-term business; not simply to appraise project risks squarely, but to assess the rewards against the other parties operating at the strategic or external edge of the project.

Development aid programmes

Aid-funded Third World development projects and programmes were meanwhile receiving quite different attention — being managed more carefully and formally, even bureaucratically. Yet, sadly, their success rates were not always much better.

Aid programmes were, and still are, financed largely by loans or grants from national development agencies such as Britain's Overseas Development Agency (ODA) and the US Agency for International Development (AID), or multilateral agencies such as the World Bank, the UN Development Programme (UNDP) or the regional developmental banks such as the Asian Development Bank. Of these, by far the largest is the World Bank (although its lending constituted barely 1% total investment in developing countries during the decade).

During the 1970s the World Bank lent over $37bn to more than 1000 operations, its level of activity in 1978–1979 being two to three times that of the late 1960s.[132] Its lending, as it grew, shifted from its 1960s infrastructure orientation to include more agriculture and rural development, education, population and nutrition, urbanization and small-scale industries. (World Bank lending for infrastructure declined from 60% in the late 1960s to 30% by the late 1970s.)

During the 1970s, attention to the importance of effective management of development programmes' implementation increased markedly. The focus, however, was on more than the simple mechanics of project management: ' . . . it was not enough to produce economic plans by central planning agencies. For achieving results, planning and implementation had to be treated as facets of an integral but wider process involving creation and strengthening of concomitant institutions and processes, and linking them together.'[133]

A major reason for the general lack of implementation success on development projects so far, it was recognized during the 1970s, was the human element. This was particularly the case where substantial social change was required. The consequent 'New Directions' approach of the 1970s was the most significant change in development management in 30 years. The thesis of the New Directions programme management was that 'other things being equal, implementation problems and failures are least likely to occur when self-sustaining behaviour change among one or more target groups is included as a success criterion for project performance'.[134] From this was to come a preoccupation with *'institution building'* — the building of technically, financially and managerially strong institutions capable of attracting resources, implementing programmes, and running the new structures as successful enterprises.

There was, it was widely argued, too large a gap between the sophisticated Western tools and techniques of management and the cultural reality of many developing countries. Host nations were often unable to deal effectively with the differing requirements of hard and soft technology; to mobilize and manage financial, human and other resources; or to develop responsive and flexible organizations. Western project management approaches, it was felt, overemphasized rules, procedures and formal structures. Too often, planning was separated from both implementation challenges and power realities. As Rondinelli remarked:[135]

> Perhaps the ultimate irony is that many developing countries have been judged backward, inefficient, and defective in public planning and administration because they cannot apply analytical and management systems techniques, the efficacy and practicality of which remain unproven even in advanced industrial nations. That better projects will emerge from proposals subjected to highly detailed technical and economic feasibility analyses, that optimal choices will emerge from appraisals using elegant rate of return, shadow pricing and social cost—benefit analyses, that projects will be implemented efficiently if planned and controlled through PERT, CPM and systems analysis, that greater impacts can be achieved by integrating projects within sectorial and national development plans, are merely assumed. Little evidence supports the assumptions.

Choosing the 'appropriate technology' became a popular concern in the 1970s with, among others, Schumacher arguing in his famous 1973 book *Small is beautiful*[136] that many Western-inspired projects were too big and, more importantly, that they too often used technology that was not appropriate to the needs of the poor whom the projects were intended to help.

Much of this analysis had been foreshadowed by Albert O. Hirschman in his influential 1967 work *Development projects observed*.[137] Analysing eleven World Bank projects, Hirschman concluded that too often the capacity of managers to invent remedial actions to resolve unexpected problems was overestimated. More emphasis should therefore be put on developing good implementers. Hirschman further distinguished 'supply-side' uncertainties (technology, administration and finance) from 'demand-side' (too little demand, i.e. white elephants, or too much). In singling out demand-side factors as an element in the estimation of project success, Hirschman crucially brought the *'project success'* question into a discussion that so far had been centred largely on 'project management'.

Despite the caveats and doubts, however, in the end most seemed to agree on the value of the project approach and project management. Appointment of a competent project manager early in the formulation stage was the most important factor for successful implementation, the UN had reported in 1969.[138]

Nuclear power   If the record of infrastructure and petrochemical projects in both the developed and the developing worlds was often disappointing during the 1970s, it was as nothing compared with that of another major construction sector of this time: nuclear power.

Not all power projects in the 1970s were nuclear, of course, and many of the non-nuclear (and even some nuclear) projects were not accomplished at all poorly. But the record of nuclear power projects, certainly in the USA and the UK, was throughout the 1970s and 1980s at best not good, and at worst simply appalling (note 29). The reasons for this are important to a general understanding of the discipline of the management of projects.

Nuclear power plants are highly complex large engineering systems. Some — the UK's Advanced Gas Cooled Reactor (AGR) type, for example — were so technically complex and unforgiving that they posed a level of construction difficulty that might simply have been too great to permit confident project time and cost completion. Some nuclear plants, then, have experienced massive cost and schedule overruns because of their enormous technical complexities and challenges.

Yet technical difficulties alone have not been the cause of the nuclear power industry suffering the worst cost and schedule overruns of any project business (with overruns of up to 4000% by the mid-1980s) and of the widespread plant cancellations of the late 1970s and 1980s, with the consequent huge financial losses. Though these have been awkward enough, equally or even more important have been the institutional arrangements and the social conditions under which the nuclear power industries have operated. Many of the later nuclear power projects, for instance, particularly the French, were accomplished on time and in budget largely because those building them organized the production effort on an orderly basis: regular orders; continuity of work for suppliers, owners, regulators and others; standardized design; and, at least in the late 1970s and 1980s, relatively comfortable relations with the local community (and a regimented public inquiry procedure).

Several factors underlying the poor project management performance of nuclear power can be identified. The first is its origins. Nuclear power was strongly promoted by governments (in countries all over the world). For a variety of reasons, its 'project risks' were never accurately appraised. In the USA, nuclear power was promoted by the Atomic Energy Commission (AEC), the successor organization to the Manhattan Engineering District, which was responsible for both the US military and civilian atomic programmes. Civil nuclear power was greatly pushed in the 1950s by the AEC and Admiral Hyman C. Rickover's Bureau of Ships, which in 1953 became responsible for the development of the Pressurized Water Reactor (PWR) (note 30).[139-142] The AEC involved the nuclear steam supply system (NSSS) companies intimately in the development of nuclear reactors. As a result of this experience, the NSSS suppliers felt sufficiently confident in the mid-1960s to offer fixed-price turnkey contracts to the utility companies.

Following President Eisenhower's 'atoms for peace' speech to the United Nations in December 1953, the AEC embarked in 1955 on a Cooperative Power Reactor Demonstration Program, in which several utilities worked with the AEC and NSSS companies to try out various reactor types. The utilities generally remained not overly impressed by the attractions of nuclear power, however. For although the USA's electricity demand was rising rapidly — it doubled every decade from 1939 to 1971 — it has abundant sources of fossil and hydro fuel: the economic case for nuclear power was never obvious. To improve the economic case, it was felt that the power units had to be bigger. The scale of units proposed thus increased dramatically during the 1950s and 1960s — from 300 MW in 1962 to 700 MW in 1965 and to 1150 MW in 1972.[143] Crucially, though, no-one had experience in building or operating such large units.

Up to 1965, no US utility had ordered a nuclear power station. Then, in 1965, General Electric sold a 500 MW Boiling Water Reactor (BWR) (Oyster Creek) to New Jersey Central Power and Light Electric Company on a fixed-price, turnkey basis. The sale was hailed as a breakthrough: ' . . . the first time an American utility company has selected a nuclear power plant on purely economic grounds without government assistance and in direct competition with a fossil fuel plant'.[144] A rush of orders followed: 22 units in 1966, 32 in 1967, 45 in 1968−1970, most on a turnkey basis.

It is not clear why there was now this sudden rush of orders. Two studies by the Rand Corporation[145,146] concluded that there was no overriding set of factors, although Hazelrigg and Roth in their 1982 study suggest increased demand and the financial feeling of security surrounding the utilities after 14 comfortable years (their 'golden age': 1952−1966).[147] There was also some concern over the environmental damage caused by coal-fired power generation, and no environmentalist opposition to nuclear power was yet apparent. In general, the utilities appeared to show little trepidation over the technological or financial risks posed by nuclear plants, not least perhaps because of the willingness of the NSSS suppliers to take this risk themselves. In the event, however, General Electric and Westinghouse experienced huge losses on these contracts — Rand estimated between $800m and $1bn (ref. 148, pp. 236−237) — and in 1967 the suppliers ceased to accept fixed-price contracts for nuclear work.

There was another burst of US nuclear power ordering in the early 1970s: 26, 29, 30 and 20 units being ordered in each of the years from 1971 to 1974. By then, however, severe problems were arising with such projects, and before long the industry was in very serious trouble.

Across the Atlantic in the UK at this time, the purchasers were in a much more dominant role than the suppliers; hence the suppliers were forced to accept fixed-price contracts throughout the 1960s. The UK had in fact been slightly ahead of the USA in developing production nuclear power plants in the 1950s and early 1960s. As in the USA, the programme in the UK was treated as of the utmost importance to national security: it was an act of political faith. In the USA, the choice of reactor type was dominated by the needs of the US Navy, which, as we have seen, was totally dominated in this regard by Admiral Rickover. Crucially, Rickover managed the nuclear development programme as an engineer, and a production-oriented one at that. In Britain, on the other hand, the development of reactor technology was dominated by research scientists and engineers led primarily by the Atomic Energy Authority. Britain first chose the magnox design in which unenriched uranium was moderated by graphite; this technology was soon seen as being expensive to build as well as entailing a number of operating inefficiencies. In 1966–1968, Britain switched to the AGR. The number of units Britain required, however, was far too small for the number of companies wishing to make such plant; the technology was too difficult and was unproven; construction delays were experienced; export orders did not materialize; and so great were the suppliers' contractual losses (the work being ordered by the duopsonic generating boards on a fixed-price turnkey basis) that they faced bankruptcy and consequent industrial restructuring (note 31). The Central Electricity Generating Board (CEGB) then chose PWRs, but was thwarted in realizing this choice by others in the industry. Only in 1978 were further reactors ordered — two AGRs. A third station was ordered in 1987: significantly, a PWR.

France, after beginning like Britain with graphite-moderated unenriched uranium reactors, switched in 1970 to US light-water moderated reactors. Having comparatively limited sources of natural energy, France began to build standardized PWRs at an impressive rate: 34 units of 900 MW had been begun by 1982; 20 units of 1300 MW units and one 1400 MW unit by 1986. By and large, construction times for these units were progressively and consistently reduced.

The *first* major cause of the nuclear power industry's poor project management performance, then, has been the difficulty experienced by some organizations in developing an extremely complex form of technology from the stage of highly advanced R&D to the point of commercialization. *This difficulty of commercialization was exacerbated by the political push to exploit nuclear technology and by the lack of care and sensitivity on the part of those buying and supplying the technology towards the risks posed by its development, construction and operation.*

The *second* major cause is the less excusable *series of mistakes and technical problems* that the industry seemed to attract. These, largely, should never have occurred. They had a disastrous impact

Fig. 27. Dungeness B: the constructor went bankrupt and the project was finished hugely late and over budget (courtesy United Kingdom Atomic Energy Authority)

on plant reliability, and created a possibly fatal loss of public confidence in the industry. This was exacerbated by the industry's penchant for keeping such mistakes as secret as possible.

There are, regrettably, far too many major incidents for them all to be reported here, but the following are amongst the most notorious.

- In 1975 an electrician's candle at Brown's Ferry BWR plant (two 1100 MW units) in Alabama set fire to cabling; both units, representing 15% of the Tennessee Valley Authority's power load, had to be shut down for 18 months.
- Cracked pipes were discovered in several US BWRs in late 1974; this led to the temporary shutdown of all BWRs until pipe integrity had been assured.
- UK AGRs all suffered substantial technical problems. Dungeness B experienced such severe problems that it still had not attained full load 20 years after construction began; Hartlepool B and Heysham 1 — two plants using another version of the AGR — had to have their boilers completely repositioned and redesigned two years after project work began when the initial design was deemed to be unsafe; Hinkley B and Hunterston B — a third AGR design — suffered two years' delay in re-engineering of technical problems during commissioning. As a result, when the

CEGB came to build power stations in the mid-1970s, its project management philosophy stressed 'standardization of design wherever possible and firm control of design changes during the project; discrete upgradings of technology, introduced only at reasonably long-term intervals; maintenance of stable relationships with suppliers where appropriate (i.e. replication), but competitive bidding where new features were involved; the use of design contracts where possible . . . ; the use of firm price contracts where appropriate, with appropriate incentives for timely completion [note 32]' and greater attention to management and industrial relations (ref. 108, chapter 6).

- In California, the Diablo Canyon plant was found to be sited, unknowingly, near an underwater earthquake fault; when this was discovered (just as construction was nearing completion) considerable additional strengthening of the plant was ordered, particularly in the pipe supports; unfortunately, just as fuel load was beginning in 1981 it was noticed that these supports had been put in the plant the wrong way round — the designers had got the blueprints of the two identical units back-to-front, and the strengthening had been made on a mirror-image basis of its real configuration (note 33).
- The reactor of the San Onofre plant in California was installed backwards.
- Reactor supports were installed 45° out by Brown & Root on Commanche Peak.
- Brown & Root had even worse problems on the South Texas plant it was building for Houston Power & Light which, unusually, it had agreed to do on a 'full responsibility' contract. Engineering could not keep pace with construction, while construction itself was seen to have huge deficiencies. Brown & Root was relieved of the contract and, in an out-of-court settlement, agreed in 1985 to pay $750m in damages to Houston Power & Light.

The point about these technical errors is not so much that they happened — all projects experience problems — but that they were not tolerable. The fact that they happened can be explained by the explosive growth of the industry (211 units ordered in the USA between 1965 and 1974: around 165 units, representing 60 000 MW of capacity installed by 1973 and almost the same number on order); by the lack of experience in managing such unforgiving projects on the part of the utilities, regulators and builders, at both company and individual level; and by the unappreciated extra risks involved in scaling up plant sizes so rapidly. These are all valid explanations, *but they are not acceptable.* Threat of loss of life or damage to the environment is, not unreasonably, unacceptable in an affluent, articulate democracy. The managers of the Apollo mission knew this (as the anxiety over Apollo 8 showed); the nuclear industry did not.

The concern over the poor quality of technical performance led to a dramatic rise during the decade in the practice of *Quality Assurance* (QA) in the industry. In July 1970, new US guidelines for quality assurance, 10 CFR 50 Appendix B, had come into effect. These indicated 18 areas for which the owner must be able to document that adequate processes had been followed. These requirements were initially interpreted fairly vaguely, but over the next few years came to mean that basic management and engineering actions during the whole project had to have formal documentary evidence showing that promulgated quality had been achieved. The Nuclear Regulatory Commission (NRC), which was established out of the AEC in January 1975, had a statutory responsibility to license each nuclear plant before it could begin fuel loading: the licence could only be issued after the operator had demonstrated that all regulatory requirements were complied with.

The pace of new regulations increased dramatically in the mid-1970s as the AEC and then the NRC struggled to deal with the licensing of the large number of plants, of non-standard reactor design, now proceeding in parallel. By 1976, new requirements were being issued at the rate of three per month.[148,149] The high level of uncertainty that this created had a significant impact on design and engineering. Where design was not completed, it was held back while approvals were obtained. If design work was already complete and construction under way, the result was essentially a form of concurrency and led to costly delay and refit (this is the process commonly referred to as 'regulatory ratchetting') (note 34).

The extent to which US utilities were adequately observing the QA requirements was increasingly challenged by the regulatory authorities during the 1970s and 1980s. The 1973 Brown Book study, a $3m study on reactor safety by MIT, provided potential objectors with a mass of useful information with which to challenge proposed plants, and further requirements for the plant builders to comply with.

When the Three Mile Island (TMI) plant at Harrisburg, Pennsylvania came within 60 minutes of meltdown on 28 March 1979 due to a stuck valve, the industry began to recognize the significance of society's opposition to intolerable plant performance. A ten-month moratorium on the issuing of operating licences was immediately introduced, and a new regulatory ruling was issued requiring state and local approval of emergency evacuation plans prior to licensing. QA requirements became mandatory in the USA.

Opposition to nuclear power hardened not just in the USA (note 35), which in fact has not placed a single order for a reactor since TMI, but around the world, most notably perhaps in Germany, Italy and Sweden. The shock of Chernobyl in April 1986 further reinforced community opposition to nuclear power (see pp. 160−162).

The environmentalists had in fact been treated derisively and aggressively by the industry throughout the 1970s: simply as protesters. Certainly, the mood of opposition had become so charged, both emotionally and physically, that many in industry found it difficult to accept that one might have to work positively with environmentalists to develop a *modus operandi* for these projects. In 1975 German protesters objected against a proposed PWR at Fessenheim (actually located on the other side of the Rhine in France) by invading the site and occupying it for several years. In 1976 there was a pitched battle between protesters and riot police at Creys-Malville in France. A few months later the US Clamshell Alliance organized a peaceful sit-in at the Seabrook site in New Hampshire — 1414 protesters were arrested.

Public opposition and attendant regulatory processes must therefore be the third factor militating against simple project management 'success' in the nuclear power sector. However good the classical project management practices, by the mid-1970s nuclear plant builders were operating in an increasingly constraining environment, which was becoming both progressively antipathetic to nuclear power and uneasy at the quality of the builders' own project management performance.

A *fourth* factor affecting the industry's poor project management success record was *the increasingly poor financial viability of the projects*. With the electricity generating boards in the UK run (until the early 1990s) as nationalized entities, UK financing had never been a serious issue. In the USA, however, approximately 75% of the utilities were investor-owned, electricity prices being regulated by the various state or local Public Utility Commissions (PUCs). Crucially, the PUCs typically did not permit Amortized Funds Used During Construction (AFUDC) to be charged to the customer until the plant went into operation. If the plant was delayed, therefore, the impact on the utility's revenues could be substantial.

Between 1960 and 1965, only 30% of utilities' construction funds came from external sources. By 1980 this figure had risen to 53%.[150] During the 1970s, electricity demand dropped from an annual growth rate of 7% to just 3% as the USA adjusted its energy consumption to meet the post-OPEC higher oil charges. At the same time, interest rates and inflation rose sharply. These factors taken together made external financing increasingly expensive and unattractive during the 1970s. Utility bond ratings fell accordingly (only 37% had Baa or better by 1980, compared with 89% in 1965 (ref. 150, p. 23)). Additional financing thus became increasingly difficult. To curtail the consequent stock devaluation, capital spending had to be cut back, the most obvious item to be cut being the construction of the nuclear power stations. In all 87 nuclear plants, representing 83 000 MW of capacity, were cancelled between 1975 and 1983. In effect the utilities transferred out of nuclear into coal, which from 1982 became the cheaper power plant option. (They did so, as we shall see below, very much under the stimulation of the 1978 US Public Utilities Act (PURPA), which encouraged utilities to purchase electricity from independent power producers, at 'just, reasonable and non-discriminatory rates' generally from smaller plants such as co-generation plants. This new line of energy project work became increasingly attractive to the private financial sector during this period — a trend that, as we shall see, was to be typical of many other project sectors.)

Most of the plants cancelled were in the relatively early stages of construction. Some, however were well advanced — Shoreham was virtually complete. For some utilities, cancellation was part of a prudent management exercise; for others it was the capstone of disaster. The Washington Public Power Supply System (WPPSS) was probably the greatest example of the latter. Five 1000 MW plants were being built, financed by tax exempt bonds. Costs escalated from $4bn in 1974 to $24bn by 1981. The project management problems appeared to spiral at an alarming rate: strikes were frequent; structural problems kept arising. By late 1980, WPPSS was issuing $200m in bonds every 90 days. With debts of $8bn, Units 4 and 5 were mothballed in 1981 and in 1983 work on Units 1 and 3 was stopped (construction being 63% and 76% complete). A legal judgement in 1983 that the municipal utilities were not liable to honour the bonds then caused the biggest bond default in US history. Settlements of the case subsequently totalled $750m.[151-155]

Although these facts were crucial, hardly any of them appeared in the publications of the professional project management societies, such as PMI and Internet (they *were* recognized by specialist groups such as the US Electricity Producers Research Institute (EPRI)). The new paradigm — the new range of issues — that the projects of the late 1960s and 1970s were offering was, unfortunately, hardly filtering through to the professional project management bodies at all. Indeed, it is a sad, and to my mind remarkable, fact that in general this was not to happen until well into the next decade. The new issues arguably first began to emerge, along with many others of the more strategic lessons on the management of projects, in a new grouping of project-related societies that had their origins in a slowly emerging perception around the late 1970s that large complex projects pose special challenges of initiation and management, and that these challenges were by no means well understood or being well managed. These were the macro-engineering and major project societies that began to be formed in the late 1970s and to which we now briefly turn.

Early macro-engineering interests

By the late 1980s, macro-engineering and major project societies around the world were beginning to champion the management of projects as a more strategic, top−down discipline than in the more middle-management, tools-and-techniques oriented view of the project management societies. The initiation of this movement owes much to Frank Davidson of the Massachusetts Institute of Technology.

In 1968 Davidson published *Macro-engineering: a capability in search of a methodology*.[156] Noting that large projects are multidisciplinary and that their management ought to have multidisciplinary skills, Davidson observed that society had not done a good job so far in training engineers to deal with the breadth of disciplines and interests necessary for such projects. Why not, Davidson asked, form international study groups to 'provide an informal setting for the exchange of ideas, the planning of legal, financial, economic and engineering studies, and the establishment of a constructive interdisciplinary atmosphere?' (ref. 156, p. 156). From 1970 Davidson pursued these ideas at MIT; by the end of the decade he was in the thick of organizing conferences and discussing with like-thinking men and women around the world the creation of a series of national macro-engineering and major project societies.

May 1978 saw two important conferences devoted to the subject of very large projects. Over 80 senior engineers and financiers met in Pacific Grove, California, to discuss 'planning, engineering and constructing the superprojects'. The conference furnished useful papers on, for example, financing, the nuclear regulatory environment and — particularly valuable in view of the paucity of attention reflected in the literature so far — logistics.[157] The papers, however, were notable for the almost complete absence of any analysis of the origins of superprojects or of the conditions which were needed to maintain them as relevant business phenomena (note 36).

In London, meanwhile, a two-day conference organized by a number of leading British industrialists focused on the problems and solutions of the successful accomplishment of giant projects. 'For many reasons' wrote the principal conference organizer, Allen Sykes, 'the size and complexity of capital projects are becoming much more common. Such projects pose problems which are different not only in size but also in nature from more moderately sized projects. The number of people with experience of giant projects is small: the number of people with experience of successful giant projects is even smaller.[158] The papers, which ranged from overall management through financial and legal to staffing matters, were notable for the breadth of thinking and excellence and the wealth of experience that they so succinctly covered.

The London event was so successful that those attending were convinced that the topic warranted further dedicated follow-up and study. Discussions were held with Frank Davidson. By 1980 it had been agreed to establish a major projects 'club' for senior managers, who would meet regularly to share information and pool experience on major projects. (Major projects being defined as those that require knowledge, skills or resources that exceed what is readily or conventionally available to the key participants.) From this was to come research, writing and teaching that has been influential in the development of our understanding of the discipline of the management of projects, as is noted on p. 194.

During the 1980s there were to be many issues that would require the kind of analysis the major project societies were capable of providing: synfuels, the crisis in the nuclear power industry, the effect on oil-based and mining projects of the collapse in the price of oil and other commodities, the steep drop in aid and the virtual cessation of commercial bank lending to the Third World, the problems in space, the rise of environmentalism, and the promises held out by build—own—operate project financing. Before moving on to these, however, we must turn to progress in the 1970s in one last sector — defence/aerospace.

**US defence/
aerospace**

Rondinelli had been right to question the value of many of the project management tools and techniques.[135] Even in the industry responsible for much of their invention and promotion, defence/ aerospace, during the 1970s they were too often inadequate. Although the tools were now available to do the job, the 1970s were to witness, in both the USA and the UK, a lack of commitment within the industry to using them properly.

McNamara, having ushered in a range of new management techniques (note 37), left the Pentagon in 1967. His successor as Secretary of Defense was Melvin Laird, supported by David Packard, co-founder and President of Hewlett Packard, as Deputy Secretary. The US involvement in Vietnam, pressures on the economy, failure of the Total Package Procurement concept, and continuing examples of poor system performance and problems of cost growth caused Packard in particular to act vigorously in the early 1970s to seek further improvements in defence procurement practices.

In May 1970, Packard issued a memorandum summarizing ways in which the acquisition of major defence systems could be improved. This became the basis for the new DoD Directive 5000.1 *Acquisition of major defense systems* of July 1971.[159] The under- lying philosophy of both documents was Packard's view that 'successful development, production and deployment of major defense systems are primarily dependent upon competent people, national priorities, and clearly defined responsibilities'. Emphasis was put on giving Program Managers the responsibility, authority and rewards for managing their programmes effectively. As it turned out, however, it was precisely this that proved the weakest aspect of DoD Program Management.

Cost growth, schedule delays and frequent instances of disappointing technical performance continued to arise during the decade. Studies by Rand in the 1970s, for example, continued to show little improvement in the pattern observed in the 1960s, as described on pp. 59–60 (note 38). In December 1972 a Blue Ribbon Defense Panel commissioned by President Nixon concluded that poor programme performance was caused largely by failures in management, inadequate Program Management training, insensitive and too frequent personnel rotation, and inadequate recognition of career advancement through Program Management.[160] 'With the long tradition of putting a general in charge of the battle, or putting an admiral in charge of a fleet', Packard said in 1971, 'one would think it would be easy to get the Services to accept the proposition that you should have one man with authority in charge of a weapon development and acquisition programme. We have been able to get this done in a few isolated cases, but it simply has not been fully accepted as a management must by any of the Services.'[161]

Opportunities for better formal training were increased with the establishment in July 1971 of the Defense Systems Management School (later College) to train, conduct research, and assemble and disseminate information (note 39).

However, while training was clearly necessary for improved Program Management effectiveness, it was not in itself sufficient. As the Blue Ribbon Panel observed, Program Managers had to be able to remain long enough at their posts to make an impact, and they had to believe that they would be rewarded for bringing projects and programmes in on time and in budget. Amazingly, this was not — even by the late 1980s — the case. Neither government nor industry programme managers necessarily perceived cost growth as a particular problem (ref. 161, pp. 427–435). Government personnel, from Congress down, saw defence programme priorities as maintaining America's defence capability, keeping people employed, maintaining programme funding, or in some other non-programme management way. As for the contractors, given the monopsonic nature of the industry, maintenance of customer satisfaction was generally a high priority, cost minimization and short-term profit were lower priorities (chapter 23 of ref. 161).[162–165]

In short, project management was being observed in US weapons system procurement at the technique level but not where it really counted, at the institutional–strategic level. The founding champions of modern project management, such as Groves, Schriever, Raborn, Webb and Mueller, had operated at precisely this level, stimulating and introducing as they did so detailed planning, organizational and control techniques. But the costs of such all-out project-focused initiatives were, in the 1970s (and 1980s), too high for the established military heirarchy to bear in any kind of persistent way, just as they had been in the 1950s with the rejection of the Gillette and Anderson Committees' proposals. Under the bureaucratic weight of the military, project management had become little more than a form of bureaucratic expediting (note 40).

In such circumstances, then, it can be little wonder that initiatives such as C/SCSC and incentive contracting progressed only slowly. By 1972 C/SCSC had been adopted by only 36 defence contractors. Although in principle all the Services supported C/SCSC, in practice there was an ambivalence as to the need for it, confusion over its implementation technicalities — a situation reminiscent of PERT/Cost in 1962−1964 — and an absence of clear enforcement procedures. This ambivalence was to remain through much of the 1970s, and many at an operating level opposed the method despite official high-level encouragement. The official encouragement meant, however, that by 1975 (following a GAO study of cost growth from $90m to over $500m on the Fast Flux Test Facility in Hanford) the US Department of Energy decided to install C/SCSC for all projects of $50m or more (under a scheme known as PMS — *Performance Measurement System*); by 1983, it was reported, the great majority of those using the method were finding it helpful.[166−168]

The alarming record of systems cost growth was addressed by Packard in his July 1969 memorandum, *Improvement in weapons systems acquisition*. This ordered that cost estimating be improved; contract definition be complete before full-scale development was authorized; there be better change control and increased emphasis on configuration management; and areas of high technical risk be identified and fully considered before beginning full-scale development (note 41). A Defense Systems Acquisition Review Council was established to advise on the status and readiness of all major defence systems, in particular before giving permission to move from one phase of the acquisition cycle to the next. There were also to be periodic independent reviews of such programmes by the Director of Defense Research and Engineering. In January 1972 an Office of the Secretary of Defense (OSD) Cost Analysis Improvement Group was established to provide cost estimating and analysis support to the Secretary. From this grew the important practices of *design-to-cost* (DTC) and *life-cycle costing* (LCC) in 1973 and 1976 respectively (note 42). A major review of life-cycle costs — 'costs-in-use', in construction parlance — in the mid-1970s led to a further re-evaluation of estimating bases during the second half of the decade.

Packard's approach to programme development was quintessentially sequential, grounded on the belief that one should define what one wants to do before embarking on development. This '*heel-*

to-toe' approach was best exemplified by DoD's new formalization of its attitudes to concurrency and prototype testing. On taking office, Packard had noted that all the DoD programmes then in trouble were being developed on the concurrency method (note 43). The 1970 Blue Ribbon Panel also cautioned against the practice, as did a Rand report in 1971.[169,170] '*Fly-before-buy*' was introduced as a way to evaluate hardware via competition and testing before making production selection, rather than making the selection on the basis of paper proposals (note 44).

The Blue Ribbon Panel also commented on the value of an independent weapons testing office. Despite Packard's prodding that such a testing office be established, nothing happened until Congress passed legislation mandating it in 1983; it took two more years for Secretary Weinberger to appoint someone to head it.

Packard's philosophy of delegation was frustrated with the abandonment in 1972 of the Total Package Procurement practice and the consequent return to cost reimbursement and incentive contracting, with separate contracts being written for development, production and support. This reversal occurred amid the almost unanimous agreement of both practitioners and researchers that incentive contracting rarely 'worked': in May 1968 the Logistics Management Institute identified several reasons why incentives were not a good means of minimizing cost growth (note 45);[171] studies by the Rand Corporation found that incentive contracts were expensive and did not necessarily perform better than cost reimbursement, and that in reality contracts were adjusted to follow costs rather than influence them to stay low;[172-174] even the Army itself reached similar conclusions.[175]

Convincing though such a weight of evidence is, however, the overall institutional context — long-term expectations, attitudes, priorities and rewards, and penalties — within which these different contract forms were being implemented undoubtedly influenced the effectiveness of the contracting arrangements. The UK 'large site' contracting milieu (see pp. 70-71) and the US nuclear power industry's contract practices illustrate the same point. It is interesting that for decades in Britain the environment was one of the defence industry working in cost-plus; since the early 1980s the environment has moved much more towards incentive contracting. The general feeling seemed to be, despite problems, some of which were certainly serious, that this was a much preferable contractual environment.

Frustrated and disillusioned by the resistance of the defence industry to the practices he believed succeeded so well in private businesses such as his own, Packard resigned his office in 1972.

Packard was not the only person to feel frustrated. Several industry leaders had vented their unhappiness with the complexity of defence system contracting to the House Committee on Government Operations in June 1969. As a result, Congress had established a Commission on Government Procurement, which reported on 31 December 1972.[176] The Commission's treatment of the conceptual basis of the subject — a landmark study of Systems Program Management — was exceptionally thorough, reference being made to the origins of the approach in the ballistic missile programmes and to the theoretical work of A. D. Hall,[177] Van Court Hare[178] and others in systems engineering. Among the commission's more important findings were the following.

- *Cost, capability and schedule goals are often not of equal importance, their relative weight being determined by the initial programme definition.*
- *Inadequacy of technology base, ineffective competition and premature commitment are difficulties typically faced in the initial problem definition phase.*
- Some cost growth is almost certainly inevitable, although the scale of recent cost growth had a harmful effect on force levels in general.
- Better estimating and funding could come about if there was *more thorough exploration of alternative systems*; however, this would be expensive (note 46).
- Test and evaluation should be conducted by the Services with more emphasis on operational capability.
- Overlapping production, development and testing (i.e. 'concurrency') can lead to problems.
- 'It is difficult for the program manager to exercise effectively the authority given him by charter due to excessive management layering and split policy making';[176] simplification of the programme selection process would help clarify the Program Manager's role; *there is no universal answer to the relative merits of project/matrix/functional or in-house/contracted-out organizational options*, the choice basically reflecting a fit between programme characteristics and available resources.

Significantly, particularly in view of its origins, the commission's report made no clear comment or recommendations on the two issues of most concern to industry, namely contracting and the value of DoD mandated control systems.

The report was well received by industry and the Pentagon — many of its recommendations were in fact already receiving action following Packard's initiatives. The emphasis on greater attention to *increased front-end definition and competition* (Fig. 28) resulted in the establishment of a new milestone in the acquisition process, *Milestone 0* (so called to avoid renumbering and consequent confusion). Milestone 0 involved approval of the *mission element need statement* (note 47) and authorization to proceed to concept exploration. This practice was further formalized under Office of Management and Budget (OMB) Circular A-109 *Major systems*

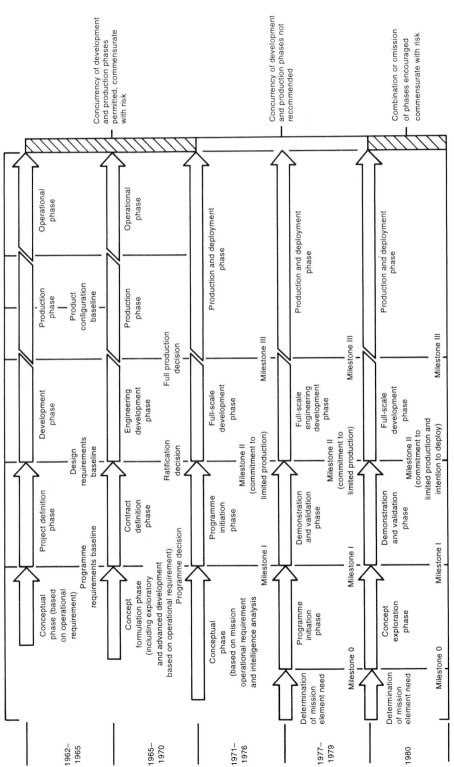

Fig. 28. Evolution of the US defence systems life cycle

acquisitions of April 1976, the major thrust of which was attention to front-end scrutiny and *avoidance of premature commitment* to full-scale development and production. (NASA followed suit by adding a *Concept* stage to the Phased Project Planning cycle.)

By the second half of the decade, a completely different set of issues was beginning to dominate the Pentagon's systems acquisition process. Programmes were taking so long to develop and were costing so much (note 48) that shorter, less costly acquisition strategies were sought. The new Under Secretary of Defense, Research and Engineering, Dr William J. Perry, thus commissioned a Defense Science Board study on how programmes could be developed in more affordable ways.

The study, undertaken predominantly by industry representatives, concluded that the acquisition cycle had lengthened excessively due to the continued accretion of procedures developed in reaction to past failures. Concurrency, the Board recommended, might be one way of accelerating the cycle. Dr Perry accepted this idea in principle, arguing in 1979 that it might be better to field an inoptimum system initially and then gradually incorporate subsystem improvements, a method said to be favoured by the Soviets.[179] The wisdom of this decision, considering the past difficulties with concurrency (and indeed those still to come, for example the UK Nimrod airborne early warning system — see pp. 154–156), must be questionable. Indeed, within five years Dr Perry was a leading figure in another study (the 1985–1986 Blue Ribbon Panel, pp. 151–152) which recommended that concurrency be avoided but that priority be given to testing systems and subsystems before proceeding with full-scale development.

In fact, another high-level report published in 1979, the Defense Resource Management Study requested by President Jimmy Carter and prepared under the chairmanship of Donald B. Rice, President of the Rand Corporation, advocated the view long held by Rand that concurrency invariably results in long and costly modification. In the same year, the General Accounting Office criticized concurrency on the XM-1 tank programme.[180] Within a decade, however, things were to change. A new approach — the new discipline of 'concurrent engineering' — was to become a bedrock of production management best practice (see pp. 295–296).

UK and European defence/ aerospace developments

While the USA struggled to master its deep-seated weapons acquisition management problems, in the UK the 1970s were to see a considerable improvement in defence/aerospace project management. In contrast to the spate of disasters of the 1950s and 1960s, most major projects completed in the 1970s were on time and in budget (note 49).

However, the decade began badly in this regard. Not only did the 1970s begin with Concorde struggling to reduce its cost and

Table 3. Phases and milestones for development and production of military equipment

NATO	Germany	France	UK	USA
Mission analysis				
Mission need document				
Mission need evaluation	Pre-concept phase	Phase préliminaire	Concept phase	Identification of a mission need
Outline NATO staff target				
Pre-feasibility				
NATO staff target	Tactical requirement	Fiche de caracter militaire	Staff target	Milestone 0
Feasibility	Concept phase	Première phase	Feasibility study	Concept exploration
NATO staff requirement	Military technical objective		Staff requirement	Milestone 1
Project definition	Definition phase		Project definition	Demonstration and validation
NATO design and development objectives	Military technical economic requirement	Fiche programme provisoire	Possibly revised staff requirement	Milestone II
		Deuxième phase		
		Rapp. prov. d'experiment		
Design and development	Development phase	Troisième phase	Full development phase	Full-scale development
		Fiche programme complète		
		Quatrième phase		
NATO production objectives	Approval for production	Fiche programme accept.	Approval	Milestone III
Production	Procurement phase	Cinquième phase	Production phase	Production
NATO in-service goals	Final report			
In-service	In-service phase	Sixième phase	In-service phase	Deployment
National Diseng-intention				

schedule overruns, but also Rolls-Royce was experiencing equally embarrassing overruns on its advanced new RB-211 fan engine.

The RB-211 was 'Rolls' most ambitious civil design and had no direct antecedents. Estimates of performance, development times and cost were based on parametric studies of the Spey and earlier, smaller turbo-fan designs. At an early stage, however, Rolls cancelled a three-shaft demonstrator engine, a decision which it later described as 'one of our greatest mistakes'.[181] The project risk was very large both technically and commercially. The RB-211 had been sold as a concept to Lockheed for a fixed unit price, which furthermore had been cut fiercely to beat off US competition. The first estimates of the cost of developing the engine were £65m, but this figure was soon seen to be far too low. By mid-1970 programme costs were already over £169m, with the project six to nine months behind schedule. The Government agreed to finance only a small part of this; additional funds were raised from the banks. Lockheed itself, meanwhile, was in serious trouble, having had to absorb a $200m loss on the C-5A contract; with orders of its Tristar flagging, for which the RB-211 was intended, the situation looked grave. By November 1970, it was apparent that Rolls could not meet its contractual obligations to Lockheed: delivery would be late (thus incurring an estimated £50m of late-delivery penalties), while Rolls would lose an additional £60m on the development contract. This was too great a cost. The Government decided to allow Rolls-Royce to go bankrupt, thereby nullifying the contract with Lockheed. Rolls-Royce was then selectively nationalized. Lockheed, needless to say, was shocked and furious, as were a good many others.

Happily, the RB-211 was largely the exception in UK defence/aerospace in the 1970s. Project management performance improved markedly during the decade, for although industrial restructuring was still causing difficulties, there was a much more professional use of project management tools and techniques in the industry as a whole.

An early indication of this was the 1971 Rayner report on the weapons development process.[182] Many of the points made by Derek Rayner, a director of the retailers Marks & Spencer, who was at the time Special Adviser to the British Government, echoed those made by Downey five years previously (and those being simultaneously espoused by Packard): the need to put *more emphasis on front-end development and to produce early prototype hardware* as the basis for reliable project cost estimates. Unlike Downey, however, Rayner dealt with the anomalies created by the differing roles of the Ministries of Aviation, Supply and Technology (noted on pp. 67–68 in connection with TSR-2). Rayner recommended that the policy and executive functions be split. The Department of Trade and Industry was given responsibility for aerospace policy, while a specialist Procurement

Executive was established within the Ministry of Defence, of which Rayner became Chief Executive (note 50).

The most significant trend of UK aerospace projects in the 1970s, however, in both the military and the civil fields, was that of international collaboration. Although championed by Plowden in 1965, moves towards international co-operation had in fact been initiated before the TSR-2 was finally cancelled. The 150 TSR-2s then on order, it was suggested, should be replaced by 50 F-111s and 100 Anglo-French Variable Geometry (AFVG) fighter–bombers. The British had proposed the AFVG to the French as a package deal with an advanced trainer, but the French unilaterally withdrew from the AFVG in July 1967, ostensibly 'on financial grounds' but in reality because Marcel Dassault wanted a swing-wing project of his own, the F1. (As a result, Britain switched to the F104-G replacement discussions that eventually led to the Tornado.) However, the trainer survived, substantially transformed, to become the Jaguar fighter/trainer. Learning from Concorde, it was seen that a separate management company was needed to control such a large collaborative project. In May 1966, an airframe company was established in Paris and an engine company was established in London. The first prototype was rolled out in April 1968 and went into operation in June 1973 (note 51).

Following the F104-G replacement studies, a Memorandum of Understanding for a new Multi-Role Combat Aircraft (MRCA) was announced in 1968. This was to be the Tornado (Fig. 29), to be developed jointly by West Germany, Italy and the UK (note 52) using an organization structure based on the experience of Jaguar. A separate company, Panavia, was established to build the plane, headed by Dr Gero Madelung, a nephew of Wilhelm Messerschmidt and an outstanding leader and engineer, and

Fig. 29. Tornado: GRMK-1 (top) and FMK-3 (bottom) (courtesy British Aerospace Defence Ltd)

composed initially of Messerschmidt, British Aircraft Corporation and Fiat. A special customer organization, NATO MRCA Development and Production Management Organization (NAMMO), was also created. Work was shared on the basis of predicted purchase quantities. Specifications were drawn largely around Britain's industrial experience and capability (thereby facilitating greatly the development of workable staff specifications).

Initially the avionics were to be a separate contract but, having learned from TSR-2, it was decided to make Panavia responsible for the avionics as well as the airframe. The engines, the RB-199, were developed separately by Turbo-Union, a company owned jointly by Rolls-Royce, Fiat and MTU (Man Turbo and Daimler Benz) after competition with General Electric, and Pratt and Witney, initially on a maximum-price basis but later as cost-reimbursable. The RB-199 was developed on a crash basis without a demonstration or definitive rig testing: this led to increased costs and some initial performance problems.

A Programme Management System was installed in 1969 which included the general repertoire of project management techniques now considered standard — Work Breakdown Structure, Programme Control Centre, Configuration Management, Systems Specification Tree, Data Management System, C/SCSC (note 53). The project was developed essentially within budget and to schedule, although inflation had increased costs (note 54). In operation, Tornado has proved excellent, as have its foreign sales.

Jaguar and Tornado illustrate the way in which international collaboration impacted on project management practices in the European aerospace community. There were also important moves towards increased collaboration in civil aerospace. These were complex and need not be traced in detail in this history of modern project management (note 55).

Collaboration in space was similarly well advanced by the early 1970s. The European Launcher Development Organization (ELDO) had been formed in 1962−1964 to develop a three-stage launcher, Europa, based on the Blue Streak rocket (which Britain had developed and — characteristically — just abandoned in mid-project). In 1973 the French proposed that there be a new European Space Agency (ESA) to develop among other things a new launch vehicle, Ariane (note 56). ESA was formally created in 1975 and was to play a significant role in the major space projects of the 1980s and 1990s. The management of the ESA projects has in general been of a very high standard, as Dr Hough's and my account of ESA's Giotto spacecraft attests (chapter 9 of ref. 108). (As that account demonstrates, the management practices of ESA owe a lot to those of NASA, and hence to the USAF and the Anderson Committee — for example in the life-cycle phasing.)

By the end of the decade, then, there were many indications

that the European aerospace industry had got its act together increasingly well, in that collaboration was now generally working effectively and successful projects were being produced. This pattern has largely persisted throughout the 1980s, in contrast, sadly, to the US space programme.

The US space programme: the Shuttle

With the landings on the moon, NASA found itself in major trouble. The country's foremost project management agency suddenly had no agreed major programmes to execute, or even a strategy for selection of possible candidates. NASA had been so hugely absorbed in the management mechanics of Apollo that efforts to develop future strategies had been seen as a distraction. The real problem, though, was not managerial short-sightedness, but funding. Space projects are exceedingly expensive. The social and economic climate of the early 1970s was very different from that of the early 1960s, and in Nixon, the agency had a very different President from Kennedy.

Nixon did two things that were to be major blows to NASA. First, and most obvious, he was exceedingly loathe to authorize substantial expenditure on space programmes. Second, and of longer-term, subtler consequence, he introduced a greater number of political appointees into the senior echelons of the agency.

Vice-President Agnew was assigned to head a task force in 1969 to develop a future plan for US civil operations in space. In September 1969, Agnew recommended three options

- an $8−10bn per year programme to include a manned mission to Mars, a lunar orbiting space station and a 50-person earth-orbiting space station, and a space shuttle
- an intermediate programme costing less than $8bn per year but including the Mars mission
- a relatively modest $4−5·7bn per year programme to include an earth-orbiting space station and a space shuttle.

In March 1970, to the surprise of many, Nixon, while affirming the space station as a longer-term aim, chose to proceed only with the Shuttle. NASA, meanwhile, had given way to Nixon's request, under pressure from the Office of Management and Budget, and cancelled the Apollo programme before it had fulfilled its planned series of missions.

Many senior members of the Nixon administration were openly hostile to the Shuttle, not least the President himself and his budget office. To strengthen the candidature of the project, NASA, somewhat desperately, accepted in a fateful decision that the Shuttle should also be used by the USAF. Politically, NASA was now very much the weaker of these two; in order to advance the programme it soon began to give way substantially to USAF requirements — a cross-range landing capability of 3000 miles; communications and avionics that were electronically 'secure' and immune to nuclear explosion; and most traumatically of all to the traditional ethos of NASA, classification of the programme.

Thomas Paine was replaced as NASA Administrator in 1971 by James Fletcher. Fletcher too was unenthusiastic towards the Shuttle, at least initially, and readily acquiesced to several redesigns aimed at reducing the programme's costs. The initial design had been for a two-stage, fully reusable manned booster as well as the orbiter, in which propellants would be carried internally, designed expressly to shuttle people and equipment up to the space station. This version was huge, however, and its estimated development cost of $10—13bn was too high for Nixon. The reusable system was thus abandoned. For the same reason (cost minimization), solid rockets were selected as boosters, instead of liquid, very much against (a now politically much weaker) von Braun's better judgement. (Liquid fuel, carried in an expendable external tank, was retained for the orbiter's engines.) An escape system for the astronauts was similarly excluded on grounds of cost.

The Office of Management and Budget insisted on having a cost-effective justification for the programme. Figures were dredged up based on absurdly high numbers of launches — everything the USA might hope to launch was assumed to go by the Shuttle. NASA's estimate for this version of the craft was about $6·5bn; ultimately the White House accepted $5·1bn.

Shortly after Carter became President in 1971, Fletcher resigned and the Shuttle came under renewed scrutiny. Major difficulties began to emerge in several areas, particularly systems design, flight controls, boosters and engine testing. Substantial cost overruns and schedule delays began to surface, causing considerable embarrassment. The initial test flights were delayed by more than two years. Fortunately, the Shuttle now had new allies in the USAF, notably the new Under Secretary, Hans Mark. As military and civilian planning became increasingly interwoven, the rising costs of the programme meant that the number of orbiters being built was reduced from five to four. Further troubles arose after the first orbiter, Columbia (Fig. 30), made the first test flight (staying within the Earth's atmosphere) in March 1979, and in so doing lost several of the tiles that comprised its insulating skin. Resolution of the tile problem was another embarrassing and lengthy affair. By November 1979 cost overruns were forecast to be $1bn (bringing the cost to $6·2bn in 1972 dollars — almost NASA's initial estimate). Carter was furious, but the programme was now receiving the full support of Defense Secretary Harold Brown and Mark, newly promoted to Air Force Secretary. The price of their support, however, was yet more Air Force control, particularly in determining the programming of operational flights.

Ronald Reagan became President in January 1981. Within three months Columbia was successfully launched. Five years later and after 20 operational Shuttle launches, on 28 January 1986 the

Shuttle Challenger exploded at 65 000 ft, 73 seconds after take-off, killing its crew of seven. The tragedy that so many had feared for so long had at last occurred.

Even as Reagan took over from Carter as President, many in NASA were deeply concerned about the viability of the Shuttle programme, and indeed about NASA's management in general. The Columbia that lifted off in 1981 was an unproven rocket system. The challenges were enormous — much greater than most people realized. No craft of anything like the orbiter's size had ever re-entered the earth's atmosphere; the consequences of engine misfiring, computer malfunction or countless other comparatively minor mishaps would be catastrophic. Yet the processes that had enabled NASA to manage Apollo so supremely well had by the end of the 1970s deteriorated drastically. There was no longer the sense of personal accountability within NASA; paperwork was not as rigorously attended to as before; the procedures for ensuring quality were sometimes ignored. Underappreciated and underpaid, NASA Shuttle staff were immensely over-pressured to get the craft up and operational.

Fig. 30. The Space Shuttle Columbia on lift-off, 25 June 1992 (courtesy NASA)

'The space agency that was a remarkably effective and very special organization had continued to deteriorate during the Carter years. By the end of 1980, NASA's capability to technically verify any contractor's work had all but vanished. By the end of 1980, the NASA that was once the toughest quality-control operation in or out of government was now depending on the military for many of its inspections. And by the end of 1980, the NASA veterans who fought the hardest for safety were leaving.'[183]

References

1. Henderson, P. D. Two British errors: their probable size and some possible lessons. *Oxford Economic Papers*, 1977, **29**, No. 2, July, 159–204.
2. Horwitch, M. *Clipped wings: the American SST.* MIT Press, Cambridge, MA, 1982.
3. Parsons, Brinckerhoff, Hall and McDonal. *Regional rapid transit 1953–55: a report to the San Francisco Bay Area Rapid Transit Commission.* San Francisco, 1962, p. 3. Quoted in Hall, P. *Great planning disasters.* Weidenfeld & Nicolson, London, 1980, p. 116.
4. Burns, L. S. Cost–benefit analysis of a housing project. *Development Digest*, USAID, 4 April 1966.
5. Divine, E. J. The treatment of incommensurables in cost–benefit analysis. *Land Economics*, 1966, Aug.
6. Hines, L. The hazards of benefit–cost analysis as a guide to public investment policy. *Public Finance*, 1962.
7. Gittinger, J. P. *Economic analysis of agricultural projects.* Johns Hopkins University Press, Baltimore, 1972.
8. Hiurichs, H. H. and Taylor, G. M. *Program planning and benefit–cost analysis.* Goodyear, Pacific Palisades, CA, 1969.
9. Kendall, M. G. *Cost–benefit analysis*, Elsevier, New York, 1971.
10. Layard, R. *Cost–benefit analysis: selected readings.* Penguin, Harmondsworth, 1972.
11. Little, I. M. D. and Mirlees, J. A. *Project appraisal and planning for developing countries.* Heinemann, London, 1974.

12. Mishan, E. J. *Cost benefit analysis*. George Allen & Unwin, 1971.
13. Pearce, D. W. *Cost benefit analysis*. Macmillan, London, 1971.
14. Prest, A. R. and Turvey. Cost/benefit analysis: a survey. *The Economic Journal*, 1965, Dec.
15. Quade, E. S. and Boucher, W. I. (eds). *Systems analysis and policy planning: applications in defense*. Elsevier, New York, 1968.
16. Sassone, P. G. and Schaffer, W. A. *Cost benefit analysis: a handbook*. Academic Press, New York, 1978.
17. O'Riordan, T. and Sewell, W. R. D. *Project appraisal and policy review*. Wiley, Chichester, 1981, p. 13.
18. Wildawsky, A. The political economy of efficiency: cost benefit analysis, systems analysis and program budgeting. *Public Administration Review*, **26**, 292–310.
19. Geistants, G. and Hauck, V. *Trans Alaskan Pipeline*. East–West Center, East–West Resource Systems Institute, Honolulu, 1979.
20. Moolin, F. P. and McCoy, F. The organization and management of large projects: realities *vs.* theory. *Proc. 1979 Project Management Institute Symp., Atlanta*, Drexel Hill, PA, 1979.
21. Reis de Carvalho, E. and Morris, P. W. G. Project matrix organizations — or how to do the matrix swing. *Proc. 1978 Project Management Institute Symp., Los Angeles*, Project Management Institute, Drexel Hill, PA, 1978.
22. Morris, P. W. G. Managing project interfaces — key points for project success. In *Project management handbook*, Cleland, D. I. and King, W. R. (eds), Van Nostrand Reinhold, New York, 1988, chapter 2.
23. Moolin, F. P. The effective project management organization for giant projects. In *The successful accomplishment of giant projects*, Sykes, A. (ed.), Willis Faber, London, 1979.
24. Kelly, J. F. *Computerized management information systems*. Macmillan, New York, 1970.
25. Bennigson, L. A. *Project management*, McGraw-Hill, New York, 1970.
26. Taylor, W. J. and Watling, T. F. *Successful project management*, Basic, London, 1970.
27. Sayles, L. R. and Chandler, M. K. *Managing large systems, organizations for the future*. Harper & Row, New York, 1971.
28. Logistics Management Institute, *Introduction to military program management*. US Government Printing Office, Washington, DC, 1971.
29. Peart, A. T. *Design of project management systems and records*. Gower, London, 1971.
30. Sapolsky, H. *The Polaris system development: bureaucratic and programmatic success in government*. Harvard University Press, Cambridge, MA, 1972.
31. Wadsworth, M. *EDP project management controls*. Prentice Hall, Englewood Cliffs, NJ, 1972.
32. Chapman, R. L. *Project management in NASA: the system and the men*. National Aeronautics and Space Administration, US Government Printing Office, Washington, DC, 1973.
33. Hoare, H. R. *Project management using network analysis*. McGraw-Hill, New York, 1973.
34. Metzger, P. W. *Managing a programming project*. Prentice Hall, Englewood Cliffs, NJ, 1973.
35. Pilcher, R. *Appraisal and control of project costs*. McGraw-Hill, London, 1973.
36. Wearne, S. H. *Principles of engineering organization*. Edward Arnold, London, 1973.
37. Whitehouse, G. E. *Systems analysis and design using network*

techniques. Prentice Hall, Englewood Cliffs, NJ, 1973.

38. Ludwig, E. L. *Applied project management for the process industries.* Gulf, Houston, 1974.

39. Archibald, R. L. *Managing high-technology programs and projects.* Wiley, New York, 1976.

40. Davis, E. W. *Project management: techniques, applications and managerial issues.* Publication No. 3, AIIE (Production Planning and Control Division), 1976.

41. Martin, C. C. *Project management: how to make it work.* Amacom, New York, 1976.

42. Peddie, R. A. *The management of high-technology projects.* Central Electricity Generating Board, Barnwood, Gloucestershire, 1976.

43. Silverman, M. *Project management: a short course for professionals.* Wiley, New York, 1976.

44. Snowden, M. *Management of engineering projects.* Newnes Butterworth, London, 1977.

45. Maciariello, J. A. *Program management control systems.* Wiley, New York, 1978.

46. Adams, J. R., Brandt, S. E. and Martin, M. D. *Managing by project management.* Universal Technology Corporation, Dayton, 1979.

47. Baumgartner, J. S. *Systems management.* Bureau of National Affairs, Washington, DC, 1979.

48. Davies, C., Demb, A. and Espejo, R. *Organization for program management.* Wiley, New York, 1979.

49. Hill, R. and White, B. J. *Matrix organization and project management.* Michigan Business Paper No. 64, University of Michigan, 1979.

50. Kerzner, H. *Project management: a systems approach to planning, scheduling and controlling.* Van Nostrand Reinhold, New York, 1979.

51. Cleland, D. I. and King, W. R. *Management: a systems approach.* McGraw-Hill, New York, 1972.

52. Johnson, R. A., Kast, F. E. and Rosenzweig, J. E. *The theory and management of systems.* McGraw-Hill, New York, 1973.

53. Kingdon, D. R. *Matrix organization: managing information technologies.* Tavistock, London, 1973.

54. Pressman, J. L. and Wildavsky, A. *Implementation.* University of California Press, Los Angeles, 1973.

55. Caro, R. A. *The power broker.* Alfred A. Knopf, New York, 1974.

56. Fox, J. R.. *Arming America: how the US buys weapons.* Harvard University, Boston, MA, 1974.

57. Squire, L. and van der Tak, H. G. *Economic analysis of projects.* Johns Hopkins University Press, Baltimore, 1975.

58. Wood, D. *Project cancelled.* McDonald and Janes, London, 1975.

59. Davis, S. M. and Lawrence, P. R. *Matrix.* Addison-Wesley, Reading, MA, 1977.

60. Delp, P., Thesen, A., Motiwalla, J. and Seshadri, N. *Systems tools for project planning.* International Development Institute, Indiana University, Bloomington, 1977.

61. Fisk, E. R. *Construction project administration.* Wiley, New York, 1978.

62. Stinchcombe, A. L. *Delays and project administration in the North Sea.* Rapport 14, Institute of Industrial Economics, Bergen, 1979.

63. Cicero, J. P. and Wilemon, D. L. Project authority: a multi-dimensional view. *IEEE Transactions and Engineering Management*, 1970, **EM-17**, 52−57.

64. Gemmill, G. R. and Wilemon, D. L. The power spectrum in project management. *Sloan Management Review*, 1970, **12**, No. 4, 15−25.

65. Wilemon, D. L. Project management conflict: a view from Apollo.

Proc. 3rd Annual Symp. Project Management Institute, Houston, Project Management Institute, Drexel Hill, PA, October 1971.

66. Wilemon, D. L. and Gemmill, G. R. Interpersonal power in temporary management systems. *Journal of Management Studies,* 1971, **8**, Oct., 315–328.

67. Bennigson, L. A. The strategy of running temporary projects. *Innovation,* 24 September, 1971, 32–40.

68. Perry, R. L., Smith, G. K., Harman, A. J. and Henrichsen, S. *System acquisition strategies.* Rand Corporation, R-733-PR/ARPA, Santa Monica, CA., June, 1971.

69. Jonason, P. Project management, Swedish style. *Harvard Business Review,* 1971, Nov.–Dec., 104–109.

70. Maeli, V. Management with hindsight: diary of a project manager. *Management Review,* 1971, **60**, June, 4–14.

71. Olsen, R. P. Can project management be defined? *Project Management Quarterly,* 1971, **2**, No. 1, 12–14.

72. Davis, E. W. and Hiedorn, G. E. An algorithm for optimal project scheduling under multiple resource constraints. *Management Science,* 1971, **17**, No. 12, Aug., B803–B816.

73. Moder, J. J., Clark, R. A. and Gomez, R. S. Application of a GERT simulated to a repetitive hardware development type project. *AIIE Transactions,* 1971, **3**, No. 4, 271–280.

74. Arisawa, S. and Elmaghraby, S. E. Optimal time–cost trade-offs in GERT networks. *Management Science,* 1972, **18**, No. 11, July, 589–599.

75. Bennigson, L. A. The team approach to project management. *Management Review,* 1972, **61**, Jan., 48–52.

76. Butler, A. G. Project management: a study in organizational conflict. *Academy of Management Journal,* 1973, **16**, Mar., 84–101.

77. Crandall, K. Project planning with precedence lead/lag factors. *Project Management Quarterly,* 1973, **4**, No. 3.

78. Davis, E. W. Project scheduling under resource constraints: historical review and categorization of procedures. *AIIE Transactions,* 1973, Dec.

79. Jennett, E. Guidelines for successful project management. *Chemical Engineering,* 9 July, 1973, 70–82.

80. Gemmill, G. R. The effectiveness of different power styles of project managers in gaining project support. *Project Management Quarterly,* 1974, **5**, No. 1.

81. Baker, B. N. and Fisher, D. Cost growth: can it be controlled? *Project Management Quarterly,* 1974, **5**.

82. Avots, I. Nuclear plant delays challenge project management. *Project Management Quarterly,* 1974, **5**, No. 1.

83. Bobrowski, T. M. A basic philosophy of project management. *Journal of Systems Management,* 1974, May–June.

84. Large, J. P. *Bias in initial cost estimates: how low estimates can increase the cost of acquiring weapons systems.* Rand Corporation, R-1467-PA & E, Santa Monica, CA, July, 1974.

85. Maciariello, J. A. Making program management work. *Journal of Systems Management,* 1974, July.

86. Thamhain, H. J. and Wilemon, D. L. Conflict management in project-oriented work environments. *Proc. 6th Annual Int. Meeting of the Project Management Institute,* 1974, Project Management Institute, Drexel Hill, PA, 1974.

87. Murphy, D. C., Baker, B. N. and Fisher, D. *Determinants of project success.* National Technical Information Services, Springfield, 1974.

88. Morton, D. H. The project manager, catalyst to constant change: a

behaviourial analysis. *Project Management Quarterly*, 1975, **6**, No. 1, 22–23.

89. Thamhain, H. J. and Wilemon, D. L. Conflict management in project life cycles. *Sloan Management Review*, 1975, Summer.

90. Barndt, S. E. Some formal education and experienced background implications for project managers. *Project Management Quarterly*, 1975, **6**, No. 4.

91. Avots, I. Making project management work — the right tool for the wrong project manager, *Advanced Management Journal*, 1975, Autumn.

92. Rondinelli, D. A. Why development projects fail: problems of project management in developing countries. *Project Management Quarterly*, 1976, **7**, No. 1.

93. Rondinelli, D. A. Project identification in economic development. *Journal of World Trade Law*, 1976, **10**, May–June.

94. Baker, B. N. and Wilemon, D. L. A summary of major research findings regarding the human element in project management. *Project Management Quarterly*, 1974, **5**, No. 2, 227–230.

95. Wilemon, D. L. and Thamhain, H. J. Leadership effectiveness in program management. *Project Management Quarterly*, 1977, **8**, No. 2.

96. Youker, R. Organizational alternatives for project management. *Project Management Quarterly*, 1977, **8**, No. 1.

97. Wiest, J. D. Project network models: past, present and future. *Project Management Quarterly*, 1977, **8**, No. 4.

98. Cook, D. L. Certification of project managers — fantasy or reality? *Project Management Quarterly*, 1977, **8**, No. 2.

99. O'Brien, J. J. Project management: an overview. *Project Management Quarterly*, 1977, **8**, No. 3.

100. Barnes, N. M. L. Cost modelling: an integrated approach to planning and cost control. *American Association of Chemical Engineers Transactions*, 1977, Mar.

101. Johnson, J. R. Advanced project control. *Journal of Systems Management*, 1977, May.

102. Cochran, E. G., Patz, A. L. and Rowe, A. J. Concurrency and disruption in new product innovation. *California Management Review*, 1978, Fall.

103. Souder, W. E. Effectiveness of product development methods. *Industrial Marketing Management*, 1978, **7**, 299–307.

104. Moolin, F. P. and McCoy, F. The organization and management of large projects: realities *vs.* theory. *Proc. Project Management Institute Symp., Atlanta*, Drexel Hill, PA, 1979.

105. Morris, P. W. G. Interface management — an organization theory approach to project management. *Project Management Quarterly*, 1979, **10**, No. 2.

106. Merrow, E., Chapel, S. W. and Worthing, C. A. *A review of cost estimation in new technologies: implications for energy process plants.* Rand Corporation, R-2481-DOE, Santa Monica, CA, July 1979.

107. Kerzner, H. Formal education for project management. *Project Management Quarterly*, 1979, **10**, No. 2.

108. Morris, P. W. G. and Hough, G. H. *The anatomy of major projects.* Wiley, Chichester, 1988, chapter 5.

109. Jacques, R. G. *Current techniques in architectural practice.* American Institute of Architects, Washington, DC and Architectural Record, New York, 1976.

110. Platt, J., The development of SEAC. *RIBA Journal*, 1969, **76**, No. 5, May, 200–202.

111. Boyce, J. R. What is the systems approach? *Progressive Architecture*,

1969, Nov., 118−121.

112. Morris, P. W. G. Influences of design upon production. *Building Technology and Management*, 1971, **9**, No. 10, 6−9.

113. Sliwa, J. Why performance specification? *Architects Journal*, 1971, **153**, No. 9, 462−465.

114. Bishop, D. Architects and productivity. *RIBA Journal*, 1966, **73**, No. 11, Nov., 513−518.

115. Bishop, D. The economics of industrialised building. *Chartered Surveyor*, 1976, **99**, No. 4, Oct., 196−205.

116. Cheney, R. H. Construction managers set design parameters. *Progressive Architects*, 1969, May, 133−142.

117. Foxhall, W. B. *Professional construction management and project administration*. The American Institute of Architects and Architectural Record, New York/Washington, 1972.

118. General Services Administration − Public Building Service. *Construction contracting systems − a report on the systems used by TVA and other organizations*. Washington, DC, 1970.

119. Carter, J. Management contracting: the Horizon project. *Architects Journal*, **157**, 14 February, 1973, 395−400.

120. Carter, J. Management contracting. *Architects Journal*, **156**, 13 December, 1972, 1371−1374.

121. Morris, P. W. G. Organizational analysis of project management in the building industry. *Build International*, 1973, **6**, Nov./Dec., 595−616.

122. National Economic Development Office. *The public client and the construction industries*. HMSO, London, 1975.

123. Department of Energy. *North Sea costs escalation study*. HMSO, 1976.

124. Crauli, O., Hetland, P. W. and Rolstadas, A. *Applied project management − experience from exploration on the Norwegian Continental Shelf*. Tapir (for the Norwegian Association of Cost and Planning Engineering), Oslo, 1986.

125. Marr, T. O. Project services concept − Merchant Field. *Proc. European Offshore Petroleum Conf.*, 1982.

126. Gaisford, R. W. Project management in the North Sea, *International Journal of Project Management*, 1986, **4**, No. 1, Feb., 5−12.

127. Hetland, P. W. What did 20 years of petroleum activities in the North Sea add to our general knowledge of project management? *Proc. Nordnet−Internet PMI Conf.*, Reykjavik, 1987.

128. Davies, J. *Client organization project management techniques in British North Sea developments*. MSc dissertation, Cranfield School of Management, 1983.

129. Graham, R. The future of project management: some North Sea experiences. *International Journal of Project Management*, 1988, **6**, No. 3, 153−163.

130. Nevitt, P. K. *Project financing*, Euromoney, London, 1983.

131. Murphy, K. J. *Macroproject development in the Third World*. Westview, Boulder, 1983.

132. *World Bank Annual Report 1980*. World Bank, Washington, DC, 1980.

133. United Nations Department of Economic and Social Affairs, Division of Public Administration and Finance. *Development administration: current approaches and trends in public administration for national development*. United Nations, New York, 1975, p. 45.

134. Ingle, M. D. *Implementing development programs: a state-of-the-art review*. Agency for International Development, Washington, DC, Jan. 1979.

135. Rondinelli, D. A. *Planning Development Projects*. Dowden, Hutchinson

and Ross, Stroudsburg, PA, 1977, p. 20.

136. Schumacher, E. F. *Small is beautiful*. Blond and Briggs, London, 1973.

137. Hirschman, A. O. *Development projects observed*. The Brookings Institution, Washington, DC, 1967.

138. United Nations Public Administration Division. Some aspects of administration of projects within the context of development planning. In *Administrative aspects of planning*, United Nations, New York, 1969.

139. Goldschmidt, B. *The atomic complex*. American Nuclear Society, La Grange Park, IL, 1982.

140. Hewlett, R. G. and Duncan, F. *Nuclear Navy 1946–1962*. The University of Chicago Press, 1974.

141. Lewis, E. *Public entrepreneurship: toward a theory of bureaucratic political power*. Indiana University Press, Lymington, IL, 1980.

142. Polmar, N. and Allen, T. B. *Rickover: controversy and genius*. Simon & Schuster, New York, 1982.

143. Bupp, I. C. and Derian, J-C. *Light water: how the nuclear dream dissolved*. Basic, New York, 1978.

144. *Annual Report to Congress for 1974*. US Atomic Energy Commission, Washington, DC, 1974.

145. Gándara, A. *Electric utility decision making and the nuclear option*. The Rand Corporation, R-2148-NSF, June, 1987.

146. Perry, R. *et al. Development and commercialization of the Light Water Reactor, 1946–1976*. The Rand Corporation, R-2180-NSF, June 1977.

147. Hazelrigg, G. A. and Roth, E. B. *Windows for innovation: the story of two large-scale technologies*. NSF 82-180-1, National Science Foundation, Washington, DC, 1982.

148. Mason, G. E., Laren, R. E., Borcherding, J. D., Oakes, S. R. and Rad, P. F. *Delays in nuclear power plant construction*. US Energy Research and Development Administration, E(11-1)-4121, Washington, DC, December 1977, p. 2–18.

149. Olds, F. C. Regulatory growth: impact on power plant planning and construction. *Power Engineering*, 1977, May, 40–47.

150. Department of Energy, *Nuclear plant cancellations: causes, costs and consequences*. DoE/EIA-0392, Department of Energy, Washington, DC, April 1983, p. 19.

151. Blumstein, M. The lessons of a bond failure. *New York Times*, 14 August 1983.

152. Lewin, T. Power group says it can't pay off $2·25 billion debt. *New York Times*, 26 July 1983.

153. Ridley, S. Nuclear power bankrupts North-West. *Environmental Action*, 1983, July/Aug.

154. Fallout from 'Whoops': a default looms casting a pall over the entire municipal market. *Business Week*, 1983, July.

155. Washington State Senate Energy and Utilities Committee. *Causes of cost overruns and schedule delays on the 5 WPPSS nuclear power plants*. Vols 1 and 2, Olympia, WA, January 1981.

156. Davidson, F. P. Macro-engineering: a capability in search of a methodology. *Futures*, 1968, **1**, No. 2, Dec., 153–161.

157. *Planning, engineering and construction of super projects. Proc. Engineering Foundation Research Conf.*, American Society of Civil Engineers, New York, 1978.

158. Sykes, A. (ed.). *The successful accomplishment of giant projects*. Willis Faber, London, 1979.

159. *Acquisition of major defense systems. Department of Defense Directive 5000.1*, Washington, DC, 1971, 13 July.

160. Blue Ribbon Defense Panel. *Report to the President and Secretary of Defense on the Department of Defense.* December 1972.

161. Quoted in Fox. J. R. *Arming America: how the US buys weapons.* Harvard University, Boston, MA, 1974, p. 455.

162. Hunt, R. G., Rubin, I. S. and Perry, F. A. Federal procurement: a study with some pertinent properties, policies and practices of a group of business organizations. *National Contract Management Journal,* 1970, Fall, 245−299.

163. Reece, J. S. *The effect of contract changes on the control of a major defense weapon system program.* Unpublished doctoral dissertation, Harvard Business School, Boston, 1970, pp. 5−38.

164. Scherer, F. M. *The weapons acquisition process: economic incentives.* Harvard Business School, Boston, 1964, p. 257.

165. Steiner, G. A. and Ryan, W. E. *Industrial project management,* Macmillan, New York, 1968, pp. 88 ff.

166. Little, A. D. *Survey relating to the implementation of cost/schedule control systems criteria within the Department of Defense and Industry.* Unpublished report for the Assistant Secretary of Defense, December, 1983.

167. Campbell, R. H. A system for measuring cost and schedule performance. *Proc. American Association of Cost Engineers Annual Symp.,* 1978, pp. 14−23.

168. Energy Research and Development Administration. *PMS system description,* RDD/PMS-1, Department of Energy, Washington, DC, 28 January 1977.

169. Acker, D. D. The maturing of the DoD acquisition process. *Defense Systems Management Review,* 1980, **3**, No. 3, 17−25.

170. Rice, D. B. *Final report, defense resource management study.* Cited in Harvey, T. E. Concurrency today in acquisition management. *Defense Systems Management Review,* 1980, **3**, No. 1, Winter, 14−18.

171. Logistics Management Institute. *An examination of the foundations of incentive contracts.* LMI Task 66−67, May 1968.

172. Fisher, I. N. *Controlling defense procurement costs: an evaluation of incentive contracting experience.* Rand, Santa Monica, CA, November 1968.

173. Alexander, A. J. Appendix B in Johnson, L. L., Merrow, E. W., Baer, W. A. and Alexander, A. *Alternative institutional arrangements for developing and commercializing breeder reactor technology.* Rand Corporation, R-2069-NSF, Santa Monica, CA, November 1976.

174. Rand Corporation. *A preliminary analysis of contractual outcomes for 94 AFSC contracts.* Rand-WN-7117, Santa Monica, CA, December 1970.

175. Army Procurement Office. *An analysis of 200 army incentive contracts.* Fort Lee, VA., March 1971.

176. *Report of the Commission on Government Procurement.* US Government Printing Office, Washington, DC, December 1972.

177. Hall, A. D. *A methodology for systems engineering.* Van Nostrand, Princeton, 1962.

178. Van Court Hare, *Systems analysis: a diagnostic approach.* Harcourt, Brace & World, New York, 1967.

179. Perry, W. J. *The FY 1980 Department of Defense Program for Research, Development and Acquisition.* Statement to the Congress of the United States, 96th Congress, First Session. 21 February 1979, pp. 11−15.

180. Stolarow, J. H. *Letter to the Honourable Harold Brown, Secretary of Defense, 12th April 1979 from Director, Procurement and Systems Acquisition Division, United States General Accounting Office.* GAO reference no. B-163058.

181. Hayward, K. *Government and British civil aerospace*. Manchester University Press, 1983, p. 103.
182. *Government Organisation for Defence Procurement and Civil Aerospace*. Cmnd 4641, HMSO, London, 1971.
183. Trento, J. J. *Prescription for disaster*. Crown, New York, 1987, p. 176.

7. The 1980s: expansion of the strategic perspective of managing projects

The twin major events of the 1980s projects world were the sharp fall in the price of oil in 1981 and the Third World debt crisis a year later. These were to lead to a dramatic restructuring of demand for much if not most construction work, and to force contractors to rethink their strategies and approaches to projects. Information technology (IT) also came to the fore, by enabling project management techniques to be used more easily and as an important class of projects in its own right.

The 1980s were to see project management begin to become a 'mature' management discipline, with degree programmes and professional certification beginning in the USA. Publications became fatter, though not necessarily sharper: while project management tools and techniques developed, largely because of technological developments in computing, the steam appeared to have left much of the writing on organizational matters. With considerable apparent consensus on how to manage several difficult types of project — defence, nuclear power, IT, R&D — and with the rise of contractor sponsored build−own−operate(−transfer) projects, the importance of managing external factors in addition to the project's technical development and implementation became increasingly evident. These important developments began a move towards broadening the subject from 'project management' to 'the management of projects'.

Before discussing these trends it may be as well, so as not to lose the thread, so to speak, to continue the review of the development of Project and Program Management in the industry where so much of project management started: defence.

US defence procurement

When Ronald Reagan became President of the USA in January 1981, he launched the biggest peacetime military build-up in American history — over a trillion and a half dollars were spent on defence during the first four years of his Presidency. This was to stretch the Pentagon's acquisition resources to the limit.

On assuming office in 1981, Defense Secretary Caspar Weinberger launched a 32-point programme to improve the DoD's procurement. By 1986, although there was some improvement, the General Accounting Office found that 23 of the 32 points were still not fully implemented, and programmes were generally less

Fig. 31. XM-1 tank which experienced a $13 bn overrun (see note 1) (courtesy Jane's Information Group)

stable than they had been in 1983.[1] In fact, the decade was to see dozens of examples of badly overrun projects and much bruising criticism of the DoD's practice of Project and Program Management.

Provoked, perhaps, by the huge sums being spent, the media were eagle-eyed for any evidence of waste or inefficiency. There was no shortage of such evidence. In the early 1980s, schedule delays of about 33% were being experienced on approximately half of DoD's programmes, with the costs of more than nine out of ten programmes exceeding their initial estimate. The average cost overrun was more than 50%, excluding the effects of quantity changes and inflation (note 1).[2,3]

In May 1985 the Pentagon admitted to having paid $659 each for seven plastic ashtrays installed in the Navy's E-2C Early Warning planes. Similar examples of gross overspending were revealed: $347 hammers, $640 toilet seats, $3046 coffee makers, and so on. There were understandable reasons why some of these costs were so high — distributed overheads, for example. Others, however, were undeniably excessive — as a consequence, for example, of unnecessarily demanding specifications and of not procuring 'off-the-shelf' items. The media, and some Congressmen, made hay with the stories. A tide of criticism mounted, as a direct result of which President Reagan ordered a Blue Ribbon Panel in July 1985 to study the entire method of DoD management and organization. The panel, which included prominent officials such as Nicholas Brady, Frank Carlucci, Barber Conable and William Perry, was headed by David Packard, and reported in 1986. It concluded that the gold-plating 'horror stories' were merely symptoms of much more severe problems in the acquisitions process. In a swingeing indictment, the panel concluded that:

With notable exceptions, weapons systems take too long and cost too much to produce. Too often, they do not perform as promised or expected. The reasons are numerous.

Over the long-term, there has been chronic instability in top-line funding and, even worse, in programs .... Federal law governing procurement has become overwhelmingly complex .... Responsibility for acquisition, execution, and accountability for its results have become vastly diluted .... Deficiencies in the senior-level appointment system have complicated the recruitment of top executive personnel with industrial and acquisition experience .... A better job of determining requirements and estimating costs has been needed at the outset .... All too often, requirements for new weapons systems have been overstated .... Developmental and operational testing have been too divorced [note 2].[4]

The principles of managing projects successfully were now essentially known, and probably had been since Polaris, Minuteman and Apollo. The key point was that *the organizational and institutional context* within which DoD projects were being undertaken was not allowing project management to be practised as effectively as it could be. Better organization of the acquisition process, more sensitive use of technology, balanced cost and performance trade-offs, greater programme stability, increased use of competition, clearer command channels, enhanced quality of personnel, more limited reporting requirements — all these, the Blue Ribbon Panel believed, were necessary institutional improvements if DoD programmes were to be better managed.

As a result of the panel's recommendations, a new post of Under Secretary, Defense Acquisition was created in 1986, and on designated 'defense enterprise programs' the DoD Program Manager was given direct access to the Secretary of Defense; for some selected projects, (carefully constrained) five-year funding was arranged; a Defense Acquisition Board replaced the Defense Systems Acquisition Board. Yet few observers expected any of these changes to make much difference, particularly as long as programmes were managed individually by the separate military arms.

J. Ronald Fox, in his 1988 book *The defense management challenge*, pursued further many of the Packard Commission's themes, although stressing relentlessly the great inadequacy of DoD policies with respect to the *training and experience of personnel* assigned to manage large development and production programmes. While DoD Program Managers had maximum responsibility, Fox observed, they had minimal authority; they spent too large a proportion of their time briefing interested parties, and they did not control contracting, or often indeed the other project management functions such as programme control, configuration management, systems engineering and product assurance.[5]

Fox distinguished two views of defence acquisition Program Management. One is the 'liaison manager' role: promoting programmes, preparing reports and briefings, negotiating with superiors and resolving engineering conflicts. The other is the 'active manager': planning and making key decisions 'associated with rigorous oversight of, negotiation with, and control of the industrial firms that perform the development and production work'; taking responsibility for cost control and applying cost reduction and productivity incentives (ref. 5, pp. 303–304). The former was the de facto DoD practice, Fox implied; the latter was what was needed. Worst of all, Fox concluded in a sustained and powerful criticism of DoD Program Managers' career development policies, there was inadequate training for 'active' Program Management and far too frequent and insensitive job rotation. The Defense Systems Management College was in practice a 'cramming' school: under pressure, despite the lip service paid to it, to reduce the length of its standard programme. As for job rotation, a 1986 General Accounting Office study found that on average Program Managers stayed only 27 months on a given programme: (ref. 1, p. 11) since DoD programmes typically last a decade or more, it can be little wonder that Program Managers often take short-term perspectives on long-term issues.

UK defence procurement

Until the 1970s, the UK's defence project management systems and tools had been 'behind' those of the USA. As noted above, for example, the MoD's *Compendium of guidelines for project management* were first published only in 1978 (although the Downey report of 1966 used many of the basic principles and practices of modern project management).

An important feature of the MoD's procurement practices, which was to cause significant problems during the decade, was the realism of early project definition work. Downey had noted the importance of the project definition phase, and had suggested that up to 15% of the total development cost should be spent in project definition. The 1971 Rayner Report suggested an even higher figure, around 15%–25%. In practice, however, British projects averaged no more than around 8% during the 1970s and much of the 1980s (note 3).

In 1983 and 1984, major steps were taken by the MoD to revise the pattern of defence procurement. An important policy document of 1983, *Value for money in defence equipment*,[6] addressed the increasingly serious problem of how the UK's defence needs could be more effectively met from its progressively limited funds. Recommendations included: increased use of competition and more vigilant cost consciousness; the avoidance of over-elaborate specifications; and greater risk and cost sharing through more international collaboration and joint ventures with industry. A few months later, in early 1984, a review of defence procurement[7] by Peter Levene for the Secretary of State for Defence made a number of recommendations along similar lines for the improvement of procurement efficiency (note 4). The clarity and promise of this approach (admittedly for a much smaller number of projects, of smaller size, than the Pentagon's) compares refreshingly with the bureaucracy and inertia so deprecated by the Packard Blue Ribbon Panel and by Fox.

In March 1985, Levene became Chief of Defence Procurement. The new policies were reflected in the defence White Paper of May 1985.[8] One of the first — and often most hotly contested — areas of change was that of increased competition. The proportion of MoD work let on a competitive basis more than doubled in the 1980s. As a result, significant price reductions were achieved and payments were geared more towards results (note 5).

Further, MoD practice was changed to letting work on a fixed- (or maximum-) price basis, after competitive tendering, and increased use was made of performance specifications, rather than detailed engineering specifications, in order to permit industry greater scope in developing cost-effective proposals. If the R&D content was high or if there were other valid reasons for uncertainty the contract might be let on a reimbursable basis and changed to an incentive form as soon as possible — the so-called *hybrid form of contract*. Thus, 'in 1979−80, 30% by value of MoD contracts and amendments were placed in a competitive environment. This increased to 38% in 1983−84, 46% in 1984−85 and some 64% in 1985−86' (ref. 8, p. 26).

The practices introduced by MoD in the late 1970s and 1980s appeared to secure a stable and viable project management framework, which encouraged attention to leadership and management and in which accountability was allocated at the project level to those responsible for doing the work and there were proper incentives and penalties and clearly identified project progression procedures and reporting requirements (note 6). Unfortunately, before the results of this new philosophy could become manifest, there was a major project management scandal — Nimrod, the UK's Airborne Early Warning (AEW) system — a project reflecting the old way of managing projects (how not to manage projects properly).

Nimrod

The Staff Requirement for a UK AEW system had been endorsed in 1975, deployment being planned for 1982. Contracts for the airframe had been awarded to Hawker Siddeley Aviation (later British Aerospace) and for the radar detection to Marconi Avionics (later GEC Avionics). No overall prime contractor was appointed, however, and separate project management teams were established within the MoD. 'Because of the operational urgency MoD opted for a compressed and overlapping development and production programme, without stage by stage reviews, including only limited expenditure on models and test equipment and allowing very little margin for unforeseen difficulty.'[9] To readers of this book, the

Fig. 32. Nimrod (courtesy Jane's Information Group)

danger signs could hardly be more obvious. The estimate for the project was £319m.

By 1979 MoD was becoming concerned about delays and cost increases. By 1983 the project was a year late, primarily due to problems with the radar, software integration and computer processing, and with management that 'had been slow to admit slippages, optimistic when revising milestones and ineffective in managing a sub-contractor.'[9] In April 1984, Marconi/GEC agreed to bear some of the costs and to move to an incentive form of contract. GEC prepared a new estimate of the projected final project costs: £192m above the then current approvals to reach the staff requirement. This was so large that, although Nimrod (Fig. 32) was now reckoned to be 80% complete, Ministers decided in December 1984 to order an independent technical audit. This concluded that there was no prospect of reaching the desired level of performance in the short term. In December 1986 the Secretary of State therefore announced the cancellation of the programme and the ordering of six Boeing AWACs, even though the cost at £860m would, after cancellation charges, be £200m more than the projected cost of completing Nimrod! The writing-off of almost £900m on the project attracted intense publicity in the UK, the MoD's project management capability coming in for particularly strong criticism.

Levene's analysis of what went wrong on Nimrod followed classic project management principles — the same, in fact, that Downey had recommended in 1966 and Rayner had repeated in 1971, but had been ignored on Nimrod in the late 1970s

(*a*) to ensure that from the earliest possible stage the contract was based on a clear specification with agreed acceptance criteria to establish that the specification had been satisfactorily met

(*b*) until that stage had been reached and confidence

established, to move ahead by comparatively short steps defined as closely as possible

(c) to establish contractual terms to put the contractor under effective discipline

(d) to appoint a single prime contractor, and, as a natural corollary

(e) to have a single project manager in MoD (ref. 9, p. 18).

Following the Nimrod debacle, a study was conducted in 1987–1988 by a team drawn from MoD and the Prime Minister's Efficiency Unit on MoD project management. The study made several dozen recommendations, the bulk of which related to management of 'the technical dimension' and the development of MoD project management expertise. In general, *the importance of the amount of technological advance* posed by a project was still under-recognized, the study found: 'feasibility is . . . often considered to be synonymous with technological possibility and is motivated by a desire to "meet the Staff Target"' (note 7).[10] Instead, the study recommended

'MoD should commit to Full Development of an equipment only when initial demonstration of hardware (or software) and its integration has produced evidence that the equipment can be developed to the required level within the time and cost proposed' (ref. 10, p. 12).

The study also proposed that *progress be measured against milestones* rather than work completed or time elapsed, and made several recommendations regarding the project management function including (*pace* Packard, Fox, *et al.*) that the chain of command be shortened and that more attention be given to the career development and training of project managers.

The Experimental Aircraft Programme and the European Fighter Aircraft

The emphasis on having tested the feasibility of the proposed technical concept was by now becoming accepted as a fundamental of good modern project management. No longer was there talk of spearhead projects, as with TSR-2 or Concorde; of massive commitment being made to untested technology, as with AGRs or the SSTs. Concurrency was widely recognized as dangerous. Prototyping was now seen as the safer route. We shall see this below in information systems and automobile projects, but even on defence projects the practice was being increasingly adopted. The European Fighter Aircraft (EFA) is a case in point.

An Experimental Aircraft Programme (EAP, Fig. 33) was proposed by the MoD in 1982 as a joint government/industry demonstration programme to develop the range of technologies needed for the new fighter aircraft scheduled for the 1990s. Attempts were made to involve the West German and Italian Tornado partners, but in the event participation was on a limited industrial scale and the programme was largely carried out by British Aerospace.

Fig. 33. EAP
(Experimental Aircraft
Programme) prototype

A contract was agreed with MoD in 1983, funded initially on a 50/50 basis with industry, with payment to be made against achievement of specific milestones. MoD management was considerably more 'hands off' than normal, project management being directed by British Aerospace. Several technologies were 'demonstrated': EAP's aerodynamically unstable configuration (to give increased agility); the fully integrated avionics and mechanical systems; carbon fibre composites used in new and more extensive ways. The software requirements of the plane were considerable: British Aerospace implemented strict controls on all software development and integration, and the software was developed satisfactorily to specification (note 8).[11,12] The engines, unlike Tornado's, had the benefit of engine demonstration programmes that had been initiated much earlier (XG20 and XG40), aimed at developing and proving the technologies that would be needed in the advanced engines of future aircraft of the 1990s. The benefits later became evident in the development of the EJ200 engine for EFA.

The EAP programme as a whole was in fact successfully accomplished on time and within budget, proving perhaps that *properly managed* — i.e. with the right techniques and project management structure — *advanced technology need not result in overruns*.

Thus, by mid-1989 it appeared that the technological challenges posed by the EFA were largely being tackled effectively (Fig. 34). But while the prospects for EFA certainly appeared good, the programme management was by no means clearly established and on its way. The French pulled out early to build their rival Rafale, hoping to lure some of the other EFA partners. (None joined, and Rafale began to look increasingly like an extremely expensive indulgence.) EFA's specifications were agreed between West Germany, Italy and Spain in September 1987; the programme was now estimated to cost £18–20bn. Organizationally, EFA was modelled closely on Tornado. Engine development posed much less risk than on Tornado (more prototype development done, less schedule urgency). There was uncertainty over the selection of

Fig. 34. The second EFA development aircraft (DA2) at British Aerospace, Warton (courtesy British Aerospace Defence Ltd)

the radar, but by far the biggest hurdle was funding and political commitment (especially in the 1990s, as the scale of the 'peace dividend' and the demands on Germany's budget increased). The technology and organization challenges had essentially been tackled; the major challenge was now the project's political environment (note 9).

Oil prices and energy projects

Meanwhile, back in the world of civil projects, the crucial development was the fall in the price of oil. Oil importers' current account had gradually improved after the first oil shock of 1973–1974, only to be set back substantially with the second shock of 1979–1980. Between 1978 and 1980, oil exporting countries' combined current account grew from $6bn to $110bn, while the non-oil developing countries' deficit increased catastrophically from $42bn to $88bn, and the developed nations plummeted from a surplus of $32bn to a deficit of $40bn. These *colossal shifts in spending power, unparalleled except in times of war*, boosted the already enormous amounts being spent on Third World and oil-related projects.

Throughout this period, as the world's economies generally performed robustly, stimulated by expansionary monetary policies, demand for oil continued to be strong. The rise in the price of oil, however, and its impact on nations' economies, made governments throughout the world acutely conscious of the importance of their energy sources and the vulnerability of their oil supplies. The expulsion of the Shah from Iran in 1979 heightened concern for oil supply security, as prices rose from $15 to $39 per barrel between January 1979 and 1981.

Unlike Britain in the early 1980s, the USA was a net importer of oil. The Iranian crisis in the spring of 1979 had created a near panic in the USA. Talk began of the need for a $100–200bn synthetic fuel programme. President Carter's administration was at this time in some despondency: his popularity was low and was suffering further as long queues of angry motorists built up at the gas pumps. After retiring to Camp David to contemplate, Carter announced on 15 July 1979, with all the zeal, he said, of the 'moral equivalent of war', an $88bn crash synfuels programme. A Synthetic Fuels Corporation was established in 1980 with two phases of funding: $20bn and 500 000 bpd for the first four years and up to $68bn and 2 million bpd thereafter. In 1981, however, the synfuels programme suffered two major changes in its project environment. First the price of oil began to fall (it was to reach around $12 −15 per barrel in 1986); second, the new administration of Ronald Reagan changed the role of the SFC from a NASA-type Program Management organization to that of an investment bank. The SFC was no longer to work as a facilitating project champion 'mobilizing a network of favourable stakeholders — absolutely critical for the success of large scale programs', but had to act as a hard-nosed investment analyst. However, it was ultimately the deteriorating financial cogency of synfuels that killed off the proposed projects. None were completed.

From an analysis of this rather sorry story, Mel Horwitch, drawing on earlier work with his colleague Gary Pralahad, concluded that for large-scale projects to be in 'convergence',[13,14] they should

- be economically rational and have positive cost−benefit relations
- have management appropriate to the project
- enjoy supportive bureaucratic−political measures
- operate in a favourable social−economic climate
- work in a favourable corporate−strategic environment.

Ken-ichi Imai, a leading figure in Japan's Ministry of International Trade and Industry, affirmed Horwitch's model in describing Japan's response to the huge rises in oil prices of the late 1970s, the so-called Sunshine and Moonlight Plans.[15] The Sunshine Plan, which aimed to make Japan self-sufficient in energy, concentrated on the development of solar and nuclear power through the use of subsidies. The programme soon ran into organizational problems, however. In particular, there was no fostering of the customer−supplier relationship. A National Energy Development Organization was set up as part of the Sunshine Plan, but experienced substantial promotional problems. Imai's analysis of the failure of this programme thus emphasizes the importance in such programmes of 'being in motion' and *user learning*. Also, the social−economic environment was not supportive of nuclear power; the management actions were not supported by research; and bureaucratic−political support waned as subsidies were removed. An important lesson, therefore, is that Horwitch's five factors are *interdependent*: the cost−benefit relation was positive as long as the political will was there; once the political will left, the social—economic opposition and lack of management back-up added to the problems created by an insufficiently robust cost—benefit return.

Virtual cessation of nuclear power plant building in the 1980s

As the Sunshine Plan suggests, the oil crisis of 1979 and the early 1980s ought to have provided a favourable economic climate for the building of additional nuclear power capacity. The fact that so little new nuclear capacity was ordered during this period (or subsequently during the decade) indicates the severity of the loss of confidence the industry had suffered. Although in 1982 the US Department of Energy was still forecasting that another 25 nuclear plants would be ordered during the decade,[16] in fact not a single order was placed. Even in France the rate of plant ordering began to be cut back substantially from 1981—1982, as it was seen that substantial overcapacity was building up. Although a long-term contract was signed between the French government and Electricité de France (EdF) in 1984, this provided for only one unit per year for the next five years.

Not only was there now both reduced demand for energy and severe lack of public confidence, there were, as the International Atomic Energy Agency reported in 1982, too many existing plants suffering

> financial, management, licensing, and technical problems. The number of such plants has grown to around 30 worldwide, corresponding to a total capacity of 27 000 MW. Of these plants 17 have never operated or were stopped indefinitely when between 30% and 100% complete: they include Bushehr in Iran and Zwentendorf in Austria. During the first half of 1982 alone, 13 US plants joined this category, primarily because of mismanagement, financial troubles, and reduced need for electric power; political uncertainty also played a part. Seven plants worldwide have been inoperable for at least two consecutive years for repair, backfitting and licensing reasons, and several are at present limited to less than half-power due to serious steam-generator problems . . . . Thus the primary motives for deciding to introduce nuclear power, reliability and economics, have not received the attention which was necessary to keep nuclear power a viable option.[17]

Confidence in nuclear power received a near-fatal blow when, on 26 April 1986, there was an uncontrollable power surge which led to an explosion at the Russian RBMK reactor at Chernobyl (Fig. 35): 'the most important man-made accident that has ever occurred.'[18] Two men were killed instantly; 29 died of radiation sickness contracted in putting out the fire in the exposed reactor core; 200—300 plant workers suffered acute radiation sickness; probably well over 7000 deaths were caused as radiation from Chernobyl was blown across and out of the USSR. There was enormous ecological and economic damage. The shock of the catastrophe to the public was huge. Many in the industry indeed wondered whether any more nuclear power plants could now be built.

Fig. 35. Chernobyl nuclear power plant, unit 4 (courtesy Vadim Mouchkin/ International Atomic Energy Agency)

Public opposition now began to take more sophisticated, though no less effective, forms than those typical of the 1970s. In the USA, opposition to the new plants came increasingly from rate payers who were suddenly faced with potentially huge rate increases (partly caused, it should be added, by the idiosyncratic Public Utility Commission rules regarding cost recovery) and who could generally see no pressing need for the extra capacity they were being asked to pay for so heavily. Political pressure in California was so strong that the Public Utility Commission allowed Diablo Canyon's plant costs to be put fully into the rate-base only if the plant performed well in operation. Voters in California voted in 1989 for the Rancho Seco plant to be shut down. Opposition on New York's Long Island to the Shoreham plant concentrated on the difficulties of evacuating the island quickly and safely in the event of an emergency; an operating licence for the $5·5bn completed plant was refused, and in 1989 the State of New York bought the plant for $1 with the intent of dismantling it, despite misgivings that were at last beginning to surface over the environmental damage of fossil fuels and the long-term need for additional US capacity.

Very few nuclear plants were built after the Chernobyl disaster. In the UK things were, of course, different. Thus, as plants were cancelled and governments fell (note 10), the UK at last decided in 1987, after the 27 month Sizewell B inquiry, to proceed with a new family of PWR nuclear power plants. Even after the Government announced its plans to privatize the electricity supply industry, it reiterated its commitment to maintaining a significant nuclear power generating capacity within Britain.

Chernobyl, unfortunately, was not the last time the 1980s would see anxiety over the environmental consequences of nuclear fuel. Towards the end of the decade, concerns over environmental damage, associated particularly with the back-end of the nuclear cycle, began to become pressing. Following Chernobyl, the US Secretary of Energy John Herrington ordered a review of the USA's 17 nuclear weapons production sites. The results appalled DoE officials. Being military, the programme had not been subject to the same regulation as the civilian nuclear power programme. By 1989 all three of the Savannah River plants, the Hanford plants and a plutonium plant in Colorado had been shut down because of safety or management problems. Consolidating and closing the complex would cost, it was estimated, in the order of $52bn; decontaminating Hanford alone would cost $47bn. The heroic era of Groves *et al.* had given way under the neglect of, in particular, the Carter and Reagan administrations to mediocrity and under-investment. The heroism and glamour had gone into building the projects: too often we fail to give the same attention to the assurance of appropriate standards of operations and maintenance.

Several lessons emerge from the unhappy experience of the building of nuclear power plants. They can perhaps be regarded as positive contributions to the development of the management of projects as a discipline, although that is hardly solace.

First, then, much is risked when *the design base* is changed in a technology-sensitive industry. This lesson is borne out

(*a*)   in France, which achieved spectacular productivity improvements by building a large number of standard PWRs

(*b*)   in the UK, which suffered terribly from the large number of different reactor types, the tendency to build production units before the new technology was proven, and a predilection to tinker with the engineering during the project, with very expensive consequences

(*c*)   in the USA, which suffered from a multiplicity of owner and architect/engineer approaches to design—construction management — rarely was an attempt made to standardize design (such as the Bechtel-sponsored standard nuclear power system (SNUPS)).

Second, the imposition of Quality Assurance as a discipline was a valuable adjunct to the early engineering management disciplines such as Configuration Management and Value Engineering, and the harbinger of the Total Quality Management approach (see pp. 243 and 290—291) which was to spread to the West from Japan in the mid-to-late 1980s.

Third, project managers could hardly hope to bring their plants in 'on time, in budget, to technical specification' if they did not also attempt to *manage in some way their external regulatory and community environment*. (Most utilities in the 1980s were attempting to do this to some extent. St Lucie 2 is one of the better known examples of a project where the utility made explicit efforts to manage its project environment (note 11).)

Fourth — although this was probably apparent to only a few at the more senior levels — it was clear in the end that *nuclear power projects had to be acceptable as 'whole entities' to the community at large*, and that there were some *serious discontinuities in the process as a 'whole'*. In particular

- except in the case of the (more successful) small countries, the production of fissionable material was inextricably tied up with national security interests, and as such it: (*a*) was subject to governmental control, (*b*) attracted habits of secrecy that repelled many of the citizens whose support would ultimately be needed for the continuation of a nuclear power programme, (*c*) generated resistance from a significant proportion of the population
- the abilities and levels of experience of both the project owners and builders, at company and individual level, and the efficacy of the organizational and contractual relationships between them, varied substantially so that there was too much unreliability in the quality of delivery of such potentially dangerous systems
- the '*back end*' of the project was seriously underestimated, in particular the financial and technical implications of decommissioning and the handling, treatment and storage of spent fuel (nuclear waste), together with the ecological, social and political costs — the back end must be properly taken into account, since projects succeed only if they do so overall, and not just in their design and construction phases.

Fifth, the success of project management directly affected the financial success of the project sponsors; their financial health in turn affected the viability of the project (note 12).

Environmental concern, Environmental Impact Assessments and the planning process

Concern over degradation of the environment increased markedly during the 1980s; with it came increased attention to the more formal management of major projects' impact on their environment. By the end of the decade concern over the global environment had been recognized as an extremely serious issue across society at large, not least to project professionals (note 13).

Consciousness of the serious threat of massive environmental damage was stirred largely by the environmental lobby movement, but received powerful support first from the Brundtland Commission's 1987 report for the UN (*Our common future*)[19] and, in 1988–1989, from the unexpected but vigorous championship of Mrs Thatcher, President Mitterand and other world leaders, including eventually President Bush. The Brundtland Commission emphasized '*sustainability*': 'a new approach in which all nations aim at a type of development that integrates production with resource conservation and enhancement, that links both to the provision for all of an adequate livelihood base and equitable access to resources' (ref. 19, pp. 39–40).

The new President of the World Bank, Barber Conable, was strongly committed to reducing poverty and protecting the environment. Conscious that some Bank projects may not have been designed with sufficient concern for environmental quality,[20] Conable established an Environmental Department to integrate environmental considerations into the Bank's overall lending and policy activities. From the Bank's reviews, two lessons in particular stood out. First, the traditional cost–benefit methodologies needed to be modified to take better account of environmental considerations and '*externalities*'. (For, despite pedantic difficulties, discount rates can be calculated to reflect the value of associated economic impacts or the knock-on consequences of a project (note 14).[21–23])

The second major factor to emerge from the Bank's reviews was the importance of interdependence, both of environmental factors and of projects. Work on the environmental planning of one project can be ruined if another project adversely affects the same factors. The $4·5bn Carajas Iron Ore project in Amazonia, for example, partly financed by World Bank and bilateral aid, was established

Fig. 36. Narmada Dam under construction, North-West India; the project created huge opposition because of its impact on the environment and local communities (courtesy New Civil Engineer)

with the utmost care in terms of its impact on the environment
— there was an in-house environmental unit and an independent
expert environmental advisory panel; environmental guides were
prepared for contractors and $13·6m was spent on developing
reserves for the Amerindians. All this was ruined when a new
ministry, Planning, suddenly created the Greater Carajas
Programme (PGC), which had involved next to no environmental
planning, and surrounded the iron ore project. The PGC-sponsored
pig-iron smelters were environmentally disastrous. 'In retrospect
a regional or sectoral approach would have been more prudent.'[24]

Carajas was not the only Brazilian project to hit the press
headlines in the late 1980s. The Kaiapó Indians toured the world
voicing their indignation at the proposed Altamira hydroelectric
scheme. This huge dam would flood 24 000 km^2 of rain forest,
obliterating forever the homelands of several thousand
Amerindians. The Kaiapó struck a sensitive topic, for dams had
come under extremely strong criticism from environmentalists
during the 1980s for the physical and social disruption they
caused.[25] Altamira did not go ahead.

The Kaiapó meeting at Altamira was in effect Brazil's first public
planning enquiry for a major project. Brazil was not alone among
developing nations in having no formal planning process. (Such
democratic processes might not always fit well with local politics!)
India, for example, which suffered the horror of the 1984 Bhopal
accident in which some 2000 slum dwellers were poisoned by
escaped gas from a Union Carbide plant, by the end of the decade
still had no comprehensive policy framework to consider the impact
of proposed major projects.[26,27]

The mechanism for doing this, which by the end of the 1980s
was being slowly implemented almost universally, was the
Environmental Impact Assessment (EIA) procedure. Introduced,
as we saw with TAPS, in the USA in 1970, EIA had been quickly
adopted by Japan, Australia, Canada, Germany, France and Eire.
From the mid-1970s the European Economic Community sought
a standard EIA procedure (since varying EIA practices could distort
competition). After a ten-year saga and over 20 drafts, an EEC
Directive was introduced in 1988. By the late 1980s it had been
adopted for certain types of project in Malaysia, Thailand, Sri
Lanka and other less developed countries.

By the 1980s EIA had come to succeed cost—benefit analysis
as the preferred project assessment technique. Following its
introduction in the 1970s, cost—benefit had been gradually
broadened, first by use of multiple objectives, different discount
rates and proxy pricing methods, and later in conjunction with
the Planning, Programming and Budgeting technique. During the
1970s, EIA itself came to be used in an increasingly broad way,
moving from an emphasis on describing the repercussions of

proposals on the ecological environment to a broader consideration of impacts on the 'social processes, cultural norms and biophysical systems'.[28]

Both developers and communities appeared to find the EIA process helpful in the articulation and discussion of the impact that a project would make on its environment. The EIA process, however, is not an automatic one — it does require active management. In the gaining of approval for a project, a '*consent strategy*' must be followed in which the 'avenues' to be followed must be determined, a policy on consultations with authorities and interest groups agreed, a policy on information release established, contentious issues identified, tactics for handling issues worked out, stances on benefits and compensation identified, and responsibilities allocated.[29]

In terms of the management of projects, the crucial point is of course that *the project is here being managed before it is even approved. Management begins as soon as the project is a gleam in someone's eye.*

The problem for developers and public alike, not least in Britain, was that planning applications were often treated as vehicles for establishing national policy. While some countries — the Netherlands for example — had an extremely tightly defined planning and regulatory process within which projects had to fit, others had a much more chaotic system. The USA was ringed with legislation laid down over the years to cover everything from zoning (the 1900s), water and air pollution (1950s and 1960s), and the environment at large (NEPA, 1970s) to hazardous waste disposal (1980s). Administration of these laws was in the hands of both federal and state agencies. There were few preset standards. Britain's planning laws rested on the 1947 Planning Act, almost all of whose assumptions had been totally abandoned by the 1980s (note 15).

No project illustrated this confusion of planning approval with policy review more clearly than the Sizewell B inquiry. The Sizewell B nuclear power station, for which a 27 month £20m public inquiry was held, was the CEGB's first PWR. Although the local authorities had indicated that they would probably accept the station, the Secretary of State for Energy called for a full inquiry, stating as terms of reference that both the 'need' and 'national interest' issues should be examined in addition to issues of local environmental impact and acceptability.[30,31]

The effectiveness of Third World development projects

The schisms and opposition over the environmental consequences of many Third World projects notwithstanding, the general understanding of what is required to ensure successful aid projects became generally well accepted during the 1980s.

The World Bank worked hard during the decade to add to our understanding of how to manage development projects. The hefty but ultimately unsatisfying *Investing in development* by Baum and Tolbert[32] reviewed the Bank's experience between 1945 and 1985. A major review by the Bank's Operations Evaluation Department in 1988 of its rural development experience[33] seemed to get nearer the mark, concluding that more attention needed to be given to the adequacy of technology and scale of development, that the project design needed to be more appropriate to the intended beneficiaries, and that more attention needed to be paid to institution building and integrated rural development ('rural development could only be pursued if various production- and consumption-orientated services were introduced concurrently and in an integrated fashion').[34]

These conclusions were of a piece with these of Jon Moris in 1981,[35] who comprehensively reviewed the challenges presented by Third World development programmes and drew on an extensive literature review to distil some general tactics and principles for effective programme development, notably:

- politics: location is a political matter; the political dimension is often under-appreciated by 'outside experts'; 'underdeveloped countries often have overdeveloped institutions'; events should be synchronized with the political timetable; effective PR should be developed
- economics and finance: cost−benefit analyses may be misleading for a large period of the project's life; loan financing should be avoided in the early stages and adequacy of funding should be ensured for recurrent (as much as for capital) costs
- technology: innovations should be kept to a minimum; the systems consequences of technology transfer should be understood
- organization: emphasis should be placed on finding the key people; people should be developed from successful projects; 'creating self-renewing leadership is the hardest step'; the greater the number of organizational levels, the greater is the uncertainty of outcome; structures that overlap bureaucratic jurisdictions should be avoided.

Samuel Paul, writing in 1982, analysed six development programmes in detail, to arrive at an essentially contingency view of programme management design. Successful programmes can be characterized initially, he observed, by a 'focus on a single goal or service, sequential diversification of goals, phased programme implementation, organizational autonomy, the use of network structures, the use of simple information systems with fast feedback, and flexible selection and training processes'.[36] However, in addition to these fundamental patterns for successful Program Management, quite different patterns of participant involvement, degrees of decentralization and use of incentives can be seen as working well. 'Program success [thus] requires a high degree of "congruence" among the strategic, structural, and process interventions initiated by program leaders [ref. 36, p. 231].'

Of all the studies of aid, none can match for comprehensiveness and thoroughness the massive 1984–1985 study *Does aid work?*, conducted under Robert Cassen's directorship.[37] Cassen and his colleagues looked at thousands of reports as well as surveying many aid activities directly. Their first, very important finding was that aid does indeed work (note 16). Cassen reviewed the performance of aid in several sectors, his comments on agricultural and industrial projects being particularly noteworthy (Fig. 37).

Cassen's analysis of so huge a class of projects provides a pithy, authoritative confirmation of the general thesis proposed in this book — that *while attention to project management tools and techniques is important to project performance, it is far from sufficient.* For as Cassen showed, management is certainly crucial, but at the broad policy as well as at the project level. The factors

Fig. 37. Lessons for managing agricultural and industrial development projects (from Cassen[37])

Agricultural projects have had a varied track record. Integrated rural development projects (creatures largely of the 1970s) suffered from weak organization and over-reliance on co-ordination between public agencies; over-risky technical proposals; and excessively high expectations pushed by over-funding. Irrigation projects showed particularly poor performance due largely to their size and complexity (construction scheduling being particularly notorious); management and maintenance requirements were too often underappreciated. Livestock projects also proved poor.

Industrial projects had, on average, a lower rate of return than agricultural projects, the principal problems being technology and management, quality maintenance, and pricing policy. There has been too great a fascination with technical innovation, on the part of recipients and, with the notable exception of the IFC, of multilateral agencies. Proven technology should be used and scaling up, or down, avoided. Development in the 1950s to 1970s favoured state-run, large-scale industrialization. On balance, this has not proved to be successful. By the 1980s the pendulum had swung towards smaller scale projects using more appropriate technology. In particular, industrial development projects in the 1980s favoured

- 'a better appreciation of the limitations of public sector bodies as implementing agents
- a much sharper focus on management capabilities
- a corresponding focus on the sectoral and sub-sectoral context of projects
- attention to the overall policy environment'.[37]

Management has often been the weakest element in industrial developments projects. 'Special effort is needed to improve project management.'[37] There should be 'a strong, committed, and financially motivated chief executive',[37] having a high degree of autonomy, able to select and build a balanced team and having a good understanding of the markets.

affecting aid success are as often to do with institutional and policy matters, with technology selection and project design, and with pricing and funding, as with what we normally consider to be classical project management. 'If there is a general weakness in the aid process other than those already dilated upon, it is that understanding of institutional, political, and social constraints to aid effectiveness lags very far behind economic and technical competence ... [ref. 37, p. 169].'

The Third World debt crisis
The slowly developing understanding of what is required to create effective development projects (indeed, the post-1984 period has been called the 'coming of age' of development project evaluation[38]) unfortunately arrived just when the volume of international lending and project activity dropped suddenly, massively and catastrophically (note 17).

The high levels of debt of the less developed countries had made their finances extremely vulnerable to external shock. Unfortunately, after the second oil price rise in 1979, instead of world trade recovering as it had done in 1976, there was recession. Real interest rates climbed, and the dollar rose steadily. At the same time, oil prices began to fall. Less developed countries began to borrow heavily to sustain their economies. Mexico alone borrowed $6·4bn in the six months before August 1982, when it announced, in a bombshell that stunned the financial world, that it was unable to raise sufficient loans to meet its upcoming debt repayments' schedule. The lending situation was transformed overnight; with world debt having grown from $130bn in 1973 to $612bn, sovereign lending by commercial banks was suddenly a business to be shunned. Within a year, 21 countries had had to postpone repayments of debts due.

Contemporaneously with this sudden cessation of commercial bank lending and collapse in the price of oil, Third World nations and their major project development programmes suffered two further setbacks. Non-oil commodity prices in general suffered their worst decline since the Second World War (26% on average in dollar terms) while levels of governmental aid began a sharp decline, partly as OECD governments cut back government spending in general and partly — perversely, considering the crystallization of development project know-how that was just emerging — as the efficacy of certain aid projects came under question.

It was under these critical conditions that the Baker Initiative was announced in October 1985, calling for the lending of some $40bn to the 15 most heavily indebted nations (note 18) in exchange for certain policy reforms. For most of the 1980s this initiative was officially held to be the preferred route for dealing with the Third World debt crisis, despite some obvious shortcomings. For example, it did nothing to tackle the debt of any of the other less developed countries, and said nothing about how to deal with existing debt. The only new commercial lending, meanwhile, was to refinance interest payments, not to finance project work. In March 1989 the new US Treasury Secretary, Nicholas Brady, announced a new initiative emphasizing debt reduction for the less developed countries. Yet by the end of the decade little had come of either initiative (although positive benefits began to work through by the early 1990s). By 1989 total Third World debt stood at over $1200bn.

Arguably of more practical impact than the Baker Initiative was the action taken by Citicorp in May 1987 to make bad-debt provisions for over $3bn of sovereign loans. This led to similar substantial provisioning in the USA and UK, an important consequence of which was the opening up of the commercial banks' ability to trade their debt. In particular, interest in debt-equity swaps increased sharply as commercial banks recognized that their existing pattern of debt already had an equity-like profile and thus might be managed more actively as such. By the late 1980s, therefore, there was increased willingness to consider equity positions in overseas projects.

With the volume of major construction project activity declining drastically from 1982 on, the major projects business of the mid-1980s had thus clearly entered a period of substantial change. Contractors retrenched severely as the volume of international work declined (by as much as one third to two thirds); huge numbers of staff were let go. For almost the first time since the Second World War, the world economy appeared to offer no prospect of steady construction growth. Contractors were suddenly unable to survive merely by responding to Requests For Proposals. Many began to look more creatively and systematically at their business development and marketing activities. Contractors began to realize that if they wished to continue working on major projects they might have to put money and effort into initiating them. Contractor-led financial engineering became an important ingredient in the initiation of projects.

These, then, were the conditions in which the build−own−operate (−transfer) (BOO(T)) form of project originated.

Origins of BOO(T) projects

The idea behind the BOO(T) form is that the contractor takes the lead in initiating the project, finding the finance, building the facility, and then owning and operating, or possibly selling/transferring back, the completed facility. In this general form, the concept had of course been applied already — housing and property development being obvious examples — but BOO(T) generally refers to sectors traditionally reserved to the state, such as infrastructure and energy. For, by a fortuitous coincidence, the BOO(T) concept had emerged just at the time that privatization was beginning to emerge as a crucial policy for the improvement of industrial efficiency (note 19).[39] Why could contractors not be offered a concession to build and operate roads, power stations, bridges, and other forms of communication and infrastructure?

BOO(T) was first initiated in a developing nation context in 1984 by Turkey's Prime Minister, Turgut Ozal, for the Akkuyu nuclear power project. (Interestingly, his original motive was the classic project one of wishing to have a single organization responsible for initiating and building the project; but Ozal also saw that the BOO(T) method would allow foreign investment to enter Turkey without upsetting borrowing restrictions; he also believed that efficiencies might be gained by having the project performed by the private sector.) Soon there was a substantial list of proposed Turkish BOO(T) projects, although, to the intense frustration of the many contractors and financiers bidding for them, progress was incredibly slow — by 1989 Akkuyu had still failed to finalize its financing.

1984 also saw the launch of two other major BOO(T) projects, both in transportation and both coming under British influence: the Hong Kong Second Harbour Crossing and the Channel Tunnel. Tenders were invited in October 1984 for the financing, design, construction and operation of a second Hong Kong harbour crossing. A contract was awarded in September 1986 to a consortium led by the Japanese contractor, Kumagai Gumi, whose bid was not the best from either an engineering or a cost view, but won on its concession terms and financing plan (note 20). (As with the Channel Tunnel (Figs 38, 39) and the later UK BOO(T) project, the Dartford Crossing, financing security was provided by government franchises and tolls — even in 'private-sector' infrastructure projects it is very difficult to do without some degree of government support.)

The origins of the Channel Tunnel project are interesting and deserve some attention, for not only is the project important, but also its initiation illustrates several lessons generic to most BOO(T) projects — particularly the difficulties of raising sufficient equity early in the project while the risks are still very high, and the problems of creating a strong owner organization where an owner as such does not already exist.

The Channel Tunnel project

Proposals for tunnelling under the English Channel became a serious possibility in 1955, when the British ceased to regard a tunnel as a threat to national security. In 1967 proposals were invited for private financing and construction of the tunnel, with 70%−90% of the loans guaranteed by the British and French governments; once operational the facility was to be government owned. British Rail was a member of the project, but was not anxious to divert its scarce funds to it and never took it particularly seriously, at least not until the UK Government issued a White Paper in 1973 that endorsed the project but added, unnecessarily,

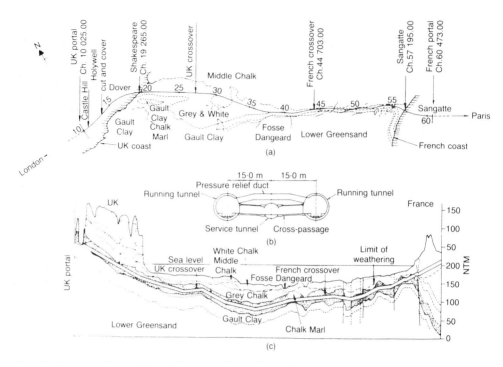

Fig. 38. Layout and geological section of the Channel Tunnel: (a) plan; (b) typical section through tunnel; (c) longitudinal section

'that a high quality railway between the Tunnel and London and the provision for through services to the provincial centres is essential for success'.[40] During 1974 the UK Government faced a rapidly deteriorating economic situation, caused largely by the first OPEC price rise (Maplin and the London Ringway motorway scheme being cancelled at this time). In the summer of 1974 British Rail revised its forecast for the high-speed rail link upwards by £130m to £330m, a far greater increase than the Government could then countenance. Unfortunately, it was not able to postpone a decision on funding, as it wished to do, since the Anglo-French Treaty had to be ratified by January 1975. The project was therefore abandoned (note 21).

Following this failure, however, studies were continued by British Rail and SNCF, the French national rail company, who published proposals in February 1979 for a rail-only single-track tunnel, British Rail suggesting that an adequate connection might now be built at the relatively low cost of £25m. The interest of several construction firms was stimulated by this new proposal. To be financially viable, the contractors felt, the cross-Channel link had to be capable of taking vehicles: the rail scheme did not allow this. One group, later to be called the Channel Tunnel Group (CTG), concluded that the scheme cancelled in January 1975 was still the most viable. Another, Euroroute, decided that the link should be a drive-through scheme consisting of bridges and an immersed tube.

The governments' response to the various proposals now being

Fig. 39. Channel Tunnel: completed running tunnel (photograph by Mike Griggs; reproduced by kind permission of Transmanche-Link)

generated was supportive, provided that — crucially, in terms of the subsequent development of BOO(T) — the scheme would be financed from the private sector. It was agreed that a joint official study should be commissioned. This appeared in 1982, recommending 'bored twin rail tunnels with a vehicle shuttle constructed, if necessary, in phases'.[41]

In June 1982 the governments accepted an offer by an Anglo-French financing group to study the feasibility of privately financing the fixed link. This reported in May 1984, concluding that the bored tunnel option was best. Since there was no natural owner for the project, the banks felt that the chance of getting a significant portion of equity into the scheme was slim. Some level of EEC or government support would be necessary, they believed, given the size and novelty of the project, but some form of risk sharing between the private and public sectors might also be possible.

The UK Government rejected this call for 'marginal guarantees' and made it clear that the project would have to be financed 'entirely without the assistance of public funds and without commercial guarantees by the Government'.[42] Observing the success of recent UK privatization schemes, CTG and the banks now concluded that perhaps the financial markets could after all fund the project. Euroroute soon announced that it too would be able to raise the necessary private funds provided certain political guarantees of non-interference could be given.

On 30 November 1984, Mrs Thatcher met with President Mitterand. To the surprise of many, the two leaders announced their enthusiasm for a fixed link between their two countries, provided it was financed, built and operated by the private sector.

The timetable set by the two governments was tight. French parliamentary elections were scheduled for March 1986 and the

French presidential election for 1988, which was also the latest year for a general election in the UK. Agreement between the governments before March 1986, and the passing of all necessary legislation before the presidential and general elections, were seen as essential to avoid the 1974 problem of political change disrupting the project. The governments decided, therefore, to issue their guidelines by the spring of 1985, which they did.

Schemes were submitted on 31 October 1985. On 20 January 1986 it was announced that the CTG's scheme had been selected.[43] One month later the Concession Agreement, granting the CTG the right to build and operate the tunnel, was concluded. In April a hybrid bill was introduced to Parliament with the aim of obtaining Royal Assent in the early summer of 1987.

Under-*staffing* posed an immediate and serious problem. Huge effort had gone into getting the concession. Now, suddenly, the winning group had to staff and organize to carry out the project. Since the project was contractor-originated, the question immediately arose (as it always does on BOO(T) projects) of how to set up a strong owner organization independent of the sponsoring contractors that could give direction, manage the contractors and ensure value for money.

CTG was split into an owner organization, Eurotunnel, and the contractors, Transmanche-Link. Staff were temporarily seconded from the promoting companies with the intention that they be replaced rapidly at CTG. The secondees, however, had to negotiate with their own companies and report to a board drawn totally from contractors and banks. At the highest level, therefore, there were conflicts of interest. And work started at a furious pace. Construction was to start in March 1986, and a construction contract therefore had to be in place very soon; a firm underwriting of funds from lending banks had to be obtained before going to the equity markets; the Termsheet for the bank lending and the underwriting, meanwhile, was not achievable until agreement had been reached with the railways.

The financing scheme proposed was one of the most complex for many years. The CTG partners contributed to the initial £50m of the project's working capital (Equity 1). Further share placings were planned for June 1986 (Equity 2) and mid-1987 (Equity 3). This programme was almost certainly over-optimistic, being driven by the original promoters' desire to minimize the money they had to put in (Equity 1) and to go to the market for Equity 2 before complaints began to be aired during the planning hearings in Parliament. The date for Equity 3 was based on the project's requirement for funds rather than the ability of Eurotunnel to prepare for such a major share issue. Equity 3 also, of course, had to be after the Treaty had been ratified, so that the political risk element would not disturb the placing.

The financing schedule was soon delayed. Suspicious that the contract terms were too easy on the contractors, the financiers insisted on their revision; as new banks and other financiers were introduced to the project, several further revisions were requested. In addition, Eurotunnel's advisers were strongly of the opinion that the contracts had to be sharper if the share prospectus was to be successful.[44] The contracts were eventually signed, after numerous lengthy and often acrimonious drafting sessions, only in mid-August 1986, some three months later than planned. This delay caused Equity 2 to be postponed to October.

The Equity 2 share placing represented the first major testing of the financial viability of the project — and the project would be nothing if it was not supported by the markets. In the event, the placing was almost a disastrous failure. The £206m sought was to be raised from institutions in Britain (£70m), France (£70m), Japan, the USA and other international markets. The French placing proved relatively straightforward. In Britain, the result was nail-biting. Subscriptions had to be paid by 2 p.m. on 29 October. By Friday lunchtime, 24 October, there was clear indication that the placing might fail. The Government later denied lobbying, but in the event £75m was raised in the UK (£75m was also raised in France) amid much talk of last minute arm-twisting by the Bank of England (note 22).

In February 1987, Eurotunnel got a new Chairman, Alastair Morton; he was faced with several immediate challenges. Most important was the re-establishment of confidence in the project among financiers to the level where the £750m of Equity 3, on which the £5bn of bank lending depended, could successfully be raised. Politically, the project still had to steer its way through Parliament, where its planning application was being reviewed. There was also the threat of the general election turning out badly for the project. In fact all these difficulties were successfully overcome within a few months: Mrs Thatcher was re-elected, Royal Assent was given in July, and the Equity 3 shares were successfully placed by November. With the money thus raised, construction of the Tunnel began in earnest.

However, there was a final, unplanned stage in the saga of raising finance and managing the Channel Tunnel project. By late 1988–early 1989 it was apparent that additional finance might be required to complete the project. By October 1989 the estimate had risen to £7bn. November 1990 saw Eurotunnel launching a rights issue to fund the £7·6bn now estimated to be required. By December 1993 the total cost looked like exceeding £10bn with a further rights issue necessary. Equally depressing, completion slipped to March–May 1994. Once again, the awful predictions of major project pundits were being proved true: a cost overrun of 100% and the project about a year late. How had this happened? Why had we still not learnt to get the management of projects right? After all, the contractors — those who 'really know' about construction — had assured the markets that the project could be built for the £4·87bn forecast in November 1987.

Essentially, the answer is to be found in that old problem of *concurrency* — of starting construction before the design is properly worked out. With the Tunnel, the problem was that the mechanical and electrical systems, the rolling stock and various safety requirements were not fully defined before the markets were approached for full funding. As the complexity of these systems grew, their costs rose. Inflation was significantly higher than forecast. Claims of £800m arose between Eurotunnel and the contractors. Conflict grew; teamwork, never particularly good, declined to the point in mid 1993 that Eurotunnel was even barred from access to the works by the contractors. Concurrency, contractual disputes, overruns: a familiar story!

The challenges faced by BOO(T) projects

The Channel Tunnel project illustrates vividly, among other things, the important and difficult requirement of creating a strong, independent project owner, and the difficulty of raising finance in the early stages of a project when the design is only elementary and the risk of failure is very high.

BOO(T) projects pose other difficulties. One is that of satisfactory definition of the interfaces between the public and private sectors. In the UK the most important obstacle to BOO(T) taking off was the Treasury's contention that financing of infrastructure projects de facto raised issues of public expenditure, even if the funds were provided by the private sector. The Treasury's view, enshrined in what became known as the Ryrie rules (note 23), was enforced so tightly for almost the entire decade that only one UK BOO(T) project apart from the Channel Tunnel was approved — the Dartford Crossing. In May 1989, however, the Ryrie rules were officially abandoned. Similar public—private sector interface issues were central on overseas projects, particularly in assessment of the impact of BOO(T) projects on ldc economies, and definition of guarantees required from the public sector, and the implications and acceptability of these.

Another difficulty is that the bid period on BOO(T) is lengthy and bid documentation is complex and expensive to prepare. There is often no guarantee that the contractor will be given an exclusive chance to build the project, even though he might have spent considerable sums preparing it: he may be forced to bid for the construction, or even see the project idea given to someone else to realize. Further, not only are the number of parties and the size of the risks great, but also the complexity of the efforts made to limit the risks is significant. On international projects, currency risks are especially significant, as is political risk.

Political risk can cover everything from the threat of the concession being revoked to a change in the national fiscal or legal base. BOO(T) projects generally last at least 15−25 years: it is not unlikely that the government of 20 years' time will be of a different political persuasion from today's and might feel little compunction in exercising its sovereign right to redefine the terms of the BOO(T) deal. Political risk is an obvious worry in Third World projects (note 24) — this is why, by the end of the 1980s, Third World BOO(T) projects had been developed only in relatively prosperous, stable Third World countries with a natural disposition towards the private sector, such as Chile, Hong Kong, Indonesia, Malaysia, Pakistan, the Philippines and Turkey. But political risk is also a factor in the developed world. The UK's decision at the eleventh hour not to proceed with the £700m Antrim power station in 1988, after bidders had incurred huge costs, illustrates this point.

Despite these difficulties, and despite the fact that the number of BOO(T) projects successfully started during the 1980s cannot, depending on definition, be much greater than a dozen, many if not most of the major players in the projects business seemed convinced by the end of the decade that BOO(T) projects represented an important element of future project business. In the developed world there was continued interest in the benefits that private-sector financing and front-end contractor involvement brought; in many Third World countries there seemed little prospect of much commercial lending for project work appearing in any other way in the near future.

The emphasis on a careful assessment of project risk in international lending, as exemplified in private sector BOO(T) project financing, is a far cry from the giddy days of Third World lending of the 1970s. It is also much saner, and must result in much better defined and organized capital projects than had often existed in past decades. BOO(T) should encourage contractors to think as owners: in making them appraise and manage a project *qua* a project it should force them to focus on the project as a whole. Financiers, in BOO(T), are held more closely to the long-term viability of the project (note 25). In systems terms, *the players are at last concentrating on the performance of the project as a 'whole'* — in theory at any rate!

The owner's role and construction management

The difficulties experienced by the Channel Tunnel in creating a strong owner organization came at a time when the construction industry — or rather, industries — was becoming increasingly aware of the importance of an effective owner to the proper management of a project. The gist of the US court and regulatory findings on the mess that the US nuclear power projects largely presented in the 1980s made this point with painful clarity. (Several billion dollars of construction costs were not allowed to be passed on to the utilities' customers, having been deemed by the Public Utility Commissions to have been incurred imprudently or

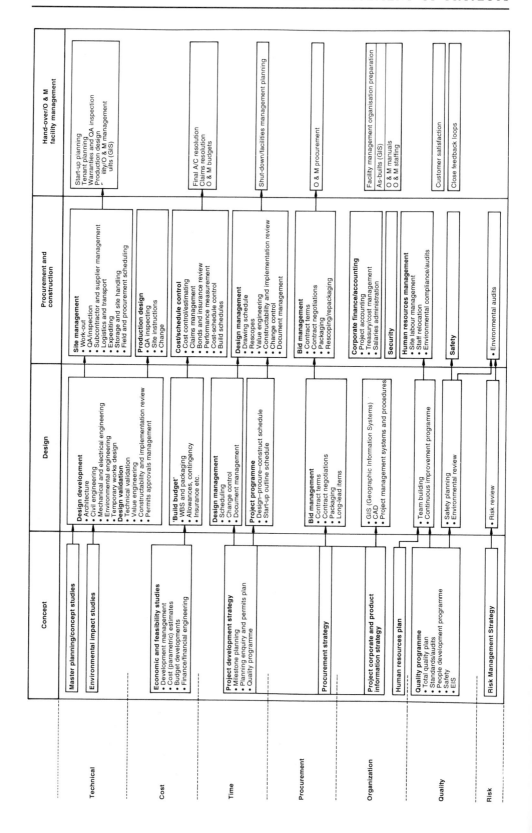

unreasonably: see the Fox and Cleland references to definitions of reasonableness and prudence (p. 319, note 15).) Most of the points made by the courts represented what any stockholder would expect of his board: contractors should be selected with due care and their work should be monitored adequately; contracts should allow adequate control and there should be proper owner–contractor interfacing; unreasonable interference in contractors' work should be avoided; and risks should be properly identified both before the final go-ahead and thereafter as the project develops. But the courts and regulatory bodies went further than this. They insisted that owners had a legal responsibility to participate actively in the project's management. The board and senior management, the courts said, must have data identifying problems before they 'begin to infect the project'; if the data fail to materialize, they have a duty to investigate. And, the courts concluded, owners must be able to distinguish between recurring patterns and non-recurring types of error.[45]

The centrality of the owner to the effective management of construction was further emphasized during the decade by the influential work of the Construction Industry Institute (CII), a body founded in the USA in 1983 following concern over almost two decades of declining productivity in construction.[46] One of the key concepts pursued by CII was constructability — the belief that lower costs, shorter durations and better use of technology could be obtained through construction-sensitive designs; better communication of engineering information; more effective use of construction techniques, subcontractors and standards; and better sequencing.[47–49] Bob Tatum and his colleagues at Stanford University developed this viewpoint within a project management framework, showing that constructability improvements could be achieved only if the specific project context and contractual approach were appropriate and effort was put into developing the project team.[50] The team dimension was further developed as another core CII concept in the mid-to-late 1980s: *'partnering'* (development of close long-term owner–contractor relationships).

There were similar trends in the UK. Many owners, particularly in the private sector, were becoming dissatisfied with the poor productivity of the UK construction industry. Studies showed that it took longer to build in the UK than in other countries, principally because of the time required in the early phases of design, pricing and obtaining statutory approvals.[51,52] Largely as a result of this dissatisfaction, the British Property Federation produced a new model form of contract in 1983–1984, the BPF system, whose essence was that the owner was to define the project specification before any construction contracts were let, after which there should be no changes; the contractor should add design details to suit his own expertise; bids should be lump-sum and should be evaluated on the basis of price, ingenuity, schedule and the contractor's design

Fig. 40 (facing page). Construction Program Management services

ideas — all of which represent familiar project management practice (note 26).

A similar initiative, largely conceived and carried through by Martin Barnes, the principal author of the BPF contract, was begun in the late 1980s to revise the standard form of engineering contract with the intention of providing greater flexibility, adhering more closely to the principles of modern project management, and using clearer and simpler language. This was to lead to the New Engineering Contract issued by the Institution of Civil Engineers in 1991.

The mid-to-late 1980s saw a large expansion of building work in the UK — both housing and commercial property. As the property market heated up, more and more pressure built up for speedier construction and better value for money. Developers demanded greater productivity from their designers and constructors. *Construction management* and *management contracting* increasingly became valued as means of achieving shorter project schedules and better integration — the better management of design being recognized as particularly critical (note 27).[53-60] 'Fast-build' was promoted as a way of getting greater speed — by starting work on early project work packages, such as foundations, superstructure, first fix joinery, etc. even though design of later activities such as M&E services and fit out and finishings was not completed. (This is importantly different from 'concurrency', where production begins before all design and testing on a work package item is finished; in process engineering the term 'fast-track' seemed to be used as a form of concurrency — work beginning, often on a firm-price basis, on construction even before all the process design had been completed.) One of the fastest growing management services in construction in the 1980s thus had its roots in exactly the circumstances in which Ramo Woolridge was selected as system integrator 30 years earlier; the need to tighten management of the project as a whole when demands for greater delivery productivity become pressing.

Project success and failure

The construction industry thus saw two strong pushes in the 1980s for more integrated project performance: construction management and BOO(T). Both stress the classic project skills of balancing technical, schedule and cost demands by use of a top–down management approach implemented by a balanced, carefully selected team, but interestingly they operate at two different levels of project management. Construction management responds to a need to enhance the internal efficiency of the building delivery system. BOO(T) raises a different question in the management of projects: a question perhaps of project effectiveness rather than efficiency. With BOO(T), the project participants have to face a longer term, more strategic set of success measures: not just whether the project will be completed on time or in budget, but whether it is commercially (and therefore socially, technically, financially, etc.) successful over the long term.

During the second half of the 1980s, considerable attention came to be given to *the question of project success*. This happened essentially at two levels. The first, chronologically speaking, was a line of enquiry based on analyses of *projects* rather than project management. Several of these are referred to above — the attempts in the 1970s by Sapolsky,[61] Marschak, Glennan and Summers,[62] and Seamans and Ordway[63] to draw lessons on the management of projects from Polaris, the DoD and NASA. This line of analysis accelerated considerably in the 1980s, with academic work by Hall,[64] Kharbanda and Stallworthy,[65] Paul,[66] Feldman[67,68] and several others analysing major projects in order to derive general lessons on what makes projects successful; there were also studies of publicly funded projects and programmes, ranging across defence (GAO[69] and NAO[70]), nuclear power,[71] R&D[72–77] and development aid.[32,35–37] (Table A.1 in *The anatomy of major projects*[78] provides a short review of several of these studies.)

The second level of success analysis was at the project management rather than the project level. The antecedents of this go back to the 1974 Murphy, Baker and Fisher study of project managers.[79] During the 1980s there were several similar surveys — for example those of Myers and Devey,[80] Might and Fischer,[81] Thamhain and Wilemon[82] and Pinto and Slevin.[83] So great did interest in this topic become that it was chosen as the theme of the 1986 Project Management Institute symposium in Montreal, most of which dealt, as one might expect, with such project management issues as team building, the use of computers, audits, and other tools and techniques. A paper by de Wit highlighted the dichotomy: 'The measurement of progress, cost, and quality is an essential part of project control but this activity should not be confused with measuring success.'[84] Different types of project have different criteria of success — so do different project stakeholders — and these change over time, de Wit pointed out.

The difference in emphasis between *project management* and the *management of projects* that these studies of success point up was to become increasingly significant in the intellectual development of the discipline. The former was the domain occupied by the project management societies; the latter — the more strategic level of analysis — was the ground taken by the major project and macro-engineering societies. Both levels of analysis are of course valid, but working in one without comprehending the other could be dangerous. As I wrote in a paper given at the 1986 PMI Symposium

There have been thousands of articles written on project management and streams of recommendations given as to the best way a project should be managed. Yet in practice the record of projects is not a good one. The classically accepted definition of project management is the accomplishment of a project within its defined technical, budgetary and schedule specifications. Yet all the studies of project schedule and cost performance indicate that overruns are the norm. Further, large projects show larger overruns.

Examination of the various studies on project overruns shows that many of the reasons for poor project performance lie in areas which are traditionally not held to be within the purview of project managers, such as inflation, government actions, poor initial project definition. Since the record of project overruns is so consistently poor, largely because of factors not traditionally the responsibility of project managers, any real attempt to improve the success of the management of projects must involve a change in project management emphasis. Project mangers must give as much and sometimes more attention to managing the impact on their projects of external factors as they do to the more commonly considered 'internal' ones such as scheduling, contracting, organization and control.[85]

Implementation and strategy — R&D, New Product Development and the automotive industry

This concern with identification of the right measures of success, and the use of these to relate operational performance to the performance of the entity as a whole, was to receive considerable attention in several other fields of management during the decade. 'Critical Success Factors', for example, became an important tool of management and information systems design for the identification of where an enterprise needs to concentrate in order to compete successfully.[86–90]

The emphasis on strategy formulation (such a vogue topic for much of the decade), while valuable, went only so far. It was no secret to practitioners that the hard part was *implementation*. That project management had something particularly valuable to contribute in this became gradually recognized by general management during the 1980s. Researchers and writers realized that basic project management concepts such as goal identification, the life cycle, scheduling and proper monitoring could be used to implement strategy and to facilitate organizational change.[91] (The literature on organizational change is particularly rich in this regard.[92,93]) This should have yielded the twin benefits of promoting project management to a wider audience, and raising the importance of strategy, success measurement and externalities to the project management community at large. Yet its impact on both fronts was minimal. The project management methodology was often used with no reference to project management. Project managers, on the other hand, were understandably more interested in the here-and-now of next steps rather than strategic questions of definition, which were generally seen as someone else's responsibility anyway.

Writings on *R&D* and *New Product Development* illustrate vividly this unfortunate tendency to compartmentalize the general insights of managing projects, although in this case, I fear, more to the cost of project management than of R&D.

De Cotiis and Dyer, for example, had defined project success by dimensions as diverse as manufacturability and business performance, technical performance, project management accomplishment, personal growth and technological innovativeness — a range of measures more attuned to the top–down 'management of projects' approach than to 'project management'.[94] Indeed, the question of success had been more thoroughly explored in R&D and new product development than in almost any other project literature, with the linkage to strategy and implementation being made forcibly by many authors, particularly Robert Cooper in his work towards the end of the decade.[95–97] Similarly, much of the literature on R&D management was concerned with relating project selection and product development to the needs of the marketplace and with the necessity of ensuring successful commercialization.[95,98,99] And writings by Balanchandra and Raelin,[73] Bedell[100] and others[101–103] dealt, almost uniquely, with the question of when to abandon a project.

One 'product development' industry in particular was quietly revolutionizing the way manufacturing was managed, and by the 1990s the developments in its practices were to begin having a radical impact on project management. This was the automotive industry, and the reason for the change was the Japanese.

During the 1980s the Japanese, led by Toyota, pioneered a new 'lean production' approach to manufacturing which contrasted radically with the traditional methods of mass production. Developed in the 1960s and 1970s largely on the basis of what were to become known as Total Quality Management principles, lean production emphasizes teamwork, catching errors before they are passed down the production line, the full involvement of

Fig. 41. Land Rover Discovery lean production line (courtesy Land Rover plc)

suppliers in achieving manufacturing improvements, and a product design process that integrates downstream production expertise into product design. Production equipment is kept sufficiently multi-purpose that considerable flexibility is built into the manufacturing line. Customers are thus offered greater choice, and products match their differing needs more fully and quickly. Further, the Japanese 'target costed' their designs to produce specific products — generally offering more attractive performance, features and style than their competitors' — for much lower cost. Product life cycle times are also shortened by a 'Fast Build' variant of concurrency known as Simultaneous Development or Simultaneous Engineering. Die production begins at the same time as body design by having both sets of designers working as a close-knit team, with rough die cuts ready to move into final cutting as soon as the final panel designs are released. In terms of managing product development, the Japanese delegated full authority to a Large Project Leader (or *shusa*). As Massachusetts Institute of Technology reported in its influential book *The machine that changed the world*,[104] in contrast to GM and most of the US automanufacturers, who used project co-ordinators for their product development programmes who had little or no formal authority, 'the shusa is simply the boss, the leader of the team whose job it is to design and engineer a new product and get it into production. In the best Japanese companies the position of *shusa* carries great power and is, perhaps, the most coveted in the company'.[104]

The cumulative impact of these new project-driven management practices was that from the mid-1980s the Japanese achieved a radical compression of product development cycles. Between 1983 and 1987 the Japanese shrank the 'time to market' for a family-sized car from 60 months (the US figure) to 46, requiring only 1·7 million engineering hours against the USA's 3 million.[105]

Industries such as the auto industry, having a high technology base or relying on major new product developments, had an obvious affinity to projects. Some, indeed had close links with the established project management world, for example aerospace and pharmaceuticals — the US Project Management Institute had had a pharmaceuticals 'special interest' group since the mid-1970s. Many, however, were relatively isolated from developments in mainstream project management: for example; in the early 1980s information technology's use of formal project management practices was surprisingly low; by the end of the decade, however, it was making a major contribution to the discipline.

Information Technology projects

Information Technology (IT) — generally taken to include both information systems and telecommunications — became recognized during the 1980s as an area of crucial importance to organizational effectiveness. Enormous sums were spent during the late 1970s and 1980s in building IT systems and facilities. The potential IT market was huge but so were the costs, and risks, of playing. For many, the R&D costs became prohibitive, and competition was often severe. In an attempt to share R&D costs, and to promote national industries, several countries instigated multi-company, pre-competitive Fifth Generation research programmes. The different ways these were managed reflect the extent to which project management principles were being recognized at this time in a wider management context.

In 1981 the Japanese announced a $900m collaborative Fifth Generation research programme to develop the technologies for the next plateau of computing capability — one which would involve Natural Language Processing (thus no longer presenting the same problems of programming to the Japanese); greater computing capacity by Very Large System Integration (VLSI); increased efficiency through Parallel Computing; Knowledge Based Computing; and Speech and Image Recognition (the common thread throughout the programme being Artificial Intelligence). The Americans and Europeans reacted quickly. The Americans established military and civilian pre-competitive research programmes — DARPA, MCC and STARS — while the EEC launched Esprit ($1·5bn) and the UK launched Alvey (£350m). France and Germany launched similar national programmes.

The Japanese programme was organized along the lines of its previous successful collaborative pre-competitive research programme, the VLSI project of 1976−1980.[106] In both cases the heart of the project was a central laboratory staffed by scientists from competing companies. *Conflict* was endemic but *was managed positively and creatively*. A *central laboratory* was used where researchers spent considerable time planning, communicating and confronting. The American MCC programme also paid much attention to *leadership* and *personnel*. Admiral Bobby Inman, recently retired as Director of the CIA, headed MCC, doing so on just two conditions: that he be in absolute charge and that he have absolute authority on personnel matters. A central laboratory was established at the University of Texas at Austin.[107]

Such a project-driven approach to Fifth Generation research compares starkly with the much more diffuse European approach. Neither Alvey nor Esprit used a central laboratory, nor was there any emphasis on creating the productive conflict that the Japanese and Americans came to prize so much.

In fact, the Europeans flew in the face of many of the project lessons of R&D management culled during the 1970s and 1980s (unlike the Japanese and Americans): they had widely varied goals, a highly diffuse geographical spread, weak personnel and team management, little active leadership, few clear schedules, and low 'productive conflict'. Alvey, unsurprisingly, was not a very successful programme.[108,109]

IT projects not only posed huge R&D and product development

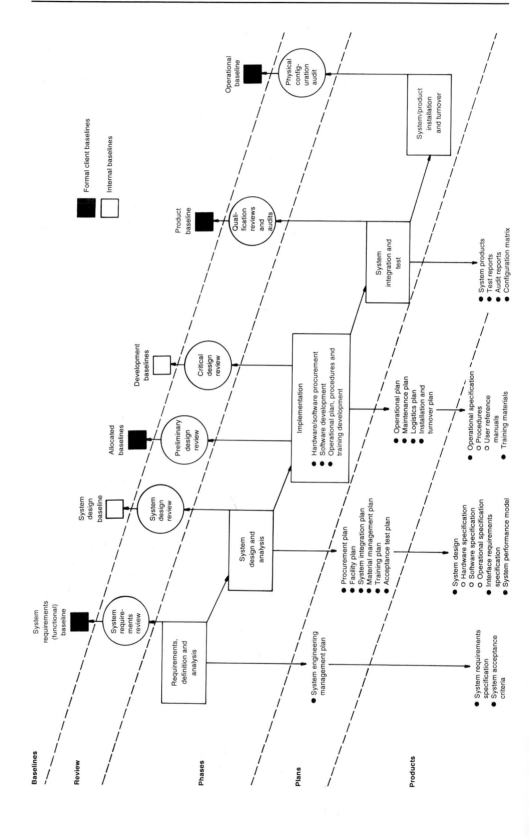

challenges, but also raised major questions of project definition and success. For IT projects were held, in the jargon of the decade, to be associated intimately with the competitive advantage of the enterprises they served.[110–112] Effective implementation of IT therefore became a much sought after capability. Yet, to the immense frustration of many, IT projects were often accomplished well over schedule and cost far too much.

The computer and telecommunications industries had of course made important contributions to the development of project management from its early years: P.V. Norden's 1960 paper, from IBM, on resource allocation was a landmark of its kind;[113] the work of A.D. Hall and others at Bell Laboratories on the development of systems engineering methodology in the 1960s was hugely influential:[114] Frederick Brooks' 1975 book *The mythical man-month*[115] is one of the best on the project management of new product development ('you slip a year one day at a time'). On the whole, however, the industry was extraordinarily slow to adopt widely the discipline of project management. Hence IT projects were often late and over budget not just because they were genuinely very hard to manage, but because most people conducting these projects in the 1970s and early 1980s simply were not using project management tools and techniques properly. The concept that a software project would follow a development life cycle was still novel to many in the industry in the mid-1970s, for example. Project-based development methodologies were only just beginning to become common in the early 1980s. Yet without a well-defined methodology it is difficult to specify user requirements unambiguously; without clearly defined requirements — and an agreed life cycle with clearly identified review points and change control procedures — it is very hard to measure progress or to control changes; and since software projects typically have much subsystem interaction, controlling this development without some form of configuration management is extremely difficult (note 28). The control of software projects absolutely requires firm project management practices.

Towards the end of the 1970s, however, substantial effort had begun to be put into the improvement of software engineering and management. Systems integration firms developed proprietorial systems development methodologies, which utilized a wide range of project management tools in a most rigorous way. DSDM (Fig. 42) was one of the best of this period. Later, other methodologies were developed, many also incorporating systems engineering capabilities. Structured programming languages such as Pascal, C, and Ada were developed in the late 1970s and early 1980s. Computer-Aided Software Engineering (CASE) tools were added to model the development process and aid in completeness and consistency checking. These broadened the scope of support from 'programming' to full 'project' requirements and led in turn

Fig. 42 (facing page). DSDM (courtesy Computer Sciences Corporation)

to the further development of project management methodologies for software projects.[116-119] The DoD propelled this effort with the development of an Ada Programming Support Environment (APSE); this was later generalized into an Integrated Project Support Environment (IPSE). In the UK, the government methodology PROMPT was introduced in the mid-1980s. Structured Systems Analysis and Design Methodology (SSADM) was introduced as the de facto UK standard for systems development. PRINCE followed in 1990 as the new UK government project management methodology.[120] (Its processes are in fact so clear and sensible that it began being used in the 1990s in a variety of non-IT project situations.)

However, the difficulty in accomplishing software projects successfully lay not only in the internal technical challenges. To be effective as an enabling technology, IT must relate effectively and intimately to the needs of the user and his organization. As these change, so, theoretically, should the information system. It would, however, be disastrous if the project definition changed every time changes (which inevitably occur quite frequently) occurred in the project's environment. Dealing with this problem has contributed extensively to our understanding of the way simplistic project management goals of 'on time, in budget, to technical specification' may have to be altered to the more subtle, top—down concern of the effective management of projects. Two practices promoted by IT managers to deal with these challenges have contributed usefully to the practice of project management: the organizational approach to tying projects into their business case, and rapid prototyping.

Project review structures involving users and the 'project sponsor' came to be seen during the late 1980s as a way of ensuring that the project was still relevant to the business case. The sponsor is the person providing the resources for the project: the person who should be responsible for ensuring that the project is successful at the business or institutional level (note 29). Similarly, the emphasis on the user involvement was taken further in information systems (IS) projects than in any other industry. Generally, users had been kept at arm's length on projects since they 'interfered with' the design. IS practice was to involve them not just at the Systems Analysis and Specification stage but formally through the Design Review process as well.[121,122] IS/IT projects also became particularly strong users of the 'Critical Success Factors' approach to identification of the project's key success requirements.

IT *rapid prototyping* emerged in the early 1980s as an alternative method to the 'heel-to-toe' evolution of a project through its life cycle, with all the lengthy checks and controls that this inevitably entails. Rapid prototyping in IT is the process of quickly developing working models of the system that can be evaluated, maybe in several different iterations, before a final version is selected.[123–129] In this way, users can quickly test a working model of the system against their perhaps inadequately perceived requirements, and developers can appraise their design and coding before the expense, time and trouble of building, installing and testing the whole system. Such 'testing' is especially valuable for high-risk, high-value systems such as decision support systems. In project management terms, rapid prototyping was particularly interesting in that it flew in the face of the simple sequential mode of development advocated by some as best system procurement practice but was allied more to the Simultaneous/Concurrent Engineering approach being developed in manufacturing.

IT's impact on project management tools

IT in the 1980s not only offered commercial and philosophical contributions to the development of the management of projects as a discipline: its technological advances at last allowed project managers to use with comparative ease many of the techniques that had previously proved too complicated or expensive for all but the more dedicated enthusiasts or well-resourced projects.

Since the inception of network scheduling in the late 1950s, schedules had had to be run in batch mode on large mainframe computers located in a special computer room. Specialized knowledge was needed to run the programs — hence the user typically did not become involved with the software, errors were frequent and often took days to correct, operation of the computer was expensive, and computer applications tended to be rigid and technique-driven rather than adapted to the need of the task in hand. All this was even truer of the more complex programs such as those for resource allocation. It is little wonder, then, that the adoption of networking and other project management techniques had been slower than the specialists had expected.[130,131]

With the arrival of Fourth Generation computing in the late 1970s and early 1980s, substantially greater capability became available. Personal computers and minis were now able to offer real computing power on site and in the office — the computer had become portable and could now be used as a decision support system, being queried directly on an interactive basis; data were held in a database management structure and so could be entered and obtained comparatively easily; a screen was located next to the keyboard, allowing the user to see and interact with his data immediately; graphics capability increased and people began to work on computer-aided design (CAD) and basic Expert Systems; and transmission capabilities increased dramatically with the introduction of better telecommunications.

Suddenly, the promises of computerized project management systems began to become a reality. By the late 1970s interactive mini-based systems were relatively common. By the late 1980s several PC-based systems were able to handle a large number of activities, costs and resources,[132–134] often in conjunction with home-office mainframes or minis as part of a distributed data networking system.

As the 1980s drew to a close, several IT barriers seemed tantalizingly close to being broken: open systems architecture; fully integrated engineering, procurement and project planning and monitoring systems, incorporating easy-to-use graphics, CAD and computer-aided manufacturing (CAM);[135,136] even Artificial Intelligence.[137-143] It would be well into the 1990s, however, before practitioners were able to work easily across these boundaries.

Project management writing in the 1980s

Table 4 lists the most significant papers written in journals on projects and project management in the decade (I should add that the selection is personal, reflecting what I believe are the more critical areas of project management writing, and that its brevity in no way reflects the actual quantity of writing that appeared).

The papers by Avots, Bu-Bushait, Dane *et al.*, Liberatore and Titus, Navarre and Schaan, and Weber provided useful summaries of what project management tools and techniques were actually being used in practice. *Risk Management* arose as a topic of interest, pioneering work being done by Ashley and Avots, Cooper *et al.*, Lichtenberg, and Perry and Hayes in particular. *Expert Systems* emerged as another area, although research was

Table 4. Key project management papers of the 1980s

Year	Organization	Tools and techniques	General management
1981		Dane *et al.*[131]	
1982		Niwa and Okumu[144] Weber[145]	Cooper[96]
1983	Hofstede[146] Morton[147]	Dunne[148] Lichtenberg[149]	
1984		Ashley and Avots[150]	Balachandra and Raelin[73] Fox[151]
1985	Might and Fisher[81]	Levitt and Kunz[152] Cooper, MacDonald and Chapman[153] Perry and Hayes[154]	Davis[155]
1986	Thamhain and Wilemon[82]	Liberatore and Titus[156]	Morris[85] Cleland[157]
1987	Gobeli[158]	Avots[132] Navarre and Schaan[159]	Ashley[160]
1988			Pinto and Slevin[83] de Wit[161]
1989	Pinto and Slevin[162]	Arditi *et al.*[163] Bu-Bushait[164]	Gareis[165] Shafer and Mantel[102]

still basically theoretical: the Levitt and Kunz, Niwa and Okumu, and Arditi *et al.* papers are among the most approachable.

In the organization area, the Gobeli and Might and Fisher papers related organization structure to project success. Thamhain and Wilemon related a wider range of organizational variables to success. Meanwhile, Morton, and Pinto and Slevin, raised and discussed the idea of the '*project champion*'. Hofstede provided an original, stimulating — and probably ultimately flawed — paper suggesting that the characteristics of different nations — Indians, Japanese, Americans, French, etc. — strongly affect their ability to work in the primarily American (goal-driven, team-oriented) project management culture.

In the more general, strategic area I should note my own paper on the role of project management in project definition, Cleland's on stakeholder management, Davis's on project evaluation, Shafer and Mantel's on project termination, and Gareis's important paper on '*management by projects*' — the idea that many general management situations can be usefully treated as project situations. Books on project management in the decade included the following, and many others

- Harrison's[166] *Advanced project management*, Keen's[167] *Managing systems development*, Peters' *Project management and construction control*[168] and Stuckenbruck's[169] (on behalf of the US Project Management Institute) *The implementation of project management* in 1981
- Kelley's[170] thoughtful *New dimensions of project management* and Ruskin and Estes' *What every engineer should know about project management*[171] in 1982
- a series of blockbusters in 1983 — Cleland and King's[172] fat *Project management handbook*, Kerzner's[173] *Project management for executives*, Kharbanda and Stallworthy's[66] interesting *How to learn from project disasters*, Stallworthy and Kharbanda's[174] *Total project management*
- Andersen *et al.*'s[175] *Goal directed project management*, Cleland's[176] large *Matrix systems management handbook*, Dinsmore's[177] useful *Human factors in project management*, Kerzner's[178] near-definitive *Project management: a systems approach to planning, scheduling and controlling*, Kerzner's and Cleland's[179] *Project/matrix management policy and strategy*, Rosenau's[180] *Project management for engineers*, Thamhain's[181] *Engineering program management* and Walker's[182] *Project management in construction* in 1984
- Meredith and Mantel's[183] text — one of the best basic ones available — *Project management: a managerial approach* was published in 1985, as were Cleland and Kerzner's[184] brave but not very successful *A project management*

dictionary of terms, Slemakers' *The principles and practices of cost schedule control systems*,[185] Stephanou and Obradovitch's[186] *Project management, systems development and productivity*, Tompkins'[187] *Project cost control for managers* and Westeney's[188] *Managing the engineering and construction of small projects*.

- Gilbreath's[189] entertaining *Winning at project management*, Lock's[190] very useful *Project management handbook* (no relation to Cleland and King's) and Kharbanda and Stallworthy's[191] *Project cost control*; Kerzner and Thamhain's[192] immensely valuable *Project management operating guidelines* and Roman's[193] *Managing projects: a systems approach* in 1986

- Silverman's[194] *The art of managing technical projects* (which seemed to be more about organizational issues than technology management), Davidson Frame's[195] *Managing projects in organizations* and Internet's[196] *Project start-up manual*

- Badiru's[197] *Project management in manufacturing and high technology operations*, Burbridge's[198] practical and useful *Perspectives on project management*, Fleming's[199] *Cost schedule control systems criteria: the management guide to C/SCSC*, Morris and Hough's[78] *The anatomy of major projects*, Roetzheim's[200] *Structured computer project management* and Stone's[201] *The management of engineering projects* in 1988

- Humphrey's[202] *Managing the software process* and Kimmons and Loweree's[203] massive, comprehensive and useful compilation of project management practice, from concept stage to operations — one of the best (and least known) textbooks on the subject, giving an enormous quantity of detail, although cast basically in an (engineering) construction context, both in 1989.

There were also several fresh editions of books already published, including those by Archibald, Cleland and King (*Systems analysis and project management*), Kerzner, Lock, and Moder *et al.*

Other important books relating to the management of projects included Boehm's[118] *Software engineering economics*, Moris's[35] *Managing induced rural development*, O'Riordan and Sewell's[30] *Project appraisal and policy review* and Kidder's[204] *The soul of a new machine* in 1981; Paul's[36] *Managing development programs* in 1982; Hayes *et al.*'s[205] *Management contracting*, Murphy's[206] *Macroproject development in the Third World* and Nevitt's[207] *Project financing* in 1983; the Warren Centre's[208] report on *Macroprojects* in 1985; Cassen *et al.*'s[37] *Does aid work?* and Whipp and Clark's[75] *Innovation and the auto industry* in 1986; and Fox's[5] *The defense management challenge*,

Karploff's[209] *Export and project finance* and O'Riordan *et al.*'s[31] *Sizewell B: an anatomy of the inquiry* in 1988.

Developments in the project management societies

As the above literature review shows, writing on project management had by now blossomed into a substantial body of useful data, much of it supplied from, and published by, the project management societies PMI and Internet. These, and indeed other project management societies which became active during the decade in Australia, Japan and India, flourished as project management became increasingly recognized across a wide range of industries as an important topic, worthy of special study and individual practice.[210–212] Given their orientation, though, most of what was discussed and published by the societies tended to be about intra-project matters (note 30). Often, as in the writings on developments in computing, this did not particularly matter. However, when the societies attempted more ambitious topics, notably, perhaps, the development by PMI of a Standard Body of Project Management Knowledge, this limitation became more important.

During the 1980s, PMI sought to define professional standards of project management. The three central planks of this effort were the definition of a common body of specialized knowledge, the establishment of an education programme, and a certification process. A Master of Project Management degree programme was established under PMI's auspices in 1984 at Western Carolina University; a formal 'Body of Knowledge' was developed between 1983 and 1986;[213,214] and a certification process, requiring evidence of an adequate knowledge base and a service record, got under way in 1984.

The 1983 Body of Knowledge identified six basic project management functions: human resources management, cost management, time management, communications management, scope management and quality management. By 1986 a seventh had been added: contract/procurement management (sic). There was still nothing, however, on finance, technology, government or the environment (either ecological or social).

Major project and macro-engineering societies

These topics were getting a broader airing in the slowly emerging stream of project societies being established out of Frank Davidson's initiatives and the success of the Giant Projects conference in London in 1978.

The Americans organized a series of prestigious seminars on macro-engineering in the early 1980s in conjunction with the American Association for the Advancement of Science.[215–218] The focus of these events was the belief that large, multi-organizational undertakings were important to society but were generally poorly understood. In 1982, The American Society for

Macro-Engineering was founded with the objective of providing a vehicle for the discussion, analysis and dissemination of information on macro-engineering. Meetings were held regularly thereafter, with articles published in the journal *Technology in Society*.[219-235] Similar macro-engineering societies were founded in Canada, Japan and Spain. A Large Scale Programs Institute based at the University of Texas at Austin, representing a network of about ten US universities researching in this area, was founded in 1984.[236] And in 1985 the Warren Centre at the University of Sydney published the results of a year-long study into macroprojects[208] — one of the most insightful, mature documents produced on the subject — maintaining thereafter a macroprojects working group.

But of all these societies, none was as active or successful as the UK Major Projects Association. Founded in 1981, the MPA built up a powerful body of knowledge on the issues affecting the successful initiation, assessment, securing and accomplishment of major projects. These lessons, derived from the confidential sharing of experience by skilled practitioners, were articulated in a series of publications and teaching programmes that emerged from Templeton College, Oxford, where the MPA is based.[237-242]

The management of macro-programmes

So far in this book we have strayed from detailed consideration of project management tools and techniques, such as C/SCSC and GERT, to reviews of the more strategic definition and management of projects, such as Apollo, the F-111 and the Channel Tunnel. We have even used the framework that has gradually emerged to critique — often using its own bullets, so to speak — the way the Pentagon procures weapons systems and the disaster (for in the end this has to be the word) that has occurred for much of the civil nuclear power business.

It is now time to end this chronological account, but in doing so let us push out the conceptual framework even further, to consider two huge programmes — one, Technopolis, an ambitious national R&D programme aimed at ensuring Japan's long-term industrial competitiveness; the second, the Space Station, our rather fumbling effort to move out into space — perhaps the biggest project of all time, and certainly one of the most confused.

Japanese 'soft' programme management and Technopolis

The project approach to large scale systems challenges described in this book, though rejected by some during the 1980s as unworkable, had one very important champion: Japan. Japan had never felt particularly comfortable with, or excelled in, the 'hard' systems approach to project management; however, particularly from the 1980s, it excelled at the 'soft' systems approach to projects and programmes. Nowhere was this more apparent than in Japan's decision in the late 1970s to become a leader in R&D. Until this time Japan had always been viewed as weak at R&D — a technology copier. With the new approach, Japan began to exhibit a remarkable goal-directed, programme-organized approach to R&D and change management, at both the micro and the macro levels (Fig. 43) At the project level, as we saw with the VLSI project, and as writings on Japanese R&D make clear,[243] this produced an approach that combined *rational analysis, complex organizational arrangements, informal but efficient information management, and a creative use of team working and conflict*

Fig. 43. Japan's parallel-track R&D projects (from Tatsuno[244])

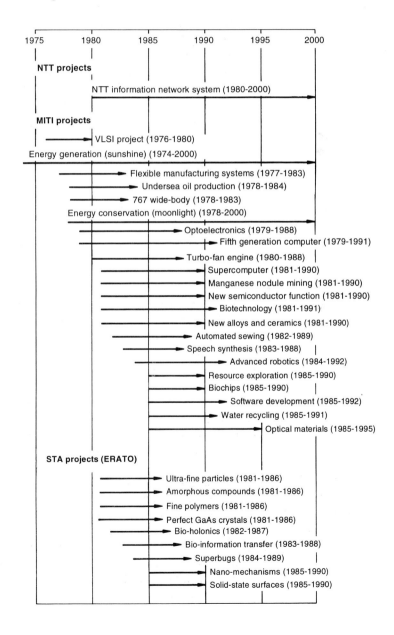

management. At the macro level, Japan has demonstrated, more than any other of the developed nation democracies, an ability to stitch together a loose, contingency-based method of planning and organization focused on defined programme tasks. Nothing illustrates this process more clearly than the Technopolis programme.[244,245]

In the late 1970s the Japanese began to look for a version of 'Silicon Valley' by which their rate of technology development could be increased. After visiting several high-technology research centres they eventually settled on a model derived in the first place from Sophia-Antipolis in France — a residential, collegiate environment in which industry, academia and government work together to create new industrial structures. The Japanese, however, made some interesting additions to this model. Coining the word 'Technopolis', they proposed the designation of one or two prefectures as technopoles. These would be created near an existing 'mother' city with a research university; at their heart would be a Technopolis zone — an industrial/research park containing industry, government and university laboratories — which would be served by recreational and housing facilities and, importantly, connected by a sophisticated system of advanced communications: high-speed rail, airports (since most of the technopoles' products are high volume/low weight), and optical fibre-based INS data networks.

Integrated communications were to be a vital part of the national R&D network. Equally importantly, the Technopolis programme was based on a regional development policy based on emerging industries (note 31). Local involvement and support for the Technopolis programme was seen to be vital: Technopolis was to be programme-focused but diffuse, long-term and flexible, well supported by local research and integrated communictions, and, equally, driven from the bottom up. Although lacking the tight organizational control associated with 'hard' programme management, the Technopolis programme shows how national endeavours can be organized around a long-term goal by the use of appropriate support groups organized around a realistic schedule.

When MITI announced the Technopolis programme in 1980, no fewer than 34 prefectures applied to be hosts for the technopoles. By 1989 there were some 27. The Japanese are realistic about the progress that will be made. They do not expect short-term miracles. By the year 2000, though, perhaps a dozen technopoles will be doing well; by 2020 perhaps 25 or so. The Japanese believe they can wait. They have a shared vision, a practical design, the money, the political and community support, and a workable implementation plan. They have a strategically sound approach for this major programme.

**The Space
Station**

To conclude this chronological section of our investigation of the management of projects, we shall return to space: fittingly, perhaps, in that so much of modern project management was developed around US rocket programmes, but also in that, while NASA exemplified in Apollo the best of *project management* as engineering management, with the Space Station (note 32) — one of the largest non-military projects of modern times — and the Shuttle, it illustrates profoundly the difficult strategic problems more typical of the *management of projects*. For by the end of the 1980s, after the Challenger crash of 1986, and with the Space Station project largely bogged down in Congressional budget difficulties, the US space programme was at best at a crossroads, at worst in a mess.

From the mid to late 1960s, cost, as we have seen, was a major problem for the USA's aspirations in space, Vice-President Agnew's 1969 proposals for the Space Station as a way-post for onward travel to the moon and Mars being rejected by Nixon as too expensive.

With the arrival of James Beggs as NASA's Administrator in 1981, the Space Station acquired a determined champion. In May 1982, Beggs formed a Space Station Task Force headed by James Fletcher to identify mission requirements and to define an initial station concept. Several foreign governments, including those of Canada, members of the European Space Agency (ESA) and Japan, conducted their own studies and exchanged findings with the Americans.

In February 1983, NASA began to prepare its 1985 budget, in which Beggs wanted first funding for the Station included. Beggs met with Reagan on 7 April. The President seemed inclined towards a Mars project but Beggs, recognizing that Congress was unlikely to accept the costs this entailed, said 'let's do the Space Station first and then we can go anywhere we want to'.[246] Beggs 'sold the Space Station to President Reagan on national security grounds as an edge on the Soviets'.[246] Yet this was precisely what the Station was not.

The trouble with the Station has always been its several different uses. Many of these were often best met by smaller cheaper craft; invariably they were harder to justify on a large, single Space Station structure than on their own (note 33). None were military. The only real reason for grouping them in a single large, expensive structure was, I believe, the long-term value of the way-station. Yet the problem was that this was extremely hard to justify to a sceptical Congress. To NASA, the Station was an article of faith. To others it was unnecessary, expensive 'big science'. The estimated cost of the Station in 1985 dollars was $12bn, of which $8bn was to be provided by NASA and $4bn by its foreign partners.

Despite the almost total opposition of his Cabinet, the President remained enthusiastic (note 34), and in his State of the Union message of 25 January 1984 announced

> Tonight I am directing NASA to develop a permanently manned Space Station, and to do it within a decade. A Space Station would permit quantum leaps in our research in science, communications and in metals and in life-saving medicines which could be manufactured only in space. We want our friends to help us meet these challenges and share in their benefits. NASA will invite other countries to participate so we can strengthen peace, build prosperity and expand freedom for all who share our goals.

A crucial assumption directly bounding the size and weight of the Space Station configuration was the Shuttle, which was to be used to carry the Station elements into orbit (and which, it will be recalled, had had to be down-sized for budgetary reasons in the early 1970s). The modular approach to the Station configuration that was thus created had an immediate impact on the question of how to assign project management responsibility for hardware development within NASA.

During the first half of 1984, NASA formulated the Station's management structure. It was decided to retain the systems engineering and integration function in-house and to allocate the four work packages to four NASA divisions. (NASA felt it unwise to rely on an external contractor for the systems engineering and integration of hardware of such a size, which was to have such a long operational life.)

Phase A of the project — the concept phase — was undertaken in 1982–1984. Phase B — definition of preliminary design — began in April 1985. Phase C — detailed design — began in the autumn of 1986, with contractors starting work in May 1987. At the end of Phase A, a 'baseline configuration' had emerged comprising a single power tower 'truss'. During Phase B, however, NASA moved to a 'dual keel' configuration which provided a stiffer frame and reduced oscillation (Fig. 44).

In April 1985, Europe and the USA agreed the basis on which they would collaborate. Europe, operating under ESA, would build and operate one of the four laboratory modules located on the Station. The European module, to be known as Columbus, would cost about $600m. Similar outlines for the Canadian remote servicing arm and the Japanese module were agreed at more or less the same time (note 35).

During the winter of 1985–1986 several serious difficulties began to affect the project. In November, Beggs was indicted for contractual improprieties connected with his previous job with General Dynamics. His successor, William Graham, was a relative newcomer to space and had been in NASA only a few weeks before Beggs went on leave of absence. On 28 January 1986, the Shuttle Challenger exploded shortly after lift-off. The American psyche was shocked, its confidence ruptured. The Shuttle fleet was immediately grounded. The ability of the USA to launch, build and service the Space Station by the scheduled date of the late 1990s was suddenly very questionable, for even assuming that another Shuttle would be built, there would be a huge backlog of delayed missions to work through.

President Reagan, predictably, reacted at his best, showing genuine sympathy and grief but affirming his belief in continued US involvement in space. Within a month of the Challenger accident, Reagan had reaffirmed his commitment to the Space Station.

As if to add insult to injury, at the end of February 1986, the Soviet Union launched Mir (Russian for 'Peace'), a new type of spacecraft intended to become the hub of the world's first permanently manned space station. Suddenly, the Soviet Union's slow but sure approach to space — consistent political support, and the avoidance of large technological leaps (such as the Shuttle) and multinational complexities (such as the Space Station) — seemed to have more to offer than America's more ambitious designs.

On 6 May 1986, James Fletcher was confirmed by the Senate

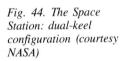

Fig. 44. The Space Station: dual-keel configuration (courtesy NASA)

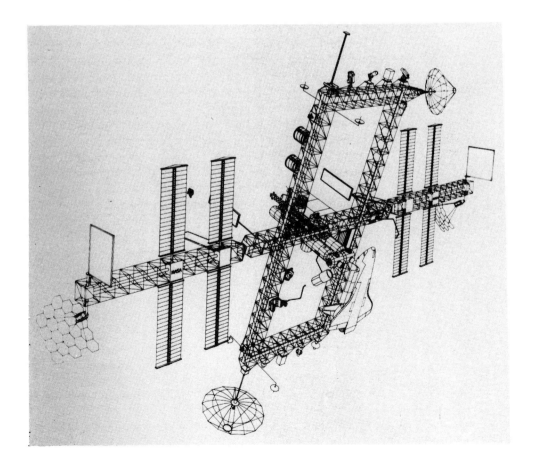

to return to NASA as Administrator. One of his first tasks was to receive recommendations from General Sam Phillips, the Program Manager for Apollo, who had been asked to review the station's overall management structure. Phillips believed that the Program Management structure would not work and that, unless changes were made, the Space Station programme would continue to experience difficulties.[247] He was also concerned that the existing division of work among the field centres did not allow clear accountability. He therefore recommended that the programme be organized into clearly definable major deliverable items, each of which would be the responsibility of a single contractor. His proposals were only partially accepted.

Things now got worse for NASA, as it became apparent that the cost of the dual-keel station had risen substantially. By January 1987 the estimate was $14·5 billion in 1984 dollars. Such an increase was unacceptable, and so in April 1987 the programme was reconfigured into two stages. Block I, the 'Revised Baseline Configuration', included the basic laboratories and modules, and the polar platform(s). The later Block II, an 'Enhanced Configuration', would have additional power and accommodation modules, a servicing bay and co-orbiting platforms. However the cost of Block I was still estimated to be $12bn.

An important implication of this reconfiguration — always implicit but now central — was the evolutionary nature of the project. The dual keel would come later; indeed, the configuration of the station would itself change as its operational needs were redefined (for example as its role as a way-post on the journey to the moon or Mars became more important). The undertaking was now not so much a straightforward project or even a programme as a major long-term mission composed (as indeed are most projects) of various operations and future project phases.

This renewed attention to long-term goals was heightened when the DoD began to become more interested in the programme. The European, Japanese and Canadian interest now became increasingly strained. The fundamental issue was how to justify the Space Station. Apollo had been initiated on the basis of the Soviet threat implied by Sputnik. The trouble was that now, almost 30 years later, the military imperative had a separate route and the interplay of military with civilian purpose was far from clear. NASA, despite Reagan's initial vagueness on the subject, had to justify the Space Station on civilian grounds; this was not easy especially given the deliberate vagueness of the programme and the scepticism of a Congress facing a very large budgetary deficit. More work was needed, it was recognized, to develop the longer term strategic 'civilian' reasons for being in space.

NASA's previous attempt to do this, in 1985 — the Paine Report (subtitled 'An exciting vision of our next 50 years in space') —

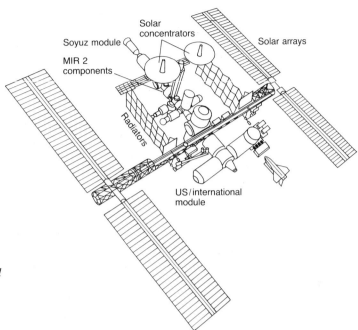

Soyuz module
Solar concentrators
Solar arrays
MIR 2 components
Radiators
US/international module

Fig. 45. NASA's global option for an international space station: November 1993

had signally failed.[248] NASA, however, had subsequently commissioned astronaut Sally Ride to re-examine its longer-term strategies. Ride analysed the pacing factors affecting four basic strategic options (note 36), and concluded first that until the mid-1990s Earth-to-orbit transportation was NASA's most pressing problem while, with regard to longer-term developments, the scientific and technological base for sending astronauts into space for long periods was currently inadequate (note 37). Lunar and Mars missions would require extraordinary allocations of resources after the mid-1990s. Hence the Station's evolution would depend critically on the option selected: 'the Planetary initiative makes few demands on the Space Station; the Mars initiative makes substantial demands'.[249]

The Ride Report was relatively warmly welcomed almost everywhere except in sections of the Congress and the White House, where, just at the time of its publication (July 1987), a complete reassessment of US space policy was initiated.

As well as the Paine and Ride Reports, the White House took note of a National Research Council assessment of the Station released in September 1987. Led by former NASA Deputy Administrator Robert Seamans, the NRC report contained a comprehensive survey of the issues facing the Space Station.[250] The Station's Block I configuration was a satisfactory starting point; deployment of the Station using the Shuttle, while not infeasible, the NRC rather amazingly concluded, would be difficult and risky — the US should develop a heavy lift launch vehicle for the late

1990s (note 38); Program Management of the Station was weak; and co-ordination with the shuttle programme could be improved. Considering that the Space Station was, in the NRC's words, 'the most ambitious and lengthy task NASA had ever undertaken', it seems incredible that the project's management could be so indicted at so late a stage of its evolution.

On 11 February 1988, the White House issued a directive on National Space Policy setting the direction of US efforts in space for the future. Leadership was to be a fundamental objective of US space activities (although, crucially, that leadership was to be selective). The Space Station, soon to be reaffirmed by President Bush and now called 'Freedom', was on.

By mid-1989, with Congress suggesting that funding to NASA be cut, and NASA in consequence talking of scaling back the now $24·7bn Station, George Bush, on the 20th anniversary of the Apollo 11 moon landing, while endorsing Mission to Planet Earth, reaffirmed the USA's intention to develop a manned lunar base as a stage on the way to a manned Mars landing by the second decade of the 21st century. All Sally Ride's options were being pursued.

Strategy was still evolving even as the project was progressing through its design. No wonder the project was in trouble — and was to remain so well into the 1990s. President Clinton ordered a radical review and scale-back of funding on taking office in 1993. On 3 November 1993 agreements were signed between Russia and the USA to merge their space station programmes — an impressive symbol of the new politics of major projects. The result should be a massive international venture leading to a space station code named Alpha, comprising components from both nations as well as Canada, Japan and Europe. Assembly is scheduled to begin in 1997–1998.

References

1. General Accounting Office. *DoD's Defense Acquisition program: a status report*. NSIAD-86-148, Government Printing Office, Washington, DC, July 1986.
2. Gansler, J. S. *Program instability: causes, costs and cures*. Defense Acquisition Study, Center for Strategic and International Studies, Georgetown University, Mar. 1986.
3. Augustine, N. Testimony before the US Senate Committee on Governmental affairs on *Acquisition process in the Department of Defense*. 21 and 27 October and 5 November 1981.
4. President's Blue Ribbon Commission on Defense Management. *An interim report to the President*. February 1986, pp. 13–15.
5. Fox, J. R. *The defense management challenge*. Harvard Business School Press, Boston, 1988, chapter 4.
6. Ministry of Defence. *Value for money in defence equipment*. HMSO, London, 1983.
7. Ministry of Defence. *Learning from experience: a report on the arrangements for managing major projects in the procurement executive*. HMSO, London, 1987, p. 9.
8. *Statement on the Defence Estimates 1985*. Cmnd 9227-1, HMSO,

London, May 1985.

9. National Audit Office. *Ministry of Defence: control and management of the development of major equipment*. Report by the Comptroller and Auditor General, National Audit Office, HC568, HMSO, London, July 1986, p. 28.

10. *Statement on the Defence Estimates 1985*. Cmnd 9227-1, HMSO, London, May 1985, p. 11.

11. Smith. M. Prize fighter. *The Engineer*, 18 June 1987, 42–47.

12. Vincent, J. The experimental aircraft programme. In *Development time scales: their estimation and control*. Royal Aeronautical Society, London, Proceedings 12 February 1987.

13. Horwitch, M. The convergence factor for successful large-scale programs: the American synfields experience as a case in point. In *Matrix management systems handbook*, Cleland, D. I. (ed.), Van Nostrand Reinhold, New York, 1984, chapter 3.

14. Horwitch, M. and Pralahad, C. K. Managing multi-organization enterprises: the emerging strategic frontier. *Sloan Management Review*, 1981, Winter, 3–16.

15. Imai, K. Japan's industrial policy for high technology industries. Institute of Business Research, Hitotsubashi University, Kunitachi, Tokyo, Discussion Paper No. 119. *Proc. Conf. on Japanese Industrial Policy in Comparative Perspective*, New York, 17–19 March 1984.

16. Department of Energy. *US commercial nuclear power: historical perspective, current status and outlook*. US Government Printing Office, Washington, DC, 1982.

17. *International Atomic Energy Association Bulletin*. Aug. 1982.

18. Fremlin, J. H. *Power production: what are the risks?* Oxford University Press, 1987, p. 283.

19. World Commission on Environment and Development. *Our common future*. Oxford University Press, 1987.

20. Searle, G. *Major World Bank projects*. Wadebridge Ecological Centre, Camelford, Cornwall, 1987.

21. Adhikari, R. Estimation of economic discount rate for practical project appraisal: the case of Nepal. *Project Appraisal*, **2**, No. 2, 1987, June, 113–122.

22. Kula, E. Future generations: the modified discounting method. *Project Appraisal*, **3**, No. 2, 1988, June, 85–88.

23. Markandya, A. and Pearce, D. Natural environments and the social rate of discount. *Project Appraisal*, **3**, No. 1, 1988, Mar., 2–12.

24. Goodland, R. The environmental implications of major projects in Third World development. In *Major projects and the environment*. Technical Paper No. 8, Major Projects Association, Templeton College, Oxford, 1989.

25. Goldsmith, E. and Hildyrad, N. *The social and environmental effects of large dams*. Wadebridge Ecological Centre, Camelford, Cornwall, 1984.

26. Bowonder, B., Prasad, S. S. R. and Reddy, R. Industrial hazards. *Project Appraisal*, **2**, No. 1, 1987, Mar., 11–20.

27. Bowonder, B. and Chetti, R. Siting of a fertilizer complex. *Third World Planning Review*, **6**, 1984, 139–156.

28. O'Riordan, T. and Sewell, W. R. D. *Project appraisal and policy review*. Wiley, Chichester, 1981, pp. 8–9.

29. Stringer, J. *Planning and enquiry process*, MPA Technical paper No. 6, Templeton College, Oxford, September 1988.

30. Layfield, F. *Sizewell B Public Inquiry*. Department of Energy, HMSO, London, 1987.

31. O'Riordan, T., Kemp, R. and Purdue, M. *Sizewell B: an anatomy of the inquiry*. Macmillan, London, 1988.

32. Baum, W. C. and Tolbert, S. M. *Investing in development*. Oxford University Press, 1985.

33. World Bank Operations Evaluation Department. *Rural development: World Bank experience 1965–86*. World Bank, Washington, DC, 1988.

34. Blackwood, J. World Bank experience with rural development. *Finance and Development*, **25**, No. 4, 1988, Dec., 12–15.

35. Moris, J. *Managing induced rural development*. International Development Institute, Bloomington, Il., 1981.

36. Paul, S. *Managing development programs: the lessons of success*. Westview, Boulder, CO, 1982, p. 229.

37. Cassen, R. & Associates. *Does aid work?* Clarendon, Oxford, 1986, pp. 11, 109 ff.

38. Cracknell, B. E. Evaluating development assistance: a review of the literature. *Public Administration and Development*, **8**, 1988, Oct., 75–83.

39. Ramanadham, V. V. (ed.). *Privatisation in the UK*. Routledge, London, 1988.

40. *The Channel Tunnel*. Cmnd 5430, HMSO, London, 1973.

41. *Fixed Channel Link: Report of UK/French Study Group*. Cmnd 8561, HMSO, London, 1982.

42. Mr Nicholas Ridley, the Secretary of State for Transport, written answer to the House of Commons. *Hansard*, 22 May 1984, col. 380.

43. *The Channel Fixed Link*. Cmnd. 9735, HMSO, London, 1986, p. 4.

44. Rowland, T. Finance — digging up the money. In *The Tunnel: the Channel and beyond*, Jones, B. (ed.), Ellis Horwood/Wiley, Chichester, 1987.

45. Speck, R. L. The buck stops here: the owner's legal and practical responsibility for strategic project management. *Project Management Journal*, **19**, No. 4, 1988, Sept., 45–52.

46. *More construction for the money: summary report of the Construction Industry Cost Effectiveness Project*. The Business Roundtable, New York, January 1983.

47. *Integrating construction resources and technology into engineering*. Report B-1 of the Construction Industry Cost Effectiveness Project, The Business Roundtable, New York, August 1982.

48. O'Connor, J. T. and Tucker, R. L. Industrial project constructability improvement. *ASCE Journal of Construction Engineering and Management*, **112**, No. 1, 1986, Mar., 69–82.

49. Tatum, C. B. and Teague, F. G. Managing the engineering–construction interface for improved construction performance. *Proc. 1981 Project Management Institute/Internet Joint Symp., Boston*, Project Management Institute, Drexel Hill, PA, 1981, 157–169.

50. Tatum, C. B. The project manager's role in integrating design and construction. *Project Management Journal*, **18**, No. 2, 1987, June, 96–107.

51. Mobbs, G. N. Investing in construction: the private sector. In Burgess, R. A. *Construction projects: their financial policy and control*. Construction Press, London, 1981.

52. Hammond, F. A. Contractual systems. In Burgess, R.A., *Construction projects: their financial policy and control*. Construction Press, London, 1981.

53. Frazio, P., Moselhi, P., Thelberge, P. and Revas, S. Design impact of construction fast type and track. *Construction Management and Economics*, **6**, No. 3, 1988, Autumn, 195–208.

54. Gray, C. and Flanagan, R. US productivity in fast-tracking starts on the drawing board. *Construction Management and Economics*, **2**, No. 3, 1984, Winter, 133–144.

55. Nahapiet, H. and Nahapiet, J. *The management of construction projects:*

case studies from the USA and UK. The Chartered Institute of Building, Ascot, 1985.

56. A comparison of contractual arrangements for building projects. *Construction Management and Economics*, **3**, No. 3, 1985, Winter, 217−231.

57. National Economic Development Office. *Fast building for commerce.* NEDO Books, London, 1988.

58. Ruby, D. I. Fast-tracking plant projects. *Plant Engineering*, 1978, 121−123.

59. Tucker, R. L. and Scarlett, B. R. *Evaluation of design effectiveness.* The Construction Industry Institute, University of Texas at Austin, July 1986.

60. Walker, A. *Project management in construction.* Granada, London, 1984.

61. Sapolsky, H. *The Polaris system development: bureaucratic and programmatic success in government.* Harvard University Press, Cambridge, MA, 1972.

62. Marschak, T., Glennan, T. K. and Summers, R. *Strategy for R&D: studies in the microeconomics of development.* Springer Verlag, New York, 1967.

63. Seamans, R. and Ordway, F. I. The Apollo tradition: an object lesson for the management of large-scale technological endeavours. *Interdisciplinary Science Review*, 1977.

64. Hall, P. *Great planning disasters.* Weidenfeld & Nicolson, London, 1980.

65. Kharbanda, O. B. and Stallworthy, E. A. *How to learn from project disasters.* Gower, London, 1983.

66. Paul, S. *Strategic management of development programmes.* International Labour Office, Geneva, 1983.

67. Feldman, E. J. Patterns of failure in government megaprojects: economics, politics and participation in industrial democracies. In *Global dilemmas*, Huntingdon, S. P. and Nye, J. S. (eds), Center for International Affairs, Harvard, and University Press of America, Cambridge, MA, 1985.

68. Feldman, E. J. *Concorde and dissent: explaining high technology failures in Great Britain and France.* Cambridge University Press, New York, 1985.

69. General Accounting Office. *Status of major acquisitions as of September 30, 1982.* GAO/NSIAD-83-32, Washington, DC, September 1983.

70. National Audit Office. *Ministry of Defence: control and management of the development of major equipment.* Report by the Comptroller and Auditor General, National Audit Office, HC568, HMSO, London, July 1986.

71. Mason, G. E., Larew, R. E., Borcherding, J. D., Oakes, R. R. and Rad, P. F. *Delays in nuclear power plant construction.* US Energy Research and Development Administration, E(11-1)-4121, Washington, DC, December 1977.

72. Baker, N. R., Green, S. G. and Bean, A. S. Why R&D projects succeed or fail. *Research Management*, 1986 Nov.−Dec., 29−34.

73. Balachandra, R. and Raelin, J. A. When to kill that R&D project. *Research Management*, 1984, July−Aug., 30−33.

74. Cooper, R. G. New product success in industrial firms. *Industrial Marketing Management*, **11**, 1982, 215−223.

75. Whipp, R. and Clark, P. *Innovation and the auto industry.* Francis Pinter, London, 1986.

76. Mansfield, E. and Wagner, S. Organizational and strategic factors associated with probabilities of success and industrial R&D. *Journal of Business*, **48**, No. 2, April, 1975.

77. Gerstenfeld, A. A study of successful projects, unsuccessful projects and projects in progress in West Germany. *IEEE Transactions on Engineering Management*, EM-23(3), August 1976, pp. 116–123.

78. Morris, P. W. G and Hough, G. H. *The anatomy of major projects*. Wiley, Chichester, 1988.

79. Murphy, D. C., Baker, B. N. and Fisher, D. Cost growth: can it be controlled? *Project Management Quarterly*, **5**, 1974.

80. Myers, C. W. and Devey, M. R. *How management can affect project outcomes: an exploration of the PPS database*. Rand Corporation, N-2196-SFC, Santa Monica, CA, August 1984.

81. Might, R. J. and Fisher, W. A. Role of structural factors in determining project management success. *IEEE Transactions on Engineering Management*, EM-32(2), 1985, May, 71–77.

82. Thamhain, H. J. and Wilemon, D. L. Criteria for controlling projects according to plan. *Project Management Journal*, **17**, No. 2, 1986, June, 75–81.

83. Pinto, J. K. and Slevin, D. P. Critical success factors across the project life cycle. *Project Management Journal*, **19**, No. 3, 1988, June, 67–75.

84. de Wit, A. Measuring project success: an illusion. *Project Management Institute Seminar/Symp. on Measuring Success*, Montreal, 1986. Project Management Institute, Drexel Hill, PA, 1986.

85. Morris, P. W. G. Research at Oxford into the preconditions of success and failure in major projects. *Proc. Project Management Institute Seminar/Symp. on Measuring Success*, Montreal, 1986, Project Management Institute, Drexel Hill, PA, 1986.

86. Boynton, A. C. and Zmud, R. W. An assessment of critical success factors. *Sloan Management Review*, **25**, 1984, 17–27.

87. Leidecker, J. K. and Bruno, A. V. Identifying and using critical success factors. *Long Range Planning*, **17**, No. 1, 1984, 23–42.

88. Rockart, J. F. Chief executives define their own data needs. *Harvard Business Review*, 1979, Mar.–Apr.

89. Shank, M., Boynton, A. and Zmud, R. W. Critical success factor analysis as a methodology for MIS planning. *MIS Quarterly*, 1985, June, 121–129.

90. Yeo, K. T. Systematic CSF analysis for strategic IT planning. *International Journal of Project Management*, **8**, No. 4, 1990, Nov., 205–213.

91. Slevin, D.P. and Pinto, J. K. Balancing strategy and tactics in project implementation. *Sloan Management Review*, **33**, 1987, Fall, 33–41.

92. Barczak, G., Smith, C. and Wilemon, D. Managing large-scale organizational change. *Organizational Dynamics*, 1989, Summer, 23–35.

93. Maidique, M. and Hayes, R. The art of high-technology management. *Sloan Management Review*, **25**, No. 4, 1984, Winter.

94. DeCotiis, T. A. and Dyer, L. Defining and measuring project performance. *Research Management*, 1979, Jan., 17–22.

95. Baker, N. R., Green, S. G. and Bean, A. S. Why R&D projects succeed or fail. *Research Management*, 1986, Nov.–Dec., 29–34.

96. Cooper, R. G. New product success in industrial firms. *Industrial Marketing Management*, **11**, 1982, 215–223.

97. Cooper, R. G. and Kleinschmidt, E. J. What makes a new product a winner: success factors at the project level. *R&D Management*, **17**, No. 3, 1987, 175–189.

98. Lovelace, R. F. R&D planning techniques. *R&D Management*, **17**, No. 4, 1987, 241–250.

99. Souder, W. E. and Mandakovic, T. R&D selection models. *Research Management*, **29**, No. 4, 1986, Jul.–Aug., 36–42.

100. Bedell, R. J. Terminating R&D projects prematurely. *Research Management*, **26**, No. 4, 1983, Jul.—Aug.

101. Buell, C. K. When to terminate a research and development project. *Research Management*, **10**, No. 4, 1967, 275—284.

102. Shafer, S. M. and Mantel, S. J. A decision support system for the project termination decision. A spreadsheet approach. *Project Management Journal*, **20**, No. 2, 1989, June, 23—28.

103. Sykes, A. Success and failure of major projects. *Project Management Journal*, 1986, Jan./Feb., 17—18.

104. Womack, J. R., and Ross, D. *The machine that changed the world*. Maxwell Macmillan International, New York, 1990, p. 112.

105. Clark, K. B., Chew, W. B. and Fujimoto, T. *Product development in the world auto industry*. Brookings Papers on Economic Activity No. 3, 1987.

106. Sakakibara, K. *From imitation to innovation: a very large scale integrated (VLSI) semiconductor project in Japan*. Sloan School of Management, MIT, Cambridge, MA, Working Paper 1490—83, October 1983.

107. Inman, B. R. Large scale collaborative research. *Colloquium on research priorities*, Working Papers 1985—87, Large Scale Projects Institute, University of Texas at Austin, March 1985.

108. Alvey IT Users. *Final Report*. National Computing Centre, Manchester, April 1988.

109. Oakley B. and Owen K. *Alvey: Britain's strategic computing initiative*. MIT Press, Cambridge, MA, 1989.

110. Parsons, G. L. Information technology: a new competitive weapon. *Sloan Management Review*, 1983, Fall, 3—14.

111. Porter, M. E. and Millar, V. E. How information gives you competitive advantage. *Harvard Business Review*, 1985, Jul.—Aug., 149—160.

112. Porter, M. E. *Competitive strategy*. Free Press, New York, 1980.

113. Norden, P. V. On the anatomy of development projects. *IRE Trans. on Engineering Management*, **EM-7**, No. 1, 1960, Mar., 34—42.

114. Hall, A. D. *A methodology for systems engineering*. US Government Printing Office, Washington, DC, December, 1972.

115. Brooks, F. P. *The mythical man-month*. Addison-Wesley, Reading, MA, 1982.

116. Benyon, D. and Skidmore, S. Information Systems Design Methodologies. *The Computer Journal*, **3**, No. 1, 1987, 2—7.

117. Boehm, B. W. *Software engineering economics*. Prentice Hall, Englewood Cliffs, NJ, 1981.

118. Martin, J. *Information engineering*. Prentice Hall, Englewood Cliffs, NJ, 1990.

119. Yourdon, E. and Constantine L. L. *Structured design*. Prentice Hall, Englewood Cliffs, NJ, 1979.

120. Central Computer and Telecommunications Agency. *PRINCE*. National Computing Centre, 1990.

121. Mumford, E., Land, F. and Hawgood, J. The participative approach to the design of computer systems. *Impact on Society*, **25**, No. 3, 1978, 235—253.

122. Mumford, E. Defining system requirements to meet business needs: a case study example. *Computer Journal*, **28**, No. 2, 1985, 97—104.

123. Andrews, W. C. Prototyping information systems. *Journal of Systems Management*, **34**, No. 9, 1983, 16—18.

124. Boehm, B. *et al.* Prototyping versus specifying: a multi-project experiment. *IEEE Transactions on Software Engineering*, **SE-10**, No. 3, 1984, 290—303.

125. Connel, J. and Brice, L. Rapid prototyping. *Datamation*, 15 August,

1984, 93–100.

126. Harrison, R. Prototyping and the systems development life cycle. *Journal of Systems Management*, **36**, No. 98, 1983, 22–25.

127. Kraushaar, J. M. *et al*. A prototyping method for applications development by end users and information systems specialists, *MIS Quarterly*, **9**, No. 3, 1985, 189–197.

128. Nauman, J. D. and Jenkins, A. M. Prototyping: the new paradigm for systems development. *MIS Quarterly*, **6**, No. 3, 1982, Sept., 29–44.

129. Willis, T. H., Huston, C. R. and d'Ouville, E. L. Project manager's responsibilities in a prototyping systems analyses and design environment. *Project Management Journal*, **19**, No. 1, 1988, Feb., 56–60.

130. Arditi, D. Diffusion of network planning in construction, *ASCE Journal of Construction Engineering and Management*, **109**, 1983, Mar., 1–12.

131. Dane, C. W., Gray, C. F. and Woodworth, B. Successfully introducing project management techniques into an organization. *Project Management Quarterly*, **12**, No. 4, 1981, Dec., 23–26.

132. Avots, I. How useful are the mass market project management systems? *Project Management Journal*, **18**, No. 3, 1987, Aug., 58–60.

133. Palla, R. W. Introduction to micro-computer software tools for project information management, *Project Management Journal*, **18**, No. 3, 1987, Aug., 61–68.

134. Thamhain, H. J. and Wilemon, D. L. Computer-aided project monitoring is coming of age. *Proc. Project Management Institute Seminar/Symp. on Measuring Success, Montreal, 1987*. Project Management Institute, Drexel Hill, PA, 1987.

135. Complex projects and new demands push software to its limits. Computers and software supplement, *Aviation Week and Space Technology*, 11 July 1988, 69–70.

136. Muspratt, M. A. Computers for the construction industry. *Project Management Quarterly*, **14**, No. 3, 1983, Sept., 45–52.

137. Arditi, D. and Patel B. K. Expert systems for claim management in construction projects. *International Journal of Project Management*, **7**, No. 3, 1989, Aug., 141–146.

138. Avots, I. Application of expert systems concepts to schedule control. *Project Management Journal*, **16**, No. 1, 1985, Mar., 51–57.

139. Barber, T. J., Marshall, G. and Boardman, J. T. A methodology for modelling of project management control in the environment. *Proceedings IEE on Artificial Intelligence in Industry*, Institution of Electrical Engineers, London, July 1987.

140. Gilmore, M. J. Knowledge based systems in construction and civil engineering, *International Journal of Project Management*, **7**, No. 3, 1989, Aug., 147–153.

141. Kangari, R. and Boyer, L. T. Risk management by expert systems. *Project Management Journal*, **20**, No. 2, 1980, Mar., 40–48.

142. Probst, A. R. and Worlitzer, J. Project management and expert systems. *International Journal of Project Management*, **6**, No. 1, 1988, Feb., 11–17.

143. Winston, P. H. *Artificial intelligence*. Addison-Wesley, Reading, MA, 1979.

144. Niwa, K. and Okumu, M. Know-how transfer methods and its application to risk management for large construction projects. *IEEE Transactions on Engineering Management*, **EM-29 (k)**, 1982, Nov., 146–153.

145. Weber, F. M. Tools for managing projects. *Project Management Journal*, **13**, No. 2, 1982, June, 46–58.

146. Hofstede, G. Cultural dimensions for project management.

International Journal of Project Management, **1**, No. 1, 1983, Feb., 41–48.

147. Morton, G. M. A. Become a project champion. *International Journal of Project Management*, **1**, No. 4, 1983, Nov., 197–203.

148. Dunne, E. J. How six management techniques are used. *Research Management*, **26**, No. 2, 1983, Mar.–Apr., 35–40.

149. Lichtenberg, S. Alternatives to conventional project management. *International Journal of Project Management*, **1**, No. 2, 1983, May, 101–102.

150. Ashley, D. and Avots, I. Influence diagramming for an analysis of project risks. *Project Management Journal*, **15**, No. 1, 1984, Mar., 56–82.

151. Fox, J. R. Evaluating management of large, complex projects: a framework for analysis. *Technology in Society*, **6**, No. 2, 1984, 129–139.

152. Levitt, R. E. and Kunz, J. C. Using knowledge of construction and project management for automated schedule updating. *Project Management Journal*, **16**, No. 5, 1985, Dec., 57–76.

153. Cooper, D. F., MacDonald, D. H. and Chapman, C. B. Risk analysis of a construction cost estimate. *International Journal of Project Management*, **3**, No. 3, 1985, Aug., 141–149.

154. Perry, J. G. and Hayes, R. W. Construction projects —know the risks. *Chartered Mechanical Engineering*, 1985, Feb.

155. Davis, D. New projects: beware of false economies. *Harvard Business Review*, **63**, No. 2, 1985, Mar.–Apr., 95–101.

156. Liberatore, M. J. and Titus, G. J. Managing industrial R&D projects: current practice and future direction. *Journal of the Society of Research Administrators*, **18**, No. 1, 1986, Summer, 5–12.

157. Cleland, D. I. Project stakeholder management. *Project Management Journal*, **17**, No. 4, 1986, Sept., 36–44.

158. Gobeli, D. H. Relative effectiveness of different project structures. *Project Management Journal*, **18**, No. 2, 1987, June, 81–85.

159. Navarre, C. and Schaan, J-L. International engineering project management: key success factors in a changing industry. *International Journal of Project Management*, 1987, Nov., 238–245.

160. Ashley D. B. Determinants of construction project success. *Project Management Journal*, **18**, No. 2, 1987, June, 69–77.

161. de Wit, A. Measurement of project success. *International Journal of Project Management*, **6**, No. 3, 164–170.

162. Pinto, J. K. and Slevin, D. P. Project success: definitions and measurement techniques. *Project Management Journal*, **19**, No. 1, 1989, Feb., 67.

163. Arditi, D., Tarim Akar, G. and Gundamar, S. Cost overruns in public projects. *International Journal of Project Management*, **3**, No. 4, 1989, Nov., 218–224.

164. Bu-Bushait, K.A. The application of project techniques to construction and research and development techniques. *Project Management Journal*, **20**, No. 2, 1989, June, 17–22.

165. Gareis, R. Management by projects: the management approach for the future. *International Journal of Project Management*, **7**, No. 4, 1989, May, 243–249.

166. Harrison, F. L. *Advanced project management*. Gower, London, 1981.

167. Keen, J. *Managing systems development*. Wiley, Chichester, 1981.

168. Peters, G. *Project management and construction control*. Construction Press, London, 1981.

169. Stuckenbruck, L. C. (ed.). *The implementation of project management: the professional's handbook*. Addison-Wesley, Reading, MA, 1981.

170. Kelley, A. J. (ed.). *New dimensions of project management*. Lexington

Books, Lexington, MA, 1982.

171. Ruskin, A. M. and Estes, W. E. *What every engineer should know about project management*. Marcel Dekker, New York, 1982.

172. Cleland, D. I. and King, W. R. (eds). *The project management handbook*, Van Nostrand Reinhold, New York, 1983.

173. Kerzner, H. *Project management for executives*. Van Nostrand Reinhold, New York, 1983.

174. Stallworthy, E. A. and Kharbanda, O. P. *Total Project Management*. Gower, London, 1983.

175. Andersen, E., Grude, K. B., Haug, T. and Turner, J. R. *Goal directed project management*, Kogan Page, London, 1984.

176. Cleland, D. I., *Matrix management systems handbook*, Van Nostrand Reinhold, New York, 1984.

177. Dinsmore, P. C. *Human factors in project management*, Amacom, New York, 1984.

178. Kerzner, H. *Project management: a systems approach to planning, scheduling and controlling*, Van Nostrand Reinhold, New York, 1984.

179. Kerzner, H. and Cleland, D. I. *Project/matrix management policy and strategy*, Van Nostrand Reinhold, New York, 1984.

180. Rosenau, M. D. *Project management for engineers*, Lifetime Learning Publications, Belmont, CA, 1984.

181. Thamhain, H. J. *Engineering program management*, Wiley, New York, 1984.

182. Walker, A. *Project management in construction*, Granada, London, 1984.

183. Meredith, J. R. and Mantel, S. J. *Project management: a managerial approach*. Wiley, New York, 1985.

184. Cleland, D. I. and Kerzner, H. *A project management dictionary of terms*. Van Nostrand Reinhold, New York, 1985.

185. Slemakers, C. M. *The principles and practices of cost schedule control systems*. Petrocelli Books, Princeton, NJ, 1985.

186. Stephanou, S. E. and Obradovitch, M. M. *Project management systems and productivity*. Daniel Spencer Publications, Malibu, CA, 1985.

187. Tompkins, B. G. *Project cost control for managers*. Gulf, Houston, 1985.

188. Westeney, R. E. *Managing the engineering and construction of small projects*. Marcel Dekker, New York, 1985.

189. Gilbreath, R. D. *Winning at project management*. Wiley, New York, 1986.

190. Lock, D. (ed). *Project management handbook*. Gower, London, 1986.

191. Kharbanda, O. P. and Stallworthy, E. A. *Project cost control*. Institution of Chemical Engineers, London, 1986.

192. Kerzner, H. and Thamhain, H. J. *Project management operating guidelines*. Van Nostrand Reinhold, New York, 1986.

193. Roman, D. D. *Managing projects. A systems approach*. Elsevier, New York, 1986.

194. Silverman, M. *The art of managing technical projects*. Prentice Hall, Englewood Cliffs, NJ, 1987.

195. Davidson Frame, J. *Managing projects in organizations*. Jossey-Bass, San Francisco, 1987.

196. Internet. *Project start-up manual*. Internet, Zurich, 1987.

197. Badiru, A. B. *Project management in manufacturing and high technology operations*. Wiley, New York, 1988.

198. Burbridge, R. N. G. *Perspectives on project managment*. Institution of Electrical Engineers, London, 1988.

199. Fleming, Q. W. *Cost schedule control systems criteria: the management guide to C/SCSC*. Probus, 1988.

200. Roetzheim, W. *Structured computer project managment*. Prentice-Hall,

Englewood Cliffs, NJ, 1988.

201. Stone, R. (ed.). *The management of engineering projects*. Macmillan, London, 1988.

202. Humphrey, W. S. *Managing the software process*. Addison-Wesley, Reading, MA, 1989.

203. Kimmons, R. L. and Loweree, J. H. *Project management: a reference for professionals*. Marcel Dekker, New York, 1989.

204. Kidder, T. *The soul of a new machine*. Houghton Mifflin, Boston, 1981.

205. Hayes, R. W., Perry, J. G. and Thompson, P. A. *Management contracting*. Construction Industry Research and Information Association, Report 100, London, 1983.

206. Murphy, K. J. *Macroproject development in the Third World*. Westview, Boulder, CO, 1983.

207. Nevitt, P. K. *Project financing*. Euromoney, London, 1983.

208. Gray, K. G., Jaafari, A. and Wheen, R. J. (eds.). *Macroprojects: strategy, planning and implementation*. The Warren Centre, The University of Sydney, 1985.

209. Karploff, I. J. *Export and project finance*. Euromoney, 1988.

210. Barber, S. Project management systems. *International Project Management Yearbook*. 1985, pp. 22−24.

211. Kahn, R. E. Tomorrow's computers — a new generation in computing. In Torrero, E. A. (ed.). *The next generation computers*. IEEE Press, New York, 1985.

212. Levine, H. PM software forum. *Project Management Journal*, **7**, No. 3, 1967, Aug., 15−17.

213. Special report: ethics, standards, accreditation. *Project Management Quarterly*, **14**, No. 3, 1983, Aug.

214. Project management body of knowledge. *Project Management Journal*, **17**, No. 3, 1986, Aug.

215. Davidson, F. P., Giacoletto, L. J. and Salkeld, R. *Macro-engineering and the infrastructure of tomorrow*. Westview Press, Boulder, CO, 1978.

216. Davidson, F. P. and Meador, C. L. *Macro-engineering and the future — a management perspective*. Westview Press, Boulder, CO, 1982.

217. Davidson, F. P., Meador, C. L. and Salkeld, R. *How big and still beautiful? Macro-engineering revisited*. Westview Press, Boulder, CO, 1980.

218. Salkeld, R., Davidson, F. P. and Meador, C. L. *Macro-engineering: the rich potential*. Westview Press, Boulder, CO, 1981.

219. Davidson, P. Macro engineering: introduction. *Technology in Society*, **6**, No. 1, 1984.

220. Hull, C. W. Macro-engineering in the 1980s. *Technology in Society*, **6**, No. 1, 1984.

221. Schillinger, A. G. Man's enduring technological dilemma: Prometheus, Faust and other macro-engineers. *Technology in Society*, **6**, No. 1, 1984.

222. McGregor, I. Euroroute. *Technology in Society*, **6**, No. 1, 1984.

223. Nakajima, M. Towards a global infrastructure. *Technology in Society*, **6**, No. 1, 1984.

224. Sellers, W. O. Technology and the future of the financial services industry. *Technology in Society*, **7**, No. 1, 1985.

225. Mazur, A. Bias in risk-benefit analysis. *Technology in Society*, **7**, No. 1, 1985.

226. Morris, P. W. G. The initiation, assessment, securing and accomplishment of macro-projects. *Technology in Society*, **7**, No. 1, 1985.

227. Bodde, D. I. The federal financing of large-scale engineering projects: new realities and their implications. *Technology in Society*, **10**, No. 1, 1988.

228. Chidgey, N. D. Macro engineering: an Australian perspective. *Technology in Society*, **10**, No. 1, 1988.

229. Fleury, P. F. The implementation of the Brazilian computer industry: its complexity and potential impacts. *Technology in Society*, **10**, No. 1, 1988.

230. Konig, C. and Thietart, R. A. Managers, engineers and government: the emergence of the mutual organization in the European aerospace industry. *Technology in Society*, **10**, No. 1, 1988.

231. Morris, P. W. G. Lessons in managing major projects successfully in a European context. *Technology in Society*, **10**, No. 1, 1988.

232. Nueno, P. The role of macro-engineering in the European economic scene. *Technology in Society*, **10**, No. 1, 1988.

233. Pettingell, W. H. Managing construction of a macro-airbase-project in the Negev: a contractor's perspective. *Technology in Society*, **10**, No. 1, 1988.

234. Seder, A. R. Building the nation's first coal gasification plant. *Technology in Society*, **10**, No. 1, 1988.

235. Kim, J. and Sung, N. G. Global cooperation: a competitive strategy for the Pacific Basin. *Technology in Society*, **10**, No. 1, 1984.

236. Large-scale Programs Institute. *Proc. Colloq. on Research Priorities for Large-Scale Programs March 21–22, 1985*. Working Papers 1985–1, University of Texas at Austin, Texas, 1985.

237. Morris, P. W. G. *Issues raised in seminars of the Major Projects Association December 1981 — June 1984*. Major Projects Association, Technical Paper No. 1, July 1985.

238. Morris, P. W. G. *The MPA on finance*. Major Projects Association, Technical Paper No. 2, July 1986.

239. Morris, P. W. G. and Hough, G. H. *Preconditions of success and failure in major projects*. Major Projects Association, Technical Paper No. 3, September 1986.

240. Allen, J. *Man-made islands*. Major Projects Association, Technical Paper No. 4, May 1987.

241. O'Riordan, T. *Major projects and the environmental movement*. Major Projects Association, Technical Paper No. 5, May 1988.

242. Stringer, J. *Planning and inquiry processes*. Major Projects Association, Technical Paper No. 6, September 1988.

243. Eto, H. and Matsui, K. (eds). *R&D management systems in Japanese industry*. North-Holland, Elsevier Science Publications, New York, 1984.

244. Tatsuno, S. *The Technopolis strategy*. Prentice Hall, New York, 1986.

245. Smilor, W., Kozmetsky, G. and Gibson, D. V. *Creating the Technopolis*. Ballinger, Cambridge, 1988.

246. Trento, J. J. *Prescription for disaster*. Crown, New York, p. 243.

247. *Space station management: an analysis of work package options submitted to the Committee on Science and Technology, US House of Representatives*. NASA, Washington, DC, 3 October 1986.

248. McDougall W. A. *The heavens and the earth: a political history of the space age*. Basic Books, New York, 1985.

249. Ride, S. K. *Leadership and America's future in space*. NASA, Washington, DC, August 1987.

250. *Report of the Committee on the Space Station of the National Research Council*. National Academy Press, Washington, DC, September 1987.

8. The Management of Projects: the new model

So, what does this saga of projects and management reveal? What lessons can we derive? Is there a pattern underlying the effective management of projects? How transferable are the insights from one field to another, between space and building, say, or nuclear power and information technology?

The development of a management discipline

The modern management of projects is a discipline that starts in the 1930s with the US Air Corps' and Exxon's project engineering co-ordinating function. Prefigured in Gulick's 1937 paper on the matrix organization, it is first put into full modern practice around 1953–1954 with the US Air Force Joint Project Offices and Weapons System Project Offices, followed in 1955 by the US Navy's Special Projects Office. All these are first and foremost organizational mechanisms for achieving *integration*. But from the integrating base comes a *systems management* practice: specify performance requirements; carefully preplan to prevent future changes; appoint a prime contractor to be responsible for development and delivery. Scheduling/risk analysis tools are developed by 1957–1958 to assist planning. CPM provides cost control and resource management capabilities; PERT is used extensively as a PR tool to help manage Polaris' external environment. And of course the men managing these missile mega-programmes are commanding personalities, welding and leading their teams, managing Congress and the Press, developing systems and procedures, creating innovative technical solutions. NASA is formed in 1958. In 1959 the Anderson Committee formalizes the systems management approach: programmes to be managed according to life-cycle stages, and more attention to be paid to front-end feasibility analysis. The decade ends with the *Harvard Business Review* publishing its first article on project management.[1]

Organizational integration is given further thrust in the 1960s as the matrix form is introduced early in the decade. By 1967–1968 Lawrence and Lorsch,[2,3] Galbraith[4] and others are explaining in precise terms the range of integrating mechanisms available and the conditions under which they should be used. Systems management procedures are elaborated further: the AFSC series (1960), AFR (1963), NASA's 500 Series (1966), AFSCM (1968), DoD 5000-1 (1971) and A-190, with its Milestone 0 (1976); and in the UK, Gibb–Zuckerman (1961), Downey (1966), and Rayner (1971). PERT/Cost (1962) is most notable for the introduction of Work Breakdown Structures. In 1964 Earned Value and Precedence are developed. Systems Analysis and PPBS arrive with McNamara from Ford in 1960. By 1963, Resource Allocation, Value Analysis and Integrated Logistics Support are being developed; GERT appears in 1966. There is still disquiet over weapons systems development effectiveness, however. Peck and Scherer (1962) suggest that development schedules are too long. Contractors are suspected of buying into long-term programmes on unrealistic initial bids with the intention of improving contract terms later. In an attempt to shift more responsibility on to industry, the Total Package Procurement concept is introduced in 1966. It is a disaster, and is abandoned in 1972. With it goes David Packard, scourge of *concurrency*, champion of heel-to-toe development. Packard has seen that the programmes with development problems are without exception those begun before development is complete and design is frozen. Building before firm design is a common practice — too common — in virtually all project industries. In some — Concorde, TSR-2, many US defence projects, nuclear power — it happens because of lack of management. In others — Mueller's response after doing a schedule risk analysis on Apollo — it is more calculated. As the 1960s close, NASA, having landed man on the moon, turns, belatedly, to the question of its longer-term strategy. The British give up trying to apply project management disciplines on Concorde, but implement them superbly on Tornado. There is an explosion of interest in project manage-ment, with professional project management societies established and books and articles published in ever growing numbers, as matrix organizations and formal projects are established increasingly in high-tech, construction, development aid and other industries and in military and civilian sectors.

1970 sees two huge, high-profile major projects — the US SST and TAPS — grounded suddenly and totally unexpectedly by environmentalist opposition. The organizational and procedures-driven approach to integration and systems management is suddenly patently insufficient. *'Externalities'* — the community, ecology, economy — must evidently be more formally integrated into the project management process. We see this in virtually every sector: transportation projects (conceived with inadequate attention to ensuring community support, as well as insufficient appreciation of technical risks), nuclear power (the degree of technology management required to satisfy community fears being completely underappreciated), North Sea (weather, inflation, finance), development projects (institutional support), Third World construction (inflation, finance), even space (funding and political support). Project management writing fails to recognize this shift, but works instead on clarifying the middle management pm issues of the 1960s: control systems, project manager power and authority (e.g. Wilemon and Gemmill[5] in 1971), conflict (Thamhain and

Wilemon,[6] 1975) and organization structure (Youker's[7] classic of 1977 and Moolin and McCoy's[8] of 1979). Management writing does not catch up with this new reality until at least the early 1980s, as Davidson founds the macro-engineering/major projects movement, Horwitch and Pralahad provide a strategic framework for initiating major projects (later to be supplemented by Merrow *et al.* at Rand, and Morris and Hough at Oxford) while Moris[9] (and later Paul[10] and Cassen *et al.*[11]) writes brilliantly on the strategic context required of development projects.

Not only is the project management community failing to address the strategic and institutional level of managing projects, but also it is still, at the start of the 1980s, completely failing to recognize that project management's success rate is abysmally low. Manned spaceflight, weapons systems development, IT projects, nuclear power, much of the oil and gas sector, infrastructure and building, Third World development projects: the record of cost and schedule overruns consistently shows high failure rates.

The mid-1980s sees substantial improvement, however. Peter Levene brings project management realism to MoD procurement. Construction management and BOO(T) introduce greater integration and owner-level focus in construction. Old problems certainly remain — see the 1986 Blue Ribbon report on US defence procurement, for example.[12] We learn how to manage technology better: prototyping and configuration (change) management become more common practice. Simultaneous Engineering and Fast Build begin to develop as alternatives to concurrency. Lean production and *Total Quality Management* (TQM) emerge. Partnering and teamwork become more accepted as important practices. Risk management becomes a distinct project management discipline. And Fourth Generation computing enables many of the cost, scheduling planning and other project management computer-based techniques to be used easily and effectively. The project management community even begins to recognize the issue of how to measure project success. A project management Body of Knowledge is published by PMI. Certification begins. Degree programmes are launched. The decade ends with Internet delegates preparing to meet in Vienna, 23 years after the first Congress there in 1967, to discuss 'Management by Projects': the contribution of project management to the general world of management.

Project management

It is clear, then, that there has been a substantial broadening of the scope of project management, as well as considerable technical development, since its initiation. The early US missile programmes of the mid-1950s were comprehensive endeavours, involving many dimensions of management, of which scheduling was only one. Engineering management was central. Yet scheduling rather than technical management was to be central to the new discipline of project management as it developed in the 1960s and 1970s. Money was not a major issue on most defence projects; nor were community or environmental pressures initially. Organizational issues, however — particular integrative organizational structures such as the matrix, team building, conflict management, and project manager issues such as leadership, power and authority — very quickly became established as important. The Apollo programme, hailed by many as the epitome of modern project management, typified the genre.

By the early-to-mid 1960s, too many people — most, perhaps — were concentrating on the management systems developed for US defence programmes and assiduously promoted by the Pentagon (as well of course as those developed by DuPont (CPM) and David Craig and John Fondahl (Activity-on-Node)), and were confusing these with what was required to manage projects. Many have felt both then and since that too much attention was given to these tools. The integration and, particularly, systems engineering origins of project management were too often overlooked. Indeed, the systems engineering origins are still virtually ignored. Even today, many experts (for example Russell D. Archibald,[13] Paul Dinsmore[14] and indeed the US Project Management Institute itself[15]) mistakenly cite these systems as the origin of modern project management.

Project management was established as a popular discipline in the late 1960s and 1970s, through the creation and activity of the US and European project management societies and, crucially, through the widespread adoption in business, government and the military of the matrix form of organization. Suddenly, thousands of professionals were pitched into task-focused, project-type situations. Unfortunately, however, project management came to focus too exclusively on the accomplishment 'on time, in budget, to technical specification' of given project objectives; too few people were concentrating on the lessons learned from projects themselves. The 'external threats' that caused such havoc from the 1970s were for many years not commented on; project appraisal, design and evaluation were conceptually treated virtually as disciplines quite different and distinct from project management. Intellectually, hardly anyone was studying the phenomena of projects — in academia no management schools were organized to study multi-organizational tasks (the concept hardly even began to make sense); what teaching there was came later (first the Defense Systems Management College and later a few schools in Europe and North America) and focused almost entirely on systems acquisition or project implementation.

The quantity of project management writings that bubbled up in the 1970s and 1980s attested to the current interest in the subject, but also reflected strongly this intra-project perspective. By now project management as a subject had 'matured' (to use the business strategy jargon): there was a Body of Knowledge, educational programmes at leading universities, people making a handsome living consulting in and supplying it, and professional societies running scholarly journals, conferences and even certificating persons 'qualified' in it. Yet by the mid-to-late 1980s much of the project management writing was in danger of becoming repetitive. The organization area in particular — not yet catching the implications of TQM and lean production — was well-trodden, and lacking the vigour it had shown 20 years previously. Work and writing in the area of planning and control seemed livelier, but largely only because of the continuing developments in Information Technology. Arguably, with the exception perhaps of Risk Management, no new principles of cost, design or schedule control have been developed since Earned Value, Configuration Management, Value Engineering, Precedence Scheduling and Resource Allocation in the mid-1960s. The driving force in the 1980s and 1990s was really in the area of computer tools: expert systems, AI, CAD/CAM, relational databases, distributed systems, Graphical User Interfaces, etc. By the end of the 1980s there was still little substantive being written or published in the mainstream project management literature on engineering, finance, contracting, or the management of community, environmental or other external factors, despite the importance of these areas in real projects. Two conclusions thus emerge from this analysis of the development of modern project management.

First, *while the subject of 'project management' is now comparatively mature*, and recognized by thousands if not millions of managers as vitally important, *it is in many respects still stuck in a 1960s time warp*. Project managers, and particularly those who teach and consult to them, generally take only a middle-management, tools and techniques view of the subject. Few address the larger, more strategic issues that crucially affect the success of projects. The question thus needs to be posed: what should the proper scope of the subject of managing projects be?

Second, therefore, if one either goes back to the origins of modern project management or simply asks the commonsense question 'What makes projects successful?', one immediately sees a vastly increased range of issues and topics that anyone concerned with projects ought to be interested in addressing. Showing this is one of the aims of this book. I have described this broader conceptual framework as *the management of projects*.

The management of projects

Tackling the topic of the management of projects is not easy. Projects are difficult to study for several reasons: they are generally multi-organizational and hence often involve sensitive issues that many people are reluctant to have publicly discussed; they are often of long duration; and the multiplicity of topics they raise requires researchers to be based more broadly than normally fits comfortably in our educational system. Nevertheless, there does seem to be a slow — very slow — academic awakening of interest in project-based undertakings, and several schools around the world are beginning to increase their studies in this area. Perhaps also, before long, the steadily rising numbers of project management courses will begin to expand their focus.

What, then, should the discipline of the management of projects encompass? At the conclusion of *The anatomy of major projects*, George Hough and I presented, in fig. 12.1, a model that organized the factors we had identified as preconditions for project success into a logical framework of analysis. Following the logic of that model, and bearing in mind the experiences of the first decades of the modern management of projects as recounted in this book, I propose the following framework for the discipline of the management of projects (Fig. 46).

First, a project will be in great danger of encountering serious problems if its definition is not right and is not developed properly, if its *objectives, standards, technical base* and general *strategic planning* are inadequately considered or poorly developed, or if

Fig. 46. The Management of Projects — diagram showing the principal items that must be managed for a project to be successfully accomplished

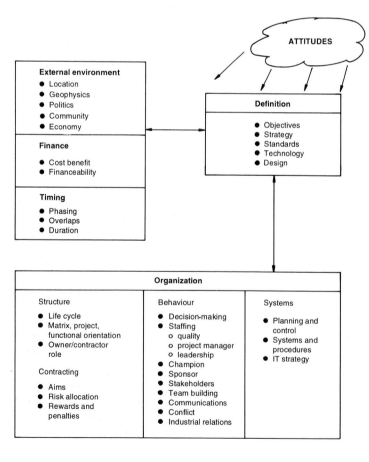

its *design* is not firmly managed in line with its strategic plans.

Second, the project's *definition* both affects and is affected by its *external environment* (such as politics, community views, economic and geophysical conditions, availability of *financing*, and *project phasing and duration*), therefore these interactions must be managed actively and well. (Many of these interactions operate, of course, through the forecast performance of the product(s) that the project will deliver once completed.)

Third, the project's definition, its interaction with these external, financial and other matters, and its implementation will be much harder to manage and may be seriously prejudiced if the *attitudes* of the parties essential to its success are not positive and supportive.

Fourth, realization of the project as it is defined, developed, built and tested involves

- the crucial skill of moving the project at the appropriate pace through its development life cycle — doing the right thing at the right time (neither too soon nor too late) through careful planning and integrative decision making
- organizing the project properly, both internally and with regard to outside parties, and getting the right balance between the owner (qua sponsor and operator) and the project implementation specialists
- having contracts that adequately reflect the project objectives, are motivational, and appropriately reflect the risks involved and the ability of the parties of bear these risks
- having experienced, strong people who will drive the project forward and lead those involved with and working on the project, but also establishing checks and balances between their enthusiasm and the proper caution of the project's sponsors
- treating project personnel as team members, with great emphasis on active communication and productive conflict
- using techniques and having tools for project planning, monitoring and reporting which properly identify the real technical, financial, schedule and other issues, are user-friendly, and allow project staff to develop the project effectively and to predict final outcomes reliably.

How do 50 years of experience support this view of the key aspects of the management of projects?

Project definition   *A project will be in great danger of encountering serious problems if its objectives, standards, technical base and general strategic planning are inadequately considered or poorly developed, or if its design is not firmly managed in line with its strategic plans.*

Objectives   Consider first how clear, agreed and communicated objectives may increase a project's chances of success. The Manhattan Project — 'First we had a clearly defined, unmistakable, specific objective'

(p. 17) — may have been extraordinarily difficult scientifically, technically and organizationally, but everyone working on the project knew clearly what its objective was (to develop an atomic bomb). Apollo was exactly the same: although the technological and administrative challenges were immense, the objective was startlingly clear: 'to achieving the goal, before this decade is out, of landing a man on the moon and returning him safely to earth' (p. 51).

Aristotle said that defining the problem is half the solution. He was exaggerating. A clear objective is far from a guarantee of a successful project. Not only is there a huge amount of work still to come, with ample scope for failure, but also clear, high-level objectives may obscure subtler inconsistencies, conflicts and problems. Concorde's objective was clear: 'to carry passengers across the Atlantic safely and supersonically through the world's air traffic control systems'. Underlying that seemingly simple objective was a mass of technical, environmental and other sub-objectives, most of which were not even apparent at the time the Anglo-French Treaty was signed. And as McCaskey has shown in his study of Citicorp's electronic teller project, it is often necessary *not* to define these sub-objectives too quickly, but to leave ambiguity long enough for options to be investigated and new ideas to emerge.[16]

Both Manhattan and Apollo were able to maintain support for their objectives during their development. Concorde was less successful, at least in the UK. In France, Concorde's objectives, being bound up with national technological development, were accepted by parliament and the public throughout the programme. Concorde's US rival, the SST, on the other hand, was not seen as vital and was viewed as an environmental threat by an increasingly vociferous lobby: the project's management totally failed to recognize this threat for far too long. The Space Station had considerable difficult in maintaining commitment to its objectives for other reasons. It had a clear(ish) objective: 'to develop a permanently manned space station, and to do it within a decade' (what does 'develop' really mean — surely not just design and construct?), but it was not fully supported by Congress, and suffered continuing funding difficulties. These difficulties, of course, reflected fundamental uncertainties over the real long-term strategy, or strategies, for being in space — the apparently clear objective concealed considerable strategic uncertainties (note 1). Project (or programme) objectives, then, should mesh with viable longer-term strategies — as they did with D-Day and Overlord, and appear to do in the Technopolis programme.

Once the programme is rolling, every effort must be made to communicate the validity of its objective. Often this may be done through quite subtle means. (Organization theorists refer to some of these as 'symbolic management'.[17,18]) Television, for example, was recognized as a valuable weapon in this regard on Apollo 'because of [its] publicity value and consequent funding importance' (p. 55). The management of Concorde, on the other hand, was less effective in its symbolic promotion; only in the 1980s did the symbolic value of Concorde really come to be exploited. On major infrastructure projects it is now recognized almost universally that effort must be put into 'selling' the project to the community, politicians and others. Huge effort was given to this on the Channel Tunnel, for example; indeed, John Stringer has proposed that major projects should develop a 'consents strategy' to ensure that public support is achieved.[19]

Sometimes objectives change in mid-programme, as with the US Synfuels Corporation or the Japanese Sunshine Programme, in which case the whole validity of the enterprise clearly needs to be re-examined. Sometimes the objectives *should* change, because of new conditions, but the issue is never raised. Sometimes, as Barry Turner has shown so well in his pioneering work on disasters and catastrophes, unperceived changes in objectives, or deviations from objectives, are a principal cause of failure.[20,21] As Imai[22] and Horwitch and Pralahad[23] inferred from these programmes, it is important that the project's objectives mesh with its stakeholders', and that they continue to fit stakeholders' interests as the project evolves, conditions change and the interdependencies of key systems, stakeholders and their objectives change.

Some objectives are more important than others. During the 1980s we became more sophisticated at identifying different measures of project success, and determining those that are critical (Critical Success Factors, p. 188). Intellectually, this approach was reflected in the writing on R&D, in the work of Ashley,[24] Morris and Hough[25] and others,[26–28] and in the PMI's 1986 Conference. In practical terms, we saw a trend towards better designed projects, with greater time and care (at last) being spent on front-end definition.

In many ways, of course, there is little that is really new, or even specific to 'modern project management', about these points. The Battle of Normandy illustrates excellently the search for 'critical success factors' and particularly the need to consider the broader definition of success. D-Day was a brilliant example of integrating a highly focused undertaking within a larger plan. Ruses such as the Pas de Calais feint were used to ensure its success; its planning and execution were concerned wholly with ensuring the longer-term success of the campaign.

Strategy   This history of the management of projects has demonstrated consistently the importance of a comprehensive definition of the project, and of spending time planning at the 'front end' of the project before implementation.

It is important to be clear about what really constitutes the project. Building the Space Station requires the Shuttle. Only the National

Research Council spotted that the likelihood of the Shuttle fleet being grounded during the early stages of Station construction, and the danger of the Station then falling to earth, had not been considered (chapter 7, note 38). This obvious system linkage was not considered prior to the Challenger disaster, since the Shuttle was not fully integrated into the Station definition and its planning. It was Teller who pointed out the interrelations of the submarine and missile rates of technology change that led to Polaris. The nuclear power programmes in the UK and the USA suffered from dramatically shortsighted definition, for example in the organizational capacity of the industry to build efficiently the large numbers of plants that were suddenly ordered and, particularly, the failure to take adequate account of 'back-end' problems of decommissioning and nuclear waste. Conversely, there was no need to tie 'a high quality railway between the Tunnel and London and the provision of through services to the provincial centres' to the Channel Tunnel project as the UK Government did in 1973 (p. 171), thereby grafting on to the project the piece that would lead directly to its cancellation 14 months later.

Every project or programme should have a clearly worked-out strategy covering all the issues necessary for implementation of the project, and all areas that can affect its viability. This strategy should be written down and communicated to the key players on

Fig. 47. Project management basic implementation process

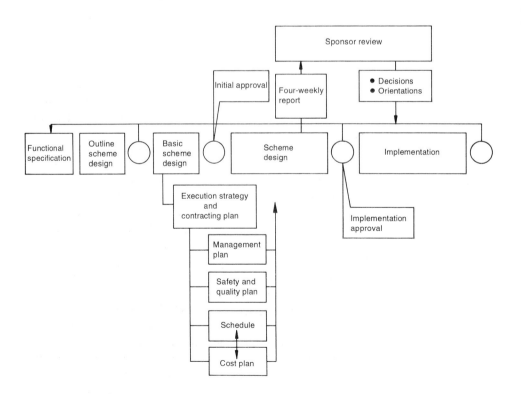

the project who will be in some way responsible for its implementation. The strategy document should not be too long. It should be reviewed regularly, and certainly at the key schedule milestones. Where aspects of the strategy are judged risky, back-up strategies should be identified.

Topics that should typically be covered in the strategy document include

- clear identification of sponsor and project objectives
- statements on how these are to be achieved
- environmental issues and strategy
- quality policy and programme
- safety policy
- owner's role and the role of third parties, e.g. consultants and contractors
- financial/economic objectives, financial strategy, funding strategy, cost planning
- legal and insurance issues and strategy
- technical strategy, technical policy, design philosophy
- project/work breakdown structure
- milestone/high-level schedule
- risk management strategy
- contracting/procurement strategy
- logistics policy
- employment and industrial relations strategy
- communication policy, particularly external policy
- information technology strategy.

Some of the most valuable work on the need for comprehensive planning has come from the areas of development and aid projects, R&D and New Product Development. In each of these the need to relate project performance across a broad range of parameters to long-term product success is paramount; many are sufficiently short-term and/or small-scale that, unlike electricity power generation, say, the results become blindingly evident remarkably quickly. Hirschman's 1967 *Development projects observed* (p. 118) was one of the first writings to pull the 'project success' question explicitly into 'project management'.[29] The 1980s' insights of Cassen[11] and Moris[9] (pp. 167–169) encapsulate almost everything that anyone of good sense would expect regarding what it takes to produce successful development projects. In the way they relate project implementation performance to environmental and market success, these works are matched closely by Cooper's,[28] Mansfield and Wagner's[30] and others' on New Product Development (pp. 181–183). In construction, the emergence of limited-recourse financing, and to an extent BOO(T) projects, has similarly had the valuable effect of forcing all parties to concentrate on the total range of factors that must be got right if the project as a whole is to be successful. Work on project success in the 1980s[24,31,32] had the same intent (pp. 181–182).

The lean production strategies pioneered by Toyota and Honda and being emulated by the US and European auto industries demonstrate a coherent and radical approach to New Product Development (pp. 183–184). The Japanese, as in their VLSI programme, emphasize strong project management leadership coupled with teamwork, open communications and productive conflict. These new strategies are used to allow hugely shortened tooling and prototyping times by overlapping design and production (Simultaneous Engineering) without the dangers of implementing untested technology or design, as in the old concurrency model.

Some of the pronouncements made in the 1980s on what is required to manage weapons projects effectively seem notably sensible too: *'Better organization of the acquisition process, more sensitive use of technology, balanced cost and performance trade-offs, greater program stability, increased use of competition, clearer command channels, enhanced quality of personnel, more limited reporting requirements'* (ref. 12, p. 143); or Levene's[33] *clear and not over elaborate specifications; agreed acceptance criteria; carefully defined, short development stages; effective contractual terms; a single prime contractor and a single project manager having greater responsibility and accountability; more attention to staff career development and professionalism; greater risk and cost sharing and collaboration between industry and government, with more responsibility moved to industry; greater competition, cost consciousness and fixed price contracting* (pp. 153–156 and p. 324, note 4).

The fact that almost everyone knows there will still be problems in the years to come in defence contracting may only go to show the limits of good intentions. After all, as long ago as 1959 the Anderson Committee was demanding that more time and effort be spent on front-end planning! Downey said the same thing, yet by the mid-1980s the MoD was still being criticized for not spending long enough in the early project stages validating the project's technical feasibility (p. 156). How many times during the years surveyed in this history were projects embarked on with far too little examination and thorough preparation — Concorde; TAPS; the sudden, herd-like ordering of over 210 US nuclear power plants between 1966 and 1974; many Third World projects of the 'loan pushing' 1970s and early 1980s? Let us hope that the progressive adoption of the Environmental Impact Assessment process may now be forcing managers to plan more comprehensively and communicate more effectively in these early project phases before committing to full project implementation.

Standards   Defining the standards of performance required of the project is an essential early step that has a major impact on the conduct of the entire operation. Standards, of course, refer to the whole range of system performance, not just to technical performance.

Personal conduct, finance, care for the environment, for example: all are crucial to the project's management. Indeed, during the latter part of the 1980s this concern for total performance became an increasingly vogue topic as TQM spread from Japan into US and European industry. TQM was first taken up in the high-technology manufacturing industries, but soon spread into the services sectors and the less obviously high-tech construction industries. 'Partnering' was one obvious example. The themes of focusing on customer requirements, Continuous Performance Improvement, teamwork and total organizational commitment, all of which are core to TQM, are hugely important to the effective management of projects: we shall examine them in the next chapter when we look at issues for the 1990s and beyond.

Nevertheless, it is the area of technology and the specification of technical standards that has dominated the development of the modern discipline of the management of projects during its first 30−40 years. Indeed, the very foundation of the discipline — systems management — has the specification of technical performance requirements at its base. Yet we saw in Atlas and Polaris how within two years the divorce of specifiers from implementers became dangerous. The trouble with the systems engineering approach is that the specifiers are easily led into developing unrealistic, overambitious expectations. Insufficient time is too often spent validating the specification: Nimrod was a famous example of overambitious technological specification; the F-111 was a project developed under specifications that were compromised, confused, inappropriate and impractical. The specifier may feel that he cannot trust the implementer to deliver real value for money (the post-Bloodhound $3000 coffee-maker syndrome). There is the temptation to shift too much risk to the supplier (the Total Package Procurement problem, and still a common practice in much of the engineering construction industry and, arguably, in the MoD). There are indications, fortunately, that these lessons are at last being learned. More care is now being given to technology validation and prototyping — and indeed to brief/bid validation — before launching into implementation; risk allocation is becoming more sophisticated. Let us hope that this trend persists: cardinal point specifications remain best project management practice in many organizations.

If people are not clear on what they want, if their ideas change, if trust is absent or risk badly allocated, then the specifications will probably not be consistent or appropriate, and implementation difficulties will almost certainly result.

Technology　Project management is a discipline developed in industries where technology development has been central. Until the 1980s at least, the dominant technical issue on most major projects was how to manage the degree of 'technology advance' (how to determine the appropriate amount of technological reach) without automatically incurring schedule slippages or cost overruns. Too often, in the 1960s particularly, major advances were initiated with only the briefest of recognitions of the challenges posed — as in Concorde, the RB-211, BART and the British Advanced Gas Cooled nuclear reactors, for example. Rand,[34-38] among others, studied this problem extensively (pp. 59, 129 and p. 322, note 38), Marschak *et al.*[39] eventually concluding that 'you can't have your cake and eat it'. Either you make only a small commitment at the outset while you verify the technology and get your estimates about right, or you commit to the programme early before you have validated the technology, in which case you must not be surprised if you subsequently exceed your estimates.

Of course it is worse when you have large technical uncertainty but great schedule urgency — where you may be forced to move into development or implementation/production before the technological uncertainties are ironed out — the concurrency situation; which has virtually been guaranteed to cause project implementation problems. ('On taking office, Packard had noted that all DoD programmes then in trouble were being developed on the concurrency method' (p. 131).)

Part of the difficulty has been that technology from the 1950s to the 1970s was often proceeding in quantum leaps. Developments now are generally more predictable. Although the rate of change of many technologies today is as large as 20, 30 or 40 years ago, or even larger, the technologies now are generally more familiar. Then, they were often of a new kind — electronics, nuclear, new metals and drugs, new aerodynamics. Today we are more familiar with the developmental risk posed by the new technology. Certainly, the philosophy of advancement today is closer to the 'building block' approach than to the 'spearhead' (p. 67); a philosophy where risks — technical and other — are carefully assessed as the project evolves; where prototypes are used extensively to demonstrate the technology (the Experimental Aircraft Programme, automobiles, drugs, IT, etc.); where close teamwork adapts the old, bald concurrency to the Total Quality driven approach of Concurrent Engineering.

An important consequence of today's way of thinking is that one does not always seek very advanced technology — any project financed on a limited-recourse basis, for example, will work hard to eliminate unproved technology from the project. That the 'best may be the enemy of the good' is as true for a plane (Concorde) as for the Third World (Schumacher's 'appropriate technology'; Moris's 'keep innovations to a minimum' (p. 167)). Since one should 'freeze' the design before implementation goes too far, large technology advances inevitably push out the development cycle (unless concurrency is used, with the risks and skills that this entails). Large technological advance is also often increasingly expensive, as the US B2 bomber or the telephone switches developed in the 1980s, for example, demonstrate (note 2). Again, this makes the case for a cautious approach to the employment of large technology advances on projects.

While aerospace offers a rich opportunity to explore the problems of technology (as indeed do many other fields: pharmaceuticals, autos, IT, rail, etc.), it is in the nuclear industry that some of the clearest and most painful lessons have been signalled. These are worth dwelling on for a moment.

The nuclear power industry, at least in the USA and the UK, never properly appraised either the size or the extent of the technology challenges it was launching. My account of the UK's decision to choose the AGR over the BWR in *The anatomy of major projects*[25] illustrates this painfully, as does the disastrous award to Atomic Power Company of the Dungeness B contract and the later radical but untested alterations in boiler positioning adopted by British Nuclear Design and Construction — both examples costing many hundreds of millions of pounds. Hence the CEGB's reaction in the early 1970s (to seek wherever possible 'discrete upgradings of technology, introduced only at reasonably long-term intervals; maintenance of stable relationships with suppliers . . . [and] standardization of design wherever possible' (p. 123)). This, of course, was precisely the strategy that was adopted in France.

The case of Heysham 2, along with Torness the last of the UK's AGRs, makes the same points in different ways. Heysham 2 adopted this strategy with almost total single-mindedness, but two relatively small technical errors slipped through unchecked to cause substantial delay and overspend. Heysham 2 was nearly two years late, first because of a problem of vibrating control rods in the nuclear core and later because the computer systems were not ready in time. The rattling of the control rods was caused by one of the very few design modifications to the first generation AGRs that was not rig-tested. The computer systems were late because they had not been subject to the same rigorous design, programme management and change controls as the rest of the project. Lessons: technology must be tested; the definition and management of the project must be comprehensive.

The situation in the USA was not much better; in fact in many ways it was worse. The industry was at least blessed in having an engineer (Rickover) rather than scientists as its presiding genius. But while Rickover and the production engineers at Westinghouse, General Electric, Stone & Webster and Bechtel moved the industry quickly into a civilian power—production mode, the Atomic Energy Commission, as the nation's regulator, failed to recognize the size of the technology risk, to control the ordering of units, or to ensure an adequate quality and regulatory framework from the outset. A proper risk assessment was not undertaken; the projects were not looked at a sector level or as a total programme (note 3).

The lessons, then, from the nuclear power industry with regard to technology are: first, *define the system properly*; second, *assess the technological risk comprehensively*; third, *develop strategies for dealing with the resultant risk*, for example, QA procedures fully established from the outset, personnel adequately trained in the technology and its management, fall-back strategies, stable relationships with key suppliers, and proper testing of proposals.

(Turner,[20,21] Perrow,[40] Collingridge[41] and others, in examining failure in large-scale technological systems, have contributed to the discussion of the management of technology. Collingridge contends that many large technology programmes — nuclear power, system building, large irrigation systems, the Shuttle, videotext — moved too quickly from small beginnings to large, inflexible projects, with long lead times, high capital and support infrastructure requirements and over-centralized organizations. This is probably a biased view: Apollo and North Sea oil certainly do not bear out his general thesis. Perrow concentrates on how disaster has often occurred where the level of system complexity exceeded management's ability to manage the system. Turner has shown similarly how catastrophes have often been the result of an organizational failure to recognize and/or respond to emerging signals of major problems. The lessons of all three authors are of a piece with those of this study: keep projects as small and modular as possible, fully assess the risk in advance, test before implementing, and have management attuned to the size and complexity of the system and the degree of turbulence associated with it (note 4).)

The R&D world offers further lessons on the management of technology. Allen, Allison and others have written many papers on the organization of R&D labs, stressing particularly the importance of communications. The VLSI and Fifth Generation programmes illustrate the same things.[42-44] The best programmes emphasized the importance of a central lab where ideas could ferment and be challenged, where productive conflict could be generated, and where there was good personnel management and strong leadership. The Japanese 'lean production' approach to management (pp. 183–184) makes the same point.

Careful definition, comprehensive planning, thorough risk analysis, better use of prototypes, careful progressing of development, thorough early testing, great care in managing concurrency/ simultaneous development, stable but challenging relationships with suppliers, good communications, conflict managed as a source of ideas and development — all these painfully learned lessons are now generally accepted strategies for managing technology effectively.

Technology, in fact, is generally no longer the major challenge to projects that it used to be. The challenges in the 1980s and 1990s are not so much technology development issues as the softer project

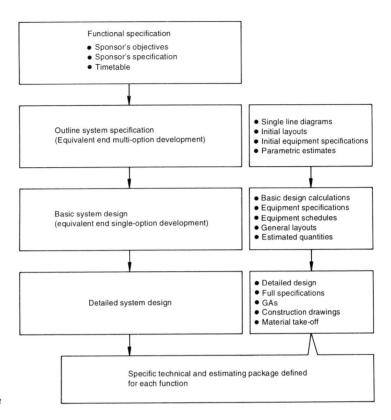

Fig. 48. The Systems Engineering approach

definition issues of overall strategy and specification trade-offs, funding, organization and people.

Design

New ideas are always being developed; there is always a possibility for the design to be enhanced that little bit more. A crucial, central challenge in the effective management of projects is the resolution of the conflicting need to meet the schedule and keep within budget with the desire to get the technical base that bit better.

In teaching, I often compare the Fulmar project with the computerization of the UK PAYE tax system (COP) (ref. 25, chapters 6 and 7). Fulmar, a £417m North Sea oil project, let its fabrication contracts per schedule even though the design was in some areas only 35% complete. Steve Matheson, the COP project manager, on the other hand, held back from writing any software code until the technical base of his project was absolutely firm. Many of Fulmar's contracts experienced 100% cost overruns; COP came in on time and in budget. In reality the comparison is less black-and-white (for example, how was Fulmar to know what 100% complete was?) but the cases make the very important point that proceeding on the basis of an imperfectly secure project definition — of putting schedule requirements above technical — can be very dangerous.

Managing the development of the project definition, in a timely, cost-effective way, with minimum changes, towards ends that reflect the customer's real needs, is central to the management of projects. It is the essence of design management. At its base is a schedule and change-control process based on the project's life cycle. The aim is *an orderly progressing of the project's design and technical basis through a sequence of review stages, the level of detail becoming progressively higher as the project progresses, with strict control of technical interfaces and over any proposed changes* (through Configuration Management/Change Control (note 5)). It is an idea as old in systems management terms as the USAF Joint Project Offices of 1953. NASA promulgated the practice as central to its project management process when it published its Phased Program Planning approach based on the 1960 375 Series procedures and the Anderson Committee recommendations. It is the basis of the structured programming methodology for software development projects. Thus, disciplines as widely different as space and aeronautics, process engineering and electrical and software engineering now generally employ project development methodologies that emphasize careful, discrete upgradings of technology, thorough review of cost, schedule and performance implications, and rigorous control of subsequent proposed changes. Of the disciplines surveyed in this book, perhaps only civil engineering and architecture/building had in the late 1980s and early 1990s (despite the growth of management contracting and construction management, and the emergence of new contract forms such as the British Property Federation and New Engineering Contract) yet to adopt so rigorous a 'project development' methodology. However, the growth of design and build as a way of getting tighter organizational integration between design and production was accelerating rapidly in building and civil engineering by the late 1980s; indeed, as we shall see in the next chapter, a feature of the 1990s is greater design accountability for overall project efficiency (cost, time, operational performance, etc.).

The gradual creation of the design concept is only a part of the total design process, however. Testing of the design is also important, and has been seen more than once in this book to have a significant impact on the effectiveness of the overall programme. Software development methodologies have system testing — verification and validation — as an integral part of the project management process. Prototyping, a form of product testing, has become accepted practice where technological uncertainty exists, particularly as a way of addressing the concurrency problem. Operational feedback, whether from prototypes or final production products, has slowly been recognized as a necessary part of good project management; this applies for cost information as well as for technical and other performance data.

In construction, the commercial pressures of cost have generally been stronger than those of operational performance. While Value Analysis was brought into DoD by McNamara in the early 1960s, it was only really in the 1980s that it became established in the construction industries. Yet the process of systematically searching out higher functionality for lower cost during design and implementation — the basis of Value Engineering (Fig. 49) — is now an effective core construction management practice. And while Costs-in-Use is an old construction industry term, effective closing of the feedback loop between actual costs and design — as is meant for example in the Design-to-Cost or Target Costing idea — was still more the exception than the rule in the late 1980s.

So, there is evidently still work to be done in developing the 'internal' skills of managing the project design. Equally, plenty of work remains in managing more effectively the interaction between the project's definition and its external constraints.

External factors, finance and timing

A project's definition both is affected by and affects its external environment. Several external factors may be identified, but I have chosen to dwell on the project's political context, its relationship with the local community, the general economic environment, and its location and the geophysical conditions in which it is set. The

Fig. 49. FAST (Functional Analysis System Technique) diagram as used in Value Engineering. This breaks down the task to be performed into basic and supporting functions. Their effectiveness in performing these functions is then analysed (adapted from Sievert[46])

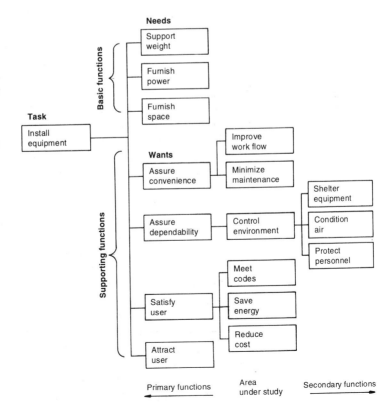

project's definition is also affected by, and affects, the *cost—benefit* relation, the pattern of *financing* and the *durations* required for the various project phases.

Location and geophysical characteristics

The project's location and geophysical characteristics affect its technology and design, the nature of its impact on the local community and political processes, and its implementation and scheduling challenges.

Once the nature of the technical challenges has been recognized properly, project personnel have generally proved impressively capable of surmounting them. Working in space, in the North Sea, in the Alaskan wilderness — such challenges are meat and potatoes to project people! Of course, the physical challenges are often not appreciated properly. Mistakes of this kind in the nuclear power industry really are unforgivable: Zimmer, in the USA, for example, should not have been built in inadequate ground conditions; neither should the stations now mothballed near Rio de Janeiro in Brazil or outside Manilla in the Philippines. As I have noted many times, too many projects move too quickly into implementation without sufficient initial definition and study. Given such proper identification and definition, however, the physical environment has hardly ever proved an insurmountable problem.

Project personnel have had more difficulty in recognizing the effect of the physical environment on budgets and schedules, and in dealing with the project's impact on the physical and community 'environment' and, in consequence, the political processes that regulate the conditions under which projects are executed. The initial estimates for TAPS, for example, were hopelessly inadequate to the challenge of building in the Alaskan wilderness. The early North Sea oil estimates hugely underestimated the costs of construction in these hostile waters. The plans for the Space Station are still ambitious in terms of the 'known unknowns' of building in the dangerous environment of space. But an even greater difficulty for project managers has been in recognizing the socio-political response to what is being proposed. It is to this political dimension that we should now turn.

Politics

There is, as far as I am aware, no discussion in the project management literature *per se* of the impact of politics on projects, or how to manage a project's political environment. There are certainly subcultures of literature that deal with the politics of various kinds of project, most obviously defence but also transportation, (nuclear) power, information technology and R&D. And although it may be validly argued that, since politics is after all about building constituencies and creating influence, the whole corpus of political science is relevant to managing 'external factors', the fact remains that the literature relating the management of projects to politics is very slight. Yet the link is very strong.

Many of the projects reviewed in this book, being major ones, were strongly and obviously affected by political forces. The

impetus for systems management developed on the US ballistic
missile programmes, for example, came out of political concern
over threatened Soviet capability, as indeed was the case for all
US space activity up to the landing on the moon of Apollo 11.
(Space has always needed a political champion.) Defence/aerospace
projects are particularly vulnerable to political 'interference'.
National transportation projects and R&D programmes, and many
energy, oil and petrochemical projects, operate only under the
dictate of the politician. The civil nuclear power business was
heavily pushed politically ('Atoms for Peace'). Third World
development projects are especially prone to political influence.
('Location is a political matter; the political dimension is often
under-appreciated by "outside experts"; underdeveloped countries
often have overdeveloped institutions; events should be timed to
the political timetable; develop effective PR'[9] (p. 167).) Even
where the public sector is supposedly liberated to the private, as
in BOO(T), political guidance and guarantees, and encouragement,
are needed, as we saw in the discussion on the Ryrie rules, Antrim,
the Turkish BOO(T)s, the Channel Tunnel, etc. (Consider the role
of Mrs Thatcher and President Mitterand in promoting the Channel
Tunnel and its enabling legislation.)

Must non-major projects also be conscious of the political
dimension? Basically, even small projects live under regulatory
and economic conditions directly influenced by politicians, so yes,
they must. And even intra-organizationally the project manager
must secure 'political' support for his project — as, on their larger
projects, did Groves and Schriever, for example. ('Schriever won
the overwhelming (Air Force) "political" support he needed (just
as Groves had had to earlier for the Manhattan Project)' (p. 23).)

What lessons can we derive, then, on managing the political
dimension?

The major lesson for those managing projects is that to be
successful, one must manage *upwards* and *outwards*, as well as
downwards and sideways. The project manager should be attuned
to the changing political winds around him or her. He or she should
court the politicians, helping allies by providing them with the
information they need to champion his or her programme. (Ed
Patton, the Chairman of Alyeska, moved to Washington, DC to
help lobby for TAPS's Authorization Act; Florida Power and Light
established an office opposite the Nuclear Regulatory Commission
headquarters to facilitate the licensing of St Lucie 2.) At best, the
politician will be fighting for your project. Without such
management guidance, however, he or she may decide against the
project or, equally bad, as we saw with Nixon and the US SST,
postpone a decision and create a delay, or, as with Nixon and the
Shuttle, set an unrealistic budget limit (note 6).

Second, do not ignore potential adversaries. As Horwitch
and Pralahad[45] showed in their study of the development of

the US Groceries Bar Code, one should co-opt people. Draw them in. (The Environmental Impact Assessment process is showing how substantive dialogue can help reduce potential opposition.) The USAF managers of the US SST failed totally in this regard. In truth, perhaps, no-one could have reconciled the SST to the environmentalist opposition that was welling up in 1970. Certainly Halaby, McKee and Jewell, and indeed the National Academy of Sciences, failed to 'read' the significance of the opposition that was rising, just as the Concorde people similarly failed. (Although Magruder did an excellent job in managing the opposition to the project when it was really too late. There are times when it may be just too difficult to neutralize environmentalist opposition.)

Environmentalist and community issues

In the USA, two of the largest and most prestigous projects — TAPS and the SST — were unexpectedly halted in 1970 by environmental opposition. Traditional project management tools and techniques proved totally inadequate to the challenge of ensuring the projects' survival. In the UK, community opposition to London's ringroads and third airport turned the siting of these projects into little more than a farce. Before the 1970s were out these forces effectively killed off another major project sector — nuclear power.

1970 was a turning point in the management of projects in that, at least from that year, the environment and the environmentalist movement were clearly forces not to be ignored. Unfortunately, ignore them is just what most project people did, at least until 1987–1989 when Mrs Brundtland, Mrs Thatcher, Barber Conable and others suddenly made them 'establishment'. Now, at last, most project staff realized that they must *find a way of involving the community positively in the development of their project*. To ignore the community and leave everything to big planning inquiries like Sizewell B is to leave it too late. (Community opposition was to disrupt completely British Rail's plans for a high-speed rail link in the early 1990s.) A 'consents strategy' (p. 166) must be devised and implemented. The dialogue and planning to ensure proper understanding and to gain consent must be comprehensive, linking with other related sectors and projects (otherwise the environmental planning may be rendered ineffective by neighbouring schemes, as happened for example in Carajas). The Environmental Impact process should be used as a means of planning and explaining the project strategically.

Getting the support of the local community is particularly important in projects where the local community is the user, so to speak, for example in development projects and Information Technology. Ever since the New Directions movement it has been accepted that 'self-sustaining behaviour among one or more target groups [must be] included as a success criterion' (p. 117), yet 17 years after Hirschman wrote those words Cassen observed that 'understanding of institutional, political, and social constraints to aid effectiveness lags very far behind economic and technical competence' (p. 169). Even by the late 1980s planning inquiries were unknown in the very great majority of ldcs. In information systems projects, on the other hand, involvement of the user in agreeing the system specification had, by the early 1980s, become a key feature of competent project management: the practice of IT rapid prototyping was developed, as we have seen, as a way of testing and tying in the user to the system design and implementation.

This therefore rather argues against the 1970s practice of building large homogeneous projects that may be insensitive to local variations in demand. Certainly in the 1980s there was a move towards building projects in phases, ensuring that each phase fits local market requirements. Another feature of the 1980s was a trend towards providing greater product adaptability by allowing greater opportunity to tailor the end design to a customer's own requirements. One sees this most notably, perhaps, in the growth of shell and core construction in building, where the basic structure is built but the 'fit-out' of internal finishes to a customer/user's individual requirements is left until he or she is firmly identified and has specified his or her needs. Software shows a parallel trend, with report writing capabilities allowing considerable flexibility to sort and select from the core database structure.

Conceptually, too, the 'local community' can be the potential 'consumer' or purchaser for the project. A market survey to see how viable the project economics are is an essential part of the project's management. Since 'market' conditions change periodically, the market check should be carried out regularly: the opportunity to change the product exists at least up to the full production or development stage, as the R&D literature points out (p. 183).

The economic environment

Changes in economic circumstances affect both the cost of the project's inputs and the economic viability of its outputs. Projects in the 1970s, for example, suffered severe cost increases as a consequence of inflation; Concorde was substantially less attractive commercially because the large and unexpected rise in the price of fuel oil could not be compensated by changes in fares. All energy sector projects, as well as oil-based projects in the petrochemical and transportation industries, were affected drastically between 1968 and 1985 as oil moved from $1−$2 to $33−$35 per barrel before falling back to $12−$16. TAPS was undertaken precisely on the basis of a rising oil price, as were the first and second generation North Sea oil projects; nuclear power became less and less attractive as the price of oil fell. Both the quantity and quality of Third World projects were substantially affected by the sudden flood of petrodollars seeking projects in the 1970s.

The more economically demanding conditions of the 1980s almost certainly improved the quality of project management. In the building industry, high interest rates forced significant productivity improvements (including propelling the development of construction management). Project financing led to a greatly improved discipline of project appraisal and management ('ten years ago, there was little examination [by the banks] of the viability of projects' (p. 326, note 25)).

It is not particularly that we have better tools today for managing the economic environment. As before, we test the project in terms of various scenarios, use sensitivity analyses of shadow prices, examine currency risk, obtain forward contracts where possible, and so on. The big difference today compared with 20 years ago is that then we assumed conditions would not vary too much in the future; now, after the economic dislocation of the 1970s and 1980s, we are much more cautious. *As it is with technology, then, so it is with economics: in appraising and managing our projects today we are more cautious as regards the future; much less inclined to take a chance.* We prefer the projects to be smaller and of shorter duration. We are generally reluctant to proceed at all unless the risk is adequately covered — which is why 'major projects' became harder to finance during the 1980s.

Cost—benefit and other appraisal techniques

Clearly, the project must show a positive benefit over its cost. In the areas of cost—benefit discounting and other appraisal techniques, our tools have moved forward in the past 15—20 years. The Roskill Commission's examination of the third London airport site exposed the limits of cost—benefit analysis as contrived in its pure form in the 1960s. Externalities and longer-term social factors are now recognized as important variables that can dramatically affect the attractiveness of a project. (This is not to say that there may not be great debate over whether or not to include such factors, and, if they are included, to what degree.) By the 1980s, basic techniques of the 1960s had been replaced by a broader set of economic and financial analyses arrayed, in the community context, under the Environmental Impact Assessment (EIA) procedure.

Initially resisted by many in the project community, the great value of the EIA process is that it allows consultation and dialogue between developers, the community, regulators and others, and ensures that time is spent at the 'front end' in examining options and ensuring that the project appears viable. Through these twin benefits the likelihood of community opposition and unforeseen external shocks is diminished, and project developers are forced to spend time planning at the front end — precisely the stage of the project that they traditionally rushed, despite the obvious dangers — and communicating their ideas clearly to those who will be affected. For *not only has lack of time spent at the front end been a problem too often in the past: so also has lack of effective communication.* A positively presented proposal can make all the difference in a cost—benefit analysis being positive.

Financing

In many of the sectors and projects in which project management was developed, money was often a secondary factor. Its place in formal project management theory is thus not as prominent as it ought to be, given its normal significance.

In defence/aerospace the military imperative meant that cost control generally received only secondary attention (*see* PERT/Cost, pp. 44−45) although clearly Congressional funding had always to be watched, as the US SST showed. (Webb's securing of several billion dollars of contingency funding for Apollo in 1960 was both politically daring and of great value to the programme later.) Hence, despite the many studies by Rand on the question of cost overruns on defence projects, the situation was never really going to change much so long as the work was performed under predominantly cost-reimbursable contracts administered by defence personnel who did not necessarily see cost growth as a serious problem (p. 129). As soon as the criticality of the programme began to diminish, however — as soon as the military imperative began to wane — funding issues became more important, as the US space programme after Apollo and the Pentagon's budgetary difficulties in the early 1990s demonstrate. This rule applies to virtually all the sectors reviewed in this book. Only in extraordinarily special circumstances does funding not significantly influence projects' design and implementation.

There is ample evidence of the way in which finance can affect a project's management. BART is an example of a project critically affected by the availability — or rather, unavailability — of municipal funding. The development of the North Sea oil province shows how national governmental fiscal policies can affect project viability: the generous allowances the Norwegian and UK governments provided to North Sea developers played an extremely important role in stimulating the development of the province. (These, together with the design uncertainties and the rapidly rising price of oil, explain of course the anxiety of the private sector to develop these fields quickly.) US nuclear power projects also demonstrate a strong influence of finance on project performance. The utilities' costs of financing were already rising dramatically as interest rates rose steeply, and their bond ratings fell when they began to experience progressive technical difficulties which caused longer and longer project delays, making the plants increasingly expensive to finance. Ultimately, the cost of finance for many US utilities became just too great (pp. 125−126). (The situation in Britain was different, the industry being favoured by government-imposed nuclear-friendly discount hurdles.)

There has been a change in the forms of financing available for projects over the past few decades. The 1970s saw an adoption of limited-recourse financing, which improved significantly the rigour and breadth of project appraisal and finance. The 1980s saw a marked shift from public- to private-sector funding. By the second half of the 1980s, limited-recourse financing, BOO(T),

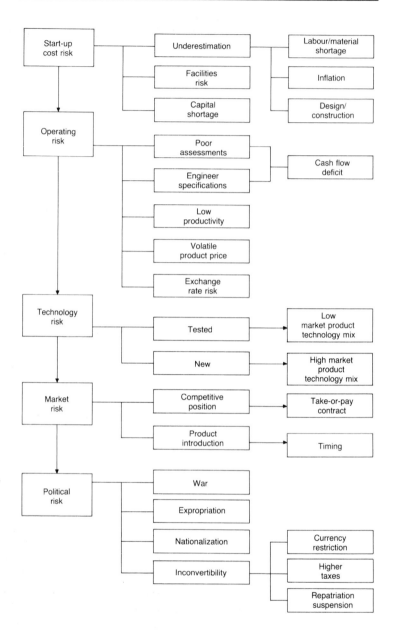

Fig. 50. Risk identification in Project Finance (from Woody and Pourian[47])

debt—equity swaps and barter arrangements, as well as some sophisticated co-financing arrangements using bilateral and multilateral aid and/or export credits, had brought private-sector money into the financing of projects in a way that was undreamt of 20 years previously. Financial engineering had become a necessary ingredient for many, if not most, major projects.

While private-sector financing has undoubtedly been beneficial, it is no panacea. There is a belief, for example, that projects built under private-sector funding inevitably demonstrate better financial discipline. This is not necessarily so. The record of privately funded, but sovereign guaranteed, Third World lending in the 1970s was, overall, simply appalling — involving, for example, weak project appraisals, loan pushing, cost and schedule overruns and white elephants. Private-sector financing institutions had little or no incentive to ensure that the projects were viable, and stated repeatedly that they were not interested in the quality of their borrowers' management. Provided they feel that their financial position is secured, many commercial banks may not care particularly about the viability of the project. The distinction should therefore be made between the disciplines of private-sector funding *per se* and of private-sector owner- or sponsor-led funding. Where the sponsoring organization must survive in the commercial world and the project is subject to the disciplines of the market place, there is much greater care in ensuring project viability. This, of course, is the benefit of limited-recourse financing: it ties the financing tighter into the sponsoring organization and project viability.

By tying private-sector responsibility more tightly into projects, new disciplines of realism and prudence have been brought to bear in the identification and appraisal of projects. Private funding disciplines have improved the general practice of project definition. By the late 1980s, there was a much better understanding of how to manage the pre-feasibility and feasibility front-end stages of a project, and this understanding began to appear on public-sector projects too.

The raising of the finance for the Channel Tunnel from the capital markets in 1986−1987 (pp. 174−176) is a classic illustration of how all the elements shown in Fig. 46 interact on a project, in this case around the question of finance, and how well-identified problems may still go unaddressed. To raise the initial finance required for the project (£6bn), certain technical work had to be done: planning approvals obtained, contracts signed, political uncertainties removed, etc. Since the project was raising most of its funding externally, a significant amount of boot-strapping was required (no pun intended): these tasks could be accomplished only if some money was already raised, and so on. Actions had to be taken by a certain time or the money would run out. (As it was, the delay in contract negotiations, and hence of Equity 2, was very serious.) Further, a key parameter of the project's viability was the likelihood of its slippage during construction. A slippage of three to six months meant not just increased financing charges, but the lost revenue of a summer season of tourist traffic. In fact, as we know, the schedule did slip and additional funding became necessary. Partly, the reason was the incomplete and inadequate technical definition on which the funds were raised. Insufficient allowance was made for items yet to be defined. Other factors, to which we shall return, were the organizational ones of an insufficiently robust owner organization (at least initially) and a construction team locked into the project in unproductive conflict with the owner.

The importance in the Channel Tunnel financing of its schedule raises the factor to which we next turn: phasing and timing.

Phasing and timing

Determining the overall timing of the enterprise is crucial to calculating its risks and the dynamics of its implementation and management. The preparation for the D-Day landings clearly illustrated the balance that must be struck between the strategic outlining of the schedule (the desire for a summer campaign in Normandy), the tactical constraints (for example high tides), and the scheduling of preparatory activities (most critically, obtaining the requisite number of landing craft).

The time available for each of the basic stages of the project, together with the amount and difficulty of the work to be accomplished in those phases, heavily influences the difficulty of the task to be managed. Manhattan, Atlas and Apollo all had extremely difficult technical challenges to be overcome relatively quickly. The objective and strategic schedule for these projects were clear, however, and the protagonists could focus on resolving the technical issues within the project constraints. The Space Station is very different. Uncertainty existed for a considerable time as to its objectives, strategic schedule and technology. With an insecure programme objective, and insecure political sponsorship, the Station slipped its schedule considerably during the 1980s and was in fact completely reconfigured in the 1990s.

Mueller's schedule risk analysis on Apollo was particularly interesting in that his response to a likely schedule overrun was primarily organizational: reduce the number of test flights, improve quality assurance, push responsibility further down the organization (the 'subsystem manager' concept — p. 54). This high-risk approach — essentially a form of concurrency — differed significantly from the more prudent 'heel-to-toe' philosophy espoused, for example, by Packard and the Rand Corporation. In the latter view technological risk is minimized through testing before committing to production ('fly before buy'). Yet Mueller showed that there may be times when the schedule is so important that this preferred sequencing of project activities may need to be shortened (without jeopardizing safety!) by increasing technical management and quality assurance and by overlapping the schedule stages.

Prototyping is a central feature of the 'sequential' development approach. As we have seen, it has played an important part in the successful development of Tornado, the European Fighter Aircraft and other modern aircraft projects, and is now an established technique in information systems development — particularly high-risk ones. Simultaneous Development/Concurrent Engineering, as pioneered by the Japanese in 'lean production', goes one stage further in that it additionally introduces team design in which there is full and open communication between production managers and product designers, as well of course as prototype testing, manufacturing, flexibility and strong project management leadership.

Several lessons have emerged from this history, therefore, on how to deal with the challenge of managing urgent projects, particularly when the technology and design are not yet fixed.

(a) Ensure the objective is clear; establish a strategic development schedule; do not omit any of the stages of the project life cycle.

(b) Have a competent project team in place from the outset, working positively towards the project objectives; include downstream production specialists in the design group.

(c) Do a thorough risk analysis; use known technology and/or standardization and design replication as far as possible; avoid unnecessary technical and other risks.

(d) Test the technology before committing to production (prototyping). Avoid outright concurrency unless prepared to take the risk of failing and of having to pay for the cost of rework, but explore the possibilities of Simultaneous Development/Concurrent Engineering.

(e) Avoid making technical or design changes once implementation had begun. Choose design parameters sufficiently broad to permit development and detailing without subsequent change ('Fast Build'). Exert strict change control/configuration management.

(f) Order long-lead items early.

(g) Prefabricate and/or build in as predictable an environment as possible; get the organizational factors (including labour relations) right to support optimum productivity.

(h) Put in strong management leadership to ensure the proper integration at the right time of the things which must be done to make the project a success — teamwork, schedule-conscious decision-making, etc.

Attitudes   *The project's definition, its interaction with external, financial and other factors, and its implementation will be much harder to manage, and quite possibly prejudiced, if the attitudes of the parties essential to its success are not positive and supportive.*

Projects demand significant effort, under difficult and even hostile conditions, often without the benefit of high personal financial reward. (In fact, as Frank Moolin of TAPS often pointed out, project people work feverishly to put themselves out of a job!) Unless there is a major commitment to making the project a success, unless the motivation of everyone working on the project is high, and unless attitudes are supportive and positive, the chances of success are substantially diminished.

Perhaps nothing illustrates these factors more obviously than accounts of war and wartime 'projects' — certainly we see them constantly, at both the General Staff and field levels, in the accounts of D-Day and Overlord. They were paramount on the Manhattan Project. Admiral Raborn exploited them to the full on Polaris ('Those working on it showed a deep commitment to the programme's success' (p. 27)): the SPO was deliberately created as an elite group, with great attention to personal fulfilment. NASA realized them brilliantly on Apollo. And, as George Hough and I showed in our studies of Giotto and the computerization of the UK tax system,[25] probably neither of these later projects would have been a success without an explicit commitment to success and supportive, positive attitudes from senior managers and the principal organizations working on the projects. In a different way, the Japanese have shown how commitment needs to be mobilized in parallel at city, regional and national levels in order to make an ambitious 'soft systems' major project like Technopolis work.

It is particularly important to project success that there be commitment and support at the top; without it the project is probably doomed. The study of the Advanced Passenger Train in *The anatomy of major projects* illustrates this clearly (ref. 25, chapter 4). The Shuttle had a terrible time because of the lack of real commitment and enthusiasm of Presidents Nixon and Carter. The Channel Tunnel, conversely, would never have gone ahead without the support of François Mitterand and Margaret Thatcher. (We shall return shortly to definitions of leadership and championing, and the role of these in projects.)

However, while commitment is important, it must be *commitment to viable ends*. Great leaders can become great dictators; the history of the 20th century has shown how commitment and positive attitudes to clear goals can lead to economic ruin and the murder of millions. It is important, then, if sensible projects are to be initiated that they not be insulated from criticism ('much of [this criticism] improved the performance of Polaris' (p. 26)), even though it may occasionally prove awkward. The US SST and Concorde, for example, might not have been such disasters if more attention had been paid earlier to the environmental question. As Williams[48] has powerfully argued, the UK nuclear industry owes many of its difficulties to the closed, secret nature of British governmental working in general and the nuclear industry in particular. Better, then, as we have seen, to co-opt critics, to bring their questioning into the project as an integral part of its development. This, essentially, is the way the Environmental Impact Assessment process works.

As well as being open to criticism, viable projects should encourage 'open' communication, with a minimum of distortion on the 'channel'. The F-111 illustrates what can happen when senior parties are not communicating clearly, and end up committing to different things while ostensibly sharing the same specifications.

Open communication is an essential part of TQM, Japanese R&D practice and lean production management.

Two management topics became increasingly important during the 1980s: Quality and Safety. Both are central to project success. Both have positive attitudes on the part of all — but particularly of senior management — as essential features. Neither is new, but their impact on the projects' world increased sharply during the decade, and their impact in the 1990s is likely to be increasingly important. (They are discussed in chapter 9.)

The principles of Total Quality can hardly be faulted: namely that by

- understanding the customers' needs
- measuring and designing performance and quality standards into the total production process
- having everyone engaged in the process attuned to the customers' needs and to the level of quality being achieved throughout the organization, and having everyone continuously working to raise this level

one satisfies one's customers better, waste is reduced and performance and profitability are increased. So basic, so fundamental is this philosophy that it can work only if everyone in the organization is committed to it. It absolutely requires positive, supportive attitudes on the part of everyone.

Safety is the same. It is an attitude of mind; a whole approach to work. As with quality, everyone must be committed to safety, and the commitment must start at the top.

Quality and safety were — and are — intrinsic to the NASA culture, although the agency's overriding commitment to them seemed to decline during the 1970s. Commitment can easily fall off — indeed it will fall off — if senior management is not committed or does not ensure that staff attitudes and actions remain supportive.

Before one goes very far, discussion of attitudes and commitment, of criticism or communications, leads to project organizational issues such as project leadership, team management, industrial relations, and owner—supplier contractual and organizational relationships. It is to these organizational issues that we now turn.

Project organization

As the strategic definition of the project becomes firm, one begins to move more rapidly into implementation. Project management, I have suggested, has in the past been more concerned with the process of implementation — with scheduling, control, teamwork, organization structure, leadership and so on — than with strategic definition. This book has shown that this alone is too limited a scope to assure successful projects. Ensuring a supportive environment and managing the development of the project's definition are equally vital.

This section of the chapter could itself perhaps be entitled 'project implementation', but this would prolong a misperception, i.e. that implementation, or project management, really begins only after the project definition and its relation with the various external factors has been defined. In fact, of course, *implementation begins as soon as the project is conceived*. Even the pre-feasibility period has to be implemented. Obviously, however, as the definition is firmed up, and funding and various approvals are obtained, the amount of action increases: contracts are let, more people become involved, the rate of expenditure rises dramatically.

The management actions that now come more to the fore, to complement those of project definition, scheduling, finance and so on, are largely organizational. By this I mean those connected with the project structure, its staffing, and its systems.

Structure I: Moving the project effectively through its development cycle

A crucial skill of the project executive is to move the project at the appropriate pace through its development cycle, doing the right thing at the right time (not too soon) — the 'organizational metronome' of Sayles and Chandler[49] — *through careful planning and decision making*.

Much of the central contribution of modern project management is, of course, to do with time−phasing, getting the rate of development right, scheduling the right review dates, dealing with the problem of urgency, and so on. The standard development cycles published by the USAF/DoD (the Anderson Committee and the AFR and AFSCM series) and by NASA (the 500 series and later the Phased Program Planning sequence) were crucial milestones of 'strategic' importance in the development of project management.

Packard, like many project commentators, fought long and hard against rushed programmes where implementation began before the project's definition and technology were secure. As George Hough and I showed on our study of Giotto, the trick in successful implementation is to have a sense of urgency — to keep the project 'on a roll' — without rushing to the point of making bad judgements or omitting steps ('schedule-conscious decision-making', in Admiral Sir Lindsay Bryson's judicious phrase[50]). Each stage of the project should be carefully and thoroughly investigated, with — as this book has highlighted — as much effort given to the early stages ('consents management', technology testing, etc.) as to the later, and all dimensions of the project's management being considered, not just the technical (i.e. finance, planning, legal and contractual, organizational, environmental, etc.).

Fig. 51 (facing page and pages 246−248). Project life cycles

The key is to *have a comprehensive master schedule for the project to ensure that all factors are considered by the right people at the right time*.

1. Standard product development life-cycle showing development and operations phases.

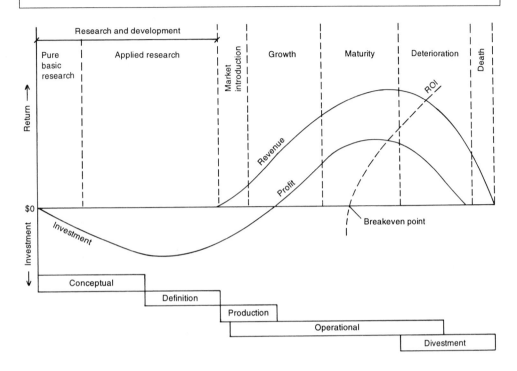

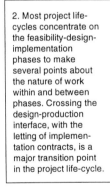

2. Most project life-cycles concentrate on the feasibility-design-implementation phases to make several points about the nature of work within and between phases. Crossing the design-production interface, with the letting of implementation contracts, is a major transition point in the project life-cycle.

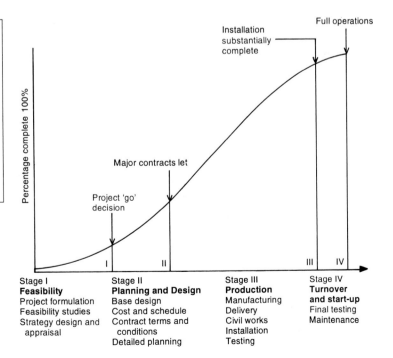

Stage I **Feasibility**	Stage II **Planning and Design**	Stage III **Production**	Stage IV **Turnover and start-up**
Project formulation	Base design	Manufacturing	Final testing
Feasibility studies	Cost and schedule	Delivery	Maintenance
Strategy design and appraisal	Contract terms and conditions	Civil works	
	Detailed planning	Installation	
		Testing	

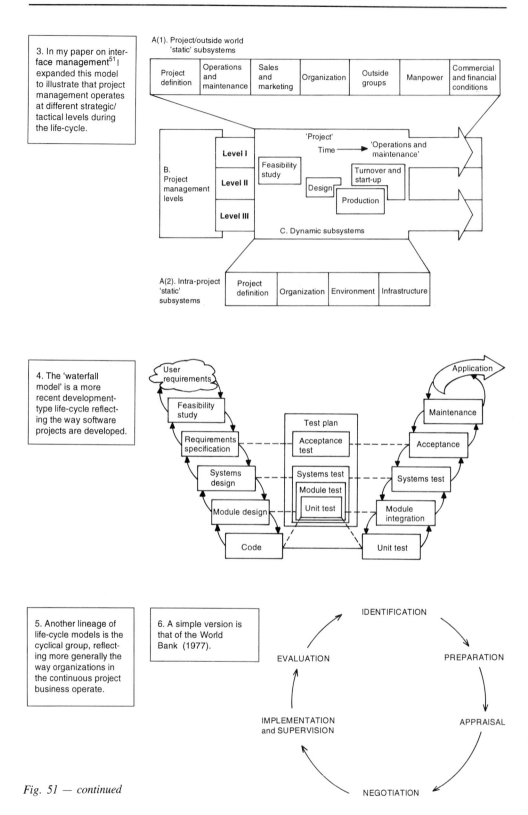

3. In my paper on inter-face management[51] I expanded this model to illustrate that project management operates at different strategic/tactical levels during the life-cycle.

A(1). Project/outside world 'static' subsystems

| Project definition | Operations and maintenance | Sales and marketing | Organization | Outside groups | Manpower | Commercial and financial conditions |

B. Project management levels

Level I
Level II
Level III

'Project'
Time →
Feasibility study
Design
Production
'Operations and maintenance'
Turnover and start-up

C. Dynamic subsystems

A(2). Intra-project 'static' subsystems

| Project definition | Organization | Environment | Infrastructure |

4. The 'waterfall model' is a more recent development-type life-cycle reflecting the way software projects are developed.

User requirements
Feasibility study
Requirements specification
Systems design
Module design
Code

Test plan
Acceptance test
Systems test
Module test
Unit test

Application
Maintenance
Acceptance
Systems test
Module integration
Unit test

5. Another lineage of life-cycle models is the cyclical group, reflecting more generally the way organizations in the continuous project business operate.

6. A simple version is that of the World Bank (1977).

IDENTIFICATION
PREPARATION
APPRAISAL
NEGOTIATION
IMPLEMENTATION and SUPERVISION
EVALUATION

Fig. 51 — continued

7. Wearne[52] developed this version for capital construction projects.

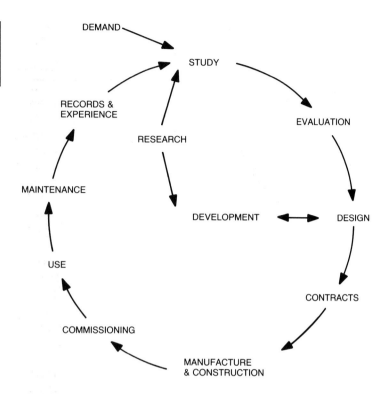

8. The Pentagon's basic cycle reflects particularly the funding and approval process.

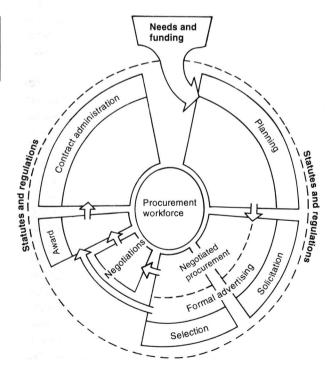

Fig. 51 — continued

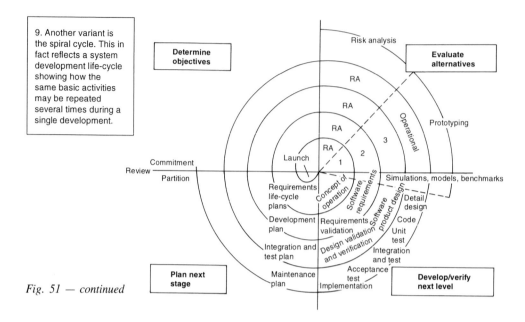

9. Another variant is the spiral cycle. This in fact reflects a system development life-cycle showing how the same basic activities may be repeated several times during a single development.

Fig. 51 — continued

Structure II: Integration

The project should be organized properly, both internally and with regard to outside parties.

Russell D. Archibald,[53] in a classic piece of project management writing, described the essentials of project management organization as

- having a *project manager as the 'single point of integrative responsibility'* (note 7)
- an independent planning and control group to co-ordinate project planning and provide independent project status information
- decentralization of project work to functional groups.

The introduction of formal integrating structures, beginning with the project co-ordinator in the 1930s, was the original starting point of modern project management. Initially, the major challenge was the introduction into hierarchically structured organizations of a 'horizontal' co-ordinating mechanism. By the late 1960s, researchers such as Lawrence and Lorsch, Thompson, and Galbraith had been able to demonstrate when such 'horizontal integrating mechanisms' were best used, and which type would be most appropriate — liaison, expeditor, special teams, co-ordinator, project manager, full project matrix (p. 75). Essentially one would move along this continuum as the project increased in size, urgency or complexity. (We saw how in Apollo increased quality requirements forced additional staffing at the workshop level, thereby creating a larger, more decentralized organization and hence the move to the matrix structure). However, the choice of which of these forms to implement will depend greatly on the background of the organization(s) involved — the people, culture, systems, and so on. Thus the US Congress concluded in 1972 that 'there is no universal answer to the merits of project/matrix/functional or in-house/contracted-out organizational options, the choice basically reflecting a fit between program characteristics and resources available' (p. 132).

One pattern that has emerged for virtually all projects is that once 'downstream implementation' begins — after project definition is basically completed and contracts for implementation are let — the amount of work and management control and co-ordination will increase substantially. There is often a swing at this point from a more functional, or vertical, orientation to a predominantly project, or horizontal one: the so-called 'matrix swing' (Fig. 52). Generally, this happens at about the 15% point of project completion (pp. 104 and 153).

Achieving this change in organizational structure inevitably requires attention to be paid to the 'softer', people issues, so that the project suffers as little as possible. Changing structure involves changing roles and responsibilities. Teams will reform, new personalities will emerge, egos will be affected. The change must be handled carefully: a swing, not a switch.[54,55]

The provision of a separate integrating body has been a practical emanation of this theory of project integration. We first saw it as the Systems Support Contractor introduced by Schriever on the Atlas programme in 1954. The emergence of Construction Management and Management Contracting in the 1960s and early 1970s was a similar, although not quite equivalent, development in construction. The Project Services Contractor of the 1970s was another example. Systems Integration Contractors became common in the Information Technology industry in the late 1970s. All these supply additional integration to some degree. Their distinctions lie basically in the scope, and kind, of services they perform (for example, how deeply they are involved in design) and the nature of their contractual arrangements with their employer.

An important principle established by Lawrence and Lorsch was that integration does not normally mean smoothing over differences. Distinctions should be maintained, even reinforced. Typical major interfaces are those between

- designers and builders
- specifiers and implementers
- owners and project managers.

The distinction between the role of owner as sponsor and future operator and the role of the project management team as designer or builder is particularly important. (Failing to achieve this has been one of the biggest problems of BOO(T) projects, as we saw for example with the Channel Tunnel.) Generally, the owner must involve himself to some degree in issues of project implementation;

Fig. 52. The matrix
swing (from Reis de
Carvalho and
Morris[54])

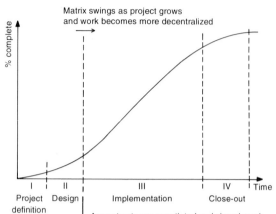

In the early, strategic stages of the project there is a need for *strong centralized functional decision-making*

● decide contracting strategy

    basic engineering
    equipment supply

● basic engineering elaboration
● prequalification of bidders
● development and installation of control systems
● budget and schedule preparation
● project organization design and implementation

As contracts are negotiated and signed, work expands, the organization grows and decision-making becomes decentralized—the swing to a project orientation increases rapidly. Project Managers are given clear scope, cost and schedule targets to achieve as the matrix moves from a primarily functional orientation to a more project one. Even so, a number of major functional decisions may still be pending—the swing does not happen overnight.

Project issues that may be still outstanding at the Phase II/III interface

● top level negotiations
● finance/governmental work
● organization expansion
● administrative items
● finalization of project control procedures

Research on the appropriate degree of project orientation in a matrix

1. Brown[56] was the first to suggest that the degree to which a matrix is project or functionally oriented ($\omega°$) may vary.
2. Davis and Lawrence[57] implied that a mature matrix condition is when $\omega = 45°$. This, they said, usually takes 2-3 years.
3. Whitmore[58] reckoned it required 12-18 months.
4. Reis de Carvalho and Morris[54] proposed that in project matrices the time required to 'swing' the matrix is determined by the project schedule.
5. UK and US researchers digging deep into the 'required amount of co-ordination' question, came up with the following.
 - Morris[59] found that special co-ordinating roles, such as task forces, are a function of the speed of the project, the degree of uncertainty, and the type of inter-dependence (one- or two-way) between the parties being co-ordinated.
 - Wearne[60] found that the degree of project responsibility ω was a function of the frequency, variety and uncertainty of the decisions to be made.
 - Davis and Lawrence[57] give three factors that call for matrix organizations: need for a dual focus of control, pressure for shared resources and, following Galbraith[4], the need to process a lot of information to deal with uncertainty, complexity and interdependence.
 - Morris[61] concluded that the key factors pressing for a project focus are project speed, size and complexity, which includes type of interdependence; technical complexity; uncertainty; and geographical, schedule, technical and contractual differentiation.

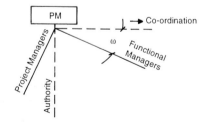

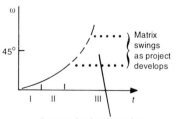

Degree of swing depends on
project size, speed and complexity

Structure III: The owner's role

determining the right degree of owner involvement emerged during the 1980s as a new and important issue of project organization.

Successful project realization involves striking the right balance between the owner, in his capacity of sponsor and operator, and the project implementation specialists.

This book has demonstrated repeatedly the decisive influence that the owner's actions can have on the conduct of a project. Logically, this can hardly be a surprise. He who is spending the money ought to be able to influence significantly the way it is spent. But the problem in the project business is that undertaking projects is something many owners do only infrequently. It is not their primary business. They look to the project implementation companies as the professionals. However, too often these companies have been more concerned to maximize their role as, say, designers or contractors than to develop a top−down, owner's view of project management. Indeed, it has been rare to find companies with the professional 'formation' of a project manager. Firms have instead been basically contractors, designers, lawyers, financiers, etc. Only in the late 1970s and 1980s have professional project management firms slowly emerged.

In some sectors, of course, this problem has been less acute. Oil, gas and petrochemicals, for example, are industries with substantial production companies that are experienced in capital development projects and understand project management well. The military has a continuous programme of capital expenditure, albeit, as we have seen, with its own problems of project management (pp. 150−156). For the rest, though, there has been either a substantial absence of any owner organization (e.g. in building) or a split between the owner's role as operator and as project manager. This split role has been particularly evident in most of the utilities — power, water, telecommunications, and transport — where it has been compounded by their strong require-ment and organizational commitment to ensuring operational safety and efficiency (often across very large organizational structures). These organizations have experienced most strikingly of all the tensions between the owner's roles as operator and as project manager.

The systems approach of the USAF made a significant contribution to clarifying the proper owner−implementer role, namely that there should be clear definition of what the owner requires (the specification), and a single organization responsible for delivering it. Further, at its best, what the systems approach says is that *everything that might affect the desired outcome of the project must be properly attended to and integrated at the right time during the project's development*. Ultimately, this is an extremely powerful concept, indicating that anything which has a bearing on project success can (and indeed should) be considered, and put into action. It is, however, hugely ambitious and, not surprisingly, has failed to materialize more often than it has succeeded — particularly in the earlier years of project management, before these ideas had been articulated and disseminated widely. Hence, for example, the difficulties in project specification that we saw earlier, of inadequate technology management and project control and, in the case of the USAF, the over-bureaucratic, hands-off approach to project management so effectively critiqued by Fox (the 'liaison' as opposed to 'active' manager role (pp. 152–153)). NASA avoided this deadening route, particularly on Apollo, by combining the procedural disciplines of the systems approach with an innovative, active, involved owner project management style which got the very best out of industry and academia. NASA, however, while scoring superbly in the 1960s on such key owner issues as quality, safety and risk management, was really a massive project management organization rather than a long-term owner–operator.

NASA and the US Department of Defense of the 1960s not only performed better as owner–project managers than their European counterparts, but also were miles ahead of the construction industry practice of the time in either the UK or the USA. Things were to change only slowly in construction. By 1988, however, they had changed sufficiently for US power plant owners to be censured by the courts for not fulfilling their 'legal responsibility to participate actively in the project's management' (p. 179).

The US court decisions of the 1980s raise starkly the issue of the extent to which an owner should be involved in the management of his project. Generally, owners have three roles. The first is to ensure that the project as conceived and realized meets its objectives. This is the *sponsor*'s role: that of ensuring that the plant makes the profit required or that the weapons system performs properly, or that the aid or welfare programme delivers real benefit. The second is the task of ensuring that once handed over to operations, the product will perform optimally. This is the *operator*'s role: it covers a variety of factors, by far the most critical of which are technical efficiency, safety and environmental performance. The third is that of the *builder*, or project manager: ensuring that the project is realized effectively and efficiently. It seems to me that in principle these duties should be performed entirely by the owner, subject only to the extent to which he does not — or should not — have the resources or the skills, outlook or experience to perform them adequately. For an owner, the role of sponsor is the most critical. If he is not capable of performing this adequately, his responsibilities to his shareholders cannot be met properly (note 8). Moreover, the owner ought also to have a good appreciation of the operating requirements of his business, so that even if outside assistance has to be contracted he can be assured that the system is being properly run. Least critical, probably, is his project management role, although here too the owner has a fiduciary responsibility to avoid waste and inefficiency, as reflected in the US court decisions.

Some degree of owner involvement in project implementation is generally necessary since, if no project management expertise is maintained in-house, active, directive decision-making of the kind we have seen to be necessary in demanding project management situations will not be available (unless it is imported as a pm consultant/contractor). On the other hand, if operators who are not really in the implementation business get into it, and staff and manage their projects with people more attuned to the owner's operating culture, there is a danger that the owner's staff may involve themselves too much and refine design and construction decisions at the expense of effective project implementation. This is the challenge, for example, that the British electrical power industry wrestled with from the 1950s to the 1990s, and that many businesses face in implementing Information Technology.

This dilemma is not easy to solve. There is in fact no standard answer — what is right will be right for a given mix of project characteristics, organizations and personalities (as the US Congress found in 1972). But it is evidently extremely important that those involved in a project bear these points in mind. 'Everything that might affect the desired outcome of the project must be properly integrated at the right time during its development'.

As a minimum, then, *owners should concentrate on predetermined milestone review points* — the key markers in its development that one wants the project to have satisfactorily reached at a certain stage — *scheduling them properly and reviewing the project comprehensively as it passes across each of them.* There should be a broad, comprehensive plan and schedule of what needs to be considered at each stage of the project; there should be comprehensive project reviews of these plans at each of the project's major milestone review points; at these, critical questions on all aspects of the plan should be raised by the full range of people connected with the project — implementers, owner—operators, financial specialists, environmentalists, opponents and so on (note 9).

Structure IV:
Contracting

Contracts should adequately reflect the project objectives, be motivational, and appropriately reflect the risks involved and the ability of the parties to bear these risks.

The previous chapters illustrated several contracting arrangements that were massively biased and involved some questionable contracting practices. It cannot have been healthy, for example, for the defence/aerospace business to have continued for so long in a cost-reimbursable mode, despite the doubtless valid claim that the monopsonic nature of the industry made contractors careful to deliver best practices for their customers (p. 322, note 45). There is now general consensus that firm price contracting

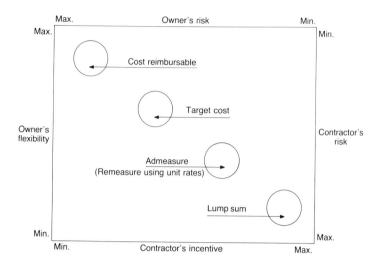

Fig. 53. Owner–Contractor risk-contracting relationship (after Thompson[62])

leads to better cost-control discipline. The fact that most US nuclear power projects were also carried out on a cost-reimbursable basis cannot have been healthy. On the other hand, simply putting the risk on to contractors can be equally wrong. There was some very large and inequitable shifting of risk on to contractors who were in no position to bear it in, for example, the process industries (UK nuclear power) and with the Total Package Procurement concept. And it was not until the mid-1980s, perhaps, that much of the unease about contractors making large profits on fixed price work, as in Bloodhound, began to dissipate. This history clearly shows that the key to better contracting lies in the better assessment and allocation of risks.

Following the work of various researchers,[25,62–64] several principles of sound contracting can now be listed.

- Risks should be borne by those best able to bear them.
- Risks should be allocated so that they are motivational.
- Sufficient effort should be given by the parties to the contract to identifying their joint aims on the project — since attitudes are so important, it is better to work out how to make the contract a success than how to 'do down' the other party.
- Fixed- or firm-price contracting provides maximum incentive and flexibility for the contractor and minimum for the owner.
- Cost-reimbursable contracting provides minimum incentive and flexibility for the contractor and maximum for the owner.
- In cost-reimbursable situations the owner must be prepared to exercise active management involvement.
- In high-risk situations, a firm-price contract should attract a high-risk premium, i.e. a guaranteed price should be a high one (other things being equal).
- There is a variety of incentive-type contracts, ranging from

target forms to unit rate (or schedule of rate) reimbursement forms.

- Both fixed-price and incentive-type contracts work best where the project scope and technical and other risks are relatively assessable (note 10).
- Contract types can be changed during the course of a project; indeed there is often a case for switching from a reimbursable type to a fixed-price type as the project scope and other risks are more fully worked out (the method known as convertible or hybrid contracting).
- Competition in general is healthy and leads to efficient contractor selection; however, adequate time should be allowed for bid preparation and owners should not be simplistic in evaluating bids.
- There are several dimensions on which bids may be competitively evaluated: price is just one of them and price alone may not be a good yardstick — quality of the technical proposal and experience, workload and quality of management are other important dimensions.

Recent UK moves in defence/areospace (the Levene reforms) and construction (BPF and the New Engineering Contract) are moving industry norms of contracting slowly towards these and other principles of good project management. Contracts reflect legal tradition, however, and the change may be slow.

A new contracting philosophy began to emerge in the late 1980s: *partnering*. Pioneered by the Japanese in the auto industry (note 11), and stemming largely from their Total Quality Management philosophy of business, partnering involves establishing long-term relations between suppliers and clients, with the aim of achieving continuous performance improvements through closer identity of interests and joint programmes aimed at improving productivity. By the end of the 1980s partnering was only beginning to be established in the West as a powerful contracting approach, and indeed was being resisted by some as ill-founded and wrong. Its potential is discussed in chapter 9 (p. 294).

Staffing I: Leaders, champions and managers

Projects need strong, experienced people to drive them forward and lead those involved.

Not only must the project be efficiently administered, there should be a high standard of leadership so that people, both within the project and outside, accept its goals and work enthusiastically towards its realization. Management drive of an extraordinary order may often be necessary to get the project moving and to produce results of outstanding quality on time and within budget. To assure the necessary resources and support, the project may need championing both within the sponsoring organizations and externally, within the community. *But there should be checks and balances between the enthusiasm and drive of the project's champions, leaders and managers and the proper conservatism of its sponsors.*

The major projects recounted in this book reveal a string of huge personalities leading their projects forward to completion and success: Eisenhower ('it remains impossible to conceive of any other Allied soldier matching his achievement'); Schriever ('quickly proved himself not just an able administrator but also a forceful and effective leader — a personable, intelligent, and patient man, he was to employ all his skills of leadership in the months to come'); Raborn ('outstanding as a champion, leader and manager of the Polaris programme'); Webb ('another of the mould familiar in this account of the origins of modern project management: tough, charismatic, politically astute, "a genius for extemporization" '); Madelung of Panavia ('an outstanding leader and engineer'); Patton of TAPS ('decisive leadership and drive'); Morton of Eurotunnel — and so on.

These forceful leaders were successful but, as has already been remarked, leaders may lead in directions that come to be regretted. Equally, the high failure rate associated with projects — particularly major ones — suggests that the challenges which major projects present may often be too great for the people we put in to manage them.

Or is it the organizational or institutional context that proves too intractable? Time and again we see projects getting into difficulties because of organizational constraints and cultures that individuals are not able to overcome. The successful project may require a visionary to change perceptions in order to steer those around him, or her, to work in new and unusual ways; this takes time and may not be achievable within the project's schedule.

And visionaries do not grow on trees: perhaps there are just not sufficient leaders around for the projects we have. Maybe Dixon's point is valid, that we are not trained to manage very difficult or demanding situations (note 12). Or, as Peter has suggested,[65] perhaps people rise to their level of incompetence, this becoming apparent only after the mistakes have been made. Or, more often, is it not that projects require different leadership skills at different stages of their development, and that these may not be present in the incumbent management? As with McKee and Maxwell on the US SST, people with the right skills may be put in at the wrong level or for the wrong part of the project life cycle.

In any event, it is clear that *the presence of an experienced, forceful leader, able to establish direction, decide on action, organize resources and motivate all those involved is one of the most essential requirements for a successfully managed project.*

We can in fact distinguish several management roles that must be filled on a project if it is to be successful (some of which may be performed by the same person). First is the *manager*: someone who gets others to do what he cannot do alone. The project manager is a manager of resources. The organizational metronome is, in Sayles and Chandler's[49] words, getting others to do what has to be done, at the right time, in order for targets to be efficiently met. Gaddis[1] was one of the first to comment comprehensively on the challenges typically faced by the project manager: issues such as style, decision-making and the development and balancing of authority and responsibility.

('Organization Behaviour' (OB) factors such as these became particularly important as matrix organizations began to be more widely used and as project managers found themselves no longer working in seamless, single-shot undertakings, such as the 1950s missile programmes, but buried deep within organizational politics, fighting for resources. Toyota's Large Project Leader (Shusa), compared with General Motor's project co-ordinator management of new model development, is a case in point (note 13). A particular OB challenge in matrix organizations is the potential conflict between individuals and their functional and project 'bosses' (note 14).)

We see now that several other project leadership and management roles must be distinguished. It may, for example, be useful to note a *Project Director* function, particularly in the matrix form. The Project Director is the chief project manager, on a par with the other directors in the (project) organization. He acts as functional head of the project managers, ensuring that they follow proper practices and procedures, resolving resource disputes, and representing their case against other functional departments.

Then there is the leadership function. A *leader* is someone who gets people to follow him. Because of the enormous energy that projects require, and their political and interpersonal challenges, practitioners have in the past emphasized the central importance of leadership on projects. Leaders are important, certainly, but, as I have remarked, it is necessary to distinguish between simply leading people and effective project leadership. One can lead people into a swamp; effective project leadership is leading people to produce a successful project.

A leader should be distinguished from a *champion*. A champion espouses a cause; he obtains the resources needed to accomplish the project. A champion, as Geoffrey Morton pointed out,[66] needs to shape perceptions, create values, garner constituencies. The champion's role is clearly political; symbolic actions are used to communicate perceptions. Much of the champion's work will be external as well as internal. There may well be more than one champion. The Channel Tunnel project needed Mrs Thatcher and President Mitterand (to 'pull') and Sir Alastair Morton (to 'push').

With many projects, of course, the failure has been to have virtually no effective champions, leaders or even managers, rather than not to have enough of the right type. Concorde is a notable example. For much of the period of this book, building projects typically went ahead without either champions, leaders or even project managers. MoD projects, particularly à la Gibb—Zuckerman, had few; DoD projects of the 1980s still suffered from having 'liaison managers' rather than 'active managers'.

A manager/director, leader and champion will all, inevitably, be promoting their project. It is very difficult to expect someone whose job is so involved in creating the conditions for success to stand back and objectively critique the chances of success. This is the project sponsor's role. The project *sponsor* 'is the person providing the resources for the project: the person who should be responsible for ensuring that the project is successful at the business or institutional level' (p. 188). This is a function we examined extensively in discussing the owner's role. The sponsor, akin to the Chairman of the Project Board, has to take a hard objective look at whether the project is meeting its objectives. If necessary he must be prepared to cancel or modify the project rather than to continue pouring good money after what might prove to be bad.

Even the sponsor may find it difficult to bring the right balance of wisdom to bear at the various stages of the project while remaining sufficiently uninvolved to maintain the objectivity needed to cancel, cut back or propel the project where necessary. Should not NASA, for example, have stood back in the mid-1960s and begun working harder, more effectively and more tenaciously to address and secure its post-Apollo strategy? Allen Sykes[67] has suggested the Project Directorate as a means of getting this objectivity — a group of experienced wise people whose compensation is, ideally, so structured that it will make little or no difference to them financially whether or not the project goes ahead, who meet periodically to review and critique progress on the project and who are charged with calling for changes, including the project's cessation, if this is what in their opinion is required.

Staffing II: Team management

Project personnel should be treated as members of a team, with great emphasis on active communication and productive conflict.

Team members include both professional staff and blue-collar workers. Several projects in this history suffered severely from industrial disputes. The advent of site and industry agreements, the gradual acceptance at the workshop/site level of the need to improve productivity, discipline and communication between workers and management — much of this being achieved only in the 1980s — have meant that industrial relations are currently much less of a problem than they were in previous decades.

Much of the pressure to increase productivity has come from Japanese industry, which has been unrelenting in seeking out new markets, understanding and meeting customer requirements, shortening product development times and keeping costs low through dramatically improved productivity.

The Japanese have in many respects taken the lead also in demonstrating the value of open communications and commitment to shared aims; their practices have largely proved as workable in the West as in Japan, at least on the shop floor. Where the Japanese seem even further ahead, however, is in the remarkable way they seem able to gain consensus across whole institutions: the implementation of Technopolis compared with, say, the British New Town programme illustrates vividly the great effort in consensus building of the Japanese (note 15).

At the same time, Japan's VLSI and Fifth Generation research programmes show how the Japanese value intense, productive conflict — to a degree the Europeans, in particular, have often missed. These programmes emphasized tight organization structures, focused yet broad research goals, active project direction and management, and the working out of conflict in an open manner. Alvey, Esprit and many other European R&D programmes were much looser on nearly all counts. (And while sceptics may question how successful the Japanese programmes really were, most would agree that they were in any event more successful than the Europeans'.)

This view of the Japanese attitude towards conflict fits closely with that discovered by Thamhain and Wilemon[6] as being preferred by project managers (Fig. 54); curiously though, it does not fit with the general picture of the Japanese and other Eastern cultures which prefer 'compromise' to 'confrontation'. Certainly, the prevailing project practice for maximizing team effectiveness is to encourage open communication while at the same time stimulating an objective confrontation of issues (note 16).

Conflict is of course inevitable in projects. Technical performance, cost and schedule are generally in some conflict, as are the different functions and different parties to a contract

Fig. 54. Conflict management methods (source: Thamhain and Wilemon[6])

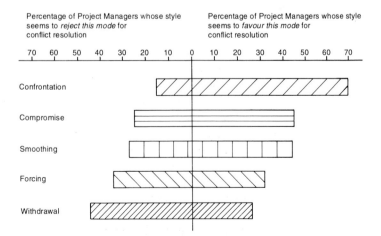

to some degree. Recognizing this, managers can structure, staff and handle their projects to benefit from the conflict rather than suffer from it. Team 'characters' can be selected along the lines suggested by Meredith Belbin,[68] for example (Fig. 55). Indeed, it is an obvious but often overlooked truism of staffing that different (project) situations required different skills. There is no such thing as a totally 'universal' project manager — the manager of a small

Fig. 55. Belbin's team types[68] (courtesy Heinemann)

Type	Typical features	Positive qualities	Allowable weaknesses
Company worker	Conservative, dutiful, predictable	Organizing ability, practical common sense, hard-working, self-discipline	Lack of flexibility, unresponsiveness to unproven ideas
Chairman	Calm, self-confident, controlled	Capacity for treating and welcoming all potential contributors on their merits and without prejudice; strong sense of objectives	No more than ordinary in terms of intellect or creative ability
Shaper	Highly strung, outgoing, dynamic	Drive and a readiness to challenge inertia, ineffectiveness, complacency or self-deception	Proneness to provocation, irritation and impatience
Plant	Individualistic, serious-minded, unorthodox	Genius, imagination, intellect, knowledge	Up in the clouds, inclined to disregard practical details or protocol
Resource investigator	Extroverted, enthusiastic, curious, communicative	Capacity for contacting people and exploring anything new; ability to respond to challenge	Liable to lose interest once the initial fascination has passed
Monitor–evaluator	Sober, unemotional, prudent	Judgement, discretion, hard-headedness	Lacks inspiration or the ability to motivate others
Team worker	Socially oriented, rather mild, sensitive	Ability to respond to people and to situations, and to promote team spirit	Indecisiveness at moments of crisis
Completer–finisher	Painstaking, orderly, conscientious, anxious	Capacity for follow-through; perfectionist	Tendency to worry about small things; reluctance to let go

R&D project will require different characteristics from, say, the owner's project manager of a large steel mill. Similarly with other members of the project team.

Team building, using a variety of techniques including the 'Project Start-Up' idea (note 17), can enhance team identity — time can be purposefully set aside to allow team members to examine their roles as a social unit rather than simply as individual experts. On projects this is often especially important, since most people are newly brought together to work on a brand-new, demanding task, generally to tight time and cost constraints.

The same holds for matrix organizations — personnel generally have to adopt new roles and styles of behaviour as the matrix, or the project, develops. As writers in the 1970s taught us, implementing a matrix takes time: time must therefore be allowed. As TAPS and Açominas demonstrate (pp. 102–104), the trick is to phase this matrix growth to the project schedule. (Samuel Paul said very much the same thing for Third World development projects, although not specifically in a matrix context (p. 167).) To do this, one needs to employ OB techniques in order to adapt people's expectations, working practices, organization culture, etc. in time with the project schedule. Once again, this demonstrates that proper integration, from the earliest phases of the project, requires comprehensive planning of all that is necessary to make the project a success.

Not only can (and must) attitudes be moulded, but skills can be taught. Training has assumed an increasing importance in the world of projects as managers have realized the great range of skills now required on modern projects, and the high likelihood of staff moving into positions for which either they do not have the skill or training, or knowledge sufficiently up-to-date or focused. Training, during the 1980s, became accepted as part of the normal business of running projects.

Equally, longer-term career planning is important. One of the major deficiencies identified by Fox and others in defence procurement has been the inadequate length of time 'in post' of DoD procurement managers, and their lack of a satisfactory career structure. Other industries, too, are slowly waking up to this issue. Educating people in the management of projects and ensuring they pass on their experience to others, and keeping good people motivated and even retaining them as projects finish, are among the biggest challenges facing the world of projects.

Systems: Project control tools

Tools for planning, monitoring and reporting a project's performance should be user-friendly and allow the real technical, financial, schedule and other issues to be tracked so that the project can be developed effectively and final outcomes predicted reliably. Control will be improved through solid baseline management and firm control of performance trends.

Project management tools have of course been in existence for ages. It is said, although I cannot personally confirm it, that a form of bar chart is to be found on a temple column in Luxor, Egypt (approximately 1500 BC)! Clearly, anyone constructing a building of any complexity, or indeed conducting a campaign or any other form of project, will have used visual aids and other planning and control tools. Modern project management tools, however, form a distinct set and have their origins almost entirely in the 20th century.

Project management planning and control tools were essentially products of the Operations Research (OR) era of the 1950s. The tools have subsequently been criticized by those who found OR academic and abstruse. Many people rejected for many years the oversold aims, disciplines and methods of the more complex tools and procedures, particularly Performance Measurement (C/SCSC) and change control. Even network scheduling was rejected by many as overly complex (note 18), although by and large PERT and CPM most readily demonstrated the benefits of modern project management tools, and for many others network scheduling still occupies the centre ground of what project management is all about. It is, however, essentially the wrong place to start in examining how project management tools can help manage projects better.

Figure 56 suggests that a better approach may be to think about: first, what needs to be done; second, who is going to do what; third, when the actions are to be performed; fourth, how much is required to be spent in total, how much has been spent so far,

Fig. 56. The project planning process

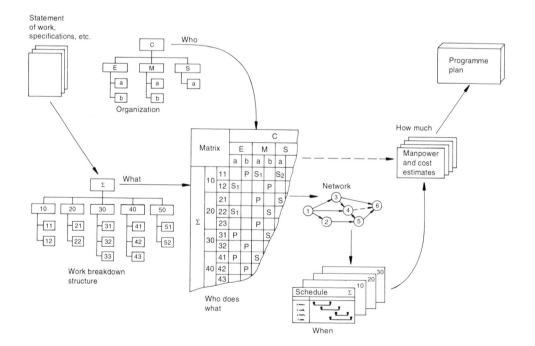

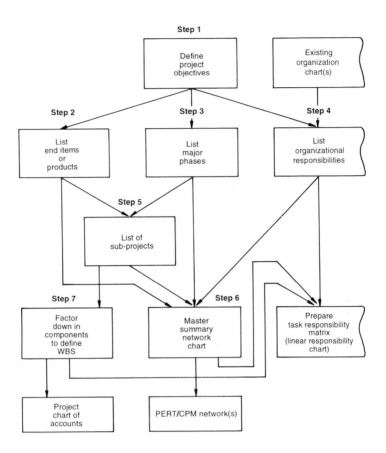

Step 1

Define
project
objectives

Existing
organization
chart(s)

Step 2

List
end items
or
products

Step 3

List
major
phases

Step 4

List
organizational
responsibilities

Step 5

List of
sub-projects

Step 7

Factor
down in
components
to define
WBS

Step 6

Master
summary
network
chart

Prepare
task responsibility
matrix
(linear responsibility
chart)

Project
chart of
accounts

PERT/CPM network(s)

*Fig. 57. The project
definition process*

and how much has still to be spent ('to go'). This at least is the
classic project management approach which has existed since the
early 1970s. A more up-to-date version, following the lines outlined
in this book, would include risk analysis on several dimensions,
such as finance, engineering and politics (as proposed by Cooper
et al., project financiers and others) and would probably also
include several possible scenarios. Figure 57 recasts the sequence
in another, slightly fuller form. Both figures essentially represent
the 'project management' view of modern project control tools
and techniques.

Central to this sequence is the *Work Breakdown Structure* (WBS):
a 'product-oriented family tree of hardware, software, services
and other work tasks which organizes, defines, and graphically
displays the product to be produced, as well as the work to be
accomplished to achieve a specified product'.[69] The WBS
essentially analyses and classifies by product element. It has taken
a surprisingly long time to become accepted in project industries:
it was only just entering building and civil engineering in the late
1980s, and many IT project personnel were still unfamiliar with
it then. It is, however, absolutely fundamental in that it

- provides a logical, coherent, complete statement of what the project comprises
- allows a coding system to be developed which enables cost, schedule, technical and other data to be identified and cross-related across the project.

Without a WBS it is very difficult to communicate a clear view of the total scope of the project and to organize the various project data in a consistent way. It is fundamental to project control.

The *Organization Breakdown Structure* (OBS) specifies which organizational groups are responsible for which parts of the WBS (Fig. 58). Not only is this useful as an analytical aid, but also it facilitates coding where, for example, cost data are to be organized by supplier rather than product element (per the WBS). (This is very common, particularly where work is let on a fixed-price basis; in such a case it is often not possible for the project owner to get cost information, say, on a detailed project element basis.)

The *Task Responsibility Matrix* is like the OBS, but in particular it makes clear who is responsible for what and can clarify (Fig. 59) the nature of the various responsibilities — supervision, first-line implementation, etc. Tony Walker has claimed that it has a major role in construction.[70] In fact, it can be very useful in a variety of project situations.

As regards *scheduling*, the Gantt chart is good for presentation. It does not, however, show the interrelationships that will exist on a project. To explore these, networks are needed. Network scheduling is particularly useful in planning; excessive use in monitoring and updating formerly proved burdensome, but recent technology developments — Windows, Graphical User Interfaces, etc. — have made it extremely easy to work with networks.

Multi-level scheduling — the practice of nesting schedules within each other to represent different levels of detail — is a particularly useful way of handling scheduling detail. Network schedules may thus be used in different ways at different levels. The use of networks to identify milestone review points is particularly valuable, and, as we saw earlier in this chapter, milestone scheduling is important at the owner level of project control. Also, since the level of detail of work to be accomplished in the short term will generally be greater than that later on, one often has detailed short-term schedules moving into more broadly detailed medium- and long-term schedules. In fact this applies to WBS work packages too. Since time is constantly moving forward, the level of detail 'scrolls to the right', hence giving rise to the 'rolling wave' concept of project planning (Fig. 60).

The probabilistic network techniques such as GERT and VERT (pp. 79−81) are conceptually extremely interesting. In practice, however, their high cost and complication has constrained their use, at least up to the late 1980s: we shall see shortly that things

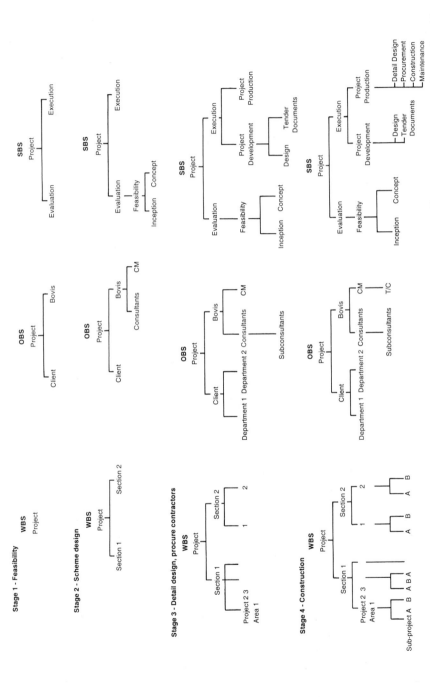

Fig. 58. The WBS–OBS–SBS relation: a WBS should be prepared in advance of the network to allow summary reports to be produced by area, group or project or by sub-area, sub-group or sub-project for all stages in the project; an OBS should be prepared to allow data to be summarized by major element, package, consultant, client, etc. for all stages in the project; a Stage Breakdown Structure (SBS) code should be assigned to each activity on the network (e.g. feasibility, design, procurement, construction, close-out) to allow data to be summarized by project phase

○ Does the work
▲ Approves
▼ Recommends
● General oversight
◆ Direct oversight
△ Boundary control
□ Monitoring
◇ Maintenance
■ Consultation - gives instructions and information
▽ Consultation - gives advice and information
⊗ Output notification mandatory

	Client							Consultants									
								Engineers						Architect		QS	
Major task	Parent company	Local board of directors	Responsible director	Project engineer	Department managers	Specialist staff	Workforce	Senior partner	Project manager	Manager structural engineering	Job structural engineer	Manager services engineering	Job services engineer	Partner architect	Job architect	Partner quantity surveyor	Job quantity surveyor
1. Identify need for project		●▲	◆▼	△□◇	○	▽											
2. Define outline requirements		●▲	◆▼	△□◇	○	▽		▽									
3. Establish budget estimate		●▲	◆▼	△○				▽									
4. Presentation for inclusion in five-year plan	▲	●▼	◆	△○													
5. Programme proposals				▲■●				◆▽	▼△○	▽		▽		▽		▽	
6. Contractual proposals				▲■●				◆▽	▼△□◇	▽		▽		▽		○	
7. Spatial proposals				▲■●	▽	▽	▽	◆▽	▼△□◇	◆	○	◆	○	◆	○	▽	▽
8. Technical proposals (structural)				▲■●	▽	▽	▽	◆▽	▼△□◇	◆	○	▽	▽	▽	▽	▽	▽
9. Technical proposals (services)				▲■●	▽	▽	▽	◆▽	▼△□◇	▽	▽	◆	○	▽	▽	▽	▽
10. Technical proposals (architectural)				▲■●	▽	▽	▽	◆▽	▼△□◇	▽	▽	▽	▽	◆	○	▽	▽
11. Financial proposals				▲■●				◆▽	▼△□◇	▽	▽	▽	▽	▽	▽	◆	○
12. Consolidate brief		▲	▼	▼●				◆▽	▼△○	▽	▽	▽	▽	▽	▽	▽	▽
13. Capital expenditure presentation	▲	▼	▼	▼○													
14. Programme details				▲▽				●	▼△○	▽	▽	▽	▽	▽	▽	▽	▽
15. Working drawings				▲▽■				●	▼△□◇	◆	○	◆	○	◆	○	▽	▽
16. Technical details (structural)				▲▽■				●	▼△□◇	◆	○	▽	▽	▽	▽	▽	▽
17. Technical details (services)				▲▽■				●	▼△□◇	▽	▽	◆	○	▽	▽	▽	▽
18. Technical details (architectural)				▲▽■				●	▼△□◇	▽	▽	▽	▽	◆	○	▽	▽
19. Contract details				▲▽				●	▼△□◇	▽	▽	▽	▽	▽	▽	◆	○
20. Contract documentation				■				●	▼△□◇							◆	○

Fig. 59. Task responsibility matrix (after Walker[70])

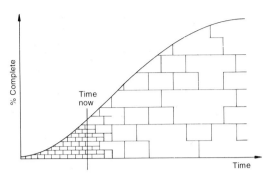

Fig. 60. The 'rolling wave' concept: as time moves on, the definition of future project work can be broken down more accurately into smaller pieces; the detail of WBS/OBS definition increases as the project moves forward

are beginning to change in the 1990s. These probabilistic techniques are assuming particular importance in *Risk Analysis*.

Risk Analysis emerged in the mid-1980s as an important part of project control. Starting with the pioneering work of Chapman, Cooper, Thomas, Hertz and others,[71,72] it later became more readily accessible through the sale of commercial risk analysis project packages such as K&H, Opera, @ Risk, etc. Meanwhile, the rise of project finance, BOO(T) and more sophisticated contracting led to a readier appreciation of the importance of analysing risk. By the late 1980s it had just about been accepted that risk identification and assessment, followed by the elaboration of a strategy to deal with the risks identified, is an essential feature of good project management practice (note 19).

Much has been written about *cost control*: about the need to obtain realistic estimates, whether or not to include allowances for inflation and contingencies, and how to measure performance. In terms simply of tools and techniques, as opposed to philosophy, the important point is that financial measures of progress must be based on physical accomplishment. It is the comparison of the physical rate of progress and the estimate that is important, not some accounting version that is confused by advances, retentions, delays in invoicing, etc. This idea has in fact been around in the construction industries for generations. The Schedule of Rates/Bill of Quantities method and the remeasurement process exemplify it almost perfectly. In more recent project management history, the *'Earned Value'* system takes the same idea but applies it to non-construction industries, notably aerospace and information technology. It has been used in the process industries for some time. *Performance Measurement* is used by many synonymously with earned value, in many ways erroneously, although this is not important. Performance Measurement is the generic term for the procedure of integrating cost and schedule control through the use of the three measures BCWS, BCWP and ACWP (p. 46). It had

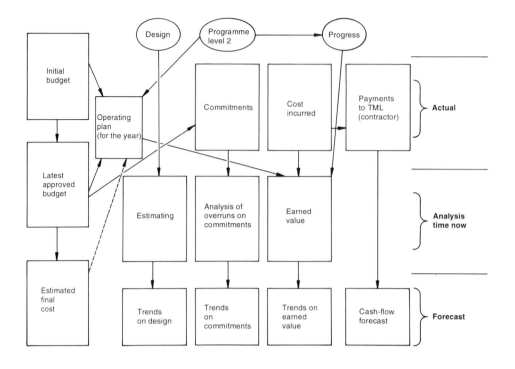

Fig. 61. Eurotunnel's cost management system

been used in a number of process industries in the 1970s and 1980s, but was only just arriving in building and civil engineering by the late 1980s. Eurotunnel, for example, employed it for the control of the civil engineering work on the Channel Tunnel project (Fig. 61).

Not only must performance be based on physical progress, but also, as Raborn and Petersen were so keen to show on Polaris, maximum attention must be given to forecasting where the costs are going to end. There must be detailed treatment of changes (actual, proposed and anticipated), and costs-to-complete should be estimated both on an ongoing basis and periodically.

The WBS, OBS, Task Responsibility Matrix, schedules and estimates, then, provide a solid baseline against which project progress can be compared, and from which the *trend of the project* towards its completion 'on schedule, in budget, to technical specification' can be calculated.

Technical performance has traditionally proved the hardest area to manage successfully in projects. The US Navy, for example, never got far with this dimension of PERT (the Reliability Maturity Index (p. 31)). This book has dealt extensively with the importance of design management and change control, technology management, configuration management, etc. However, it is not project management, but the commitment to Total Quality, that is doing most to manage the technical dimension successfully. Quality Assurance and Quality Management Systems are ensuring that the things which need to be done, to ensure that the project is completed as specified, are done; but Total Quality is revolutionizing the way we approach performance. Springing, as we have noted, from the pioneering work of Deming, Juran, and the Japanese, but first seen fully in the project world in the missile and nuclear power sectors with QA, the commitment to achieving Total Quality has provided a comprehensive approach for the realization of the desired technical parameters, as we shall see in the next chapter.

Our vision of how project management tools and techniques may be developed and be of use in projects has consistently outstripped technology's ability to perform. It was 25 years (up to the emergence of Fourth Generation computing, when network scheduling became user-friendly) before networks became widely and positively used. It will probably have taken another 25 years (i.e. until the late 1990s) for risk management, stochastic scheduling, CAD links and Fifth Generation benefits to work their way into the mainstream of project management applications.

Conclusion

But these are only some of the changes of the 1990s to which we must now turn in concluding this study. What are the trends likely over the next decade or two? How will projects develop? What developments in the art and science of the management of projects are coming?

References

1. Gaddis, P. O. The project manager. *Harvard Business Review*, 1959, May–June, 89–97.
2. Lawrence, P. R. and Lorsch, J. W. *Organization and environment: managing differentiation and integration.* Harvard University Press, Boston, MA, 1967.
3. Lawrence, P. R. and Lorsch, J. W. Differentiation and integration in complex organizations. *Administrative Science Quarterly*, **12**, No. 1, 1967, 1–47.
4. Galbraith, J. R. *Achieving integration through information systems.* Working Paper No. 361-68, Alfred P. Sloan School of Management, Massachusetts Institute of Technology, 1968.
5. Wilemon, D. L. and Gemmill, G. R. Interpersonal power in temporary management systems. *Journal of Management Studies*, **8**, 1971, Oct., 315–328.
6. Thamhain, H. J. and Wilemon, D. L. Conflict management in project life cycles. *Sloan Management Review*, 1975, Summer.
7. Youker, R. Organizational alternatives for project management. *Project Management Quarterly*, **8**, No. 1, 1977.
8. Moolin, F. P. and McCoy, F. The organization and management of large projects ... realities vs theory. *Proc. Project Management Institute Symp.*, Drexel Hill, PA, 1979.
9. Moris, J. *Managing induced rural development.* International Development Institute, Bloomington, IL, 1981.
10. Paul, S. Managing development programs: the lessons of success. Westview Press, Boulder, CO, 1982.
11. Cassen, R. *et al. Does aid work?* Clarendon, Oxford, 1986.
12. President's Blue Ribbon Commission on Defense Management. *An interim report to the President,* 28 February, 1986.

13. Archibald, R. D. The history of modern project management: key milestones in the early PERT/CPM/PDM days. *Project Management Journal*, **18**, No. 4, 1987, Sept., 29–31.

14. Dinsmore, P. C. *Human factors in project management*. American Management Association, New York, 1984.

15. Snyder, J. R. Modern project management: how did we get here — where do we go? *Project Management Journal*, **18**, No. 1, 28–29.

16. McCaskey, M. B. *The executive challenge*. Pitman, Boston, MA, 1982.

17. Pfeffer, J. Management as a symbolic action: the creation and maintenance of organizational paradigms. In *Research and organizational behavior*, Stair, B. M. and Summings, L. L. (eds), JAI Press, Greenwich, CT, 1981.

18. Pondy, L. R., Morgan, G., Frost, P. J. and Dandridge, T. C. (eds), *Organizational symbolism*. JAI Press, Greenwich, CT, 1983.

19. Stringer, J. *Planning and inquiry process*. MPA Technical Paper No. 6, Templeton College, Oxford, September 1988.

20. Turner, B. The organizational and interorganizational developments of disasters. *Administrative Science Quarterly*, **21**, 1976, Spring, 378–397.

21. Turner, B. *Man-made disasters*. Taylor & Francis, London, 1979.

22. Imai, K. *Japan's industrial policy for high technology industries*. Institute of Business Research, Hitotsubashi University, Kunitachi, Tokyo, Discussion Paper No. 119, prepared for Conf. on Japanese Industrial Policy in Comparative Perspective, New York, March 1984.

23. Horwitch, M. and Pralahad, C. K. Managing multi-organization enterprises: the emerging strategic frontier. *Sloan Management Review*, 1981, Winter, 3–16.

24. Ashley, D. B. Determinants of construction project success. *Project Management Journal*, **18**, No. 2, 1987, June, 69–77.

25. Morris, P. W. G. and Hough, G. H. *The anatomy of major projects*. Wiley, Chichester, 1987.

26. Baker, N. R., Green, S. G. and Bean, A. S. Why R&D projects succeed or fail. *Research Management*, 1986, Nov.–Dec., 29–34.

27. Balachandra, R. and Raelin, J. A. When to kill that R&D project. *Research Management*, 1984, July–Aug., 30–33.

28. Cooper, R. G. New product success in industrial firms. *Industrial Marketing Management*, **11**, 1982, 215–223.

29. Hirschman, A. O. *Development projects observed*. The Brookings Institution, Washington, DC, 1967.

30. Mansfield, E. and Wagner, S. Organizational and strategic factors associated with probabilities of success and industrial R&D. *Journal of Business*, **48**, No. 2, 1975, Apr.

31. de Wit, A. Measuring project success: an illusion. *Proc. 1986 Project Management Institute Symp.*, Montreal, Project Management Institute, Drexel Hill, PA, 1986.

32. Morris, P. W. G. Research at Oxford into the preconditions of success and failure in major projects. *Proc. 1986 Project Management Institute Symp.*, Montreal, Project Management Institute, Drexel Hill, PA, 1986.

33. Ministry of Defence. *Learning from experience: a report on the arrangements for managing major projects in the procurement executive*. HMSO, London, 1987.

34. Harman, A. J. assisted by Henrichsen, A. *A methodology for cost factor comparison and prediction*. Rand Corporation, R-6269-ARPA, Santa Monica, CA, August 1970.

35. Perry, R. L., Smith, G. K., Harman, A. J. and Henrichsen, S. *System acquisition strategies*. Rand Corporation, R-733-PR/ARPA, Santa Monica, CA, June 1971.

36. Large, J. P. *Bias in initial cost estimates: how low estimates can increase*

the cost of acquiring weapon systems. Rand Corporation, R-1467-PA&E, Santa Monica, CA, July 1974.

37. Marshall, A. W. and Meckling, W. H. *Predictability of the costs, time and success of development.* Rand Corporation, P-1821, Santa Monica, CA, March 1965.

38. Perry, R. L., Smith, G. K., Harmon, A. J. and Henrichsen, S. *System acquisition experience.* Rand Corporation, RM-6072-PR, Santa Monica, CA, November 1969.

39. Marschak, T., Glennan, T. K. and Summers, R. *Strategy for R&D: studies in the microeconomics of development.* Springer Verlag, New York, 1967.

40. Perrow, C. *Normal accidents: living with high risk technologies.* Basic Books, New York, 1984.

41. Collingridge, D. *The management of scale: big organizations, big decisions, big mistakes.* Routledge, London, 1992.

42. Allen, T. J. *Managing the flow of technology transfer and the dissemination of technological information within the R&D organization.* Massachusetts Institute of Technology Press, Cambridge, MA, 1977.

43. Allison, D. *The R&D game.* Massachusetts Institute of Technology Press, Cambridge, MA, 1969.

44. Sakakibara, K. *From imitation to innovation: a very large scale integrated (VLSI) semiconductor project in Japan.* Sloan School of Management, MIT, Cambridge, MA, Working Paper 1490-83, October 1983.

45. Horwitch, M. and Pralahad, C. K. Managing multi-organization enterprises: the emerging strategic frontier. *Sloan Management Review*, 1981, Winter, 3−16.

46. Sievert, R. W. A review of value engineering as an effective system for planning building projects. *Project Management Journal*, **22**, No. 1, 1991, Mar., 31−38.

47. Woody, W. B. and Pourian, H. Risk assessment and options in project finance. *Project Management Journal*, **23**, No. 4, 1992, Dec., 21−28.

48. Williams, R. *The nuclear power decisions. British policies 1953−78.* Croom Helm, London, 1980.

49. Sayles, L. R. and Chandler, M. K. *Managing large systems. Organizations for the future.* Harper & Row, New York, 1971.

50. Bryson, L. Large scale project management. *IEEE Proceedings*, Part A, **129**, No. 8, 1982, Nov., 625−629.

51. Cleland, D. I. and King, W. R. (eds). *The project management handbook.* Van Nostrand Reinhold, New York, 1983.

52. Wearne, S. H. *Principles of engineering organization.* Edward Arnold, London, 1973.

53. Archibald, R. D. *Managing high-technology programs and projects.* Wiley, New York, 1992, p. 5.

54. Reis de Carvalho, E. and Morris, P. W. G. Project matrix organizations — or how to do the matrix swing. *Proc. 1978 Project Management Institute Symp.*, Los Angeles, Project Management Institute, Drexel Hill, PA, 1978.

55. Morris, P. W. G. Managing project interfaces — key points for project success. In *Project management handbook*, Cleland, D. I. and King, W. R. (eds), Van Nostrand Reinhold, New York, 1982.

56. Brown, W. P. D. *Exploration in management.* Heinemann, London, 1960.

57. Davis, S. M. and Lawrence, P. R. *Matrix organizations.* Addison-Wesley, Reading, MA, 1977.

58. Whitmore, K. R. *Matrix organizations in conventional manufacturing — marketing companies.* Sloan School of Management, MIT, Cambridge, MA, MS thesis, 1975.

59. Morris, P. W. G. Systems study of project management. *Building,* **226,** Nos 6816, 6817, 1974.

60. Wearne, S. H. *Principles of engineering organization.* Arnold, London, 1973.

61. Morris, P. W. G. An organizational analysis of project management in the building industry. *Build International,* No. 6, 1973.

62. Thompson, P. A. *Organization and economics of construction.* McGraw-Hill, London, 1981.

63. Ibbs, C. W., Back, W. E., Kim, J. J., Wall, D. E., De La Garza, J. M., Hassanein, M. A., Schran, S. M. and Twardock, R. K. *Determining the impact of various construction contract types and clauses on project performance.* Department of Civil Engineering, University of Illinois at Urbana-Champaign, March 1986.

64. Perry, J. G. and Hayes, R. W. Risk and its management in construction. *Proceedings of the Institution of Civil Engineers,* Part 1, 1985, Feb.

65. Peter, L. J. and Hull, R. *The Peter principle: why things always go wrong.* Souvenir, London, 1969.

66. Morton, G. M. A. Become a project champion. *International Journal of Project Management,* **1,** No. 4, 1984, Nov., 197−203.

67. Sykes, A. Reducing neglected risks on giant projects. In *New dimensions of project management.* Kelley, A. J. (ed.), Lexington Books, Lexington, MA, 1982.

68. Belbin, M. *Management teams: why they succeed or fail.* Heinemann, London, 1985.

69. Department of Energy. *Mini-PMS guide.* Washington, DC, 1977, pp. 40, 41.

70. Walker, A. *Project management in construction.* Granada, London, 1984.

71. Cooper, D. F. and Chapman, C. B. *Risk analysis for large projects,* Wiley, Chichester, 1987.

72. Hertz, D. B. and Thomas, H. *Risk analysis and its applications.* Wiley, Chichester, 1983.

9. And now?

The 1990s opened with project management experiencing strong and healthy growth. Developments in Information Technology were substantially improving the power and ease of use of project control tools, and the subject was broadening, to include the more strategic and external issues such as concept planning, system definition, politics, finance and environmental issues, into the newer field of 'the management of projects'.

Nothing ever remains stationary. The context in which projects are being formed and managed is constantly changing, and indeed in the 1990s it is changing at a rate not experienced in over 40 years. The political situation of the 1990s is dramatically new and fluid. Business and finance are having to operate in conditions of unprecedented uncertainty. Social pressures are mounting sharply. A number of environmental issues have become very serious. Technology continues to develop rapidly. And the practice of management is changing.

Managers of projects must adapt to these new conditions or face the likelihood of producing unsuccessful projects, just as before, when their predecessors took insufficient account of their projects' environments. The mechanics of project management are still important, but the broader multi-functional, goal-oriented approach to projects, blending strategic and tactical issues around life-cycle development, is today needed more than ever for their successful management.

So, how will the management of projects develop over the next 10−20 years?

A changing context

Modern project management, as we have seen, emerged, largely in the defence/aerospace sector, in a period that was more inflexible and less complex and where events changed less rapidly than today. The two superpowers were locked in mutual stand-off. There was a rising scale of technological capability and 'enemy threats'. Engineering and urgency were the two paramount defence/aerospace project parameters. Similarly in the power sector, there was little emphasis on cost minimization: projects were generally large and monolithic. Oil and gas were developed on the back of rapidly rising product prices. Technology and speed came first. Projects often had large matrix organizations involving complex contractual and organizational processes.

Only in the 1970s did environmental issues and finance begin to arise formally as serious factors that could fundamentally affect the way projects are put together and executed. The impact of these on projects and their arrangement over the past 20 years is described in chapters 6−8. Organizationally, too, projects on average got smaller and more emphasis was placed on entrepreneurship, leadership and championing.

The 1990s are carrying these trends further, and at a much faster rate. And as we move into the 21st century, frequent change will become even more pervasive. Political change will be more common; the larger number of democracies will mean more frequent changes in government; social, demographic and economic pressures will grow. Environmental issues will increasingly crowd in on us. Financial and economic uncertainty will become a major dimension of project planning. Technology and communications will become even more global.

What is the outlook in the sectors of most interest to project people? While some trends can be identified, our ability to forecast accurately very far into the future is extremely limited. Few foresaw the severity of the worldwide economic depression of the early 1990s, the property collapse of Western Europe, North America and Japan, the dramatic decline of the defence industries, or the retrenchment in space. Nevertheless, we can hazard some projections.

Sector outlooks

The trends over the next decade or so in the major project industries will probably be along the following lines.

Space

Telecommunication and earth observation satellites will continue as important commercial sectors in space. The launch business will continue to be highly competitive, with the USA's R&D edge essentially subsidized by its military programmes. ESA's manned space ambitions will be cut back; the USA's will too, but less for cost reasons (technical difficulties will come into play to delay programmes and drive up costs). It seems very unlikely that man will be back on the moon by 2020 (compare p. 202).

Defence/aerospace

The defence industries will experience their worst business downturn since 1945. With the end of the Cold War, defence budgets will probably be cut by around 20% in real terms over the decade. Programmes will be cancelled, trimmed or drawn out. Defence requirements will shift towards dealing with the consequences of smaller, more localized and more frequent conflict than was typical of the 1945−1990 period (note 1). As a result, new types of operating requirement will emerge that are less aligned to the long-range strategic systems of the Cold War era and more to lighter, cheaper, more tactical and flexible systems. There will be emphasis on sophisticated intelligence and support systems, and a new breed of 'nice' weapons (destroying enemy capability with minimum loss of life) as well as 'smart' ones. Cost growth will continue to cause problems due, for example, to programme stretch-outs and an increasingly expensive labour base. There will be considerable restructuring in the industry.

Civil aviation   Competition in the civil aviation sector will continue to be extremely intense. Although there will be major growth in civil air transport — perhaps a doubling between 1990 and 2010, and a concomitant programme of airliner development — the cyclical nature of demand will lead to increases in both international competition and collaboration. Financing will be a crucial element of project development; increased use will be made of the international capital markets. Demand for 600−800-seater super jumbos and the replacement for Concorde will harden towards the end of the 1990s, by which time prototype studies should be well in hand. Japanese and US manufacturers look likely to strengthen their position in engine production, largely through their current substantial R&D programmes.

Airports $250−$350bn is said to be needed for airport upgrading worldwide between 1990 and 2010. IATA estimates that about 34 of Europe's 46 airports will run out of runway capacity by 2000. Worldwide, 35 new airport projects are already under way, with 50 new runways and 150 runway improvements. An important component of the commercial air infrastructure to be upgraded will be Air Traffic Control. Environmental opposition to airport expansion will be more vigorous than ever. Much of the 1990s will be spent, for example, in planning and arguing over the expansion of London's Heathrow (compare p. 96).

Ground transportation   There will be substantial investment in major ground transportation systems, particuarly rail (high-speed, heavy and light). Road charging will become more widespread. The first really commercial attractive electric car will appear early in the 21st century. There will be increased interest in multi-modal transportation planning (road, rail, water, air, and also pipeline and telecommunications) for commercial, logistical and environmental reasons. Industrial and business parks and com-munities — even a few business cities/technopoles — will increasingly be built at these nodal points.

The built environment   The oversupply of commercial office space in OECD countries of the early 1990s will take much of the decade to work through. Commercial building's major growth markets will thus be places where there is still economic growth and no overhang. The largest such region is South-East Asia. Housing, health, education and other public sectors (e.g. prisons) will be significant building markets. In all cases there will be evidence, probably on average only relatively mild, of interest in new technologies (principally materials and IT), integrated front-end planning and Program Management, and longer-term oriented procurement practices.

Power   Demand for electricity will grow at about the same rate as GDP (p. 285), despite some attempts to increase conservation and energy efficiency. Gas will increase as a source of electricity: there is more of it, it is cheaper than oil, it is more efficient and it is environmentally cleaner. Coal will seem attractive in many instances as an alternative to oil. The greenhouse consequences work against it, although modern desulphurization technology makes it less unattractive. The likelihood of nuclear energy returning in any large way will in the short term be crucially constrained by the availability of cheap, environmentally clean gas, and even clean coal, as alternatives. Over the next 10–15 years, most nuclear power work will be in Japan (which aims to increase its nuclear-generated power from 27% to 43% by 2010), South Korea, Indonesia, China, and possibly East Europe/Former Soviet Union (FSU). The really interesting question will be what happens when existing nuclear power capacity needs to be replaced. At present, 73% of France's capacity is nuclear, 21% of the UK's, 22% of the USA's. Safer, smaller plants will probably be built. Attempts to develop fast breeder plants still seem a long way from commercial production: fusion is even further off, and more expensive. Renewable energy is likely to be only a marginal source. Hydroelectricity, although potentially significant in some countries, represents only 1% of total capacity; it also has questionable environmental costs in many instances.

The environmental costs of energy production will be increasingly scrutinized, and there will be strong pressure to minimize them. There are already obvious conflicts between society's needs for power and the costs to the environment; these are likely to grow. It seems unlikely that market forces will generate enough pressure to reduce energy consumption, produce cleaner fuels or encourage the use of renewable sources over the next 20 years. If the environment–energy balance is to be improved, it will be more through political acts such as taxation than the cost of supply, at least over the next 25–30 years.

Oil, gas and chemicals

The price of oil is not likely to rise significantly during the next 20 years, basically because of the existence throughout this period of adequate supplies and the reluctance of oil exporting countries to curtail production. (The latest forecasts indicate adequate oil reserves for at least the next 40–45 years and gas reserves for at least 55–60 years). The current trend of developing non-OPEC fields will continue during the 1990s. There could be a 5%–10% switch from oil to gas over the next 10–20 years.

Capacity in the refined products and chemicals sectors will be restructured substantially during the next decade or two. There is currently overcapacity in Europe, and considerable new capacity in South-East Asia. Asian ethylene production, for example, will increase from just under one million to 2·4 billion tonnes per annum by the year 2000; 34% of world petrochemical demand in 2000 will be in the Asia–Pacific region. The environmental respectability of oil, gas and chemicals will continue to need to improve. Society will increasingly move to penalize polluting industries.

Pharmaceuticals

The pharmaceutical sector will thrive over the next 20 years, although cutbacks in US and European medical spending may lead to some dampening of 1980s' growth rates. There continues to be enormous demand for a wide range of pharmaceutical products, and continuing developments in molecular chemistry and biogenetics mean a wealth of new products will be produced over the next few decades. Competition will be intense, the key dimension being R&D and product-to-market times. A dominant feature of pharmaceuticals is regulation, and we can expect some harmonization of international regulatory standards leading to cheaper, more predictable development programmes.

Automobiles   For projects, autos represent perhaps the most interesting industry for the 1990s. Pushed by the Japanese, the industry has had to respond to fierce, globally competitive standards of product design, flexible production and quality (p. 184). Worldwide overcapacity for the 1990s is estimated at 10 million vehicles with all manufacturers having to increase investment, cut costs drastically and offer increased product flexibility. There is, as a consequence, immense pressure to integrate customer and manufacturing requirements into design to produce products that offer increasingly high value yet are still profitable. Management techniques such as Total Quality, competitive benchmarking, Design-for-Manufacturability and Assembly, lean production and simultaneous engineering, all fundamental to the future of the management of projects, to say nothing of teamwork, Computer Integrated Engineering, etc., are probably being pushed faster and further in the automobile industry of the early 1990s than in any other.

Computing   Technological developments in computing will continue to be dramatic for the foreseeable future: 64 Mb chips will be introduced in the mid-1990s — there will in fact be a quadrupling of chip density approximately every four years at least into the early 21st century. Optical computing could make a massive impact on processing efficiency by the late 1990s. Microprocessor architecture will be progressively rationalized to provide hugely increased functionality on single chips. Enormous developments will be made in software: Artificial Intelligence, object-oriented programming, neural networks, client—server architecture. The move to open systems will be largely complete by the mid-1990s. Competition will be extraordinarily intense, with many major companies disappearing. Hardware supply companies will turn increasingly into software companies, either because of the significance of standards (e.g. IBM's OS2 versus Microsoft's Windows NT) or because of a general emphasis on systems integration, or both.

These developments will drive computers to be dramatically more powerful and cheaper. Users will decentralize their IT more and more. *Computing, and telecommunications, will become even more powerful and necessary elements of company and project management.*

Telecommunications   Fierce competition and continued industry restructuring will also be a feature of the telecommunications industry. Spending on new

switching and transmission equipment will increase by at least
33% worldwide between 1990 and 2000. Installation of broad-
band cabling (optical fibre, ISDN (note 2), etc.) will be the
dominant transmission activity over the next 10–20 years, creating
what has been described as the largest machine in the world —
the global telecommunications network! Huge sums will be spent
on software development to provide 'intelligent' value-added
services such as electronic mail, electronic data interchange,
freephone services and remote access to a multitude of databanks
and services; a major portion of this work will be in conforming
to different national protocols. There will be a continued liberation
from public-sector control. Substantial new capacity will be added
in East Europe, the FSU, Asia and Latin America. Cellular
technology will continue to expand rapidly. Call costs will drop
dramatically.

Future trends   Plausible though these forecasts may be, they do not actually
take us very far in looking at the practice of managing projects
in the 1990s and the 21st century. They are at best very general;
at worst they may be wrong — by omission if not by commission.
The unexpected will happen; somewhere, somehow it will affect
these forecasts.

A richer, tighter insight into future trends in the management
of projects can be obtained by interweaving this industry sector
approach with an examination of the way the *processes* of managing
projects are developing. We shall do this by considering in turn
the political, social, environmental, economic and financial,
organizational, and technological contexts of projects. Finally, we
shall turn to the outlook for the discipline of the management of
projects itself — the institutional dimension.

**The political
context**

A map of the world in the 1990s is as different from that of the
1970s as the map of the 1970s was from that of the 1920s. The
big difference is the collapse of the Soviet Union and the supremacy
of capitalism (or if not quite the victory of unbridled capitalism,
at least the implosion of communism). The world of the 1990s,
as a result, is one where borders are now being redrawn, and often
fought over. This is an era of growing nationalism — of tribalism
even, coupled with massively powerful weapons. Yet it is a
heightened nationalism operating within a communications and
trading network in which people, ideas and markets are interlinking
globally on a scale and at a speed unprecedented.

The USA and Japan will continue to be the world's economic
giants, although China may grow to be the world's biggest economy
by the end of the first quarter of the 21st century. Europe will
continue to grow prosperously, but in a more differentiated manner
than the USA or Japan. Europe will be a patchwork of nations
for many years yet, and nationalism, and local politics, will
continue to be particularly potent. Demographic pressures on

European countries will be a serious issue. The right wing of national politics will be a stronger, more threatening pressure than at any time since 1945. Central Europe and the FSU will continue to splinter into nationalist groupings.

There is a real likelihood of the world dividing into three principal economic blocks: Europe, the USA and the Far East. Almost half the world's population will be outside these blocks by the early 21st century. Within them there will be a gradation of prosperity, with the USA, Northern Europe and Japan supplying higher value-added products and services and the poorer regions providing more low-cost production. North Africa will probably become de facto part of the European trading block, providing a low-cost base to Northern Europe.

The rate of economic growth during the 1990s will critically affect the extent to which these economic blocks become protectionist. The situation in the early 1990s has been one of low growth in Europe and the USA, and trade barriers have been erected accordingly. The challenge for political leaders will be to avoid this danger and achieve 'managed free trade'. If they fail to achieve this, the danger will be of a 'Cold Peace' — a balance of power based not on ideology, as in the period from 1930 to 1990, but on economics.

China, Japan, Taiwan, Korea and South-East Asia will be *the* region of major economic growth over the next quarter century or more. By 2000 the Asia—Pacific Economic Co-operation region may have been formed as a fully-fledged trading block; by 2010 its combined output may equal the combined output of the USA and Europe. China may split into a prosperous coastal southern area, including Hong Kong, and a slower, more conservative area in the central and northern parts. This break up may not be without conflict. The new China will become a massive importer of capital and will industrialize rapidly. A Chinese Economic Area (CEA) comprising China, Hong Kong and Taiwan could account for 6%—7% of world trade by 2000 and 20% by 2030, the OECD predicts. Tension between Japan and the CEA will mount progressively, with Japan having a lower growth rate, a much smaller population — 128 million against 1·2 billion — and a much smaller military capability. Japan will probably increase its military strength during the 1990s as a result.

By the early 21st century Russia will probably be a controlled social market economy acting as a land bridge between Europe and Asia. Eastern Russia, indeed, will probably itself be a part of the Asian economic boom. The FSU and Central Europe will represent significant opportunities for major projects, but political risk will be the major constraining factor for many years to come.

Like the FSU, Australasia and Canada will continue to offer significant natural resource project opportunities. Canada, as such, may not survive another decade: at least not in its pre-1990 form.

Instead, it may split into smaller regions, following the pattern set in Central Europe in the early 1990s, relying on the American Free Trade Area (AFTA) for its economic livelihood. By the early 21st century AFTA will probably comprise the USA, Canada, Mexico, Chile, Argentina and Panama, and perhaps Brazil.

The USA will be *the* global power. Its orientation may be more truly global than at any time in its history, partly because of its worldwide prominence but specifically because it will be less preoccupied with East—West divisions than it was during the Cold War. Latin America will slowly pull itself out of debt and dictatorship and will probably see substantial economic growth: there will be major project opportunities on the continent.

Conflict will continue in the Middle East for many years yet, but quite what will happen is difficult to forecast. Many parts of Africa, sadly, will be a social and environmental disaster — look at the trajectories of AIDS, famine, drought, war and disease. The continent is vast, however, and there are several indications that the damage done by centralized, state economic management is now being repaired. The big question in Africa, of course, is what will happen in South Africa: whatever does happen will have a significant knock-on effect south of the equator.

The greater overall volatility of the political environment will generally mean that greater attention is paid to political risk analysis. This will apply at both the national and local levels. It will range from dramatic threats such as nationalization and appropriation (as with oil in Zaire in 1992) to subtler issues of electoral timing or different tax rates of new governments. Political risk insurance will continue to be important, and we can be sure that innovations in policies, products, and instruments will continue to be made in both the private and public sectors, i.e. the export credit agencies and Multilateral Investment Guarantee Agency (MIGA) and Guaranteed Return on Investment Principle (GRIP) (note 3). The additional costs, both direct and indirect, of this risk and its insurance will be an element of the overall financial engineering increasingly required of projects.

The move towards more competitive and open markets and away from 'closed' state-controlled ones will result in project sponsors and their advisers — designers, economists, contractors, bankers, etc. — paying more attention than at any time since the First World War to the financial viability of projects. This trend will continue at least for the next several years. The late 1980s and early 1990s essentially saw the discrediting of state intervention: the 1990s are likely, however, to see a consolidation of liberal, or even social, capitalism as opposed to total reliance on open market forces, not least as the difficulties of readjustment in the FSU and Central Europe and other socialist economies — particularly the less developed countries — become apparent.

Privatization and BOO(T) projects will continue to be important in the years ahead. Although their track record was not good in the 1980s, their basic attractiveness to governments will ensure a continuing demand for them in both developed and developing countries. While government practices and procedures may have worked against such projects at times in the 1980s, the trend will be for these constraints to be reduced rather than tightened.

The trend towards greater democracy, at all levels of society, which should continue at least throughout the 1990s, will mean that projects must continue to engage in greater public consultation and dialogue. The Environmental Impact process will continue to be important as a means of describing the proposed project and its likely impact on society. Other forms of intermediation, such as public affairs consultancies, will become increasingly important.

The social context

Society is always changing. The 1990s look like being more conservative than the 1980s. Much of the developed world is facing a prolonged recession. Employment will continue to be a major issue. Poverty and particularly population growth will be important factors dragging down many societies and constraining initiatives and projects for much of the decade. Of every 20 children born in the 1990s, 19 will be born in a developing country. The very high population growth of Africa, India and Latin America will not abate in the next 10–20 years. Dealing with massive urban conglomerations such as Cairo, Calcutta, Mexico City, São Paulo, Seoul and Shanghai will be major challenges for decades to come. Health and welfare concerns will generally heighten as populations age, social medicine comes under increased budgetary pressure and immigration builds up from wherever there is conflict, poverty or starvation — not least North Africa, Central Europe, Central America and South-East Asia. The welfare state will be partially rolled back in Northern Europe. Crime, the UN predicts, will have increased by 60% between 1975 and 2000; prison populations will double. Terrorism will increase, as will drug abuse, and state pressures to counteract them.

It is not a particularly cheerful prospect: depressingly reminiscent of the 1930s except, of course, that nothing is ever quite the same as it was. Women will generally continue to play an increasing role in employment and to take important positions in politics, business and the more formal side of society in general. Our democratic institutions are now more robust, thanks not least to television. Electronic communications, and indeed air and other means of rapid transport, have shrunk the world (note 4). We are more and more a global village and, as a result, democracy is in better shape than ever — a new and evolving form of democracy, perhaps, but people's opinions cannot be bulldozed quite as before. They can be manipulated perhaps, but not ignored.

Development of people will receive more and different emphasis. Development strategies are now according much greater

significance to human resources.[1,2] (A World Bank review[3] of all
its projects since its inception in the 1940s concluded that the two
major factors associated with project success were emphasis on
people development and allowing prices to operate at internationally
competitive market levels.) Education, particularly at the primary
and post-experience ages, will be recognized to be of more crucial
importance. The fuller participation of all in the development
process — whether a city building, a new product, a health
programme or anything else — is now widely recognized as more
likely to lead to success.

All this paints a powerful picture for the management of projects.
People demand consultation and the right to have their say; they
are anxious and conservative; but the communications media are
a powerful tool, for good or bad.

The lessons are obvious. The populace must be consulted. Their
real concerns must be taken note of and, as far as possible, acted
on. Opinions can be moulded. Skill should be used in forming
and channelling public sentiment. Project executives should hone
their communications skills. We have already seen the lessons many
times in this book: co-opt or ally with opinion shapers; tune in
closely to the political environment — feed politicians ideas; relate
project schedules to political timetables; contribute to the
community.

The three cardinal social dimensions for projects (at least in the
developed world) — welfare and employment, the environment,
and safety — will continue to be unrelenting. People will fight
projects that diminish their standard of living; Western society will
not tolerate a project that threatens its health and safety; society
now cares for its environment in ways and to an extent that were
unknown two decades ago. Witness to the health and safety aspect
is the progressive tightening of legislation in the West which often
impacts directly on the organization of project procurement and
the allocation of responsibilities and liabilities. The Construction
Design and Management (CONDAM) regulations being introduced
in the early 1990s into the UK construction industry, for example,
will make construction design consultants and owners significantly
more liable for construction safety. All those involved in the
management of projects ignore these issues at their cost — or rather,
theirs and the project's.

**The
environmental
context**

If environmentalism began to impact the world of projects only
in 1970, by 1990 its profile had risen to one of some urgency.
It is reasonable to predict that by 2010 the pressure for action to
protect our environment will have risen yet again. Even by the
early 21st century industrial output and energy output could have
tripled from their 1990 levels, with major, possibly appalling,
consequences for conditions in cities and countryside alike.

It is now widely, if not universally, agreed that major and

threatening changes to the earth's ecology are under way: climatic change (caused not least by atmospheric warming), ozone depletion and the destruction of major ecosystems such as the tropical rain forests. Mankind continues to add to these pressures. There is no real let-up in the rate of rain-forest depletion. Greenhouse gases will continue to increase, especially while the USA refuses to change its practices and while developing countries develop — buying more fridges, using more electricity, running more vehicles. The IPCC (note 5) has concluded that temperatures will rise $0 \cdot 3$ K per decade, leading to a corresponding rise in sea level of 6 cm per decade. Patterns of disease and climate will change. River deltas, flood plains and low-lying coastal areas will be threatened — from the Maldives to a large portion of Florida. The situation is compounded by man-made accidents, over-farming, poorly controlled urban growth and bad project siting, and many more depressing acts of extreme short-term thinking, or indeed of outright thoughtlessness.

Project participants must and will become better educated environmentally so they can better understand the impact of their actions, not just scientifically and morally, but legally and commercially. The concern with creating sustainable development that first surfaced in the 1980s will stay with us into the 21st century: Agenda 21, one of the most important outcomes of the 1992 UN Rio conference, has set the agenda for sustainable development for at least the next one to two decades; the UN Commission for Sustainable Development will monitor whether or not governments deliver. Increasing penalties will be applied to those who transgress society's increasingly severe norms of environmental impact. Already the US and UK legislation on hazardous waste, for example, has potentially massive financial implications for owners of contaminated land. Fines for pollution are also severe, and rising. Environmental monitoring and audits, ecological and environmental costing, public accountability, environmental training — all will be more common in project and non-project industries alike. This trend will be most marked in the developed world, but it is already being adopted by developing nations. The Environmental Impact Assessment process, statutory now for certain classes of projects in the developed world, will increasingly be used in developing countries and, on the basis that it genuinely represents best practice, on projects where its use is not mandatory.

Through such actions, many of the more detrimental effects of proposed new developments will be mitigated or eliminated. And while it hardly seems likely that the dangerous direction of the overall trends will be reversed in the short term, some may at least be checked. Noxious emissions and dangerous pollutants in the energy, oil, gas and petrochemicals industries are being and will continue to be reduced; exhaust emissions from road vehicles are becoming cleaner; cars and planes are becoming quieter and there will be some reduction in aircraft engine emissions; construction materials are being used with greater consideration of their origins.

One of the major environmental sectors in the next 20–40 years or more will be water. In the UK and large parts of the USA (particularly the South-West) we have already run out of immediate reserve capacity. The same is true for North and Sub-Saharan Africa, the Middle East, Pakistan and Western India. In Western Asia as a whole, demand will probably have doubled between 1980 and 2000, and here too reserve will only just service demand. Much skill will be needed to find ways of providing additional capacity without damaging existing environments too severely (and without adverse social repercussions — irrigation and hydro schemes in the Middle East, India, China and Central Europe are raising strong social and political objections).

Such projects must be engineered with an eye not only to providing new supply but also to improving existing demand. Wastage in existing systems is too high in many instances. Water quality in a great many locations needs substantial upgrading. Nitrate pollution is common in the USA, Europe and the FSU. Levels of pesticides and PCBs are too high in many East Asian, Latin American and African countries. Sewerage contamination is a massive problem. Coastal protection works, particularly in regard to the forecast rising sea levels, will be a major area of activity over the next 20–30 years.

Household, industrial and hazardous waste is another area of growing major project activity. Land and sea dumping is ceasing to be a viable option in many places. Disposal of non-hazardous waste by incineration is generally environmentally benign and seems likely to increase worldwide. Hazardous waste is one of the great untackled issues facing late 20th century society. In the opinion of many we still have inadequate plans for the long-term treatment of nuclear waste, and indeed of much industrial waste. Tyres are a major problem. Electronics is another: optical fibre, ceramics and composite materials use large quantities of toxic metals, chemicals and gases, as does the manufacture of televisions and visual display units; many of the materials cannot be decomposed, and their disposal is a substantial problem.

Sustainable development does not imply reduced development and growth: the opposite, in fact. It demands vigorous growth to reduce problems of poverty, underdevelopment and environmental degradation. But current patterns of growth must be changed to make them less resource- and energy-intensive, and less inequitable. In the developing world particularly, economic growth is — paradoxically to some — the only long-term solution to the more desperate problems, since only economic growth will ultimately lead to reduced population growth and the opportunity to build cleaner systems and a less polluting environment. The World Bank, in its 1992 Development Report,[4] argues strongly that the pricing of resources such as water, energy and timber at market levels would contribute significantly to an improved environment: under-pricing simply leads to under-investment and inadequate maintenance. Economics strongly influences the pattern of environmental damage.

The economic and financial context

As we have seen, the rate of economic growth and the degree of protectionism of the three emerging world trading blocks will be the major economic issues over the next 10–20 years. Growth requires investment, both in physical capital and people. The capacity to invest depends on the ability to mobilize internal savings and to attract new savings from abroad. Economics rather than ideology will be the dominant political imperative. Diplomatic activity, and to an extent military pressure, will increasingly be exerted towards economic and trade ends. Similarly, business investment, which could increase dramatically through the decade if economic growth develops, will be focused as much on securing market access as on low production costs (note 6).

GDP will probably continue to grow at 3%–4% per annum, as it has on average since the early 1980s. During this period, growth rates have varied substantially between the Far East and the West, however, with differences ranging from over 8% to less than 1%. The critical issue in the years ahead will be the extent to which the Western economies can recover from their low rate of growth. GDP will probably grow fastest in China (6%–10%), followed by South-East Asia (5%–7%), Japan and Latin America (4%), Europe and the USA (2%–3%), East Europe and the FSU (2%). Africa will probably have GDP of ±2%. Per capita GDP in the least developed and/or primary commodity exporting countries will unfortunately remain very low, due partly to currency depreciation but more to rising population.

If there is some degree of policy co-ordination, world trade could grow at 4·5% per annum. However, without managed free trade it could be as little as 1% — this is the disaster scenario. Developing nations will continue to export more than developed, but not to the same extent as in the 1980s (Fig. 62).

The scale of public-sector spending peaked in the 1980s. There is now a worldwide trend to reduce governments' borrowing requirements. OECD government deficits, with the exception of Japan's, will continue to be large and in need of substantial reduction for the forseeable future. Indeed, the USA's huge deficit is likely to be a cause of serious difficulties to the capital markets and hence to project finance.

Driven partly by the desire in most countries to reduce public-sector financing, projects will be financed more frequently within

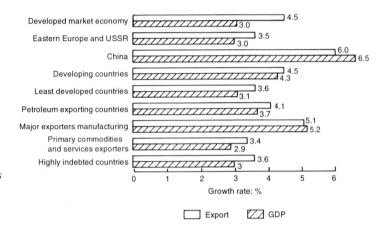

Fig. 62. Growth rates of exports and GDP, 1990–2000 (source UNDP)

the mechanics of the private sector. This move will also be a reflection of the general shift towards the disciplines of the market-place. After all, isn't it better for an infrastructure project experiencing cost overruns to have the intense management pressure on containing cost that the Channel Tunnel experienced in 1992–1993 than, say, the problems of the public-sector Thames Barrier project a decade earlier?

BOO(T) projects should therefore grow slowly in popularity during the years ahead. However, because they are complex and difficult to structure, they should be approached with caution. Their preparation cost, and often uncertainty, makes them attractive only to contractors and suppliers with a strong capital base. Nevertheless, they offer scope for creativity and their costs and risks can, in the right circumstances, be counteracted by good returns in a relatively secure (i.e. non-competitive) position.

While the marked trend towards sourcing financing from the private sector will continue, it would be naïve to believe that there will not still be a major role for public-sector funding. There are significant long-term benefits in certain sectors — notably transport, low-cost housing, public education — which are not obviously attractive to private finance: public-sector money is then the only viable major source. Public-sector involvement may also be politically necessary to ensure adequate public-sector control. And cheaper public-sector funds or guarantees will often be necessary to ensure the viability of the overall financing package. We may thus predict a continued role for public-sector funding. In fact, the norm will be a much greater mix of public- and private-sector funding than has ever been experienced before.

By the early 1990s the Third World debt crisis was largely over. With the normalization of creditor relations for Brazil and Argentina, the debt crisis for the middle income ldcs that were the original target of the Baker Initiative (p. 169) can be said to have ended. The continued actions embedded in the Brady Plan

Table 5. *International Funding Institutions 1990–99*

Institution	Commercial lending: $ billion	Soft aid: $ billion	
World Bank	210	IDA	50
Asian Development Bank	29	ADF	15
InterAmerican Development Bank	27	FSO	0·5
African Development Bank	10	AfDF	7·5
European Investment Bank	70	Lomé	22

helped ease the debt loan on these nations further. Even so, despite the general return to creditworthiness, it will be a long time before many rate even a B+ in financial terms.

For the next 40 or so poorest nations, on the other hand, the situation is still bad: for them the debt crisis is far from over. Although they spent more than half their export earnings on debt servicing in the 1980s, they were unable to pay off more than half their scheduled debts. The only way forward for such countries in the foreseeable future will be a combination of debt forgiveness, International Finance Institution (IFI) support, growth, and sound economic policies (in reverse order).

Debt relief for the poorest and most indebted countries, assessed on a case-by-case basis, is likely to happen for several countries in the 1990s. In all cases, however, from the very poor to the middle-income countries, sound economic policies and IFI support will be critical.

Official development finance, including that of bilateral agencies, can be expected to grow at an annual average rate of 2%–3% in real terms in the medium term. Currently, lending of about $441bn is forecast by the IFIs for the 1990s (Table 5).

European, Japanese and US funding for the FSU and Central Europe should be added to these figures. The EBRD (European Bank for Reconstruction and Development) is forecast to commit $15bn or so over the decade. The EC (EU), through the European Investment Bank and its Phare and Tacis programmes, is also an important source of funds for European infrastructure projects. Even more important is the European Regional Development Fund — the so-called Structural Funds — of which 15bn ECUs per year are being committed to the poorest areas of the EC. (Large though these sums are, they are significantly less than most observers' predictions of needs; such predictions are generally highly inflated, however, being based on almost open-ended shopping lists.)

The same trend towards mixed funding will apply to the IFIs as was noted for more domestic public/private-sector projects. Mixed public–private financing is not without its difficulties, however. The aims are sufficiently different that the consequent overall financing structure can be quite complex. Project promoters therefore, will often have to call on specialized and financially inventive skills.

Counter-trade, forfeiting, securitization, use of derivatives and other techniques of project and export finance will continue to be needed on many projects. Export credits will continue to play an important role in ensuring financeable projects; credit mixes will be another means whereby finance can be 'engineered' to the project's needs and the project can be engineered to the financing available.

Engineers and managers can assist bankers and accountants in creating financeable projects in many ways other than simply configuring the project to fit sources of available finance. The generally high cost of money and capital shortage will continue until at least the middle portion of the 1990s. Competitive pressures to get costs down — continuously — are and will remain a fact of business life, particularly in product-oriented project industries. As a result, *project sponsors will continue to look for real contributions from production management in reducing project costs through shorter cycle times, better inventory management and, particularly, better target-costed and value-engineered designs*. The key, as ever, is to create projects that generate the maximum 'value added', be this public sector utility or commercial return. Designers and production managers must work with sponsors and their financiers to this end to an extent that in many cases was only just starting to happen in the mid-1980s.

In the same way, designers and production managers will continue to join financiers, insurers and others in actively 'managing down' risk. For example, specifications can be changed to reduce currency risk. Shorter implementation schedules will help minimize financial exposure. Computer planning systems are being introduced combining analyses of project financial return, risk analysis and scheduling.[5]

With continued pressure on financial engineering over the foreseeable medium-term future, we can predict a continued emphasis on tighter coupling of production management, design and financing. Successful projects and products will be those that accomplish this integration.

The organizational context

The 1990s will see a *growing interest in better definition of the management required at the front-end, strategic stages of a project*. It will be more important than ever to ensure that the project is adequately defined, technically, in relation to its business viability, and in the other ways described in chapter 8. The old bad habit of 'just beginning' a project will increasingly be seen to be dangerous and inappropriate. The early planning stages are still not adequately articulated by the project management community. Organizations perform these functions but many learn by trial and error, and then have to relearn on the next project after people leave. This book has drawn several lessons on the strategic management of projects, but a good deal of further elaboration and testing remains to be done.

With the heightened emphasis on market forces, the environment and international trade, greater attention will be given to the wider, systemic influences acting on and set off by projects. There will, as a result, be a continuing move towards taking a sectoral or systems approach to project definition and management. The interrelation of the project and other parts of the community or economy, or other elements of the organizational, geographical or industrial sectors that the project covers, will increasingly be seen to be important.

As trade and ideas become more transnational, managers will increasingly have to think and operate internationally — both at the macro level, in aspects as diverse as environmental, political and economic interactions, and at the micro level in tactical issues such as global structuring of funding, international competition and sourcing of suppliers and other resources — so-called 'international vendorization'. For some this will manifest itself first at the trade block level — the EC 'single market' of 1993, for example. For others it will be translated into more global sourcing, mixing American, Far East, European, ldc, nic (note 7) and developed nation suppliers.

Projects will more frequently be carried out in modular form. Large homogeneous mega-type projects will be avoided where possible. As far as possible, the modules of the project will be self-standing, so that if the design of the whole changes, the parts themselves remain viable. This will add a new twist to the challenge of integration. The modular parts of the project must be designed so that not only are they individually viable, but also the whole works synergistically.

There is another reason why projects will generally start off smaller, or be implemented in a modular form. Recognizing the fluidity and uncertainty of today's project environment, but also the need to perform proper front-end Project Definition, owners will want to minimize the amount they need to spend before they are sufficiently confident that the project is viable and the risks are acceptable. Sponsors will show greater caution over proposed investment projects; there will be more frequent disjointed phasing as owners provide greater scrutiny and satisfy themselves that the risks are acceptable before proceeding to the next stage of design or implementation.

We can expect too to see increased attention being given to the proper role of the *owner*. This is one of the few areas in the organization of projects that is still insufficiently researched and inadequately understood. It is evident, from the historical analysis of the earlier chapters of this book if not from a wider, more general experience, that the demands made by the structure, responsibilities and performance of a project's owner can often be the dominant influence on the way the project will be managed. Just consider the impact of Groves, Schriever, Raborn, Mueller and Phillips, Patton and Moolin, and Rickover; or, conversely, the problems of TSR-2 and Concorde, the nuclear power industry, the British construction industry, the Channel Tunnel, NASA in its later years, the DoD (pp. 152−153), and the findings of the US Courts and the CII in the late 1980s (p. 179).

To an extent, the definition of an owner is clearly industry-specific. The Pentagon and MoD have well-developed views of their roles. So do most automobile manufacturers and pharmaceutical companies. In other industries, however, the owner's role may be weak (construction, for example) or changing, for example due to privatization policies or to declining opportunities (arguably the case for many of the oil majors in the next 20 years). Given that the owner can exert such a fundamental influence on the conduct of a project, what essential project management functions should he perform?

The next few years will see the project management community defining the owners' role more comprehensively: distinguishing further the role of the sponsor and the owner's project manager; elaborating which functions should be retained by the owner (for example, safety; key business functions; environmental, social and fiduciary responsibilities) and which might better be contracted to outside groups; and defining the set of project management services a competent owner should mobilize, whether totally in-house or with external assistance.[6]

We can expect a sea change in the world of projects in terms of *attitudes* and fundamental concerns over *performance*; for this we largely have to thank Japanese competition. Since the mid-1980s there has been, quite simply, a revolution in management. It is about international competitiveness and productivity, and its guiding philosophy is *Total Quality*.

Initially introduced to the Japanese by the Americans W. Edwards Deming and J. M. Juran in the early 1950s, Total Quality Management became the predominant management philosophy behind Japan's phenomenal post-war growth.[7−10] The philosophy is simple: concentrate on what the customer really wants; meet these needs as effectively as possible; strive continuously to improve performance. The approach can be embellished: be clear on what your organization's aims are and get everyone committed to them; involve the whole organization in analysing systematically how performance can be improved, in terms of both operating efficiency and effectiveness in meeting both its own aims and those of its clients; continuously improve performance (because competition is never stationary). From these come further principles. Think of customers in chains — the 'value chain' — from suppliers and subcontractors to customers and users: look at how value and productivity can be increased at each link in the chain; form long-term partnerships between customers and suppliers and work together over a sustained period to achieve measurable increases in performance (this will generally mean abandoning traditional competitive tendering); develop 'learning organizations'; analyse inefficiencies over the total production process (problems may be arising in specification or design as much as in manufacturing), base observations on quantifiable data, and engineer down the defects rate to aggressively low levels (Crosby talks of 'zero defects').[8]

The increased attention to strategic issues that Total Quality represents will even flow over into the management of projects where Total Quality is not being explicitly implemented.

- The move towards more comprehensive schedule planning and control, with more top−down emphasis and a more rapid and powerful simulation capability, will continue.
- Risk Management will become more common on projects.
- Contracting may begin to become less exclusively focused on the short term and concern itself more with the greater benefits that can result from longer term 'relationship' contracting.

The trend towards developing *comprehensive plans* covering all major aspects of the project from its earliest stages will be continued by both owners and contractors (pp. 223 and 244). Having a Project Execution Plan (PEP) from the outset will be recognized as the right way to proceed. Critical items and critical groups will be identified. Progressively more detailed schedules will be nested within the top-management-driven plan. (Computer technology is making it increasingly easy to play with parts of the schedule, by 'dragging out' certain key items, exploding them, simulating alternative (risk) scenarios, testing interlinkages, looking at the effect on key activities, resources, etc., and presenting the results in a variety of different ways.) The project strategy (PEP) should be renewed and updated regularly — either at major milestones or every four to six months.

The move towards scheduling and managing by *milestones* will be consolidated. It fits best with the life-cycle development approach, configuration management, and other project management 'best practices', and also provides the best form of control. Controlling, including paying, contractors in terms of milestone achievement is much more effective than paying by monthly valuation of work accomplished (pp. 253, 264 and p. 321, note 32).

Advances in statistical and computing techniques are creating renewed interest in GERT-like (or more accurately, *probabilistic*) *network scheduling*. These will improve our simulation capabilities and lead to a more sophisticated approach to project organization (note 8; Fig. 63).

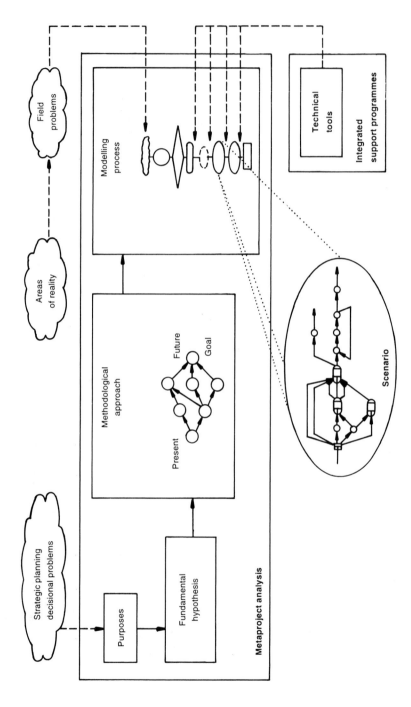

Fig. 63(a). Simplified conceptual architecture of Metaproject Analysis and its relations with problems faced and tools used

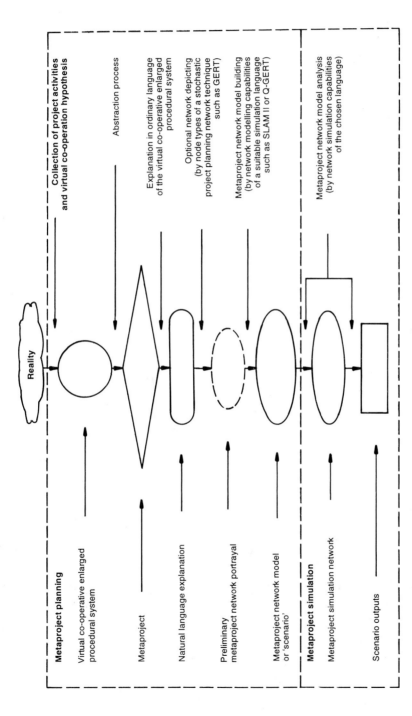

Fig. 63(b). Modelling process of Metaproject Analysis (source: Nicolo[43], courtesy Internet)

Over the next five to ten years, *risk* identification, analysis and management will come to be accepted as a normal part of the way owners and contractors approach projects. Data will be collected and stored on a wide variety of risks, categorized by type and stage of projects, organizations involved, technology, contract type, etc. Principal risks will be identified and their possible effect simulated. (Increasingly, this will be computer-assisted using Expert Systems and new statistical techniques (note 9).) The 1990s will see further development of these tools, which in turn will enrich the organizational approach to projects, allowing both better informed decision-making and more flexible organization structures.

This approach to appraising and managing risk more maturely is, as we saw in chapter 8, tied closely to one's approach to contracting. The new view of 'best practice' contracting outlined on pp. 254–255 will become increasingly widely adopted over the next 20 years. Leading procurement bodies are already beginning to promote it; its principles are at one with those of Total Quality.

One result of the new approach to contracting will be to reinforce further the advantages of long-term *relationship contracting* and multi-contract arrangements; this will often extend as far as *'partnering'*. Greater attention will be given to the objectives of the contracting parties, the nature of the services each provides, the risks they bear, and the rewards they can reasonably expect. The aim will be for

- parties to work together over a sufficiently long period for the owner to obtain quantifiable improvements in the value of services provided by his consultants, contractors and suppliers
- the risks posed by a project to be shared between the contracting parties according to their ability and willingness to bear them
- bid prices to be based on carefully worked-up proposals, prepared on the basis of reasonable information and understanding or, in the absence of this, with adequate risk or contingency allowances
- patently inadequate bids not to be accepted but to be reworked collaboratively between the owner's project management and the bidder's
- contract difficulties to be handled quickly.

It will be much worse for a contractor to lose the goodwill of a long-term client than to make a loss on one of his projects. *Alternative Dispute Resolution* (ADR) procedures will become more common as a cheaper, quicker and less destructive way of handling legal disputes than going through the courts (note 10).

As partnering was only beginning to be adopted in the projects world in the mid-to-late 1980s, by the end of the decade there had been little chance to achieve much in the way of *measurable productivity gains*. (Generally in the West in the 1980s, firms partnered and formed strategic alliances to increase market share rather than productivity; the Japanese, however, generally sought both benefits from their partnering arrangements.)

Productivity gain must be the challenge of the 1990s. Projects must emulate the '*re-engineering*' success of the manufacturing industries, organizing business processes around customer needs and results rather than around traditional functions, and consequently reducing costs dramatically by reducing waste, lost time and inefficiency.[11-14] Look at Chrysler's turn-round in the early 1990s. Considered by many to be near terminal failure in 1989, Chrysler formed project teams reducing product development times by $1\frac{1}{4}$ years, benchmarked everything from accounting to manufacturing (note 12) and cut its overhead by $4·5bn in $3\frac{1}{2}$ years. The same philosophy should be standard in the management of projects. The attitude of project management must be continuously to reduce product-to-market times and design and production costs, and to develop projects with increased value added.

Until the 1990s, project management's philosophy was based on norms. Estimators knew how much standard items cost; planners knew how long activities took. The successful companies of the 1990s, on the other hand, will be those that aggressively seek and achieve progressive improvements on those norms. This will require sharing of data between owners and supplies, joint planning and a positive can-do approach to production. Key technologies may have to be jointly identified, researched and proved. Joint R&D groups may be needed. Achieving this will require trust, continuity and openness between parties to the project. This is why partnering is so important (note 13).

The *team approach* to project design and production will become increasingly common.[15,16] Teams will be formed from all the disciplines and processes having a bearing on the total project delivery process. The team approach is integral to Total Quality; it is also the 'lean production' essence of Simultaneous Development or Engineering (also known in Production Management as 'Concurrent Engineering'). The emphasis in modern Concurrent Engineering, as in the past, is to reduce overall project durations, but there is not the same 'fast track' connotation of beginning testing and development before R&D is finalized as in the old concurrency (pp. 226, 240 and p. 322, note 43). The aim is to maximize integration of all production and development disciplines into the design process so that production can begin more smoothly and quickly than in the old sequential approach.[17-22]

A number of new engineering, technology and production management techniques are now being promoted as part of Concurrent/Simultaneous Engineering; we shall turn to these and their future role shortly when looking at the technological dimension of the management of projects. The organizational implication of modern concurrency, however, is a return to the fluidity of the task forces and the matrix, à la NASA of the early 1960s, and we can expect a continued interest in the non-hierarchical, creative, highly adaptive organization structures required for fast-evolving projects with high integration needs (something allied closely to what is more generally being promoted at 'high involvement' management[23]): a renewed emphasis on the importance of human factors in technology management — 'hu-tech' rather than just 'hi-tech' (note 14)!

Central to the new, Total Quality driven approach to project organization are positive attitudes of everyone, from receptionist to chairman, from project executive to financier. We have seen how attitudes and commitment, are vital to the successful management of projects (pp. 241–243 and 254–255). Equally, managers will have to put more effort into selecting the right persons for project positions, and induction and staff development on the job, and pay more attention to career development, particularly of staff who show promise of promotion to the higher, more strategic levels of managing projects.[24,25] More time will be spent in creating positive organizational environments through team building. The owner, in particular, will need to recognize these points and provide leadership in their implementation.

Much of this is not new; for many, little will change from the way they approached projects in the 1980s, but in the world of projects overall the emphasis on positive attitudes on all sides will be marked and will be very much for the better.

The emphasis on Total Quality that underlies so much of the new organizational basis of projects of the 1990s is so great that we can conclude that integration is no longer the dominant organizational principle for projects that it was between 1950 and, say, 1985. Although integration is still the most fundamental structural characteristic of project management and the project manager's role, the principles of Total Quality will probably become the dominant philosophy guiding best project management practice.

(An interesting twist to this view is that in a number of general management and manufacturing organizations managers are beginning to turn to *project management* as the new, all-purpose management philosophy, rejecting Total Quality, unfortunately, as too difficult. '*Management by projects*' is seen as a particularly useful way of providing a quick-fix means to pep up the organization.[26])

The technological context

Technical problems were probably the biggest cause of project difficulty for the first 30 years of modern project management. By the mid-1980s, the danger of committing to project implementation with a still unresolved high level of technical uncertainty had become widely recognized. The 1990s will see continued progress in managing technical uncertainty better, from appraisal and risk analysis to prototyping and concurrent engineering. Information management and IT will continue their extraordinarily large rate of change: the project information systems of the late 1990s will be an order of magnitude more sophisticated than those of the early 1990s.

Technology forecasting will become an integral part of most projects. Companies in the pharmaceutical, aerospace, computer, telecommunications and automobile industries, for example, routinely and systematically appraise the technology developments likely over the next five, ten and 15 years and the actions (R&D, acquisitions, technology testing, capital expansion, funding) needed to capture competitive advantage from this new technology. Future products are managed as portfolios according to their degree of technological uncertainty and the organizational relationships needed to bring them 'to market'. The organizational and control attributes of project management have a major role in accomplishing this successfully.[27–30] Core and pacing technologies are investigated. Milestones are predicted for new technology development, proving, licensing, and production to market.) Generally, the key issue is to get the product-to-market time as short as possible, provided of course that there is a benefit in doing so. This 'Time-Based Innovation' (TBI) process is by no means restricted to obviously high-tech industries, however, and an increasingly wide swathe of project sectors will adopt it in the years ahead. From the 1990s on, everyone working on the design and definition of projects should be aware of the need for and benefit of forecasting likely technological change over the following five to ten years. Very simply, if managed technology forecasting is not performed then future competitiveness will be diminished.

The risk that new and core technologies pose must of course be carefully assessed. The risk of reduced performance, delay and cost growth must be monitored from the earliest stages of project or programme identification, and then continuously updated. (This will be integrated into the strategic planning updating.) Back-up technologies must be on hand.

Continued attention will be given in the years ahead to improving the definition of performance acceptance criteria and project briefs. Criteria must be comprehensively and carefully defined in terms of performance benefit and effectiveness, cost and schedule, and risk of failure. In some cases acceptance criteria are simple measures of performance; in others, however, they are being used also as management control measures. On software projects, for example, we are beginning to see Function–Point Analysis being used increasingly frequently as a means of measuring software productivity and efficiency (note 15).

The 1990s are seeing an economic shift in many project sectors towards longer product life, with greater emphasis on reducing operating and maintenance costs. Performance specifications will reflect this, giving more attention to costs-in-use, life-cycle management, safety requirements, spares, maintenance and logistics (note 16).

Testing of generic and project-specific technology before committing to project implementation will increasingly become common practice. Prototyping, and Verification and Validation, will be built into project schedules as a routine project management function. Where the technology is primarily a design issue, prototyping will take the form of comprehensive modelling. Often this will be done electronically — so-called 'digital assembly'. Building and plant design, for example, will be modelled using CAD with comprehensive estimating, scheduling, procurement and other databank links. A 'virtual project' will in effect be created (note 17). Information systems projects will extend the modelling to full preliminary program development, following established prototyping principles (p. 188). Where design requires further testing, electronic modelling will give way to physical modelling. The prototyping will involve all principal disciplines involved in the design, test and manufacture of the product, following modern Simultaneous Engineering principles. For the social and environmental reasons discussed earlier, the safety and environmental attributes of the proposed technology and design will be major dimensions of the testing. Increased attention will be given to building feedback from operations and previous products into the prototyping.

As we have seen, the interrelation of technology, design and schedule and the way this is managed will be of continuing importance in many project industries. A product brought to market more quickly than its competitors can often afford to be less competitive on cost (and even on technical performance). Speed is thus often of overriding competitive importance. Rapid prototyping, TBI and Time-Based Manufacturing[31,32] and Simultaneous Engineering are important practices of the 1990s that will be used increasingly across a wide range of projects to achieve faster development. (The F-22 Advanced Tactical Fighter, the USAF's major systems acquisition programme identified as the 'model' for Pentagon, post Packard, acquisition for the 1990s, exhibits all 'best practice' practices centred around, in DoD's terms, Concurrent Engineering,[33,34] note 18.)

As well as the organizational attributes touched on earlier, Concurrent/Simultaneous Engineering uses the following product and technology management principles

- *Design-for-Manufacturability and Assembly*: the Buick Le Sabre, for example, was analysed in terms of quality,

reliability, durability, safety, manufacturability and ease of assembly, weight of vehicle, time to market, and total cost[18,35,36]
- *Group Technology* to ensure optimum technical compatibility: defence and civilian organizations are creating 'virtual factories' from sets of suppliers conforming to common Group Technology standards[37]
- Improving *Reliability* by reducing the number of parts, building in redundancy, increased testing, and good logistics and maintenance
- *Computer Integrated Manufacture and Design*
- Competitive *Benchmarking*
- Total Quality principles such as *Just-in-Time* and *Taguchi Quality Engineering* (note 19) to achieve more effective design and leaner production.

These and other techniques will continue to be important project management topics in the next decade. Research will continue to foster their application in all kinds of project situations, probably pushed above all by continued competitive pressure in autos, electronics and pharmaceuticals (note 20).

Design management will be given further recognition in the 1990s as schedule and technical performance requirements tighten. Design targets for cost, schedule and life-cycle support will become more stringent in industries where such practices are already used, and will be progressively adopted where they are not. There will be continued strong pressure for greater integration of design and production, and increased design accountability for better project performance. The move in construction towards Design-Build, reflecting owners' desires to achieve these basic project management principles, is an example. Reliability and systematic 'lessons learned' feedback, maintainability and product support, and Pre-Planned Product Improvement (P^3I) will become common life-cycle support practices. Design-to-Cost (first seen in the DoD in the 1960s (pp. 39 and 231)) and cost modelling will continue to be important. Scheduling of design work, and its optimal integration within the overall project schedule, will be a major project management activity. Simulation of schedule—

Fig. 64 (pages 300–301). Product life cycle technical activities flowchart (adapted from the DSMC system engineering guide 12/86)

CDR, critical design review	RFQ, request for quotation
CDRL, contract date requirements list	SDR, system design review
EDM, engineering development model	SPEC, specification
FCA, functional configuration audit	SOW, statement of work
FQR, formal qualification review	SQA, software quality assurance
IV & V, independent validation and verification	SRR, system requirement review
LCC, life cycle cost	SSR, software support equipment
PCA, physical configuration audit	TRR, test requirement review
PEP, product engineering proposal	WBS, work breakdown structure
PDR, preliminary design review	

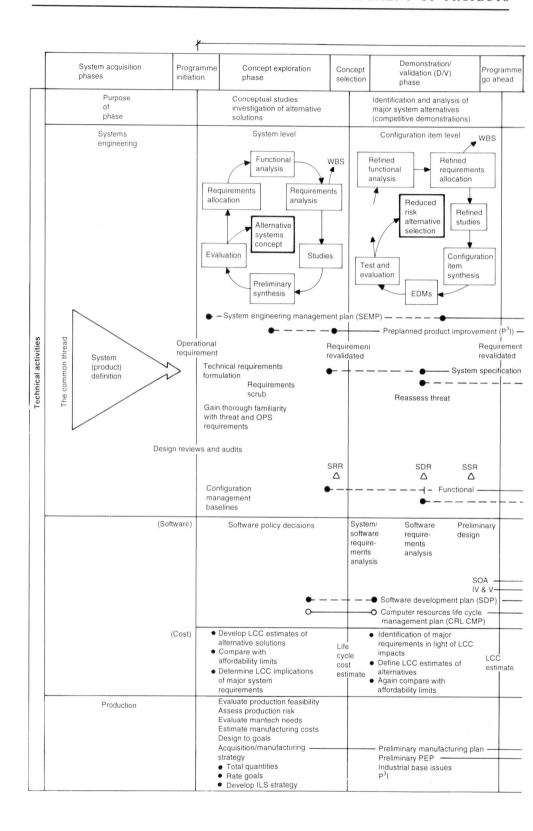

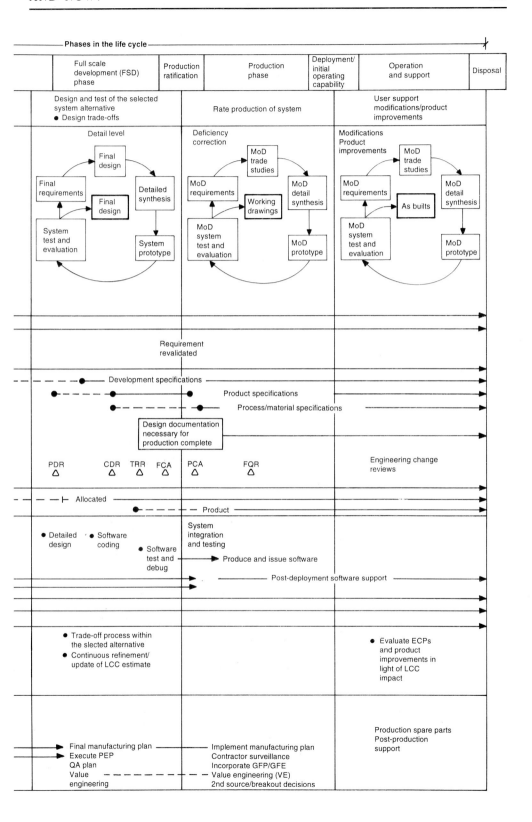

cost—performance trade-offs is increasingly valuable in assessing the cost and risk impacts of the accelerated schedule. The interest shown in the early 1990s in configuration management's enhanced role in Concurrent/Simultaneous Engineering will continue.[38]

Document management is central to effective design scheduling and configuration management. There will be substantial developments in CAD data handling tools such as PDES and STEP, so that by the turn of the century it will be common for huge amounts of data to be kept for a range of product 'attributes' on a project — physical characteristics, cost data, supplier information, and so on. While this information will be oriented around the project design, the key point in the 1990s is that increasingly all project information will be held in object-oriented databases rather than the traditional drawing-based file formats of the 1980s.

The 1990s will see a steady continuation of the trend begun in the 1980s to digitize all project data. The DoD, for example, launched its Computer-Aided Acquisition and Logistic Support project in 1992 to allow projects to be built and maintained with all data kept and cross-referenced electronically.[39] (In DoD's case this involves linking several hundred different sites.) Having data stored and integrated digitally will lead not only to cheaper and quicker procurement, but also to easier management of maintenance records, better quality information, quicker document access and greatly enriched possibilities of project modelling. However, there will still be substantial barriers to full and seamless electronic data interchange, due not so much to lack of agreement on technical standards as to the difficulty of getting legal and commercial protocols sufficiently agreed, particularly between different countries. Widespread adoption of Electronic Data Interchange (EDI), particularly in poorly regulated industries such as construction and across international protocols (note 21), will take time to come.

We can identify several *computing technologies* that will continue to improve radically the way we manage projects over the next decade. The increased use of object-oriented programming will allow more data to be cross-related more easily. Standard Query Language (SQL) and client—server technology will allow greater distribution of data handling onto PCs and networks (note 22). Groupware will increasingly allow disparate users to interconnect a wide range of systems and exchange data more easily. Developments in operating languages and standards by the end of the century will at last enable full data exchange between different systems on a project. Artificial Intelligence will progressively impact project management, moving from its current position of predominantly relatively simple analytic routines such as Expert Systems to more complex, synthesizing functions (note 23).[40–42] But for many users perhaps the most obvious and immediate developments will be in user friendliness: Graphical User Interfaces (GUIs), Windows, multimedia, voice recognition and the like, which by the early 1990s were already well on the way to revolutionizing and easing the way that users operate computers.

Add to these software developments the computer developments and telecommunications discussed above (pp. 277–278) and one can see that the likelihood of significantly greater use being made on projects of IT hardware is enormous. Multimedia, video conferencing, real-time data exchange over long distances, wireless computing in the field, powerful integrated computer–fax–telephone notebooks — all will be real and cutting-edge features of modern project IT in the late 1990s. The millennium will at last see the realization of much of the modelling power dreamt of and predicted for computers over the past 50 years.

The institutional development of the management of projects

Despite these technological and organizational developments, managing projects will not be easier in the next 10–20 years than it has been in the past. If anything it will be harder, particularly given the political, economic and financial uncertainties of the 1990s and the continuing emphasis on competitive productivity improvements.

Projects, ultimately, are managed by people. Not systems, not contracts — people. People working in organizations, doing jobs, operating systems, preparing plans, making decisions, communicating.

Selecting managers and developing them to become competent in managing the subjects and issues described in this book is a significant responsibility. Creating excellent managers, who have not just multiple functional skills but sensitivity and a perceptiveness towards the softer, more judgemental issues that are often crucial to project success, will be an outstanding requirement for the 1990s and beyond. The key lessons of the new discipline of 'the management of projects' is that the management task has suddenly and dramatically been expanded from the old, more mechanistic concept of project management.

Not everyone should expect, or be expected, to cover the gamut of issues encompassed by the management of projects. As before, many managers will do best to remain in their functions — cost, scheduling, procurement, etc. But for others, with the opening up of the discipline, there is now an immensely wider area that they can cover — finance and technology, environment and procurement, politics and organization. Moving into or out of these fields will require care and guidance. Effectiveness at senior levels of the project organization will require persons of exceptional breadth and ability. Identifying such persons, grooming them but not prematurely exposing them, will be a major task of senior management. Not much different from the traditional management function of career development and human resource management, perhaps, but now cast precisely within the broader framework of a new, richer discipline.

The principal characteristics of a person working in the management of projects in the 1990s will not be very different from those in previous decades — an ability to comprehend the technical, commercial, organizational and other issues inherent in his or her job; decisiveness; and a strong ability to get on with people. Those taking a senior position in management, however, will have to exhibit further crucial characteristics — above all, an ability to take a wide and comprehensive view of the current and upcoming issues posed by the project, and to integrate these into a focused, directed, course of action; an ability to communicate clearly and directly; and, generally, some international experience. As the 1990 Internet Expert Seminar recognized, project management tools and techniques represent only part of the knowledge and skill set required by managers of projects (Fig. 65). Much lies in understanding and being able to influence to the project's advantage the technology, business, environmental, financial and socio-political contexts of the project.

This, of course, is exactly the point made throughout this book — that to manage projects successfully managers need to attend to the wider and more strategic factors that affect project outcomes while still effectively deploying project management tools and techniques. This poses a major challenge for the professional project

Fig. 65. Principal competencies of a project manager (source: Internet, 1990)

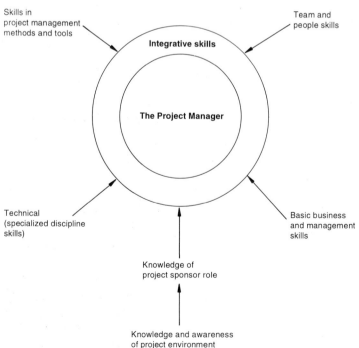

management community: although the development of managers will generally happen 'on the job' — on projects and in companies and other institutions — project organizations will always look to the academic and professional bodies for guidance on standards and materials and for expert resourcing. The professional project management societies, however, have generally been too under-resourced to provide much assistance in anything other than the more straightforward area of tools, techniques and organization-building skills.

Two things are happening in the 1990s that will change this. First, the project management societies are introducing 'certification'; in doing so they are both consciously broadening the required scope of a project manager's knowledge and experience and raising their own status within academia and the professions. Second, in recognition of the wider remit required of managers of projects, and helped by the rising profile of the project management societies, there should be increased collaboration between these societies and the other governmental and professional bodies associated with projects and management development — particularly the engineering societies and institutions, the legal and contracting bodies, and the standards institutions.

Certification was introduced first in the mid-1980s by the (US) Project Management Institute (p. 193). Since its introduction, the intellectual basis of US certification — the Body of Knowledge — has been revised two or three times (Fig. 66). Internet's most developed version, based around the UK's Association of Project Managers, was introduced in the early 1990s (Fig. 67); other European countries, notably Germany, are also developing certification programmes. The Australian Project Management Association is also considering introducing certification.

While the mechanics of certification differ between the various institutions, the aims and consequences are very similar. The aim is to provide formal recognition that an individual has reached a high level of competence in the discipline of project management; a by-product is thus the definition of the base of the discipline. This definition is provided by the Body of Knowledge. Fortunately, both the US and UK 'Bodies' have been defined in the early 1990s to reflect not just the internal processes of managing projects but also the wider organizational, technological and socio-economic contexts in which projects occur.

The Body of Knowledge had led to other important steps in the development of the discipline of project management, at least in the UK: a 'distributed' country-wide electronic library, keyed to the Body of Knowledge; accreditation services; and Continuing Professional Development programmes. Equally importantly, it has led to joint work with other professional bodies who are initiating certification programmes; several construction and IT professions, for example, began to initiate certification in the early

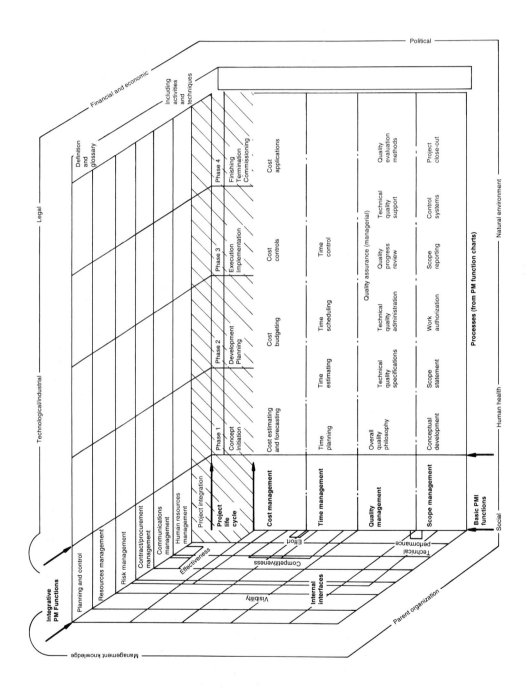

1990s but quickly realized that they could best do so by working jointly with Internet and its relevant national organizations.

These moves to formalize and strengthen the broader scope of project management, along the lines suggested by this book, are welcome. They will provide a reference for researchers, teachers and consultants in the years ahead, and help the discipline to grow healthily in the directions needed to ensure that projects are initiated, assessed, secured and accomplished successfully.

The future development of the management of projects

At its simplest, project management is very simple. It is very much like any other kind of management, except that one moves through a predetermined life cycle. Everything else, at this level, is covered by general management practices — planning, organizing, controlling and so on.

A little further investigation, however, reveals project definition, contracting, planning and measurement issues of some complexity. Considerable team leadership is also required, which is a real, distinct and enjoyable challenge for many up-and-coming middle managers.

For many, this is as far into project management as they want or need to go. Others, however, realize that there is a third level of complexity and management: the strategic level. This occupies almost entirely the front-end, definition stage of the project, but in fact continues throughout and across the life cycle. Typical important strategic issues crucial to the conduct of the project and the way it will evolve include definition, policy, strategy, technology, legal, financial, environmental, community and other issues.

Project management became public property as a new management discipline in the mid-1960s, initially only at the first level of sophistication. For most of the 1970s, public activity in project management largely involved spreading this basic message. It was only in the mid-to-late 1980s that sufficient inter-industry exchange of project management experience and practice had occurred for a multi-industry, universal model of best project management practice to emerge in any kind of robust form. And it was only in the late 1980s that the strategic dimension began to be accepted as a necessary part of the broader discipline of the management of projects.

The challenges as we approach the 21st century are substantial. As this chapter has shown, major changes in the discipline are still under way (Fig. 68). Tracking these, placing them properly in their relevant industry context, developing them, and integrating them into the general corpus of knowledge of the management of projects is the task now facing us.

Fig. 66 (facing page). The PMI Body of Knowledge (USA) (courtesy Project Management Institute)

An even bigger one will be to develop the professional and institutional environment required to nurture and develop this exciting and growing discipline. The project management societies

APM Certification Self Assessment Form

Candidate's Name: Industry:

Project Management

High			Medium			Low			
10	9	8	7	6	5	4	3	2	1	0

- Systems Management
- Program Management
- Project Management
- Project Life Cycle
- Project Environment
- Project Strategy
- Project Appraisal
- Project Success/Failure Criteria
- Integration
- Systems & Procedures
- Quality
- Safety

Organisation & People

High			Medium			Low			
10	9	8	7	6	5	4	3	2	1	0

- Organisation Design
- Control & Co-ordination
- Communication
- Leadership
- Delegation
- Team Building
- Conflict Management
- Negotiation
- Management Development

Processes & Procedures

High			Medium			Low			
10	9	8	7	6	5	4	3	2	1	0

- Work Definition
- Planning
- Scheduling
- Estimating
- Cost Control
- Performance Measurement
- Design Management
- Risk Management
- Value Engineering
- Change Control
- Procurement
- Mobilisation
- Close-out

General Management

High			Medium			Low			
10	9	8	7	6	5	4	3	2	1	0

- Operational/Technical Management
- Marketing & Sales
- Finance
- Information Technology
- Law
- Industrial Relations

APM certification involves the following.

- Candidates first rate their knowledge and experience levels on the Self Assessment Form, guided by the Help Sheets like that for Team Building, shown on the facing page.

- They then submit a 5000 word essay on a recent project management assignment, provide two references, and are interviewed by two Assessors.

Example Help Sheet for the Self Assessment Form

TEAM BUILDING

Definition

The ability to assemble the right people to join the project team and to get everybody working together for the benefit of the project. This can be achieved both in a formal manner, by use of project start-up meetings, seminars, and workshops, and in a more informal manner by getting people to work well together and gradually build a tempo in the early stages of a project. Motivating and resolving conflict between individual members of the team are important elements of team building.

Knowledge

High Level: Extensive knowledge of the literature on Organisation Behaviour, particularly in a project context including an understanding of the informal organisation, theories of group behaviour, cross cultural and multi-disciplinary team working, motivation and team building. Good knowledge of people.

Medium Level: Exposure to management writings on group working, motivation and the informal organisation, particularly in a project context.

Low Level: Some knowledge of academic writings on management. Some practical appreciation of how people work together.

Experience

High Level: Considerable experience in melding disparate personalities and people of different skills, educational backgrounds or national cultures, to work together as effectively as teams. Experience of doing this for different sized teams, of different composition, on a variety of different project types.

Medium Level: Experience in working as part of several teams in different project situations.

Low Level: Awareness of what is involved in creating a team sense of purpose and spirit on several different 'team' occasions.

References

Andersen E S, Grude K V, Haug T and Turner J R. "Goal Directed Project Management", Kogan Page, 1987

Bennigson L A "The Team Approach to Project Management" Management Review Vol 61, January 1972 pp 48-52

Davison-Frame J "Managing Projects in Organisations", Jossey-Bass Publishers, 1987

Graham R J "Project Management as if People Mattered", Prima Vera Press, 1985

Hofstede G "Cultural Dimensions for project management" International Journal of Project Management Vol 1(1) 2/83 pp 41-48

Hunt J W "Managing People at Work" (2nd edition) McGraw-Hill 1986

Fig. 67 (facing page and above). The APM Body of Knowledge (UK) (courtesy Association of Project Managers)

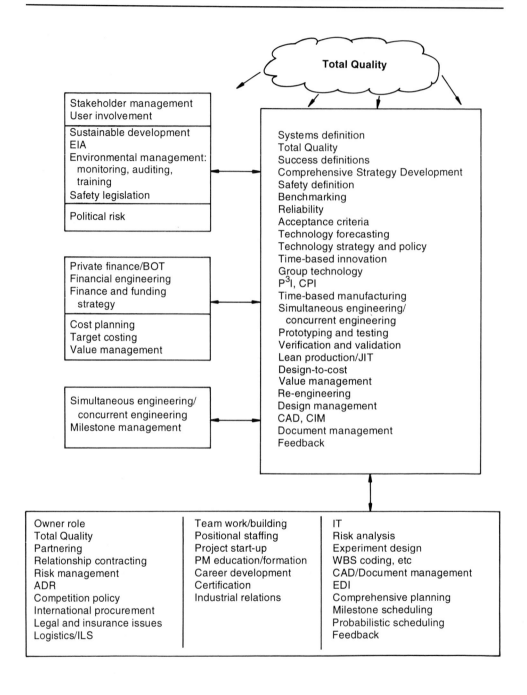

Fig. 68. Cutting-edge issues of the 1990s in the management of projects

are still weak, and are likely to remain so for some years yet. There is not yet a popular guru or a strong intellectual voice recognized by the managerially curious 'man in the street' on either side of the Atlantic.

It will come. But there is meanwhile much work for us all to do. And opportunity. And fun!

References

1. Committee for Development Planning. *Human resource development: a neglected dimension of development strategy.* United Nations publication, Sales No. E.88.II.A.II, 1988.

2. Griffen, K. and Knight, J. Human development in the 1980s and beyond. *Journal of Development Planning,* No. 19, 1989.

3. World Bank. *The challenge of development.* World Development Report 1991, Oxford University Press, 1991.

4. World Bank. *Development and the environment.* World Development Report 1992, Oxford University Press, 1992.

5. Espedal, R., Hetland, P. W. and Jordanger, I. TOPPs, a new project planning concept. *International Journal of Project Management,* **10,** No. 2, 1992, May, 102–106.

6. James, L. Outsourcing vs system integration services. *Systems Integration Business,* **25,** No. 7, 1992, July, 15.

7. Feigenbaum, A. V. *Total quality control,* 3rd edn. McGraw-Hill, New York, 1983.

8. Crosby, P. B. *Quality is free.* McGraw-Hill, New York, 1979.

9. Deming, W. E. *Out of crisis.* Massachusetts Institute of Technology, Cambridge, MA, 1989.

10. Juran, J. M. *Quality control handbook.* McGraw-Hill, New York, 1974.

11. Fitzpatrick, E. W. Information management: business re-engineering. *Journal of the American Society of CLU & ChFC,* **46,** No. 5, 1992, Sept., 34–35.

12. Hammer, M. and Champy, J. *Re-engineering the corporation: a manifesto for business revolution.* Harper Business, New York, 1993.

13. Rasmus, D. 'Re-engineering' or evolution through violent overthrow. *Manufacturing Systems,* **10,** No. 9, 1992, Sept., 52–58.

14. Wilkinson, R. Re-engineering: industrial engineering in action. *Industrial Engineering,* **23,** No. 8, 1991, Aug., 47–49.

15. Katzenbach, J. R. and Smith, D. K. *The wisdom of teams: creating the high-performing organization.* Harvard Business School, Cambridge, MA, 1993.

16. Rossy, G. L. and Archibald, R. D. Building commitment in project teams. *Project Management Journal,* **23,** No. 2, 1992, June, 5–14.

17. Cleland, D. I. Product design teams: the simultaneous engineering perspective. *Project Management Journal,* **22,** No. 4, 1991, Dec., 5–10.

18. Moskal, B. S. Product design: GM's new-found religion. *Industry Week,* **241,** No. 10, 18 May, 1992, 42–53.

19. Steudel, H. J. and Desruelle, P. *Manufacturing in the nineties: how to become a lean, mean, world-class competitor.* Van Nostrand-Reinhold, New York, 1992.

20. Wesley Allen, C. (ed.). *Simultaneous engineering — integrating manufacturing and design.* Society for Manufacturing Engineers, Dearborn, MI, 1992.

21. Inwood, D. and Hammond, J. *Product development: an integrated approach.* Kogan Page, London, 1993.

22. O'Connor, J. T. and Norwich, W. Fossil power plant schedule compression tactics: lessons from independent power producers. *Project Management Journal,* **24,** No. 3, 1993, Sept., 34–42.

23. Lawlor, E. E. *The ultimate advantage: creating the high involvement organization.* Maxwell Macmillan, London, New York, 1992.

24. Dimarco, N., Goodison, J. R. and Houser, H. F. Situational leadership in a project/matrix environment. *Project Management Journal,* **20,** No. 1, 1989, Mar., 11–18.

25. Petersen, N. Selecting project managers: an integrated list of predictors. *Project Management Journal,* **22,** No. 2, 1991, June, 21–26.

26. Gareis, R. Management by projects: the management strategy of the

'new' project-orientated company. *International Journal Project Management*, **2**, 1991, May, 71–76.

27. Erickson, T. J. Worldwide R&D management: concepts and applications. *Columbia Journal of World Business*, **25**, No. 4, 1990, Winter, 8–13.

28. Roussel, P. A., Saad, K. M. and Erickson, T. J. The evolution of Third Generation R&D. *Planning Review*, **19**, No. 2, 1991, Mar.–Apr., 18–26.

29. Starr, M. K. The role of project management in a fast response organization. *Journal of Engineering and Technology Management*, **7**, No. 2, 1990, Sept., 89–110.

30. Wheelwright, S. C. and Clark, K. B. Creating project plans to focus product development. *Harvard Business Review*, **70**, No. 2, 1992, Mar.–Apr., 70–82.

31. Musselwhite, C. W. Time-based innovation: the new competitive advantage. *Training & Development Journal*, **44**, No. 1, 1990, Jan., 53–56.

32. Turino, J. *Managing concurrent engineering — buying time to market*. Van Nostrand Reinhold, New York, 1992.

33. Cochrane, C. Defense acquisition policy. A new set of directives for 'A disciplined management approach'. *Program Manager*, 1991, May–June, 29–34.

34. Heberling, M. E., Wagner, C. F. and Rendon, R. G. The F-22 advanced tactical fighter: the Air Force Model Acquisition Program. *PM Network*, **7**, No. 9, 1993, Sept., 12–20.

35. Otis, I. Designing for manufacture and assembly to improve efficiency and quality. *Industrial Engineering*, **24**, No. 8, 1992, Aug., 60–62.

36. Skimin, W. E., Smith, D. E., Darrel, E. J. O., Krolicki, J. C. and Zenner, K. D. Scope management on an automotive tooling project. *Project Management Journal*, **22**, No. 3, 1991, Sept., 22–26.

37. De Meyer, A. *Creating the virtual factory*. Insead, Fontainbleau, 1993.

38. Sweetman, S. L. Utilizing expert systems to improve the configuration management process. *Project Management Journal*, **21**, No. 1, 1990, Mar., 5–12.

39. Nordwall, B. D. Digital data system expected to benefit defense and industry. *Aviation Week & Space Technology*, **132**, No. 6, 5 February, 1990, 66–70.

40. Currie, K. and Drabble, B. Knowledge-based planning systems: a tour. *International Journal of Project Management*, **10**, No. 3, 1992, Aug., 131–137.

41. Winstanley, G. and Kellet, J. M. A computer-based configuration and planning system. *International Journal of Project Management*, **11**, No. 2, 1993, May, 103–109.

42. Diekmann, J. E. and Al-Tabtabai, H. Knowledge-based approach to construction project control. *International Journal of Project Management*, **9**, No. 3, 1991, Aug., 169–178.

43. Nicolo, E. Metaproject analysis: a systematic methodological aid for strategic planning. *Project management without boundaries, Proc. 11th Internet World Congress on Project Management, Italy, 16–19 June*, Vol. 2, 1992.

Notes

Chapter 2

1. Noah (after the Creator himself) has claims to be one of the earliest known project managers.

2. 'The pyramid project was creating a type of community which had never existed before. Tribal villagers were welded by common work into people with the consciousness of nationhood. It was probably for the first time that they thought of themselves first and foremost as Egyptians.'[1] In the case of Stonehenge, many authors have commented on the importance of the centrality of Stonehenge's location and on the huge demands on manpower that the building of Stonehenge made, and the implications of these resource demands on the state of the secular society at that time.[2-3] (Cummins, following Atkinson, says of Stonehenge III (the famous circle of trilithons most people associate with Stonehenge) that hauling the stones from Avebury must have required the effort of at least 750 men for six to nine years with 50 masons being involved in dressing the stones. Overall, Stonehenge III 'might have occupied the entire adult population of an area of, at the very least, 260 km^2 for six to nine years.')

3. Vauban's projects were documented by an explanatory memorandum (*Mémoire*), several sheets of drawings and a covering letter (*Lettre d'envoi*). The *Mémoire* included a general background of the scheme, a detailed description of the constituent parts (including references to the drawings), cost estimates, and notes on special features and advantages of the work.

4. Meetings of civil engineers were held under Smeaton at the King's Head Tavern, Holborn, from March 1771. At Palmer's initiative, the (British) Institution of Civil Engineers was formed in 1818, with Telford becoming its first President in 1820. (That the Institution was conscious of the political dimension of projects is evidenced by the location of its headquarters — just a few hundred yards from Parliament. One of the jobs of the Engineer was, after all, to secure planning permission for his client's project; generally this was obtained from Parliament.)[5-6]

5. Paul Kennedy has a more sophisticated summary of the reasons why the General Staffs found it so difficult to break the stalemate on the Western Front: they involve crucially the *technology* of supply and communications.

   - Allied naval power could not exercise a decisive, quick impact on the Axis' large, land-based economy.
   - The 'absence of a means to achieve a real breakthrough' in the land battles simply meant that armies were decimated whenever a big push was attempted (there being no effective way to bring up supplies or reinforcements, nothing to deal with the withering counterfire, no effective battlefield communications).
   - Germany enjoyed two specific advantages: in its advances of 1914 it had captured the ridges of high ground which it then occupied while staying largely on the defensive, and it had good internal communications, allowing efficient troop deployment between its Eastern and Western fronts.[7]

6. 'This is a 90° rotated bar chart type graph with a vertical time scale, and a column (strip) for each activity in the project ... The activity

strips are ordered so that the predecessors of any given activity will always be found to its left. The activity strips each contain a movable tab whose length is proportional to the estimated duration of the activity, and whose location along the time scale denotes the scheduled start and finish time for each activity . . . The Harmonygraph is equivalent to an arrow diagram.'[8]

7. 'The nature of the inter-relation between departments organized on the basis of purpose and those organized on the basis of process may be illustrated best by considering the former as vertical departments, and the latter as horizontal departments.'[9]

Chapter 3

1. On D-Day, 72 215 British and Canadian and 57 500 American troops landed from the sea, and 23 000 Allied troops landed by air in 1087 transport aircraft and 804 gliders. The next day, a further 55 000 men were landed by sea. By then, 19 000 vehicles had been put ashore. There had been over 4000 landings supported by 1300 merchant ships and ancillary craft and over 1200 warships.[10] Seven weeks later, 1 450 000 Allied troops had been landed; the Allied armies by then required 26 000 tons of stores a day. Many of the provisions were landed on two specially built Mulberry harbours (45 000 men had been employed on their construction) which were erected within a few days of the first landings and handled 12 000 tons of supplies and 2500 vehicles per day. Six weeks after D-Day, fuel was being pumped from England to France directly through the Pipeline Under The Ocean (PLUTO).

2. Over half of one of the most authoritative recent books on this subject, *The making of the atom bomb*,[11] deals with the period preceding General Groves' posting, thus illustrating nicely one of the truisms of projects, that the early phases are immensely important, often of significant duration compared to the overall duration of the project, and generally either undermanaged or unmanaged.

3. The principles of fission had been developed in 1937 in Germany by Hahn and Strassman, with Lise Meitner (an Austrian Jewess who had fled to Sweden that year, where she worked at a distance with the other two), following Sir James Chadwick's discovery of neutrons at Cambridge in 1932 and Fermi's work identifying radioactive substances in Italy (before he too fled Fascism for the USA in 1937).

4. The time between the first chain reaction and the first nuclear explosion was $2\frac{1}{2}$ years. The Soviets took exactly the same length of time for the development of their first atomic bomb: they began work in earnest in 1942 but were interrupted by the German invasion. Their first chain reaction was in August 1949.[12] (The Soviet effort was aided immensely by information provided by the British spy Ernest Fuchs, who was intimately involved with the Manhattan Project.)

5. Concurrency, described elsewhere in this book, is the simultaneous design, development and production of a project.

6. There were extremely interesting similarities between the Soviet and US programmes. Fortescue's comparison of the two underscores the project management features of both undertakings: 'The history of the development of the Soviet atom bomb . . . reads not unlike that of the Manhattan Project. While the role of the USSR's Oppenheimer, Igor Kuratchov, might be exaggerated at the expense of Malyshev, Vannikov and Zaveniagin, the Soviet equivalents of General Groves, one gets the impression of a *very clear goal* with all *necessary resources* being devoted to its achievement; the encouragement of work on competing approaches, but all under the strict overall control of a *single person*; the closest possible cooperation between science and production, with indeed stern subordination of the former to the latter; a good understanding of the need to work towards the final goal stage by stage while integrating an

enormous number of discrete processes; and a *project structure*, in this case based on a special organization just for this project, the famous Laboratory No. 2'[13–15] [my italics].

Chapter 4

1. In fact, the development of US missiles had proceeded cautiously during the early 1950s, since there had been considerable scepticism as to the superiority of missiles over bombers due to the newness of rocket technology and the expectation that the weight of the thermonuclear warheads might prove too large for these new machines.

2. It could be argued that this is not different in principle to the way in which building and civil engineering were run. In practice the situation was soon to prove different in that the systems support contractor (*a*) was involved significantly in technical design issues, and (*b*) traded these off against schedule and other parameters. Building and civil engineering projects, being at that time generally less complex, were run by designers who concentrated more on detailed design and were not required to involve themselves as much with ongoing managerial decisions and trade-offs.

3. The power of Admiral Rickover is discussed in the context of the development of nuclear power on pp. 119 and p. 320, note 30.

4. 'Line-of-Balance' is a technique developed largely in manufacturing to optimize the balance of outputs and inputs at each successive stage of an assembly line. Studies were conducted throughout the decades following Taylor, Gantt, *et al.* on LOB. Computer programs on LOB were developed in the late 1950s and early 1960s. In construction, the technique was developed in the UK particularly for housebuilding.[16–21]

5. Engineers were asked to estimate three durations for each event or activity: the optimistic *a*, pessimistic *b* and most likely *m* times. Assuming a beta distribution, the most likely estimated time t_e is given by $(a + 4m + b)/6$.

6. The Soviet Union developed its own version of PERT, *Setevoe planirovanie i upravlenie* (network planning and management).[13,22]

7. The impact of the techniques themselves was substantial, however: the CEGB's technique brought reductions in shut-down durations first of 42%, it was claimed, and later of a further 32%.[23]

8. Schedule data were obtained via Work Study, estimating and activity network sequencing.

9. NASA's predecessor had been the National Advisory Committee for Aeronautics (NACA). NACA was solely an aeronautical research organization: it did not have the sponsoring, operational or managerial responsibilities of NASA.[24]

10. See Clarence L. Battle's *SPO code* for a vigorous and amusing view of how a Systems Program Office should be run 'at the sharp end'.[25]

Chapter 5

1. C/SCSC = Cost and Schedule Control System Criteria (this technique is explained on p. 47); SAIMS = Selected Acquisitions Information and Management System (a resource management system that obtained information from contractors' management systems in a form desired by DoD managers); SAR = Selected Acquisition Report (high-level report for the Secretary of Defense providing details on progress, problems, etc. for selected programmes).

2. MPM employed a graphical system of 'knots' (dots and circles) and 'strips' (connections between the knots in the form of lines with or without flow directions) in which the start of one activity was specified to lag a certain time after the start of its preceding activity.

3. RPS used blocks, connections and knots (branching or collecting points) to calculate the critical path(s).

4. Or Project Breakdown Structure, as Russell Archibald would prefer.

5. As witnessed for example as recently as the 1980s with the use of the 'Key Date' procedure by the CEGB, and later by Eurotunnel and other employers.[26]

6. See for example the writings by Archibald, Dinsmore and myself in the 1980s.[27–29]

7. A Blue Ribbon Defense Panel estimated that in Fiscal Year 1969 the cost of operating these mandatory management systems was $4·4bn![30]

8. Tom Wolfe's *The right stuff* provides a wonderful description of this period of NASA's man-in-space programme.[31]

9. Minuteman was the successor to Atlas: lighter and cheaper, it was solid-fuelled and could be launched within 60 seconds of an alert (hence its name) — Atlas took too long to fuel, ignite and accelerate for attack conditions. Unlike Atlas, Minuteman was not based above ground — Atlas was extremely vulnerable to first strike, and in effect offered no deterrent at all. Minuteman did. Along with Polaris and the B52, Minuteman constituted America's three-pronged delivery system for its nuclear deterrent during the bulk of the 1970s.

10. The matrix organization had recently been introduced into several arms of the US armed forces.

11. This work is best summarized by Merrow *et al.* in their two reports.[32,33]

12. Citing Polaris, Metcalfe and Rowley make a plea for a stronger project focus: 'One would like to see for each major system an Industrial Prime Contractor reporting to a full-time and very senior Project Director ... If one cannot appoint a man of the appropriate seniority, experience and ability to run full time on the Government's behalf a project costing, say, £100m or more, one cannot complain if things go wrong.'[34] One might bear this comment in mind when reviewing the Nimrod experience of 10–15 years later (pp. 154–156). The plea was to be made for some decades to follow, on both sides of the Atlantic.

13. A Ministry of Supply study of 1958 showed that for about 100 defence projects, final costs exceeded initial estimates by a factor of 2·8 on average. The main reasons were: (*a*) changes in requirements, (*b*) lack of programme definition, (*c*) incomplete appreciation by the contractor of the work necessary and (*d*) inflation.[35]

14. The estimate of what a proper fixed price should be at the initiation of the production phase of Bloodhound was extremely difficult, since the missile was one of the first to be built in Britain and there was no experience available on which to prepare an estimate. It was therefore decided to fix the price later, by agreement. The data used to determine Ferranti's price were in the end drawn from the early stages of its contract, before production costs had begun to settle down. To make it even harder to agree a proper price, the government officials had no substantive knowledge of the technology. Further, the organization of the administration of the contract was not clear. The Ministry's Director of Contracts was ultimately responsible for the contract, but he had neither the requisite technical knowledge to question the contract nor any authority over the Ministry's cost personnel. It was thus unfair to hold him responsible for the pricing of the Bloodhound contract, a fact later recognized by the Government.

15. This criticism may have been overstated: both the Treasury and the Ministry of Supply were represented on the Defence Research Policy Committee.

16. One must thus feel sceptical of Gardner's more partial account: 'The whole TSR-2 concept was a terrific challenge ... the British industry responded wonderfully to that challenge ... What, however, was beyond the British ability (or anyone else's for that matter) at the time, was to

evolve a project management system which ever looked like being able to control such a vast and complex undertaking and keep the cost within bounds. For this, some blame must lie at the door of industry ... A large share of it, however, belongs to Whitehall with its proliferation of committees, its buck-passing, and its costly [Gibb–Zuckerman] time-wasting, which latter, in the end, was to be TSR-2's undoing in that it played into the Treasury's hands.'[36]

17. The contracts for most of the TSR-2's life were cost-plus. It was the Ministry's desire that these be changed to fixed-price once the design became firm. Unfortunately, the delay in achieving the latter meant that the former was also delayed.

18. As John Simpson wrote in 1970: 'This structure ... was a subtle compromise between the Special Projects Office of having all personnel directly concerned with the project within one integrated organization, and the usual British practice of allocating all work on a departmental basis and co-ordinating projects through inter- and intra-departmental committees, which had difficulty in reaching rapid decisions. It also differed markedly from the organizational approach adopted for a contemporary weapons systems project, the TSR-2. In this, responsibility for progressing the project lay with the main civilian contractor, but in practice the fact that all official sub-contractors had contractual relations with the Ministry of Aviation meant that a real centre of responsibility for the project was never created.'[37]

19. The others were Brian Pyle and Ronald Burbridge.

20. A further NEDO report, *Engineering construction performance* of 1977,[38] demonstrated the seriousness of UK performance in relation to similar projects in the USA and mainland Europe. After lengthy negotiation the agreement was implemented in 1981, but its scope was constrained to engineering construction work, the civil engineers declining to participate. After its introduction, which coincided with a downturn in activity, the industry's record in completing projects to schedule and budget improved substantially.

21. 'It is important that the project should be clearly defined, that the definition should remain valid during the whole period of the work, that it should be understood by the project leadership, and moreover that they should be in sympathy with the definition.'[39]

22. This is true of the UK and US construction industries, but not necessarily of other countries. In Japan, for example, construction companies usually carry out both design and construction work. This makes 'the construction company itself responsible for the quality of its product and enables the company to better perform the budgetary planning, production control, and maintenance service that will most benefit the clients'.[40]

23. The principle of separating architects from builders was incorporated in the charter of the Royal Institute of British Architects in 1887. The 1931 Architects Registration Act meant that architects could not hold a position in a building firm. This prohibition, which ceased only in the 1980s, in effect formalized the separation of building design from building production.

24. The Tavistock Institute, originally interested primarily in psycho-social issues but by the late 1950s and early 1960s increasingly involved in industrial matters, was a pioneer of the 'systems approach' to organization. Elliott Jacques led much of the Tavistock Institute's early work in management, working with Wilfred Brown of the Glacier Metal Company to create a social science approach to a broad range of organizational and management issues.[41]

25. Checkland's book *Systems thinking, systems practice* provides one of the best detailed reviews of systems theory and its origins.[42]

26. Emery's term was soon to characterize the Tavistock approach; before long the 'socio-technic school' was seen to offer a sensible, comprehensive view of management that built on and superseded previous ones such as Weber's on bureaucracy, the scientific school of Taylor, Gilbreth and Gantt, the administrative school of Fayol, Urwick, Bernard and others, and the human relations school of Roethlisberger, Mayo, *et al.*

27. I would add 'organization', and would point out that, on most projects, not one of these four natural discontinuities is to be found during the design phase. This is why, unless one introduces an artificial, so to speak, review point such as NASA's First Article Configuration Review, one can find oneself moving from Scheme Design to Detail Design, with totally inadequate review and management.

28. Sayles and Chandler's example of the AEC (the US Atomic Energy Commission) as an institution that would brook no public dissent was both typical and symptomatic of the massive misreading of the nuclear industry that was being made at this time. A decade later, the nuclear power industry was in deep trouble precisely because of the factors Sayles and Chandler are here identifying (see pp. 125 and 160−163).

Chapter 6

1. There was no formal objective for the project other than the requirement 'to carry passengers across the Atlantic safely and supersonically through the world's air traffic control systems'; there were certainly no commercial objectives. For an extended account of Concorde see Feldman,[43] Hayward,[44] Knight,[45] Morris and Hough (Ref. 26, chapter 2), Williams,[46] etc.

2. By this time the manufacturers were coming under strong pressure from the Government (the Ministry of Technology) to control and report costs better. The British Aircraft Corporation (BAC) found it difficult to identify the areas to be controlled and to find suitably trained staff, however. In 1967 BAC established a Director specifically responsible for Concorde's cost control. The project was now broken down into 14 'design areas' or 'chapters', each of which was then split into 15 'task areas' and finally into 200 or so more detailed categories. The Ministry required quarterly reports, and identified over 700 milestones against which it required progress to be reported. These reporting requirements failed, however, and a simpler system was installed in 1969.

3. The British Government wanted industry to assume some financial risk for the project at this juncture, but the companies concerned made it clear they were either unable or unwilling to do this. Throughout the project, therefore, the work was undertaken on a 'cost plus fixed fee' basis. The Government attempted to introduce contracts containing firmer incentives, but with little success.

4. In particular that insufficient account had been taken of the effects of noise, access, industrial development, land acquisitions, etc.

5. The approach began by specifying objectives, generating technically feasible alternatives and then evaluating their economic and social consequences. Both direct and indirect benefits and costs were considered, from three viewpoints: the project itself (financial analysis), the economic system (public or economic analysis), and the socio-politico-economic system (social cost−benefit analysis).

6. Similar problems stalled the proposed development of a series of ring roads around London. The Government had launched a new initiative to tackle the problem of London's chronic traffic congestion in the early 1960s; it sought to use modern 'American' 'scientific' transportation planning principles and appointed Colin Buchanan to produce a report on 'traffic in towns'. To accommodate the automobile in an environmentally acceptable way, Buchanan argued, required a massive

increase in spending on urban roads.[47] The resultant London transportation plan became incorporated in the Greater London Development Plan of 1969, and was made the subject of a public inquiry headed by Sir Frank Layfield in 1970 that 'was to rival Roskill ... as the most protracted planning inquiry in British history'. The Government argued that without investment London's traffic congestion would increase to unacceptable levels; opponents, largely from local community groups, argued that the American 'scientific' approach misread traffic patterns, that it not only assumed but also created increased traffic flows and that its economic justification was awry. Over the next several months community opposition to the proposals grew, and in 1975 the newly elected Labour local government announced that it was abandoning the proposed motorways ring-way scheme (along with Maplin and the Channel Tunnel). Community opposition had been reflected in the democratic process. The Government responded to voters and chose congestion over unpopularity.

7. Cicchetti provides a critique of the cost—benefit assumptions underlying TAPS.[48]

8. A state in which the soil is permanently frozen. Building in permafrost requires special care: if the construction causes the frost to melt then, among other things, the ground becomes very soft and unstable.

9. This sentence was written before the catastrophic Exxon Valdez disaster in March 1989 in which 11 million gallons of oil were spilt into Prince William Sound, which was to heighten the already serious concern over the environmental impact of major projects (see pp. 163—166).

10. That is, the cost of building pipelines in the 48 US states south of Canada; rates were $750 000 per mile for buried-pipe and $1·5 million per mile for above-ground construction.

11. Prepared by Alyeska at a cost of $11m and 175 person years.

12. Staff of the regulatory agencies working on TAPS numbered almost 200; as of November 1975 'the average time the Authorized Officer took to review the applications and issue the 230 Federal notices-to-proceed was about 70 days; the average time the state pipeline coordinator took for the 449 state notices was about 65 days'.[49]

13. Sohio, Arco, Exxon, BP, Mobil, Union of California, Phillips and Amerada Hess.

14. 'Approximately 50% of these increases were due to inflation, 30% to environmental requirements and 20% to other items such as design changes or changes in engineering standards imposed by reviewing government agencies.'[50]

15. See Cleland[51] and Fox[52] for two views on what constitutes prudent and reasonable project management.

16. That is, *pace* Moolin and McCoy, Downey (the later Rayner and the MoD/Efficiency study (see pp. 102—104 and 153)), at about the 15% complete point.[53—56]

17. These ideas were explored in my research on the construction industry in the late 1960s and early 1970s.[57,58]

18. Whether one takes $3\frac{1}{2}$ or 4 years as the schedule overrun depends on whether or not one includes the six months mobilization period; it is said that of the £329·3m overrun, 70% was due to cost inflation (for which no allowance was included in the original budget), 5% to design enhancements, 10% to construction difficulties not covered in the contract, and 15% to poor productivity (caused by industrial relations problems or poor management or both).[59]

19. There were earlier antecedents: Bovis, for example had been acting as professional construction managers for the retailers Marks and Spencer since the 1920s (operating on a 'management fee' principle.) In the

process industries, particularly where US practice dominated, the role was similarly old — see Stone & Webster on the Manhattan Project, for instance.

20. Robert F. Hastings wrote in the *Architectural Record* in November 1968 of the need to balance Decision, Design and Delivery: to give management attention to the decision to build and to the purpose, scope and configuration; the design of the building; and the delivery (construction) of the building.[60]

21. The principal concepts underlying these construction management approaches entirely reflected the ideas on integration being expressed by management theorists at about this time (p. 74): 'The owner ... is the key member of the project development team. Only he can select and organize the professional team, define his own needs, set his priorities and make final decisions ... the project team must have all the capabilities required to deal with all the project problems; all of these capabilities should be brought to bear at the earliest possible time; the project should be regarded and managed as a single, integrated and continuous process from programming through design and delivery.'[61]

22. NPV is the future net cash flows of a project discounted (at the cost of capital) to their *present value* equivalent, less the capital cost of initiating the project.[62,63]

23. The PSC approach was developed more readily in the North Sea than in the building and civil engineering industries since in the process industries there was more of a tradition of project management, and owners were generally better staffed with experienced people. This support function practice was often deployed in a similar way on developing country projects. Where there was a strong technology transfer requirement this arrangement often led to a 'shadow management' function.

24. A sovereign guarantee is a guarantee given by a sovereign nation.

25. Take-or-pay is in effect an unconditional guarantee: the purchaser will pay even if the product or service is not available.[64]

26. In the North Sea, the UK and Norwegian governments were able to give assurances as to the validity of licences that satisfied the financiers. The UK Government, however, changed the taxation regime for North Sea oil quite significantly between 1970 and 1985, and this had a marked impact on developers' plans in both general and specific terms (see for example my study ref. 26, chapter 7) of the Fulmar field — indeed, the Fulmar case shows dramatically how political decisions (or lack of them) regarding the proposed route for exporting Fulmar's associated gas affected the engineering process and, as a result, caused delays and difficulties throughout the duration of the project.

27. As Magee and Brock have noted, 'Because of the importance of speed in moving the massive inflow of petrodollars, the banks transferred their normal economic functions of project appraisal and risk screening to ldc governments through government guarantees. This bias leaned towards political operators and away from economic projects.'[65]

28. McKinsey's data do not in fact cover defence, aerospace or telecommunications; projects in these sectors absorbed huge sums.

29. Nuclear plants were built comparatively successfully in several other countries at this time — generally by experienced contractors using established technology in politically supportive environments.

30. Rickover attended a meeting of the AEC's General Advisory Committee — including Conant, Fermi, Teller and Oppenheimer — at Oak Ridge in the summer of 1947 as an observer. When the committee concluded that it would take 20 years to develop useful power from the atom, Rickover interrupted, berating those present for adopting a scientific

approach to an engineering problem. In fact, within six years Rickover had developed a prototype power plant (for the USS Nautilus). Rickover is credited with accomplishing such an impressive feat as a result of his vision, energy, drive and relentlessness; his selection and use of people; the two-hat administrative system he devised (Rickover and his staff worked simultaneously for the Navy and the AEC); and the on-the-job education and training he provided for his staff.[66–69]

31. This unhappy story is expertly documented by Hannah[70] and Williams;[71] I have examined the AGR selection and construction processes in some detail in *The anatomy of major projects* (ref. 26, chapter 6).

32. These incentives were developed by the CEGB by methods including its Key Date Procedure, which has proved particularly worthwhile. If a contractor does not achieve his scheduled progress by the contractual key date (milestone), payment is withheld. This sanction has the benefit of concentrating senior management's attention on contract performance. The same method was later used on other major projects in the late 1980s and 1990s (ref. 26, chapter 6).

33. Similar geophysical problems were encountered in Brazil, where billions of dollars were spent constructing two units near Rio de Janeiro on ground with inadequate foundation support (the project was eventually abandoned), and in the Philippines, where a plant was built on the island of Bataan too near a volcano (the completed plant was later demolished). Cincinatti's Midland plant was built on unsuitable ground, and eventually had to be abandoned in 1984 after budgets had risen from $240m to $3·1bn.

34. QA was not seen in the same mandatory context in the UK as in the USA. The UK philosophy was that the operator must satisfy the Nuclear Installation Inspectorate (NII) that the plant was safe. Rather than meet predefined standards, as in the US, UK practice was that the operator would develop safety criteria for acceptance by the NII from which guidelines would be derived for use in preparation of the plant's safety case. The NII then approved the design and issued a licence to begin construction, monitored construction and, when it was satisfied that construction was in conformance with the licensed design, permitted commissioning of the plant.

In the USA, the Nuclear Regulatory Commission defines QA as including 'those quality assurance actions related to the physical characteristics of a material, structure, component or system which provide a means to control the quality of the material, structure, component or system to predetermined requirements'. In the UK, BS 4778 defines QA as 'embracing all activities and functions concerned with the attainment of quality rather than in the narrow sense only of the provision of proof associated with the word "assurance". Thus quality assurance includes the determination and assessment of quality'.[72,73]

35. The historic Calvert Cliffs judgement of July 1971 — that the requirement for an Environmental Impact Statement, as required under the National Environment Policy Act (NEPA) had not been submitted — was a landmark, providing environmentalists with the legal teeth to fight proposed plants.

36. Cordell Hull's brief paper[74] is the sole exception. Hull concludes: 'While the number of superprojects actually being implemented is small because of the hazards and uncertainties involved, world demand for energy and mineral resources, plus the coming of age of the less developed countries, should be expected to ensure that this trend will be reversed'. Within five years this forecast would be looking rather sorry.

37. Incentive contracting, new cost-control practices, systems analysis and engineering, support for the Program Management function, PERT, Total Package Procurement, contract performance evaluation, better estimating practices.

38. Studies by A. J. Harman[75] on 25 US weapon systems projects in 1970 reported 50%−700% cost growth, due largely to the projects' size, complexity, degree of technological advance and development strategy; by R. L. Perry et al.[76] on 36 US weapons systems projects in 1971 reported 0%−220% cost overruns, due largely to technical uncertainty (30%), scope changes (50%) and underestimating (20%); and by J. P. Large[77] on eight US weapon systems projects in 1974 reported 200%−400% cost increases, due largely to the cost and technical difficulties having been underestimated.

39. The founding of DSMC, as it became known, coincided with the burgeoning activities of the project management societies such as PMI and Internet. Cross-fertilization between DSMC and these other educational/professional groups has been exceedingly limited, however.

40. As Sapolsky observed in his account of Polaris, 'The FBM [Fleet Ballistic Missile] program managements were not used as the model for the project management wave. Rather, project management was conceived, as it had been in the Air Force, as the staff coordination of development activities being performed by and under the jurisdiction of traditionally specialized line organizations.'[78]

41. A 1986 Rand report found evidence to suggest that these measures had proved effective: 'In the 1970s (unlike the 1960s) the larger programs were performing considerably better than average . . . This has sometimes been attributed to a more conservative design philosophy in the 1970s, especially for the more expensive programs, coupled with a more rigorous control of cost-generating engineering changes.'[79]

42. Designing to a cost ceiling was a practice long familiar in industry; such were the traditions of defence that it took several more years before the practice had much impact in the DoD.

43. 'As I reviewed program after program beginning in the Spring of 1969, almost all were in trouble from a common fault — production had been started before engineering development was finished.'[80]

44. Although expensive, this form of prototype competition has proved advantageous when the defence system (a) entails substantial innovation, (b) is to be produced in quantity, and (c) is characterized by a low ratio of development to total acquisition costs.

45. Contractual considerations dominate over profit; no significant correlation has been found between cost sharing ratios and overruns or underruns; incentives have not been significantly effective as a protection against cost growth; contractors establish upper limits on profit and government contracts; incentives are costly to negotiate and administer; contractors will not sacrifice performance attainment for profit; and it is often difficult to pass incentive motivation on to the people who carry out the contract on a day-to-day basis.[81]

46. It cost nearly a quarter of a billion dollars for the USAF to prepare the B-1 competition and the contractors to prepare proposals and to deal with Requests for Proposals.[82]

47. The Mission Element Need Statement identifies the mission; threat (basis for the mission); existing capabilities to accomplish mission; and assessment of need, constraints, resources and schedule to reach Milestone I. In construction terms, Milestone 0 is the end of the Prefeasibility stage. That it should have taken until 1976 for this important stage to be officially recognized by the Pentagon is amazing.

48. Development cycles had lengthened considerably; given the heating in

the economy, this had led to further cost growth. Worse, a number of very expensive programmes seemed to be experiencing their peak funding at about the same time — the so-called 'bow-wave' phenomenon. Many thus risked danger of cancellation by Congress.

49. Not all UK aerospace projects of the 1950s and 1960s were a disaster, of course. The BAC One-Eleven airliner of the early-to-mid 1960s, for example, was both a project management and a commercial success.[83]

50. It was to be some years before the new Procurement Executive would issue a comprehensive set of project management procedures, the MoD's *Compendium of guidelines for project management* being first issued in 1978. (Comparison with the first US DoD procedures is interesting, first in that the MoD's procedure appeared a full 18 years after the DoD's 375 series, and second in that their respective titles almost caricature the two nations' different approaches to the subject.)

51. Jaguar was undertaken by the BAC and Breguet (led by Henri Ziegler, an internationalist of quite different mould from Dassault). A Memorandum of Understanding was signed on 17 May 1965. Breguet, however, was taken over by Dassault in 1971, and the Dassault F1 was pitched by the new company as a competitor to the Jaguar. Although sales of the Jaguar were good, the takeover in effect kept France out of much European defence collaboration for many years to follow.

52. Canada, Holland and Belgium were also initially members of F104-G Joint Working Group, but did not ultimately join the project. The aircraft had to perform several roles, including close air support, interdiction—strike—reconnaissance and, in the UK's case, long distance over-sea patrol. That all these requirements could be met was made possible by the aircraft's swing-wing design. Inevitably, perhaps, the air forces complained that specially designed craft for each of these roles would have been preferable operationally.

53. It is interesting to observe this range of tools and techniques being employed so assuredly by British managers and their continental colleagues when, at more or less the same time, BAC was failing to implement basic project controls on Concorde.

54. There was some confusion for a while in 'the public mind' about Tornado's costs, caused partly by the substantial decline of sterling against the Deutschmark and partly by the German practice of including operating costs such as airfields, fuel, maintenance and operating personnel as well as development costs, while the British tended to cite only the last. The cost increases in Germany were to cause political uproar and lead to the resignation of two ministers.

55. The energy crisis depressed demand for civil airliners and made the European manufacturers conscious of the dangers of cutting each other's throats; the threats and attractions of the Americans were also very much on the Europeans' minds. The French showed interest in negotiating with Boeing and McDonnell-Douglas; Britain meanwhile wished to join the German—French Airbus consortium. Boeing was in discussion with British Aerospace and Rolls-Royce over participation on the new 757. In September 1978 the UK Government decided, after decisive lobbying by Chancellor Schmidt, that British Aerospace could join the Airbus A310 project; Rolls-Royce meanwhile was to develop the RB211-535 engine for the Boeing 757 (both companies being at this time nationalized). Both projects have proved outstandingly successful.

56. France was the first European country to initiate a national space programme — indeed the first in the world after the USA and the Soviet Union. France's goals always centred around security and prestige, albeit within a French-led European space hegemony. These have resulted in a particularly strong commitment to manned space.

Chapter 7

1. Some programmes were experiencing enormous overruns: Trident, $33bn increase; the F-16 programme, $33bn increase; the M-1 tank, $13bn increase; the UH-60A helicopter, $4·7bn increase; the Navy's Aegis cruiser programme, $8·4bn increase.[84] Although these figures are factually correct, for such major system procurements the great length of the programme development (often a decade or more) and the political and technological changes that occur during this period often seriously impair the usefulness of the overrun figures.

    A 1988 GAO review of recurring problems and systemic issues in US government major acquisitions during the period 1960–1987 nevertheless identified four major recurring problems — pre-emptive programme decisions, unstable top-management commitment to the system requirement or design, insufficient funding, and inappropriate external decisions (for example, on specific technology or design options). All these are factors largely outside the programme managers' immediate area of control. Inadequate testing due to insufficient funding, and priority given to maintaining schedule rather than correcting serious design problems were also noted as recurring factors; these are more within Program Management's control.[85]

2. 'Short, unambiguous lines of communication among levels of management, small staffs of highly competent professional personnel, an emphasis on innovation and productivity, smart buying practices, and most importantly, a stable environment of planning and funding — all are characteristic of efficient and successful management. These characteristics should be hallmarks of defense acquisition. They are, unfortunately, antithetical to the process the Congress and the Department of Defense have created to conduct much of defense acquisition over the years.'[86]

3. The MoD guidelines of December 1978 did not even distinguish between the successive phases of project development, although when the Guidelines were revised in November 1980 distinction was made between the Feasibility Study, Project Definition and Full Development phases. The procedures were further revised in June 1981 to impose tighter control over each phase.

4. (*a*) More attention should be paid to project management career development and increased professionalism.

    (*b*) Project managers should be given more control over, and made more accountable for, their projects and specialist support. Projects should be managed from cradle to grave. Project teams should contain specialist expertise at appropriate times and act as intelligent customers.

    (*c*) More responsibility could be moved to industry, in particular by having prime contractors take more responsibility for the overall management of the project and a greater use of 'cardinal point specifications'.

    (*d*) There should be an increased emphasis on competition and fixed prices, with strictly defined acceptance procedures.

5. The major criticism of this policy was that under the new regime the general overheads necessary for long-term R&D, and indeed bid-specific R&D, were not being recovered appropriately.[87]

6. Other initiatives promoted by Levene included an attempt to minimize the Treasury practice of departments having to 'give back' funds allocated but not spent in a budget year (the 'annuality' rule), and his development of a comprehensive top–down control and reporting information system on the status of all major MoD contracts and contractors. Prior to implementation of this system, 'there was no way in which the Chief of Defence Procurement could actually view [the major] programmes without going through a special exercise'.[88]

7. The study therefore recommended that 'The Feasibility Study ... should be replaced by a Technology Survey, which would take as a baseline the capability achievable with currently available technology or products and would define the work, cost and time necessary to develop a series of options — from the baseline to the full Staff Target — to the point of entry to Full Development.'[88]

8. 'Software', said Norman Augustine, 'almost non-existent a few decades ago, is rapidly becoming the dominant element in the design of most major high-tech systems'.[89] Indeed, some of the major project problems in the decade, such as the UK's digital telecom switch System X and the US B-1B bomber, and Nimrod of course, and even the UK's second generation AGRs, were the direct result of software difficulties — software project management is discussed on pp. 187–188.

9. In 1992 the EFA partners agreed to a cheaper, multi-option version of the plane: the so-called New EFA (NEFA).

10. The Italian coalition government of Sr Goria fell in March 1988 over a disagreement between the Christian Democrats and the Socialists as to whether the mothballed 2000 MW nuclear station Montalto di Castro, north of Rome, should be reopened. The plant was closed after a November 1987 national referendum, following Chernobyl, gave a verdict against nuclear power.

11. Florida Power and Light, the utility building St Lucie, set up a local office in Bethesda, Maryland to work with the Nuclear Regulatory Commission's headquarters' staff in obtaining the necessary licensing approvals.[90]

12. The next generation of nuclear reactors will probably be smaller, simpler and much more highly automated (and hence less prone to human error). Smaller (e.g. 250 MW) reactors, like the Swedish PIUS design, could be completely enclosed to make them inherently safe. However, the economics of competing fuels originally drove up the size of nuclear reactors (pp. 119–120): comparative cost will be a major element of the new reactors' viability.

13. With world industrial production having grown 40-fold since 1950, by the late 1980s desertification was increasing by 6 million hectares a year and deforestation by 10 million; over 20 million hectares of agricultural land was being lost to the world annually; flooding and soil erosion were on the increase, as was the proportion of the world's population without safe drinking water (60%) or sanitary facilities (75%); air pollution in major Third World cities was massive; acid rain in industrialized areas was damaging buildings, forests, rivers and lakes. Damage to the ozone layer over the poles was discovered in 1986–1987; by the end of the decade worry over the warming of the atmosphere through the 'greenhouse' effect, caused by CO_2 emissions and deforestation (leading to further desertification, rising sea level and increased flooding), had become a matter of world concern.

14. As Anderson showed in his study of afforestation in Northern Nigeria, 'If the additional benefits of tree planting such as associated increases in livestock weight brought on by improved dry season fodder, the avoided damage from desertification ... the improvements in yields due to shelter-belt activities, farm forestry effects on soil nutrient, recycling and moisture retention, as well as many other identifiable benefits and costs ... were taken into account then the overall picture would be completely different.'[91]

15. The first assumption of the 1947 Act was that the task of planning was to control and direct in the public interest spontaneous private developments; in the economic climate of the 1980s, control had to make way for stimulation. The second was that planning control was necessary to protect the countryside from urban encroachments; agriculture in the

1980s—1990s seemed a greater enemy of the countryside than did the town. The third was that local authorities were expected to combine land use planning with their own investment plans; 45 years later the intentions of the public sector could no longer be assumed to be consistent with the plans of local authorities. Lastly, decisions on planning permission were supposed to have no effect on the value of land; in the 1990s it was recognized that planning gain need not accrue to the community.[92]

16. Particularly on financial, poverty-alleviation, institution-building and self-reliance-inculcating grounds, although less in assisting women and not damaging the environment. (The developed world has not done particularly well on these two either.)

17. This section on BOO(T) and the Third World debt crisis is more fully analysed in Morris and Suratgar's 'Equity and the LDC debt crisis'.[93]

18. Argentina, Bolivia, Brazil, Chile, Colombia, Ecuador, Ivory Coast, Mexico, Morocco, Nigeria, Peru, Philippines, Uruguay, Venezuela, Yugoslavia; the Initiative was named after US Secretary of the Treasury James Baker, who called for this action at the 1985 World Bank—IMF meeting in Washington DC.

19. It can be argued that there was little relation between the two. As Rowland[94] has shown, Margaret Thatcher's decision to finance the Channel Link entirely from the private sector appears to predate the formal commitment to a programme of privatization; in any case, privatization was certainly not behind the Hong Kong Second Harbour Crossing or the US PURPA schemes.

20. BOO(T) was more common in Japan, where such projects are known as 'Third-Sector' projects. The Trans Tokyo Bay Highway is an example.

21. This highly compressed account of the history of the 1960—1975 period of the project is taken from chapter 2 of *The anatomy of major projects*;[26] a fuller account of the 1980—1987 initiation of the Channel Tunnel project is given in ref. 95.

22. To the City investors, the offer had been both unusual and risky. The scale of the project was vast; the payback exceptionally long; the shares were not to be listed until 1987 and there would be no dividend until 1994; the investment was neither purely project nor concessionaire — the offer suggested too little return for the former and too much for the latter. These were serious risks: planning delays were possible; there could be a change in government and the political risks in general were high; there was still the echo of the Thames Barrier, Humber Bridge, the power-station industry and other large project overruns; and there was the risk of the future failure of Equity 3 or the loan syndication.

23. These were that for a project to be financed by the private sector it must (*a*) not add to the overall level of expenditure planned for the sector, (*b*) reflect government priorities, (*c*) show cost efficiencies compared with the traditional public-sector approach.

24. The multilateral and bilateral agencies moved significantly in the late 1980s to help minimize the extra risks associated with BOO(T) projects. A new organization of the World Bank family, the Multilateral Investment Guarantee Agency (MIGA), was signed into effect in 1988 to provide insurance for a wide range of non-commercial risk. The International Finance Corporation developed a similar scheme for commercial risks: Guaranteed Return on Investment Principle (GRIP). Some of the export credit and aid agencies similarly came during the late 1980s to define their packages more closely towards project risk identification and to accommodate the needs of BOO(T) more specifically.

25. 'Ten years ago, there was little examination of the viability of projects. Today's philosophy, whether it is project finance or ECGD [Expert Credits Guarantee Agency], is that you are supporting corporate clients.'

Rowlinson,[96] Barclays Bank).

26. Both the architect and the quantity surveyor suffered in the BPF form
— the architect was no longer automatically the project leader, as in
other building contract forms; Bills of Quantities and the monthly
measurement were omitted, being replaced by Schedules of Rates
(prepared by the contractor) and stage (milestone) payments.

27. Construction Management is generally considered as the provision of
construction know-how on a consultancy basis, the contracts with the
trades contractors being directly with the client; Management Contracting
is where the trade contracts lie with the management contractor.[97–100]

28. Jenkins and Wetherbe found in 1984 that two-thirds of the 72 software
projects they surveyed required a redoing of the requirements analysis
effort, either because something was omitted or because something
changed in the application environment or in the way the end users
expected to work with the system.[101]

29. His role, which is akin to the Chairman of the Board, is different from
that of the project *champion* (a role which, as we see later, was to be
stressed early in the 1990s in the project management literature).

30. Thus, for example, in June 1988 Hill, Russell and Smith[102] wrote
absurdly that 'the importance of strong, competent, project management
involvement during the pre-project phase of a project is only recently
being recognized' — this statement is neither intellectually correct nor
historically true, as this book has shown.

31. Unlike MITI's New Industrial Cities programme of the 1960s, which
was based on the then dominant industries and withered as these industries
declined.

32. An extended account of this mega-project, up to December 1988, is given
in ref. 103.

33. The Station would allow observation of the earth's environment and the
universe; it could provide opportunities for commercial space endeavours;
it would serve as a repair base to maintain, upgrade and fix spacecraft
and to service satellites; it could provide a staging point for spacecraft
on missions to the moon, Mars, or the asteroids; and it would have
important benefits of prestige and as a way of building international
co-operation.[104]

34. 'In the final analysis, the President felt deeply that we could not pre-
ordain a pessimistic future by simply not providing the infrastructure
necessary to ensure that optimistic estimates of space uses would actually
materialize.'[105]

35. These agreements by no means resolved all the outstanding issues,
however. Many important matters were left to be resolved during Phase
B. Among the issues that required additional clarification were
agreements over what functions should be allocated to which (national)
parts of the Station, the legal mechanisms to ensure control over
technology transfer and to cover patent rights for intellectual property
developed on the Station, agreements over management rights and cost-
sharing responsibilities for operating the Station, and several major
technical matters such as radiation protection for crew members and the
development of less corrosive rocket fuel.

36. 'Mission to Planet Earth' — to study and characterize earth on a global
scale; 'Exploration of the Solar System' — to retain US leadership in
exploration of the outer solar system and regain US leadership in the
exploration of comets, asteroids and Mars; 'Outpost on the Moon' —
to establish a permanent lunar presence and begin to prospect the moon's
resources; and 'Humans to Mars' — a Mars landing leading to the
eventual establishment of a permanent base.

37. Areas such as robotics, propulsion, minerals extraction, the physiological

consequences of microgravity, radiation exposure, and routine and emergency health care aboard spacecraft were particularly in need of further study.

38. The Block I configuration required 20 Shuttle flights for station assembly: 13 for the manned base, two for outfitting, one for the platform and four for logistics. The NRC also did a risk analysis on the likelihood of a Shuttle failure and the implications of this to the programme. They found that the chances of the Shuttle suffering a prolonged grounding were as high as one in eight; crucially, if this were the case during the early phases of the Station's construction in space there would not be sufficient angular momentum to keep the Station in space long enough before gravitational pull would drag it into the Earth's atmosphere, leading to burn-up and destruction. As a result of this analysis it was concluded that there always had to be an extra Shuttle available as back-up.

Chapter 8

1. Perhaps transportation projects invariably set up such strategic uncertainties: many road building projects reflect similar ones. The decision to build more roads to ease congestion may only bring more cars on to the roads ('the American "scientific" approach not only assumed but also created greater traffic flows' (p. 318, note 6).

2. The USAF's 1989 request for funding for the B2 'stealth' bomber programme — a $550m-a-piece plane, developed in secrecy on the concurrency basis, whose mission was essentially either to force the Soviet Union to spend money it did not have on developing new radar to detect the plane, or to bomb Russian rubble hours after the US missile attack — would, at $8bn a year, have exceeded the entire annual defence budget of all but the world's 12 'top defence spending' nations.

   The digital switches of the early 1980s were requiring up to $1bn to develop; to recoup such an investment needed a market of at least $14bn, yet the total North American, European and Japanese markets were estimated to be only around $15bn, $10·6bn and $4·6bn respectively. There were just too many companies. Meanwhile, product life cycles were reducing sharply, from an average of eight to two years. Against such a background, the industry experienced major structural reorganization.

3. It was a challenge to launch nuclear power at all; it might have been impossible if full consideration had been given to the whole fuel cycle. Anyway, the energy business rarely seems to work like that: look at the problems of calculating the ecological costs of fossil fuel which the 1990s are attempting to address.

4. The last attribute may seem arbitrary, but it is intended to reflect both the insights of the socio-technic/systems theorists of the late 1960s,[106–108] whose theoretical foundations underlie so much of modern project management (as we saw in chapter 5), and those on strategy and organizational level, as developed for example in my work on interface management.[109]

5. Configuration Management differs from Change Control (and Configuration Control) in that it is employed to *minimize* unnecessary change; Change/Configuration Control is more concerned with administering project changes.

6. In the same vein, for large projects it is not overly cynical to suggest that, if possible, the programme be lashed up with some international collaboration (preferably a Treaty: Concorde survived in this manner; there is no doubt that the Space Station has benefited from its arrangements with ESA, Japan and Canada).

7. In his 1992 edition of this famous book,[110] Archibald changes the elements of the project management triad to 'identified points of

integrative project responsibility', 'integrative and predictive planning and control systems' and 'the project team'.

8. The British government's Competition and Purchasing Unit clearly defined the role of the project sponsor in its 1992 note No. 33.[111]

9. The 'other major contribution [of the 1962 DoD–NASA Guide, *PERT/Cost system design*] was its conceptual emphasis on milestone and interface planning' (p. 45). See also the Key Date Procedure etc. (p. 321, note 32). The team 'audit' is used by some to apply to this process: I see an audit as being separate from this milestone review, although it may usefully be related to it; an audit is additionally usually carried out by a third party.

10. The doubts expressed by researchers in the late 1960s and early 1970s over the use of incentive contracts (p. 131) thus seem in retrospect probably more to be due to the cultural climate of the institutions administering the contracts than to be definitive statements on the matter.

11. Although the TQM approach to partnering fits well with the Japanese business philosophy, as we saw in the Japanese car industry's adoption of 'lean production', it also fits comfortably into the clannish nature of Japanese business. Japanese construction contracting, for example, is largely based on 'families' of main contractors and subcontractors.

12. Dixon conducted a detailed review of military leadership.[112,113] Militarism, he concluded, tends to appeal to persons neurotically absorbed with sex, dirt, aggression, self-esteem and death. Unfortunately these traits tend to work against effective leadership! These flaws may be exacerbated by the speed of modern communications, the need for large staffs, and the mass of technological resources now at a commander's disposal. Industry, of course, appeals to a much broader range of people, but top management is typically authoritarian (in large part at least), stress is common and often prolonged, and the opportunity for rivalry is considerably greater.

13. While several writers addressed these issues in the 1960s to mid-1970s, it is only really as a consequence of lean production and Total Quality that interest in this area is reviving in the early 1990s. We return to this topic in chapter 9.

14. The best way to resolve this apparent conflict is for the functional staff to 'contract out' their services to the projects, agreeing price and schedule for services rendered, and negotiating variations accordingly.

15. The Japanese do not always do this well, of course. Norita and Kansai airports, for example, suffer severe constraints on passenger and aircraft access because of the objections of farmers and others in the local community.

16. Thamhain and Wilemon's research showed project managers as preferring all five conflict management modes: confrontation, compromise, smoothing, forcing and withdrawal.

17. The Project Start-Up idea was pushed heavily within the project management community during the 1980s, principally by the Danish project management society, or rather by its President, Morten Fangel.[114] Start-up meetings are designed as a mixture of basic project induction courses, group development exercises (a team-building opportunity to get to know colleagues' strengths and weaknesses, personalities, etc.) and basic project and management planning sessions, focusing on project procedures, organization structure, systems, schedules, budgets, etc. In the USA in the 1990s, the US Army Corps of Engineers adopted a similar practice, under the confusing label of 'partnering' (p. 330, note 10).

18. Remember, e.g., the critiques by Avots, Bu-Bushait, Dane, Geddes, Liberatore and Titus, Marquis, Navarre, and others (pp. 79 and 190).[115–122]

19. By the early 1990s, formal Risk Analysis was mandatory on all MoD projects, for example.

Chapter 9

1. The consequences of such 'smaller' regional conflicts could nevertheless be dramatic: nuclear weapons, enriched uranium and nuclear knowledge are leaking out of the Former Soviet Union (FSU) in the early 1990s at an alarming rate, particularly to the Middle East. Similarly with chemical weapons: 1000 lbs of potassium cyanide, the deadliest nerve gas in the world and enough to kill the entire population of the FSU, disappeared from Kyrgyzstan in 1992.

2. Integrated Services Digital Networks — broad band digital technology communication allowing voice, data and image communications to be carried on the same information highway. The aim is for the networks to connect internationally, allowing seamless multimedia information transfer. Sophisticated networks should be in place in Europe, USA and Japan by the early-to-mid-1990s.

3. The World Bank's and IFCs' political risk insurance instruments (see p. 326, note 24).

4. Electronics is profoundly altering the way our society not only behaves, but also organizes itself. The Technopolis concept has become fashionable in the 1990s: much of Central Europe and the FSU is promoting 'intelligent' business-park-based technologies as nodes for economic rejuvenation. Al Gore and Bill Clinton promoted information superhighways and government-led technology and business programmes as fundamental to their 1992 campaign. Telecommuting is leading to more and more executives, technologists and other knowledge-intensive workers working substantially from home rather than the office. This is producing large shifts in the geographical structure of population and the age structure of the urban population. The next 20−30 years will see new infrastructure being put in place to service the new dispersal of settlements; this may prove a preoccupying issue in many regions.

5. Intergovernmental Panel on Climate Change, sponsored by the UN Environment Program and the World Meteorological Organization.

6. The much-touted globalization of business will obviously be harder to create if the economic blocks become more protectionist.

7. Nic = newly industrialized country, e.g. Taiwan, as opposed to less developed country (ldc).

8. Packages such as OPERA and Lotus @ Risk, which allow consideration of a range of activity time values, are becoming more commonly used on projects. For example, Nicolo[123] has extended the use of GERT to a 'metaproject' planning methodology, while PERT-like capabilities have been applied to 'influence diagrams' for a range of project evaluation situations using software known as Dynrisk.[124]

9. Expert Systems, for example documenting practical knowledge of the likely source of risk and the consequence of combining risk factors, are beginning to extend influence diagramming. Systems have been developed for analysing general influence diagrams (e.g. by Niwa and Okuma[125] and Diekmann[126]) and, specifically, for detecting construction risk and analysing contractual arrangements (Expert Risk).[127] 'Fuzzy logic' is sometimes used on these programmes as a useful tool to express the uncertainty inherent in the risk analysis.[127]

10. Interestingly, partnering and the ADR process has been especially championed in the USA by the public sector, the US Corps of Engineers in particular. Partnering to the Corps, however, is in fact more like the European Project Start-Up idea (p. 261): essentially a two-to-three-day workshop after contract award during which a common spirit and common aims between all parties are established.

11. Even the Space Station became re-engineered. In June 1993 President Clinton ordered the Station to be redesigned to a $10·5 bn configuration ($16·5 bn including the European and Japanese modules). The savings were to come not just from a drastic reduction of size and functionality but also from simplifying the Station's management structure from eleven levels to five. At the same time, the management style was to be changed with work concentrated into interdisciplinary integrated production teams responsible for specific goals, such as putting together payloads for the Space Shuttle.[128]

12. Benchmarking is the process of identifying the best standard of performance in a particular function in an industry (often unrelated to the one in which the firm operates), taking that as the benchmark standard best practice and then seeking ways to upgrade the firm's performance in this function to that of the benchmark standard.

13. There are those who promote partnering as an exclusive relationship between an owner and a single contractor, consultant, or supplier, at least within the industry sector or market being served. This argument really only applies where there is truly commercially sensitive information, for example, where contractors hold licences on particular process technologies. Many will argue that production planning norms are commercially sensitive data too, but in reality they are not sufficiently sensitive to warrant an exclusive relationship. Partnering in the 1990s, therefore, will be based more frequently on strategic alliances between small clusters of highly compatible firms, accustomed to working together, and trusting each other in the use of information that they will exchange on the basis of the grouping as a whole achieving progressive improvements in performance. (Data management becomes important when working in this way. We see later in chapter 9 that Information Technology in the 1990s is greatly increasing integrated data management capabilities. This will be one of the important areas of development in project management technology in the next few years.)

14. Another interesting consequence of Concurrent Engineering is the attention to product launch. This is commercially so critical, particularly if competitors are close on the heels of the new product or if operators have to debug the rushed product, that project teams continue in place for some time to hone product performance.

15. Function-Point Analysis indicates software cost−benefit. It measures five things: inputs, outputs, inquiries, files and interfaces. These are weighted according to the complexity of writing the software needed to implement them, files being weighted highest, inputs and inquiries lowest. By calculating the software's cost per function, a measure of software development productivity can be achieved.[129,130]

16. The term Integrated Logistics Support is common in defence/aerospace and, like several other defence/aerospace terms, is being progressively adopted first in obviously high-tech industries and later in others. A particular feature of ILS is its emphasis on the logistics of operations — reliability, replacements, maintenance, etc.[131]

17. The idea of a 'virtual organization' based on partnerships, group technology and an information systems infrastructure is increasingly being suggested as an organizational model for the 21st century.[132]

18. 'Concurrent engineering differs from the traditional weapon system development process in that it requires the appropriate functional disciplines, such as engineering, procurement, test, and logistics support, to work interactively to conceive, develop and implement new weapon system programs ... instead of trying to force-fit designed products into existing manufacturing and logistical support processes, program managers are implementing an integrated product development

approach that moves previously "downstream" product considerations "upfront" to the product development phase.'[133]

19. The Taguchi method aims to gain maximum benefit from small changes in input factors. The challenge is to find which input changes these are. The Taguchi method varies several inputs simultaneously while allowing analysis to be performed on each input individually. It does so by designing tests ('experiments') which balance the effects of different inputs in turn.[134,135]

20. The US National Research Council thus identifies research in the following areas as crucial to future US manufacturing capability: intelligent manufacturing control, reliability and maintenance, materials, the product realization process and manufacturing skills.[136]

21. EDI has been used most in the motor, electronics, transportation, tourism, defence/aerospace, retailing, pharmaceuticals, insurance, banking and health industries.

22. SQL — Standard Query Language — is a standard relational database format allowing data to be addressed and stored in a common manner across a wide variety of different operating environments. Client—server technology is a way of holding base software on a host machine (the server) while taking just the programs and data needed to perform a local set of routines on to a local, generally smaller computer (the client). This allows cheaper and more efficient processing.

23. Automatic testing, configuration and document control, specification and standards selection and verification, scheduling and modelling, semi-automated software development, robotics, and voice and handwriting recognition will see further development which will positively contribute to project management in the 1990s. There will be many other examples.

References

1. Mendelssohn, K. *The riddle of the pyramids.* Praeger, New York, 1974, p. 153.
2. Atkinson, R. J. C. *Stonehenge.* Penguin, Harmondsworth, 1979.
3. Fox, C. *The personality of Britain: its influence on inhabitant and invader in pre-historic and early historic times.* Cardiff, 1959.
4. Cummins, W.A. *King Arthur's place in prehistory.* Alan Sutton, Stroud, 1992.
5. Straub, H. *A history of civil engineering.* Hans E. Rockwell, Leonard Hill, London, 1952, p. 120.
6. Watson, G. *The civils: the story of The Institution of Civil Engineers.* Thomas Telford, London, 1988, pp. 6–14.
7. Kennedy, P. *The rise and fall of the great powers.* Unwin Hyman, London, 1988, pp. 259–260.
8. Moder, J. J. and Phillips, C. R. *Project management with CPM and PERT.* Litton, 1964; 3rd edn, Van Nostrand Reinhold, New York, pp. 10–11.
9. Gullick, L. Notes on the theory of organization. In *Papers on the science of administration,* Urwick, L. (ed.), Colombia University Press, New York, 1937, pp. 1–46.
10. Ehrman, J. *Grand strategy.* Vol. 5, HMSO, London, 1956.
11. Rhodes, R. *The making of the atomic bomb.* Simon & Schuster, New York, 1986; Penguin Books, Harmondsworth, 1988.
12. McDougall, W. A. *The heavens and the earth: a political history of the space age.* Basic Books, New York, 1985, p. 48.
13. Fortescue, S. Project Planning in Soviet R&D. *Research Policy,* **14,** 1985, 267–282.
14. Golovin, I. *Academician Igor Kuratchov,* Mir, Moscow, 1969.
15. Holloway, D. *Entering the nuclear arms race: The Soviet decision to build the atomic bomb 1939–45.* Working Paper No. 9, International

Security Studies Program, the Wilson Center, Washington, DC, 1979.

16. Buffa, E. S. Sequence analysis for functional layouts. *Journal of Industrial Engineering,* **6**, No. 2, 1955, Mar.–Apr.

17. Hegelson, W. B. and Birnie, D. P. Assembly line balancing using the ranked position weight technique. *Journal of Industrial Engineering,* **12**, No. 6, 1961, Nov.–Dec.

18. Kilbridge, M. D. and Wester, L. A heuristic method of assembly-line balancing. *Journal of Industrial Engineering,* **12**, No. 40, 1961, July–Aug.

19. Schoderbek, P. P. and Digman, L. A. Third generation PERT/LOB. *Harvard Business Review,* 1967, Sept.–Oct.

20. Tonge, F. Summary of a heuristic line-balancing procedure. *Management Science,* **7**, No. 1, 1960, Oct.

21. Calvert, R. E. *Introduction to building management.* Newnes-Butterworth, London, 1964.

22. Campbell, R. W. Management spillovers from Soviet space and military programmes. *Soviet Studies,* **23**, 1972, 586–607.

23. *Maintenance intensification.* Memo GO/18/OR, Central Electricity Generating Board, London, 1957.

24. Rosholt, R. L. *An administrative history of NASA, 1958–1963.* National Aeronautics and Space Administration, Washington, DC, 1966.

25. Battle, C. L. SPO code. In *Systems management,* Baumgartner, J. S. (ed.), The Bureau of National Affairs, Washington, DC, 1979, pp. 106–109.

26. Morris, P. W. G. and Hough, G. H. *The anatomy of major projects.* Wiley, Chichester, 1988, chapter 6.

27. Archibald, R. D. Project interface management: a key to more effective project management. *Proc. 9th World Congress on Project Management,* 4–9 September, 1988, Zurich, Internet.

28. Dinsmore, P. D. *Human factors in project management.* Amacom, New York, 1984.

29. Morris, P. W. G. Managing project interfaces — key points for project success. In *Project management handbook,* Cleland, D. I. and King, W. R. (eds), Van Nostrand Reinhold, New York, 1988, pp. 16–55.

30. Blue Ribbon Defense Panel. Report to the President and Secretary of Defense on the Department of Defense. *Staff report on major acquisitions process.* Appendix E, Government Printing Office, July, 1970, p. 45.

31. Wolfe, T. *The right stuff.* Farrar Strauss, Giroux, New York, 1979.

32. Merrow, E., Chapel, S. W. and Worthing, C. A. *A review of cost estimation in new technologies: implications for energy process plants.* Rand, R-2481-DOE, Santa Monica, CA, July 1971.

33. Merrow, E., Chapel, S. W. and Worthing, C. A. *Understanding the outcomes of a megaproject: a quantitive analysis for very large civilian projects.* Rand, R-3560-PSSP, Santa Monica, CA, 1988.

34. Metcalf, H. and Rowley, D. Project management of bloodhound. Comparative project management, The Institution of Mechanical Engineers Symposium, *Institution of Mechanical Engineers Proceedings* 1968–69, **183**, Part 3K, p. 9.

35. *Report of the Steering Group on Development Cost Estimating,* Vol. 1, Ministry of Technology, HMSO, London, 1969, p. 3.

36. Gardner, C. *British Aircraft Corporation.* B. T. Batsford, London, 1981, pp. 101–102.

37. Simpson, J. The Polaris Executive: a case study of a unified hierarchy. *Public Administration,* 1970, Winter, 384.

38. National Economic Development Office. *Engineering construction performance.* HMSO, London, 1977.

39. Gott, H. H. The engineering of large projects, Comparative Project Management, The Institution of Mechanical Engineers Symposium, *Institution of Mechanical Engineers Proceedings* 1968–69, **183**, Part 3K, pp. 30–41.

40. Hasegawa, F. *Built by Japan: competitive strategies of the Japanese construction industry.* Wiley, New York, 1988.

41. Brown, W. *Exploration in management.* Penguin, Harmondsworth, 1965.

42. Checkland, P. *Systems thinking, systems practice.* Wiley, New York, 1981.

43. Feldman, E. J. *Concorde and dissent: explaining high technology failures in Great Britain and France.* Cambridge University Press, New York, 1985.

44. Hayward, K. *Government and British civil aerospace.* Manchester University Press, 1983.

45. Knight, G. *Concorde: the inside story.* Weidenfeld & Nicolson, London, 1976.

46. Williams, H. *A promise unfulfilled.* Paul Ian Allen, London, 1985.

47. Ministry of Transport. *Traffic in towns.* HMSO, London, 1963.

48. Cicchetti, C. J. *Alaskan oil: alternative routes and markets.* Johns Hopkins University Press, Baltimore, 1972.

49. Government Accounting Office, HMSO, London.

50. US Comptroller General. *Trans Alaskan Oil Pipeline — progress of construction through November 1975.* Report to Congress, February 1976, Government Printing Office, Washington, DC.

51. Cleland, D. I. Prudent and reasonable project management. *Project Management Journal,* **16**, No. 4, 1985, Dec., 91–97.

52. Fox, J. R. Evaluating management of large, complex projects: a framework for analysis. *Technology in Society,* **6**, 1984, 129–139.

53. *Report of the Steering Group on Development Cost Estimating.* Ministry of Technology, HMSO, London, 1969.

54. Moolin, F. P. and McCoy, F. The organization and management of large projects ... realities *vs* theory, *Proc. Project Management Institute Symp.*, Drexel Hill, PA, 1979.

55. Ministry of Defence, HMSO, London, 1988.

56. *Government Organisation for Defence Procurement and Civil Aerospace.* Cmnd 4641, HMSO, London, 1971.

57. Morris, P. W. G. An organizational analysis of project management in the building industry. *Build International,* No. 6, 1973.

58. Morris, P. W. G. Systems study of project management. *Building,* 1974, Jan.

59. Gilbert, S. and Horner, R. *The Thames Barrier.* Thomas Telford, London, 1984.

60. Hastings, R. F. Proposal: a new and comprehensive system for design and delivery of buildings. *Architectural Record,* 1968, Nov.

61. Foxhall, W. B. *Professional construction management and project administration.* The American Institute of Architects and Architectural Record, New York/Washington, 1972, pp. 57–58.

62. Merrett, A. J. and Sykes, A. *The financial analysis of capital projects.* Longman, London, 1963.

63. Brierley, R. A. and Myers, S. W. *Principles of corporate finance,* McGraw-Hill, New York, 1988.

64. Nevitt, P. K. *Project finance,* Euromoney, London, 1983, p. 14.

65. Magee, S. P. and Brock, W. A. Third World debt and international capital market failure as a consequence of redistributive political risk sharing. In *World debt crisis,* Claudon, M. P. (ed.), Ballinger, Cambridge, MA, 1986.

66. Blair, C. *Admiral Rickover and the atomic submarine.* Henry Holt, New York, 1954.

67. Hewlett, R. G. and Duncan, F. *Nuclear navy 1946–1962.* The University of Chicago Press, 1974.

68. Hazelrigg, G. A. and Roth, E. B. *Windows for innovation: a story of two large-scale technologies.* National Science Foundation, 82-180-1, Washington, DC, 1982.

69. Polmar, N. and Allen, T. B. *Rickover: controversy and genius.* Simon & Schuster, New York, 1982.

70. Hannah, L. *Engineers, managers and politicians.* Macmillan, London, 1982.

71. Williams, R. *The nuclear power decisions. British policies, 1953–78.* Croom Helm, London, 1980.

72. British Standards Office *Glossary of terms used in QA.* BS 4778, HMSO, London, 1978.

73. Nuclear Regulatory Commission. *Quality assurance.* 1984.

74. Hull, C. In *Planning, engineering and construction of super projects. Proc. Engineering Foundation Research Conf.* American Society of Civil Engineers, New York, 1978, 39.

75. Harman, A. J. assisted by Henrichsen, A. *A methodology for cost factor comparison and prediction.* Rand, R-6269-ARPA, Santa Monica, CA, August 1970.

76. Perry, R. L., Smith, G. K., Harman, A. J. and Henrichsen, S. *System acquisition strategies.* Rand, R-733-PR/ARPA, Santa Monica, CA, June 1971.

77. Large, J. P. *Bias in initial cost estimates: how low estimates can increase the cost of acquiring weapon systems.* Rand, R-1467-PA&E, Santa Monica, CA, July 1974.

78. Sapolsky, H. *The Polaris system development: bureaucratic and programmatic success in government.* Harvard University Press, Cambridge, MA, 1972, pp. 199, 200.

79. Rich, M. and Dews, E., with Batten, C. L. *Improving the military acquisition process — lessons from Rand Research.* Rand, R-3373-AF/RC, Santa Monica, CA, 1986.

80. Packard, D. Defense industry must do a better job. *Defense Industry Bulletin,* 1971, Fall, 4.

81. Logistics Management Institute. *An examination of the foundations of incentive contracts.* LMI Task 66-67, May 1968.

82. Logistics Management Institute. *Contractor costs during proposal evaluation and source selection, B-1 program.* LMI Task 071-2, 31 August, 1971.

83. Gardner, C. *British Aircraft Corporation.* B. T. Batsford, London, 1981, chapter 9.

84. *SAR program acquisition cost summary, 31 December 1980.* Procurement Programs (P-1), Department of Defense, Washington, DC, 10 March 1981, as reported in *New York Times,* 26 July 1981.

85. *Major acquisitions: summary of recurring problems and systematic issues 1960–1987.* General Accounting Office, GAO/NSIAD-88-135 BR, Washington, DC, September 1988.

86. President's Blue Ribbon Commission on Defense Management. *Formula for action.* Government of the USA, April 1986.

87. Public Accounts Committee. *16th report on MoD annual major projects statement.* Session 1984–85, HMSO, London, 1985.

88. Committee of Public Accounts. *Control and management of the development of major equipment.* House of Commons Committee of Public Accounts 6th Report, HC104, HMSO, London, 18 February 1987, p. 2.

89. Augustine, N. R. *Augustine's laws*. Penguin, Harmondsworth, 1987, p. 151.

90. Derickson, W. B. St Lucie Unit 2 — a nuclear plant built on schedule. *Proc. 1983 Project Management Institute Symp.*, Houston, October 1983.

91. Anderson, D. *The economics of afforestation: a case study in Africa*. World Bank Occasional Papers, New Series No. 1, Johns Hopkins University Press, Baltimore, 1987.

92. Nuffield Foundation. *Town and country planning*. London, 1987.

93. Morris, P. W. G. and Suratgar, D. Equity and the LDC debt crisis: equity in Third World project financing with particular reference to build−own−operate projects. *Technology in Society*, **10**, 1988, 353−373.

94. Rowland, T. Finance — digging up the money. In *The tunnel: the Channel and beyond*, Jones, B. (ed.), Ellis Horwood/Wiley, Chichester, 1987.

95. Morris, P. W. G. *The Channel Tunnel 1980−87*. Templeton College Management Research Paper, Oxford.

96. Rowlinson, M. Project financing. *Euromoney*, 1988, Aug., 4.

97. Adrian, J. J. *CM: the construction management process*. Reston Publishing Company, Reston, VA, 1981.

98. Dearle and Henderson. *Management contracting: a practice manual*. E. & F. N. Spon, London, 1988.

99. Hawes, R. W., Perry, J. G. and Thompson, P. A. *Management contracting*. Report No. 100, Construction Industry Research and Information Association, London, 1983.

100. Sidwell, A. C. An evaluation of management contracting. *Construction Management in Economics*, **1**, No. 1, 1983, Spring, 48−55.

101. Jenkins, A. M. and Wetherbe, J. C. Empirical investigation of systems development practices and results. *Information and Management*, **7**, 1984, 73−82.

102. Hill, K. W., Russell, J. G. and Smith, T. J. The pre-project project management role. *Project Management Journal*, **19**, No. 3, 1988, June, 41−47.

103. Morris, P. W. G. *The Western Space Station: a study in the initiation of major projects*, Templeton College Management Research Paper, MRP 88/5, June 1988, Oxford.

104. *The Space Station: a description of the configuration established at the Systems Requirements Review (SSR)*. National Aeronautical and Space Administration, Washington, DC, 9 September 1983.

105. *The Space Station: a description of the configuration established at the Systems Requirements Review (SSR)*. National Aeronautical and Space Administration, Washington DC, June 1986.

106. Burns, T. and Stalker, G. M. *The management of innovation*. Tavistock, London, 1961.

107. Emery, F. E. and Trist, E. L. The causal texture of organizational environments. *Human Relations*, **18**, No. 1, 1965, 21−32.

108. Miller, E. J. and Rice, A. K. *Systems of organization — the control of task and sentient boundaries*. Tavistock, London, 1967.

109. Morris, P. W. G. Managing project interfaces — key points for project success. In *Project management handbook*, Cleland, D. I. and King, W. R. (eds), Van Nostrand Reinhold, New York, 1988.

110. Archibald, R. D. *Managing high-technology programs and projects*. Wiley, New York, 1992.

111. Public Competition and Purchasing Unit. *Project sponsorship*. HM Treasury, HMSO, London, 1992, Guidance Note 33.

112. Dixon, N. F. *The psychology of military incompetence*. Jonathan Cape, London, 1976.

113. Dixon, N. F. Some thoughts on the nature and causes of industrial incompetence. *Personnel Management*, **14**, No. 12, 1982, Dec., 26–30.

114. Fangel, M. *Project start up*. Internet, Zurich, 1985.

115. Avots, I. Why does project management fail? *California Management Review*, 1969, Fall.

116. Bu-Bushait, K. A. The application of project techniques to construction and research and development techniques. *Project Management Journal*, **20**, No. 2, 1989, June, 17–22.

117. Dane, C. W., Gray, C. F. and Woodworth, B. Successfully introducing project management techniques into an organization. *Project Management Quarterly*, **12**, No. 4, 1981, Dec., 23–26.

118. Dunne, E. J. How six management techniques are used. *Research Management*, **26**, No. 2, 1983, Mar.–Apr., 35–40.

119. Geddes, P. How good is PERT? *Aerospace Management*, **4**, 1961, Sept., 41–43.

120. Liberatore, M. J. and Titus, G. J. Managing industrial R&D projects: current practice and future direction. *Journal of the Society of Research Administrators*, **18**, No. 1, 1986, Summer, 5–12.

121. Marquis, D. C. A project team plus PERT = success. Or does it? *Innovation*, 1969.

122. Navarre, C. and Schaan, J-L. International engineering project management: key success factors in a changing industry. *International Journal of Project Management*, 1987, Nov., 238–245.

123. Nicolo, E. Metaproject analysis: a systematic methodological aid for strategic planning. *Project management without boundaries*, Proc. *11th Internet World Congress on Project Management*, Italy, **2**, 1992.

124. Skogen, S. and Huseby, A. B. Dynamic Risk analysis — the dynrisk concept, *International Journal of Project Management*, **10**, No. 3, 1993, Aug., 160–164.

125. Niwa, K. and Okuma, N. Know-how transfer method and its application to risk management for large construction projects. *IEEE Transactions on Engineering Management*, **EM-29**, No. 4, 1982, 146.

126. Diekmann, J. E. Risk analysis: lessons from artificial intelligence. *International Journal of Project Management*, **10**, No. 2, 1992, May.

127. Kangari, R. and Boyer, L. T. Risk management by expert systems. *Project Management Journal*, **10**, No. 2, 1989, Mar., 40–48.

128. Re-engineering the engineers. *The Economist*. 26 June, 1993, 107.

129. Betteridge, R. Successful experience of using function points to estimate project costs early in the life cycle. *Information and Software Technology*, **34**, No. 10, 1992, Oct., 655–658.

130. Dale, C. J. and van der Zee, H. Software productivity metrics: who needs them? *Information and Software Technology*, **34**, No. 11, 1992, Nov., 731–738.

131. Finkelstein, W. and Guertin, J. A. R. *Integrated logistics support, the design engineering link*. IFS Publications, London, 1988.

132. The virtual corporation. *Business Week*, 8 February, 1993.

133. Heberling, M. E., Wagner, C. F. and Rendon, R. G. The F-22 advanced tactical fighter: the Air Force Model Acquisition Program. *PM Network*, **7**, No. 9, 1993, Sept., 12–19.

134. Santell, M. P., Jung, J. R. and Warner, J. C. Optimization in project coordination scheduling through application of Taguchi methods. *Project Management Journal*, **23**, No. 3, 1992, Sept., 5–16.

135. Turner, J. R. *The handbook of project-based management*. McGraw-Hill, London, 1993, pp. 174–176.

136. National Research Council. *The competitive edge: research priorities for US manufacturing*. National Academy Press, Washington, DC, 1991.

Selected bibliography

Descriptions of projects or project industries

Acker, D. D. The maturing of the DoD acquisition process. *Defense Systems Management Review, 1980*, **3**, No. 3, pp. 17–25.

Baum, W. C. and Tolbert, S. M. *Investing in development.* Oxford University Press, 1985.

Caro, R. A. *The power broker.* Knopf, New York, 1974.

Cassen, R. & Associates. *Does aid work?* Clarendon, Oxford, 1986, pp. 11, 109 ff.

Clark, K. B. and Fujimoto, T. *Production development performance.* Harvard Business School Press, Boston, 1991.

Fallon, I. *Paper chase.* Harper Collins, London, 1993.

Feldman, E. J. *Concorde and dissent: explaining high technology failures in Great Britain and France.* Cambridge University Press, New York, 1985.

Fox, J. R. *Arming America: how the US buys weapons.* Harvard University, Boston, 1974.

Groves, L. M. *Now it can be told: the story of the Manhattan Project.* Harper, New York, 1962 (reprinted De Capo Press, New York, 1983).

Hall, P. *Great planning disasters.* Weidenfeld & Nicholson, London, 1980.

Horwitch, M. *Clipped wings: the American SST.* MIT Press, Cambridge, MA, 1982.

Irving, C. *Wide body: the making of the 747.* Hodder & Stoughton, London, 1993.

Kharbanda, O. B. and Stallworthy, E. A. *How to learn from project disasters.* Gower, London, 1983.

McDougall, W. A. *The heavens and the earth: a political history of the space age.* Basic Books, New York, 1985.

Moris, J. *Managing induced rural development.* International Development Institute, Bloomington Il, 1981.

Morris, P. W. G. and Hough, G. H. *The anatomy of major projects.* Wiley, Chichester, 1987.

Murray, C. and Bly Cox, C. *Apollo: The race to the moon.* Secker & Warburg, London, 1989.

Paul, S. *Strategic management of development programs.* International Labour Office, Geneva, 1983.

Putnam, W. D. *The evolution of air force system acquisition management.* Report R-868-PW, Rand Corporation, Santa Monica, CA, 1972.

Sapolsky, H. *The Polaris system development: bureaucratic and programmatic success in government.* Harvard University Press, Cambridge, MA, 1972.

Seamans, R. and Ordway, F. I. The Apollo tradition: an object lesson for the management of large-scale technological endeavours. *Interdisciplinary Science Review*, 1977, p. 280.

Trento, J. J. *Prescription for disaster.* Crown, New York, 1987.

Williams, R. *The nuclear power decisions. British policies 1953–78.* Croom Helm, London, 1980.

Systems acquisition and project management

Archibald, R. D. *Managing high technology programs and projects.* Wiley, New York, 1976. (Second edition, 1993.)

Bennigson, L. A. The strategy of running temporary projects. *Innovation*, 24 September, 1971, 32–40.

Blue Ribbon Defense Panel. Report to the President and Secretary of Defense on the Department of Defense. *Staff report on major acquisitions process.* Government Printing Office, July 1970.

Bryson, L. Large scale project management. *IEEE Proceedings*, Part A, **129**, No. 8, 1982, Nov., 625–629.

Cleland, D. I. and Kerzner, H. *A project management dictionary of terms.* Van Nostrand Reinhold, New York, 1985.

Cleland, D. I. and King, W. R. *Systems analysis and project management.* McGraw-Hill, New York, 1968.

Crauli, O., Hetland, P. W. and Rolstadas, A. *Applied project management — experience from exploration on the Norwegian Continental Shelf.* Tapir (for the Norwegian Association of Cost and Planning Engineering), Oslo, 1986.

Davidson, F. P. Macro-engineering: a capability in search of a methodology. *Futures*, 1968, **1**, No. 2, Dec., 153–161.

Dinsmore, P. *AMA handbook on project management.* AMA Publications, New York, 1993.

Fangel, M. *Project start up.* Internet, Zurich, 1985.

Finkelstein, W. and Guertin, J. A. R. *Integrated logistics support, the design engineering link.* IFS Publications, London, 1988.

Gaisford, R. W. Project management in the North Sea. *International Journal of Project Management*, 1986, **4**, No. 1, Feb., 5–12.

Gareis, R. Management by projects: the management approach for the future. *International Journal of Project Management*, **7**, No. 4, 1989, May, 243–249.

Graham, R. The future of project management: some North Sea experiences. *International Journal of Project Management*, 1988, **6**, No. 3, 153–163.

Gray, K. G., Jaafari, A. and Wheen, R. J. (eds). *Macroprojects: strategy, planning and implementation.* The Warren Centre, The University of Sydney, 1985.

Heberling, M. E., Wagner, C. F. and Rendon, R. G. The F-22 advanced tactical fighter: the Air Force Model Acquisition Program. *PM Network*, **7**, No. 9, 1993, Sept., 12–20.

Hetland, P. W. What did 20 years of petroleum activities in the North Sea add to our general knowledge of project management? *Proc. Nordnet — Internet PMI Conf.*, Reykjavik, 1987.

Horwitch, M. and Pralahad, C. K. Managing multi-organization enterprises: the emerging strategic frontier. *Sloan Management Review*, 1981, Winter, 3–16.

Jennett, E. Guidelines for successful project management. *Chemical Engineering*, 9 July, 1973, 70–82.

Johnson, R. A., Kast, F. E. and Rosenzweig, J. E. *The theory and management of systems.* McGraw-Hill, New York, 1973.

Keen, J. *Managing systems development.* Wiley, Chichester, 1981.

Kerzner, H. *Project management: a systems approach to planning, scheduling and controlling*, Van Nostrand Reinhold, New York, 1984.

Kimmons, R. L. and Loweree, J. H. *Project management: a reference for professionals.* Marcel Dekker, New York, 1989.

Liberatore, M. J. and Titus, G. J. Managing industrial R&D projects: current practice and future direction. *Journal of the Society of Research Administrators*, **18**, No. 1, 1986, Summer, 5–12.

Major acquisitions: summary of recurring problems and systematic issues 1960–1987. General Accounting Office, GAO/NSIAD-88-135 BR, Washington, DC, September 1988.

Martin, C. C. *Project management: how to make it work.* Amacom, New York, 1976.

Merrow, E., Chapel, S. W. and Worthing, C. A. *Understanding the outcomes of a megaproject: a quantitive analysis for very large civilian projects.* Rand, R-3560-PSSP, Santa Monica, CA, 1988.

Ministry of Defence. *Learning from experience: a report on the arrangements for managing major projects in the procurement executive.* HMSO, London, 1987.

Ministry of Technology. *Report of the Steering Group on Development Cost Estimating.* HMSO, London, 1969.

National Audit Office. *Ministry of Defence: control and management of the development of major equipment.* Report by the Comptroller and Auditor General, National Audit Office, HC568, HMSO, London, July 1986.

O'Brien, J. J. Project management: an overview. *Project Management Quarterly,* 1977, **8**, No. 3.

Olsen, R. P. Can project management be defined? *Project Management Quarterly,* 1971, **2**, No. 1, 12–14.

Paul, S. *Managing development programs: the lessons of success.* Westview, Boulder, CO, 1982.

Perry, R. L., Smith, G. K., Harman, A. J. and Henrichsen, S. *System acquisition strategies.* Rand Corporation, R-733-PR/ARPA, Santa Monica, CA, June, 1971.

Rich, M. and Dews, E., with Batten, C. L. *Improving the military acquisition process — lessons from Rand Research.* Rand, R-3373-AF/RC, Santa Monica, CA, 1986.

Rondinelli, D. A. Why development projects fail: problems of project management in developing countries. *Project Management Quarterly,* 1976, **7**, No. 1.

Speck, R. L. The buck stops here: the owner's legal and practical responsibility for strategic project management. *Project Management Journal,* **19**, No. 4, 1988, Sept., 45–52.

Thamhain, H. J. *Engineering program management.* Wiley, New York, 1984.

Turner, J. R. *The handbook of project-based management.* McGraw-Hill, London, 1993.

Organization

Archibald, R. D. Project interface management: a key to more effective project management. *Proc. 9th World Congress on Project Management,* 4–9 September, 1988, Zurich, Internet.

Baker, B. N. and Wilemon, D. L. A summary of major research findings regarding the human element in project management. *Project Management Quarterly,* 1974, **5**, No. 2, 227–230.

Battle, C. L. SPO code. In *Systems management,* Baumgartner, J. S. (ed.). The Bureau of National Affairs, Washington, DC, 1979, pp. 106–109.

Belbin, M. *Management teams: why they succeed or fail.* Heinemann, London, 1985.

Bennigson, L. A. The team approach to project management. *Management Review,* 1972, **61**, Jan., 48–52.

Butler, A. G. Project management: a study in organizational conflict. *Academy of Management Journal,* 1973, **16**, Mar., 84–101.

Cicero, J. P. and Wilemon, D. L. Project authority: a multi-dimensional view. *IEEE Transactions and Engineering Management,* 1970, **EM-17**, 52–57.

Cleland, D. I. Product design teams: the simultaneous engineering perspective. *Project Management Journal,* **22**, No. 4, 1991, Dec., 5–10.

Cleland, D. I. Project stakeholder management. *Project Management Journal,* **17**, No. 4, 1986, Sept., 36–44.

Cleland, D. I. and King, W. R. (eds). *The project management handbook.* Van Nostrand Reinhold, New York, 1983.

Davis, S. M. and Lawrence, P. R. *Matrix organizations.* Addison-Wesley, Reading, MA, 1977.

Dinsmore, P. D. *Human factors in project management.* Amacom, New York, 1984.

Gaddis, P. O. The project manager. *Harvard Business Review*, 1959, May–June, 89–97.

Galbraith, J. R. Environmental and technological determinants of organizational design. In *Studies in organization design*, Lorsch, J. R. and Lawrence, P. R. (eds). Irwin-Dorsey, Homewood, Il., 1970, chapter 7.

Gemmill, G. R. The effectiveness of different power styles of project managers in gaining project support. *Project Management Quarterly*, 1974, **5**, No. 1.

Gemmill, G. R. and Wilemon, D. L. The power spectrum in project management. *Sloan Management Review*, 1970, **12**, No. 4, 15–25.

Gobeli, D. H. Relative effectiveness of different project structures. *Project Management Journal*, **18**, No. 2, 1987, June, 81–85.

Gulick, L. Notes on the theory of organization. In *Papers on the science of administration*, Urwick, L. (ed.). Institute of Public Administration, Columbia University Press, New York, 1937, pp. 1–46.

Hayes, R. W., Perry, J.G. and Thompson, P. A. *Management contracting*. Construction Industry Research and Information Association, Report 100, London, 1983.

Hofstede, G. Cultural dimensions for project management. *International Journal of Project Management*, **1**, No. 1, 1983, Feb., 41–48.

Katzenbach, J. R. and Smith, D. K. *The wisdom of teams: creating the high-performing organization*. Harvard Business School, Cambridge, MA, 1993.

Lawlor, E. E. *The ultimate advantange: creating the high involvement organization*. Maxwell Macmillan, London, New York, 1992.

Lawrence, P. R. and Lorsch, J. W. The new management job: the integrator. *Harvard Business Review*, 1967, Nov.–Dec.

Mansfield, E. and Wagner, S. Organizational and strategic factors associated with probabilities of success and industrial R&D. *Journal of Business*, **48**, No. 2, April, 1975.

Marquis, D. G. and Straight, D. M. *Organizational factors in project performance*. Working Paper No. 133–65, Sloan School of Management, Massachusetts Institute of Technology, August 1965.

Middleton, C. J. How to set up a project organization. *Harvard Business Review*, 1967, Mar.–Apr., **45**, 73–82.

Might, R. J. and Fisher, W. A. Role of structural factors in determining project management success. *IEEE Transactions on Engineering Management*, EM-32(2), 1985, May, 71–77.

Moolin, F. P. and McCoy, F. The organization and management of large projects . . . realities *vs* theory. *Proc. Project Management Institute Symp.*, Drexel Hill, PA, 1979.

Morris, P. W. G. Managing project interfaces — key points for project success. In *Project management handbook*, Cleland, D. I. and King, W. R. (eds). Van Nostrand Reinhold, New York, 1988, pp. 16–55.

Morton, D. H. The project manager, catalyst to constant change: a behaviourial analysis. *Project Management Quarterly*, 1975, **6**, No. 1, 22–23.

Morton, G. M. A. Become a project champion. *International Journal of Project Management*, **1**, No. 4, 1983, Nov., 197–203.

Petersen, N. Selecting project managers: an integrated list of predictors. *Project Management Journal*, **22**, No. 2, 1991, June, 21–26.

Reis de Carvalho, E. and Morris, P. W. G. Project matrix organizations — or how to do the matrix swing. *Proc. 1978 Project Management Institute Symp., Los Angeles*. Project Management Institute, Drexel Hill, PA, 1978.

Rossy, G. L. and Archibald, R. D. Building commitment in project teams. *Project Management Journal*, **23**, No. 2, 1992, June, 5–14.

Sayles, L. R. and Chandler, M. K. *Managing large systems: organizations for the future.* Harper & Row, New York, 1971.

Tampoe, M. and Thurloway, L. Project management: the use and abuse of techniques and teams (reflections from a motivation and environment study). *International Journal of Project Management,* **11**, No. 4, 1993, Nov., 245–250.

Tatum, C. B. The project manager's role in integrating design and construction. *Project Management Journal,* **18**, No. 2, 1987, June, 96–107.

Thamhain, H. J. and Wilemon, D. L. Conflict management in project life cycles. *Sloan Management Review,* 1975, Summer.

Thamhain, H. J. and Wilemon, D. L. Criteria for controlling projects according to plan. *Project Management Journal,* **17**, No. 2, 1986, June, 75–81.

Youker, R. Organizational alternatives for project management. *Project Management Quarterly,* 1977, **8**, No. 1.

Tools and techniques

Ashley, D. and Avots, I. Influence diagramming for an analysis of project risks. *Project Management Journal,* **15**, No. 1, 1984, Mar., 56–82.

Bu-Bushait, K. A. The application of project techniques to construction and research and development techniques. *Project Management Journal,* **20**, No. 2, 1989, June, 17–22.

Cooper, D. F. and Chapman, C. B. *Risk analysis for large projects.* Wiley, Chichester, 1987.

Crandall, K. Project planning with precedence lead/lag factors. *Project Management Quarterly,* 1973, **4**, No. 3.

Currie, K. and Drabble, B. Knowledge-based planning systems: a tour. *International Journal of Project Management,* **10**, No. 3, 1992, Aug., 131–137.

Dane, C. W., Gray, C. F. and Woodworth, B. Successfully introducing project management techniques into an organization. *Project Management Quarterly,* **12**, No. 4, 1981, Dec., 23–26.

Davis, E. W. Project scheduling under resource constraints: historical review and categorization of procedures. *AIIE Transactions,* 1973, Dec.

Delp, P., Thesen, A., Motiwalla, J. and Seshadri, N. *Systems tools for project planning.* International Development Institute, Indiana University, Bloomington, 1977.

Fleming, Q. W. *Cost schedule control systems criteria: the management guide to C/SCSC.* Probus, 1988. (Second edition, 1993.)

Geddes, P. How good is PERT? *Aerospace Management,* 1961, **4**, Sept., 41–43.

Gilmore, M. J. Knowledge based systems in construction and civil engineering. *International Journal of Project Management,* **7**, No. 3, 1989, Aug., 147–153.

Hertz, D. B. and Thomas, H. *Risk analysis and its applications.* Wiley, Chichester, 1983.

Kangari, R. and Boyer, L. T. Risk management by expert systems. *Project Management Journal,* **10**, No. 2, 1989, Mar., 40–48.

Kerzner, H. and Thamhain, H. J. *Project management operating guidelines.* Van Nostrand Reinhold, New York, 1986.

Marquis, D. C. A project team plus PERT = success. Or does it? *Innovation,* 1969.

Moder, J. J., Clark, R. A. and Gomez, R. S. Application of a GERT simulator to a repetitive hardware development type project. *AIIE Transactions,* 1971, **3**, No. 4, 271–280.

Moder, J. J., Phillips, C. R. and Davis, E. W. *Project management with CPM, PERT and precedence diagramming.* Van Nostrand Reinhold, New York, 3rd edn, 1983.

Nicolo, E. Metaproject analysis: a systematic methodological aid for strategic planning. *Project management without boundaries, Proc. 11th Internet World Congress on Project Management, Italy, 16–19 June*, Vol. 2, 1992.

Niwa, K. and Okumu, M. Know-how transfer methods and its application to risk management for large construction projects. *IEEE Transactions on Engineering Management*, **EM-29**, (k), 1982, Nov., 146–153.

Perry, J. G. and Hayes, R. W. Construction projects — know the risks. *Chartered Mechanical Engineering*, 1985, Feb.

Pritsker, A. A. B. *Modelling and analysis using Q-GERT networks*. Wiley, New York, 1977.

Probst, A. R. and Worlitzer, J. Project management expert systems. *International Journal of Project Management*, **6**, No. 1, 1988, Feb., 11–17.

Sweetman, S. L. Utilizing expert systems to improve the configuration management process. *Project Management Journal*, **21**, No. 1, 1990, Mar., 5–12.

Thompson, P. A. and Perry, J. G. *Engineering construction risks*. Thomas Telford, London, 1992.

Vazsonyi, I. L'histoire de grandeur et la decadence de la methode PERT. *Management Science*, 1970, **16**, No. 8, Apr., B449–B450.

Weber, F. M. Tools for managing projects. *Project Management Journal*, **13**, No. 2, 1982, June, 46–58.

Wiest, J. D. A heuristic model for scheduling large projects with limited resources. *Management Science*, 1967, **13**, No. 6, Feb., B359–B377.

Wiest, J. D. Project network models: past, present and future. *Project Management Quarterly*, 1977, **8**, No. 4.

Wiest, J. D. and Levy, F. K. *A management guide to PERT/CPM*. Prentice Hall, Englewood Cliffs, NJ, 1969.

Technology and R&D

Andrews, W. C. Prototyping information systems. *Journal of Systems Management*, **34**, No. 9, 1983, 16–18.

Baker, N. R., Green, S. G. and Bean, A. S. Why R&D projects succeed or fail. *Research Management*, 1986, Nov.–Dec., 29–34.

Balachandra, R. and Raelin, J. A. When to kill that R&D project. *Research Management*, 1984, July–Aug., 30–33.

Benyon, D. and Skidmore, S. Information Systems Design Methodologies. *The Computer Journal*, **3**, No. 1, 1987, 2–7.

Boehm, B. W. *Software engineering economics*. Prentice Hall, Englewood Cliffs, NJ, 1981.

Brooks, F. P. *The mythical man-month*. Addison-Wesley, Reading, MA, 1982.

Buell, C. K. When to terminate a research and development project. *Research Management*, **10**, No. 4, 1967, 275–284.

Central Computer and Telecommunications Agency. *PRINCE*. National Computing Centre, 1990.

Cooper, R. G. New product success in industrial firms. *Industrial Marketing Management*, **11**, 1982, 215–223.

Cooper, R. G. and Kleinschmidt, E. J. What makes a new product a winner: success factors at the project level. *R&D Management*, **17**, No. 3, 1987, 175–189.

Harrison, R. Prototyping and the systems development life cycle. *Journal of Systems Management*, **36**, No. 98, 1983, 22–25.

Inwood, D. and Hammond, J. *Product development: an integrated approach*. Kogan Page, London, 1993.

Jenkins, A. M. and Wetherbe, J. C. Empirical investigation of systems development practices and results. *Information and Management*, 7, 1984, 73–82.

Maidique, M. and Hayes, R. The art of high-technology management. *Sloan Management Review*, **25**, No. 4, 1984, Winter.

Martin, J. *Information engineering*. Prentice Hall, Englewood Cliffs, NJ, 1990.

Moskal, B. S. Product design: GM's new-found religion. *Industry Week*, **241**, No. 10, 18 May, 1992, 42−53.

Roussel, P. A., Saad, K. M. and Erickson, T. J. The evolution of Third Generation R&D. *Planning Review*, **19**, No. 2, 1991, Mar.−Apr., 18−26.

Wheelwright, S. C. and Clark, K. B. Creating project plans to focus product development. *Harvard Business Review*, **70**, No. 2, 1992, Mar.−Apr., 70−82.

Womack, J. R., and Ross, D. *The machine that changed the world*. Maxwell Macmillan International, New York, 1990.

Yourdon, E. and Constantine, L. L. *Structured design*. Prentice Hall, Englewood Cliffs, NJ, 1979.

Timing and phasing

Cochran, E. G., Patz, A. L. and Rowe, A. J. Concurrency and disruption in new product innovation. *California Management Review*, 1978, Fall.

Harvey, T. E. Concurrency today in acquisition management. *Defense Systems Management Review*, 1980, **3**, No. 1, Winter, 14−18.

Musselwhite, C. W. Time-based innovation: the new competitive advantage. *Training & Development Journal*, **44**, No. 1, 1990, Jan., 53−56.

O'Connor, J. T. and Norwich, W. Fossil power plant schedule compression tactics: lessons from independent power producers. *Project Management Journal*, **24**, No. 3, 1993, Sept., 34−42.

Skelton, T. M. and Thamhain, H. J. Concurrent project management: a tool for technology transfer, R&D-to-market. *Project Management Journal*, **24**, No. 4, 1993, Dec., 41−48.

Turino, J. *Managing concurrent engineering — buying time to market*. Van Nostrand Reinhold, New York, 1992.

Wesley Allen, C. (ed.) *Simultaneous engineering — integrating manufacturing and design*. Society for Manufacturing Engineers, Dearborn, MI, 1992.

Finance and project appraisal

Davis, D. New projects: beware of false economies. *Harvard Business Review*, **63**, No. 2, 1985, Mar.−Apr., 95−101.

Hirschman, A. O. *Development projects observed*. The Brookings Institution, Washington, DC, 1967.

Little, I. M. D. and Mirlees, J. A. *Project appraisal and planning for developing countries*. Heinemann, London, 1974.

McCarthy, S. C. and Tiong, R. L. K. Financial and contractual aspects of build−operate−transfer projects. *International Journal of Project Management*, **9**, No. 4, 1991, Nov., 222−227.

Mishan, E. J. *Cost benefit analysis*. George Allen & Unwin, 1971.

Nevitt, P. K. *Project financing*. Euromoney, London, 1983.

O'Riordan, T. and Sewell, W. R. D. *Project appraisal and policy review*. Wiley, Chichester, 1981.

Orman, G. A. A. New applications of risk analysis in project insurances. *International Journal of Project Management*, **9**, No. 3, 1991, Aug., 131−139.

Prest, A. R. and Turvey. Cost/benefit analysis: a survey. *The Economic Journal*, 1965, Dec.

Woody, W. B. and Pourian, H. Risk assessment and options in project finance. *Project Management Journal*, **23**, No. 4, 1992, Dec., 21−28.

Overruns and project success

Ashley, D. B. Determinants of construction project success. *Project Management Journal*, **18**, No. 2, 1987, June, 69–77.

Avots, I. Why does project management fail? *California Management Review*, 1969, Fall.

Baker, B. N. and Fisher, D. Cost growth: can it be controlled? *Project Management Quarterly*, 1974, **5**.

Cleland, D. I. Prudent and reasonable project management. *Project Management Journal*, **16**, No. 4, 1985, Dec., 91–97.

DeCotiis, T. A. and Dyer, L. Defining and measuring project performance. *Research Management*, 1979, Jan., 17–22.

Department of Energy. *Nuclear plant cancellations: causes, costs and consequences*. DoE/EIA-0392, Department of Energy, Washington, DC, April 1983.

de Wit, A. Measuring project success: an illusion. *Project Management Institute Seminar/Symp. on Measuring Success, Montreal*, 1986. Project Management Institute, Drexel Hill, PA, 1986.

Fox, J. R. Evaluating management of large, complex projects: a framework for analysis. *Technology in Society*, **6**, 1984, 129–139.

Ibbs, C. W., Back, W. E., Kim, J. J., Wall, D. E., De La Garza, J. M., Hassanein, M. A., Schran, S. M. and Twarduck, R. K. *Determining the impact of various construction contract types and clauses on project performance*. Department of Civil Engineering, University of Illinois at Urbana-Champaign, March 1986.

Mason, G. E., Laren, R. E., Borcherding, J. D., Oakes, S. R. and Rad, P. F. *Delays in nuclear power plant construction*. US Energy Research and Development Administration, E(11-1)-4121, Washington, DC, December 1977.

Morris, P. W. G. Research at Oxford into the preconditions of success and failure in major projects. *Proc. Project Management Institute Seminar/Symp. on Measuring Success, Montreal*, 1986. Project Management Institute, Drexel Hill, PA, 1986.

Murphy, D. C., Baker, B. N. and Fisher, D. Cost growth: can it be controlled? *Project Management Quarterly*, **5**, 1974.

Perry, R. L., DiSalvo, D., Hall, G. R., Harman, A. L., Levenson, G. S., Smith, G. K. and Stucker, J. P. *System acquisition experience*. Rand Corporation, RM-6072-PR, Santa Monica, CA, November 1969.

Pinto, J. K. and Slevin, D. P. Project success: definitions and measurement techniques. *Project Management Journal*, **19**, No. 1, 1989, Feb., 67.

Education

Cook, D. L. Certification of project managers — fantasy or reality? *Project Management Quarterly*, 1977, **8**, No. 2.

Kerzner, H. Formal education for project management. *Project Management Quarterly*, 1979, **10**, No. 2.

Project management body of knowledge. *Project Management Journal*, **17**, 1986, Aug.

Special report: ethics, standards, accreditation. *Project Management Quarterly*, **14**, No. 3, 1993, Aug.

General

Deming, W. E. *Out of crisis*. Massachusetts Institute of Technology, Cambridge, MA, 1989.

Hammer, M. and Champy, J. *Re-engineering the corporation: a manifesto for business revolution*. Harper Business, New York, 1993.

Juran, J. M. *Quality control handbook*. McGraw-Hill, New York, 1974.

Turner, B. *Man-made disasters*. Taylor & Francis, London, 1979.

World Commission on Environment and Development. *Our common future*. Oxford University Press, 1987.

Index